MARVEL
DOCTOR STRANGE
PRELUDE

WRITER: **WILL CORONA PILGRIM**
ARTIST: **JORGE FORNÉS**
COLORIST: **JESUS ABURTOV**
LETTERER: **VC'S TRAVIS LANHAM**
EDITORS: **EMILY SHAW & MARK BASSO**

INFINITE COMIC
WRITER: **WILL CORONA PILGRIM**   STORYBOARD ARTIST: **GEOFFO**
ARTIST: **JORGE FORNÉS**   COLORIST: **JESUS ABURTOV**   LETTERER: **VC'S TRAVIS LANHAM**
PRODUCTION: **ANNIE CHEUNG**   PRODUCTION MANAGER: **TIM SMITH 3**   EDITORS: **MARK BASSO & EMILY SHAW**

DOCTOR STRANGE CREATED BY **STAN LEE & STEVE DITKO**

MARVEL STUDIOS
DEVELOPMENT & PRODUCTION MANAGER: **KEVIN WRIGHT**
SVP PRODUCTION & DEVELOPMENT: **STEPHEN BROUSSARD**
PRESIDENT: **KEVIN FEIGE**

COLLECTION EDITOR: **JENNIFER GRÜNWALD**
ASSOCIATE EDITOR: **SARAH BRUNSTAD**   EDITOR, SPECIAL PROJECTS: **MARK D. BEAZLEY**
VP, PRODUCTION & SPECIAL PROJECTS: **JEFF YOUNGQUIST**   SVP PRINT, SALES & MARKETING: **DAVID GABRIEL**

EDITOR IN CHIEF: **AXEL ALONSO**   CHIEF CREATIVE OFFICER: **JOE QUESADA**
PUBLISHER: **DAN BUCKLEY**   EXECUTIVE PRODUCER: **ALAN FINE**

MARVEL'S DOCTOR STRANGE PRELUDE. Contains material originally published in magazine form as MARVEL'S DOCTOR STRANGE PRELUDE #1-2, MARVEL'S DOCTOR STRANGE PRELUDE INFINITE COMIC #1, DOCTOR STRANGE: THE OATH #1, DOCTOR STRANGE (2015) #1, STRANGE TALES #110 and #115, and MARVEL PREMIERE #14. First printing 2016. ISBN# 978-1-302-90109-7. Published by MARVEL WORLDWIDE, INC., a subsidiary of MARVEL ENTERTAINMENT, LLC. OFFICE OF PUBLICATION: 135 West 50th Street, New York, NY 10020. Copyright © 2016 MARVEL No similarity between any of the names, characters, persons, and/or institutions in this magazine with those of any living or dead person or institution is intended, and any such similarity which may exist is purely coincidental. **Printed in the U.S.A.** ALAN FINE, President, Marvel Entertainment; DAN BUCKLEY, President, TV, Publishing & Brand Management; JOE QUESADA, Chief Creative Officer; TOM BREVOORT, SVP of Publishing; DAVID BOGART, SVP of Business Affairs & Operations, Publishing & Partnership; C.B. CEBULSKI, VP of Brand Management & Development, Asia; DAVID GABRIEL, SVP of Sales & Marketing, Publishing; JEFF YOUNGQUIST, VP of Production & Special Projects; DAN CARR, Executive Director of Publishing Technology; ALEX MORALES, Director of Publishing Operations; SUSAN CRESPI, Production Manager; STAN LEE, Chairman Emeritus. For information regarding advertising in Marvel Comics or on Marvel.com, please contact Vit DeBellis, Integrated Sales Manager, at vdebellis@marvel.com. For Marvel subscription inquiries, please call 888-511-5480. **Manufactured between 7/29/2016 and 9/5/2016 by R.R. DONNELLEY, INC., SALEM, VA, USA.**

10 9 8 7 6 5 4 3 2 1

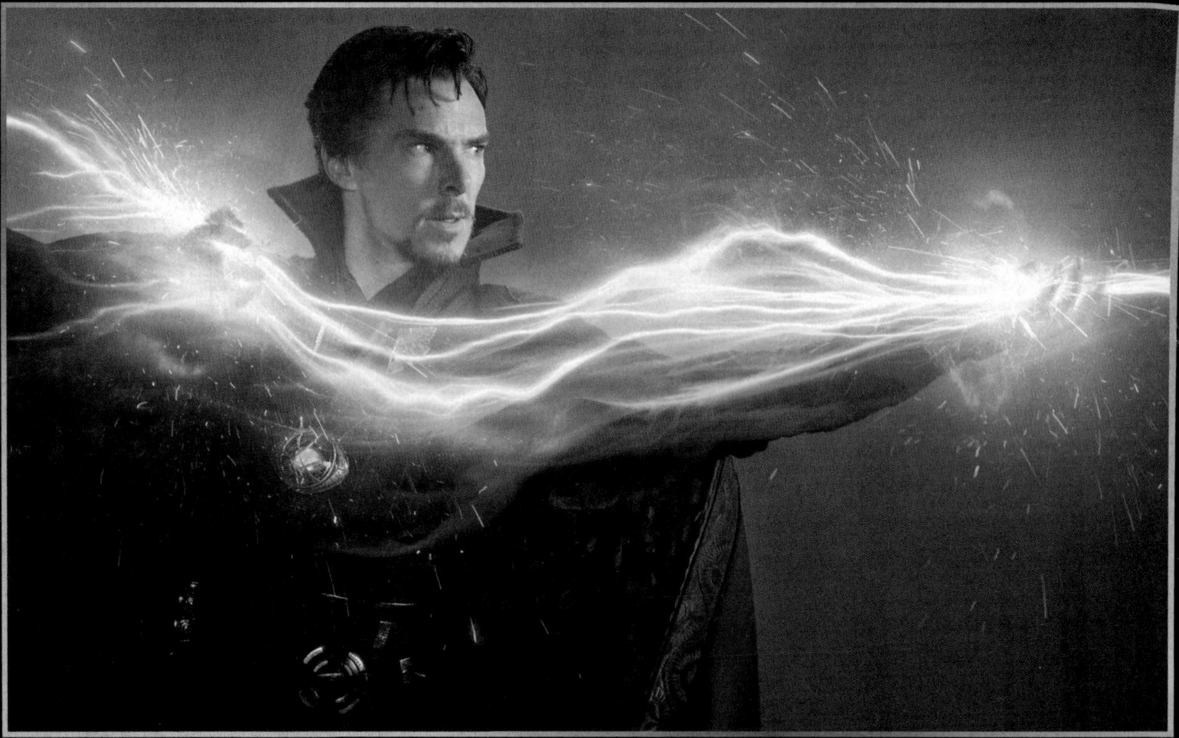

MARVEL'S DOCTOR STRANGE PRELUDE #1

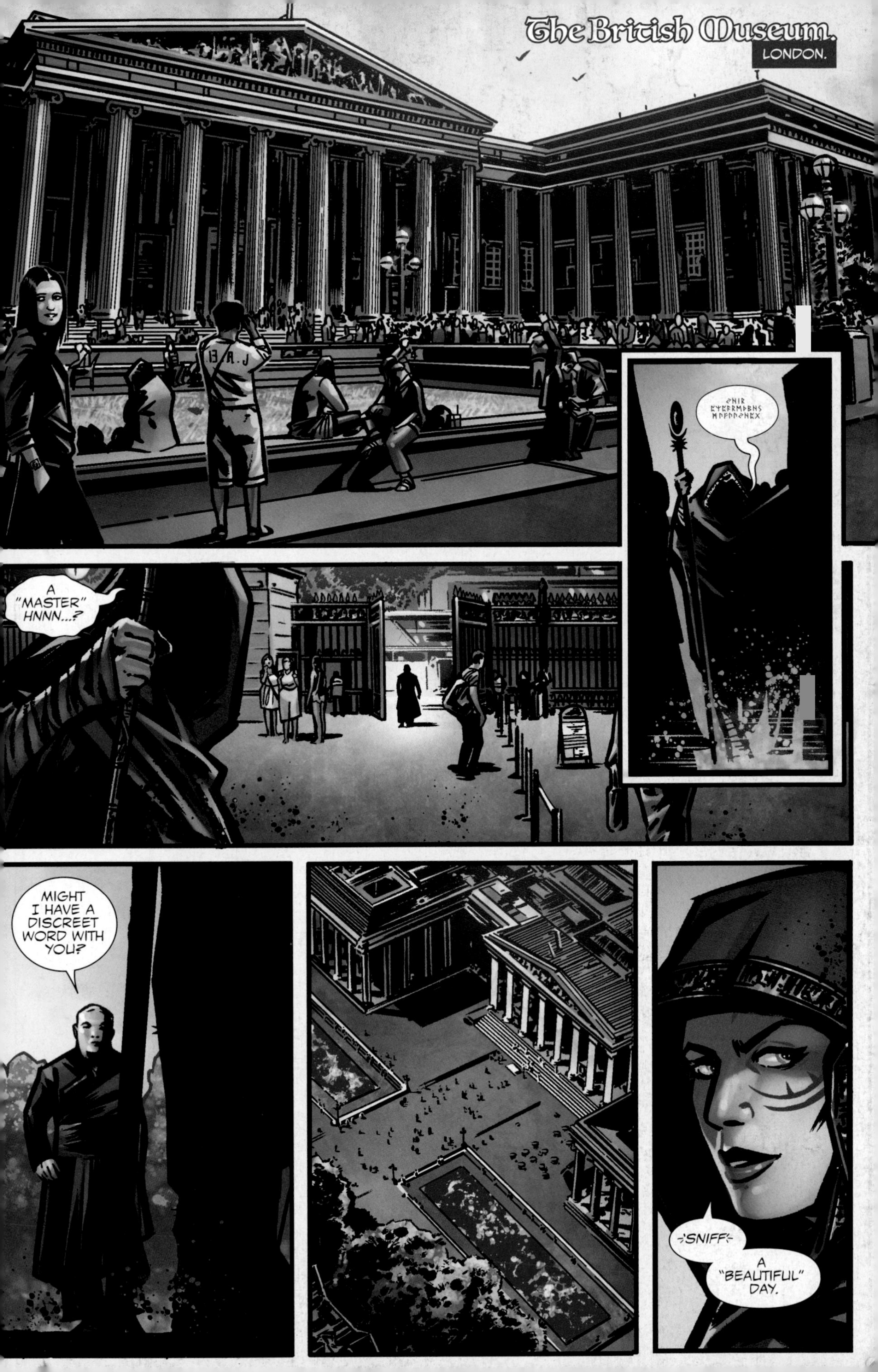
The British Museum.
LONDON.
A "MASTER" HNNN...?
MIGHT I HAVE A DISCREET WORD WITH YOU?
-SNIFF-
A "BEAUTIFUL" DAY.

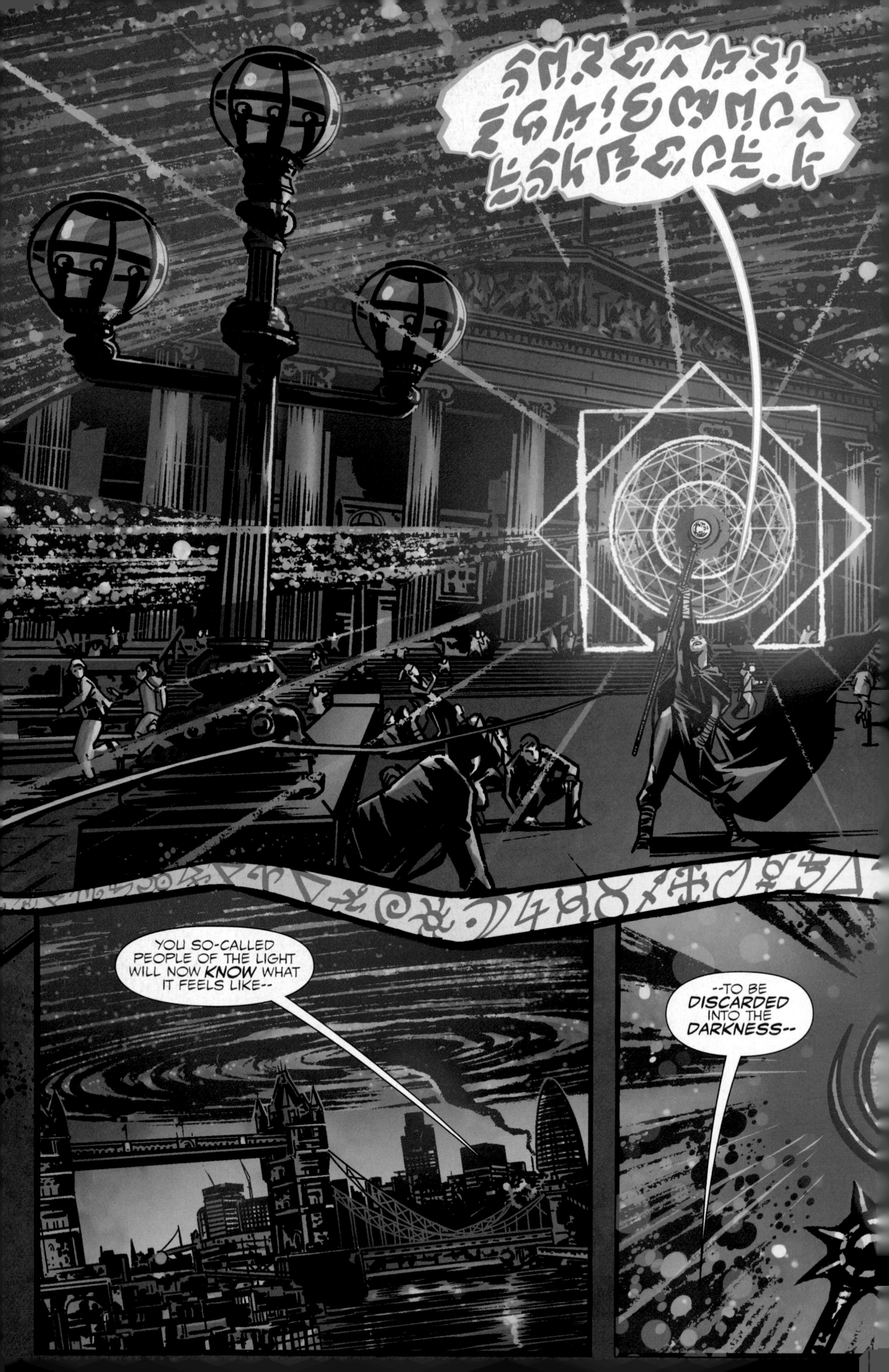
YOU SO-CALLED PEOPLE OF THE LIGHT WILL NOW KNOW WHAT IT FEELS LIKE--
--TO BE DISCARDED INTO THE DARKNESS--

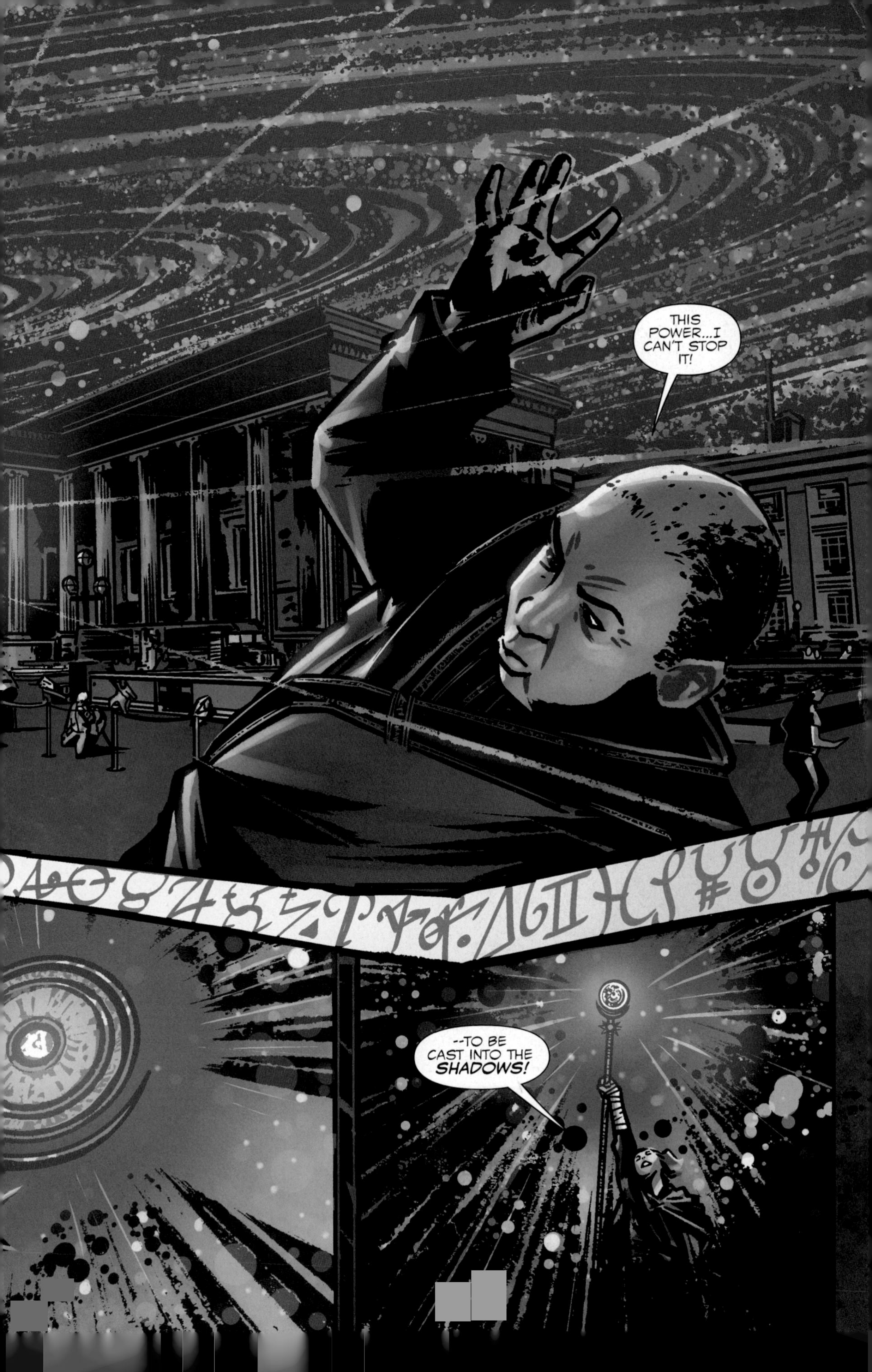
THIS POWER...I CAN'T STOP IT!
--TO BE CAST INTO THE SHADOWS!

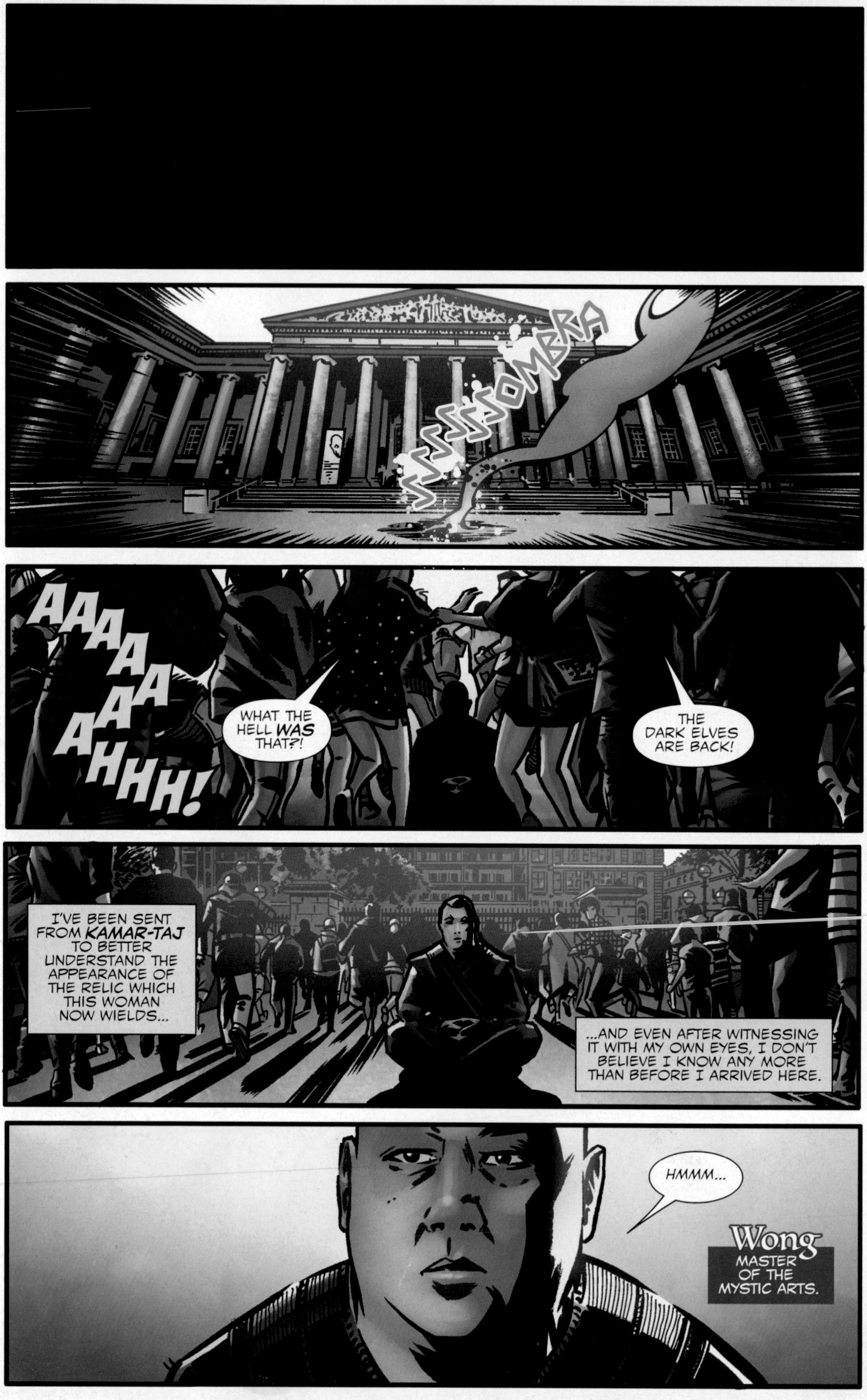
SSSSSOMBRA
AAAAAAAHHHH!
WHAT THE HELL WAS THAT?!
THE DARK ELVES ARE BACK!
I'VE BEEN SENT FROM KAMAR-TAJ TO BETTER UNDERSTAND THE APPEARANCE OF THE RELIC WHICH THIS WOMAN NOW WIELDS...
...AND EVEN AFTER WITNESSING IT WITH MY OWN EYES, I DON'T BELIEVE I KNOW ANY MORE THAN BEFORE I ARRIVED HERE.
HMMM...
Wong
MASTER OF THE MYSTIC ARTS.

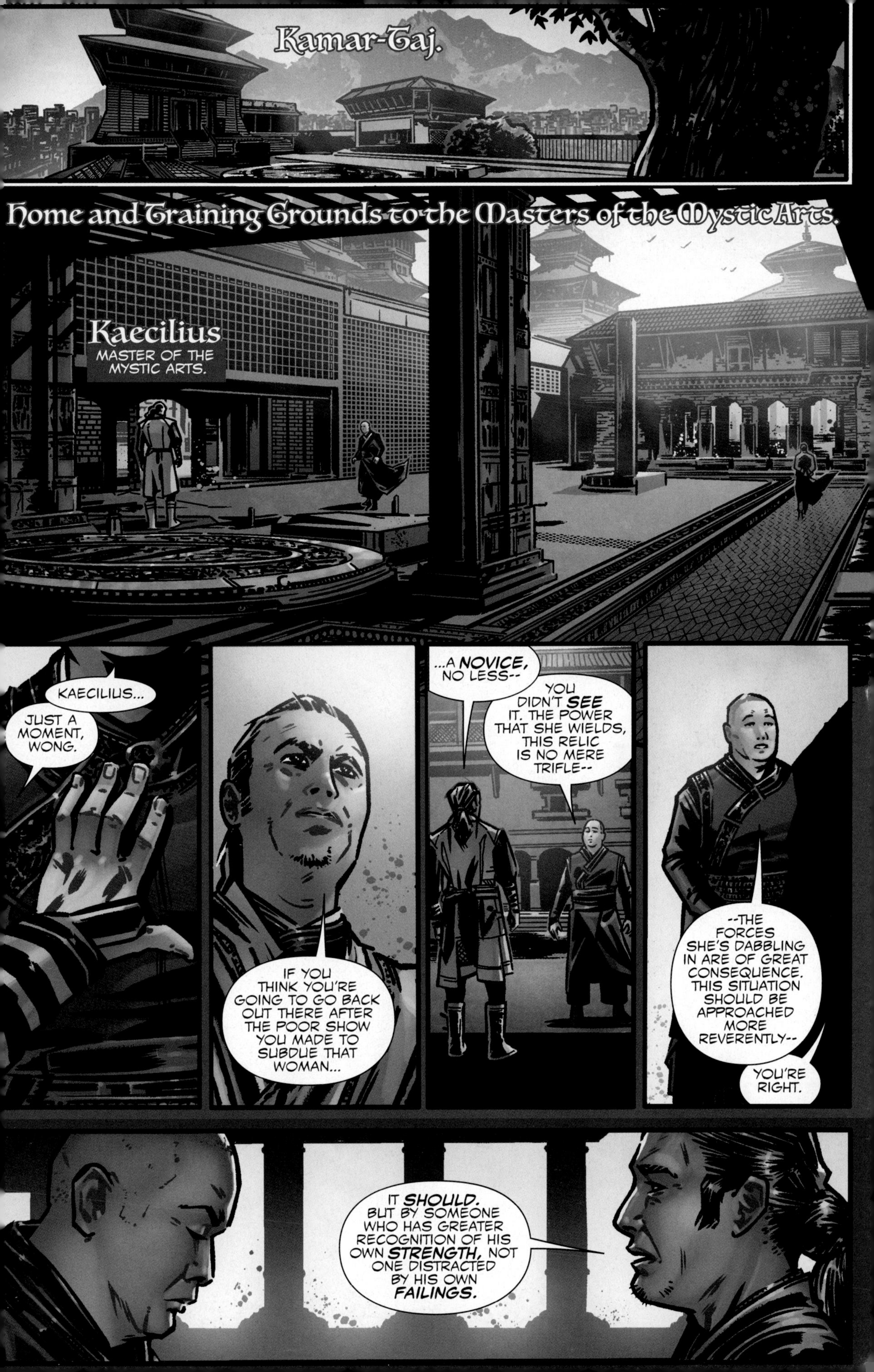

Kamar-Taj.
Home and Training Grounds to the Masters of the Mystic Arts.
Kaecilius
MASTER OF THE MYSTIC ARTS.
KAECILIUS...
JUST A MOMENT, WONG.
IF YOU THINK YOU'RE GOING TO GO BACK OUT THERE AFTER THE POOR SHOW YOU MADE TO SUBDUE THAT WOMAN...
...A NOVICE, NO LESS--
YOU DIDN'T SEE IT. THE POWER THAT SHE WIELDS, THIS RELIC IS NO MERE TRIFLE--
--THE FORCES SHE'S DABBLING IN ARE OF GREAT CONSEQUENCE. THIS SITUATION SHOULD BE APPROACHED MORE REVERENTLY--
YOU'RE RIGHT.
IT SHOULD. BUT BY SOMEONE WHO HAS GREATER RECOGNITION OF HIS OWN STRENGTH, NOT ONE DISTRACTED BY HIS OWN FAILINGS.

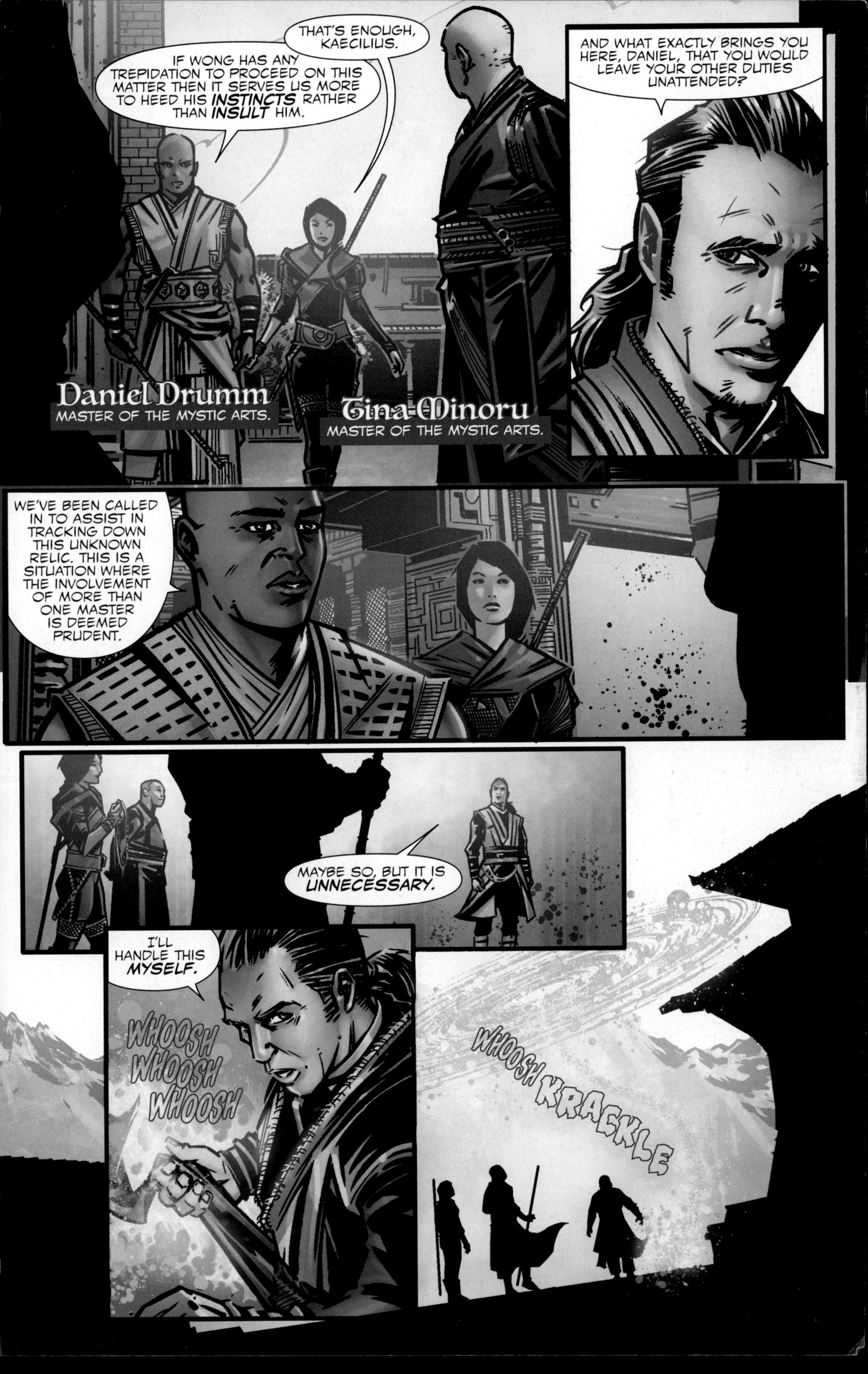

THAT'S ENOUGH, KAECILIUS.
IF WONG HAS ANY TREPIDATION TO PROCEED ON THIS MATTER THEN IT SERVES US MORE TO HEED HIS INSTINCTS RATHER THAN INSULT HIM.
Daniel Drumm
MASTER OF THE MYSTIC ARTS.
Tina Minoru
MASTER OF THE MYSTIC ARTS.
AND WHAT EXACTLY BRINGS YOU HERE, DANIEL, THAT YOU WOULD LEAVE YOUR OTHER DUTIES UNATTENDED?
WE'VE BEEN CALLED IN TO ASSIST IN TRACKING DOWN THIS UNKNOWN RELIC. THIS IS A SITUATION WHERE THE INVOLVEMENT OF MORE THAN ONE MASTER IS DEEMED PRUDENT.
MAYBE SO, BUT IT IS UNNECESSARY.
I'LL HANDLE THIS MYSELF.
WHOOSH
WHOOSH
WHOOSH
WHOOSH KRACKLE

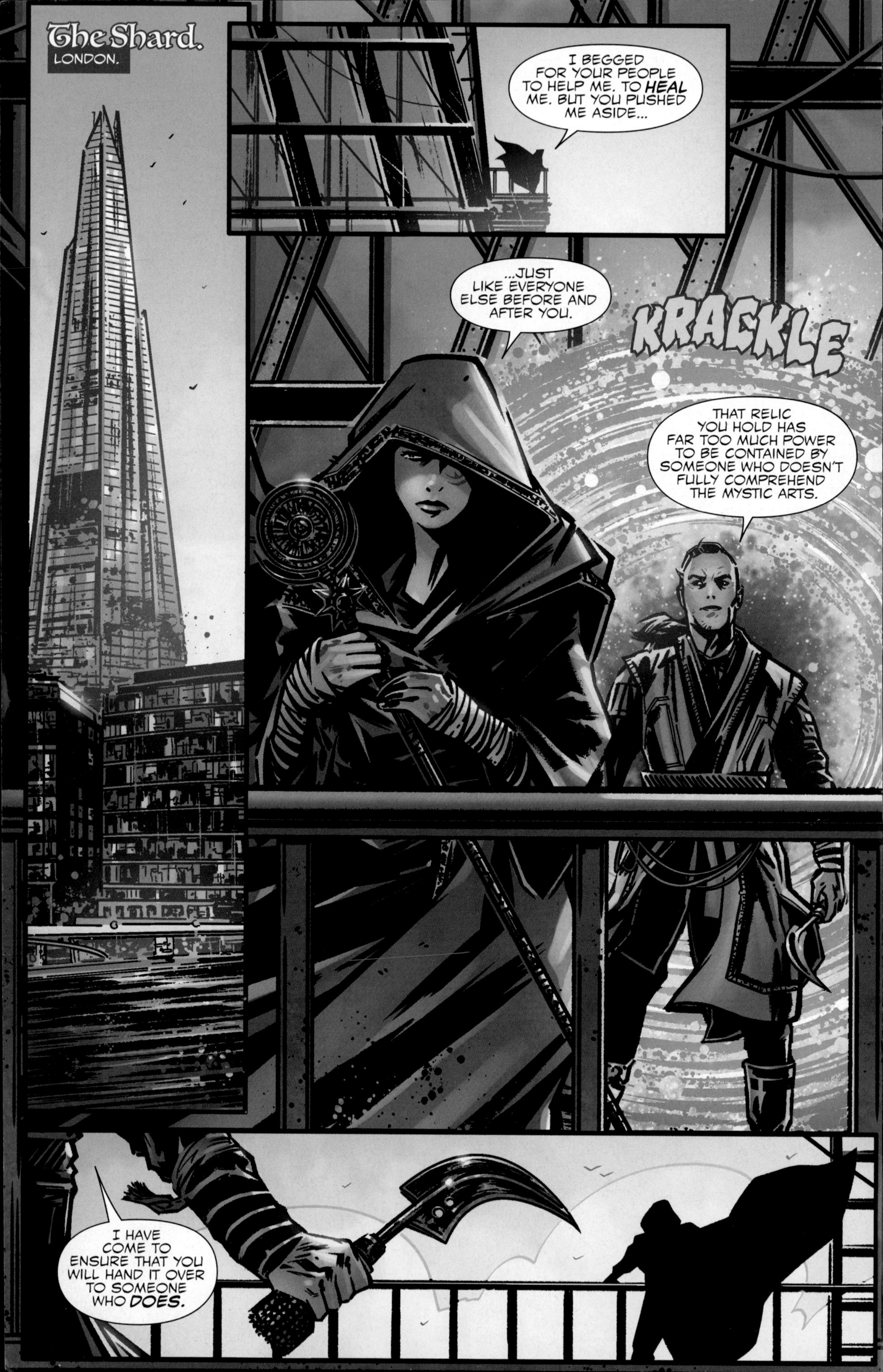
The Shard.
LONDON.
I BEGGED FOR YOUR PEOPLE TO HELP ME. TO HEAL ME. BUT YOU PUSHED ME ASIDE...
...JUST LIKE EVERYONE ELSE BEFORE AND AFTER YOU.
KRACKLE
THAT RELIC YOU HOLD HAS FAR TOO MUCH POWER TO BE CONTAINED BY SOMEONE WHO DOESN'T FULLY COMPREHEND THE MYSTIC ARTS.
I HAVE COME TO ENSURE THAT YOU WILL HAND IT OVER TO SOMEONE WHO DOES.

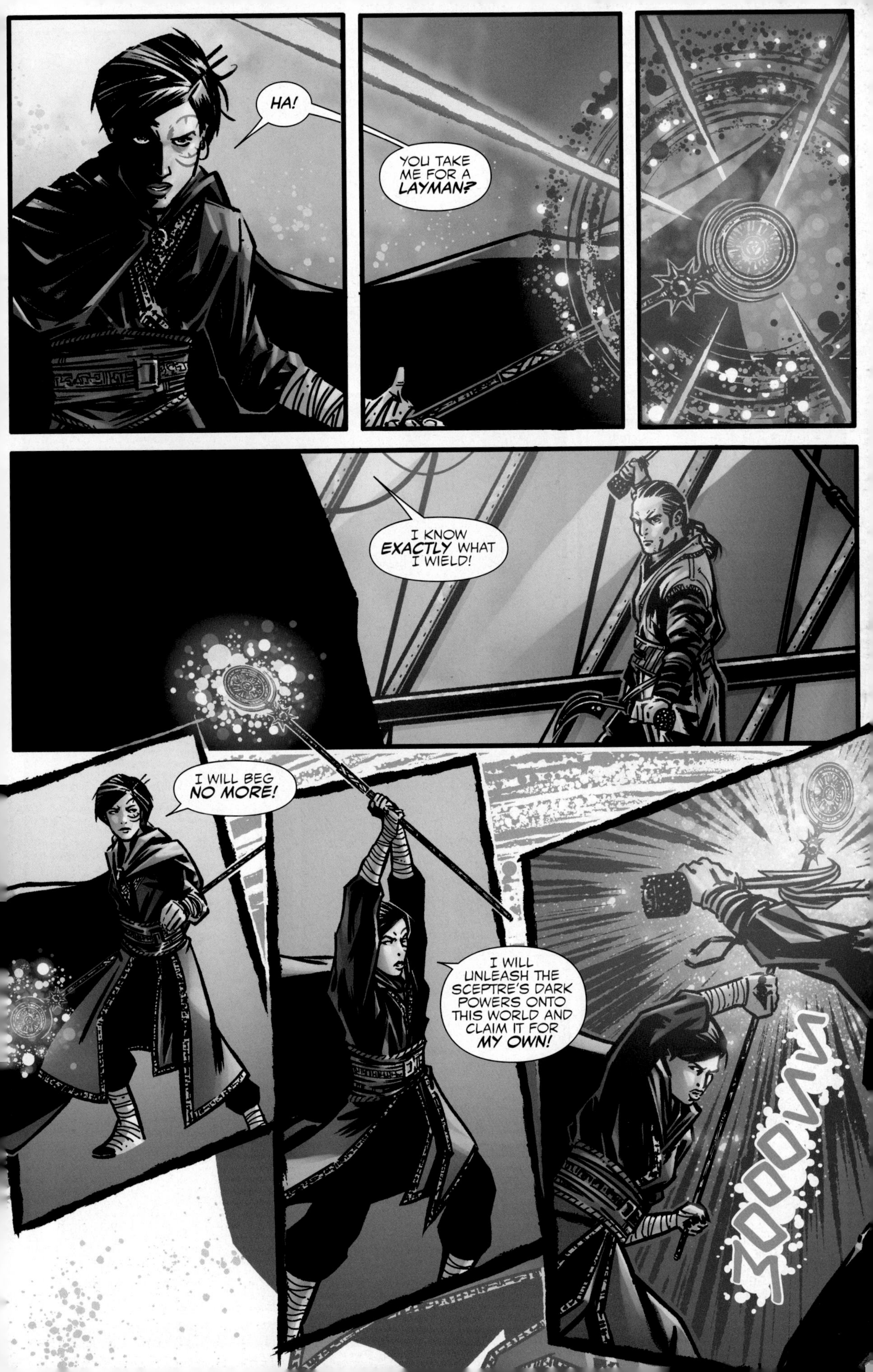
HA!
YOU TAKE ME FOR A **LAYMAN?**
I KNOW **EXACTLY** WHAT I WIELD!
I WILL BEG **NO MORE!**
I WILL UNLEASH THE SCEPTRE'S DARK POWERS ONTO THIS WORLD AND CLAIM IT FOR **MY OWN!**
ZOOOM

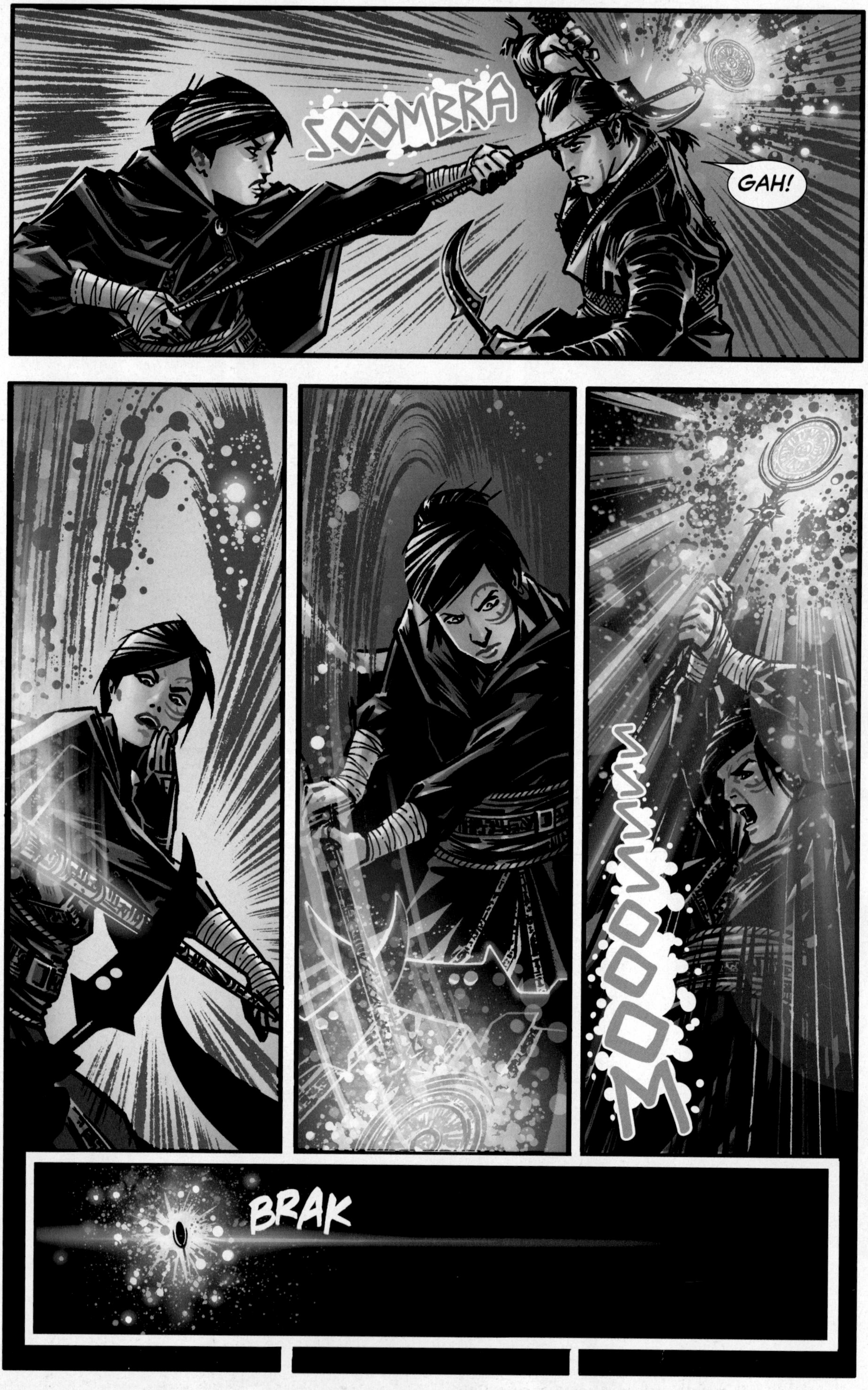
SOOMBRA
GAH!
VVVVVVOOOOM
BRAK

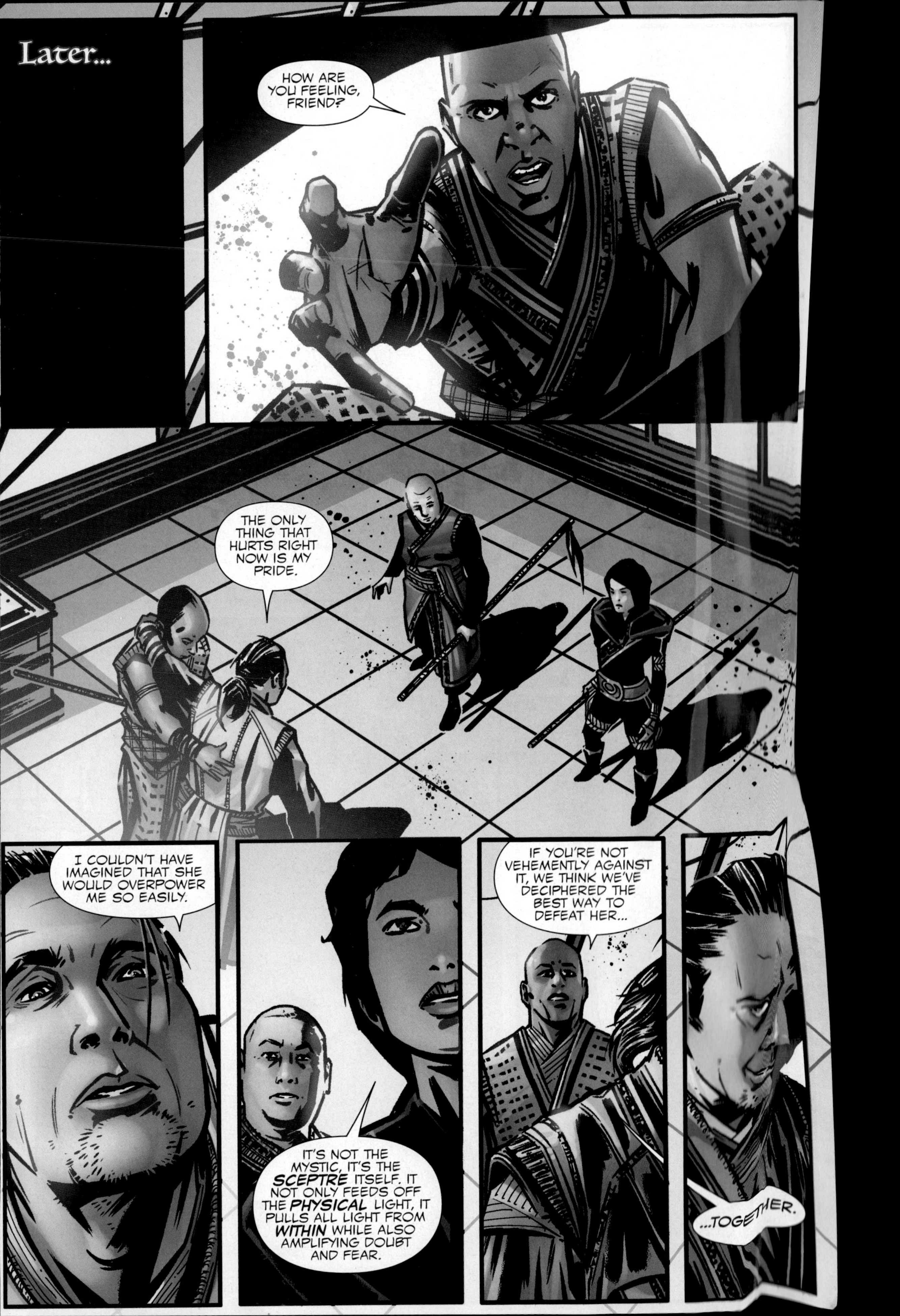
Later...
HOW ARE YOU FEELING, FRIEND?
THE ONLY THING THAT HURTS RIGHT NOW IS MY PRIDE.
I COULDN'T HAVE IMAGINED THAT SHE WOULD OVERPOWER ME SO EASILY.
IT'S NOT THE MYSTIC, IT'S THE SCEPTRE ITSELF. IT NOT ONLY FEEDS OFF THE PHYSICAL LIGHT, IT PULLS ALL LIGHT FROM WITHIN WHILE ALSO AMPLIFYING DOUBT AND FEAR.
IF YOU'RE NOT VEHEMENTLY AGAINST IT, WE THINK WE'VE DECIPHERED THE BEST WAY TO DEFEAT HER...
...TOGETHER.

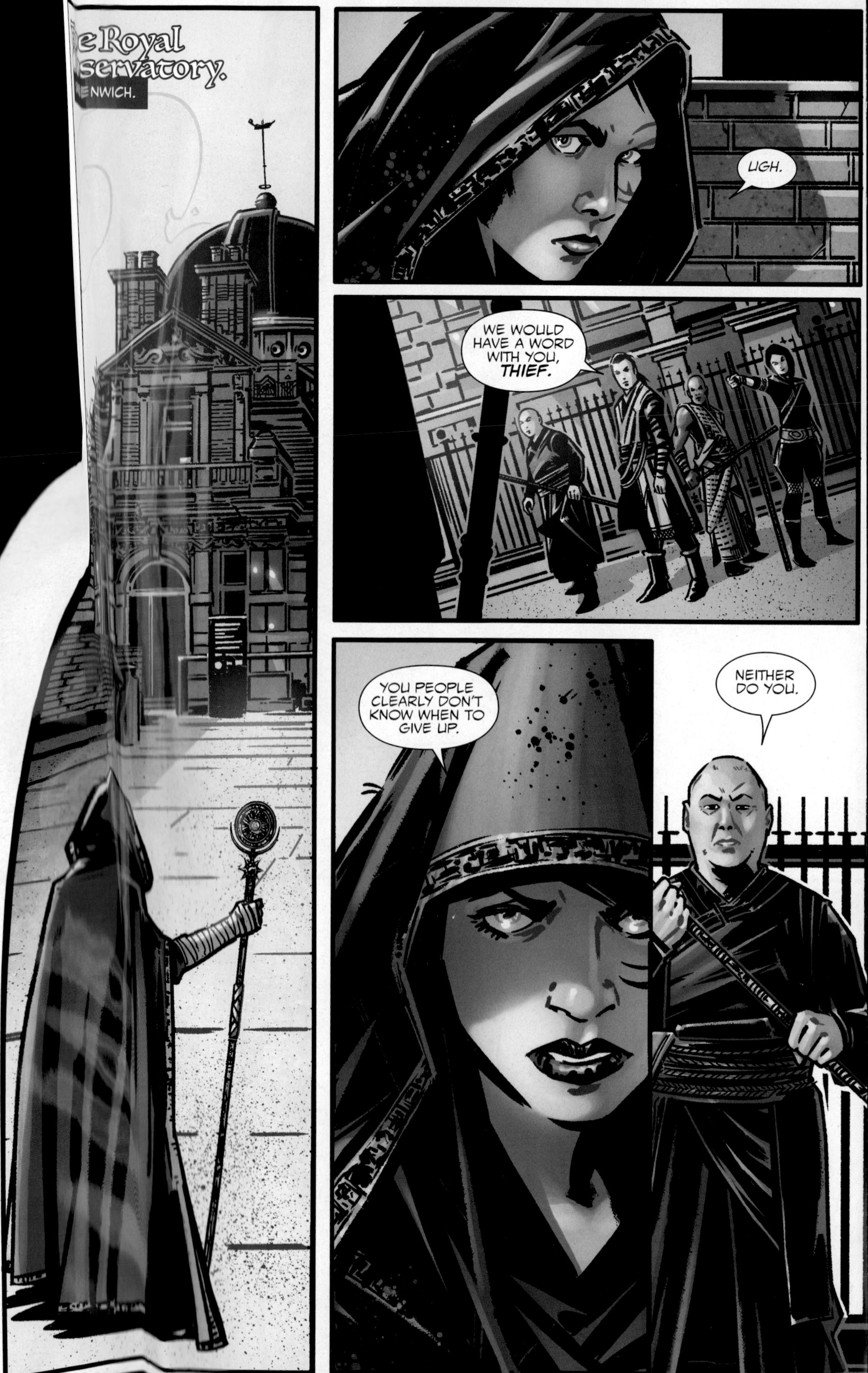
e Royal
servatory.
NWICH.
UGH.
WE WOULD HAVE A WORD WITH YOU, THIEF.
YOU PEOPLE CLEARLY DON'T KNOW WHEN TO GIVE UP.
NEITHER DO YOU.

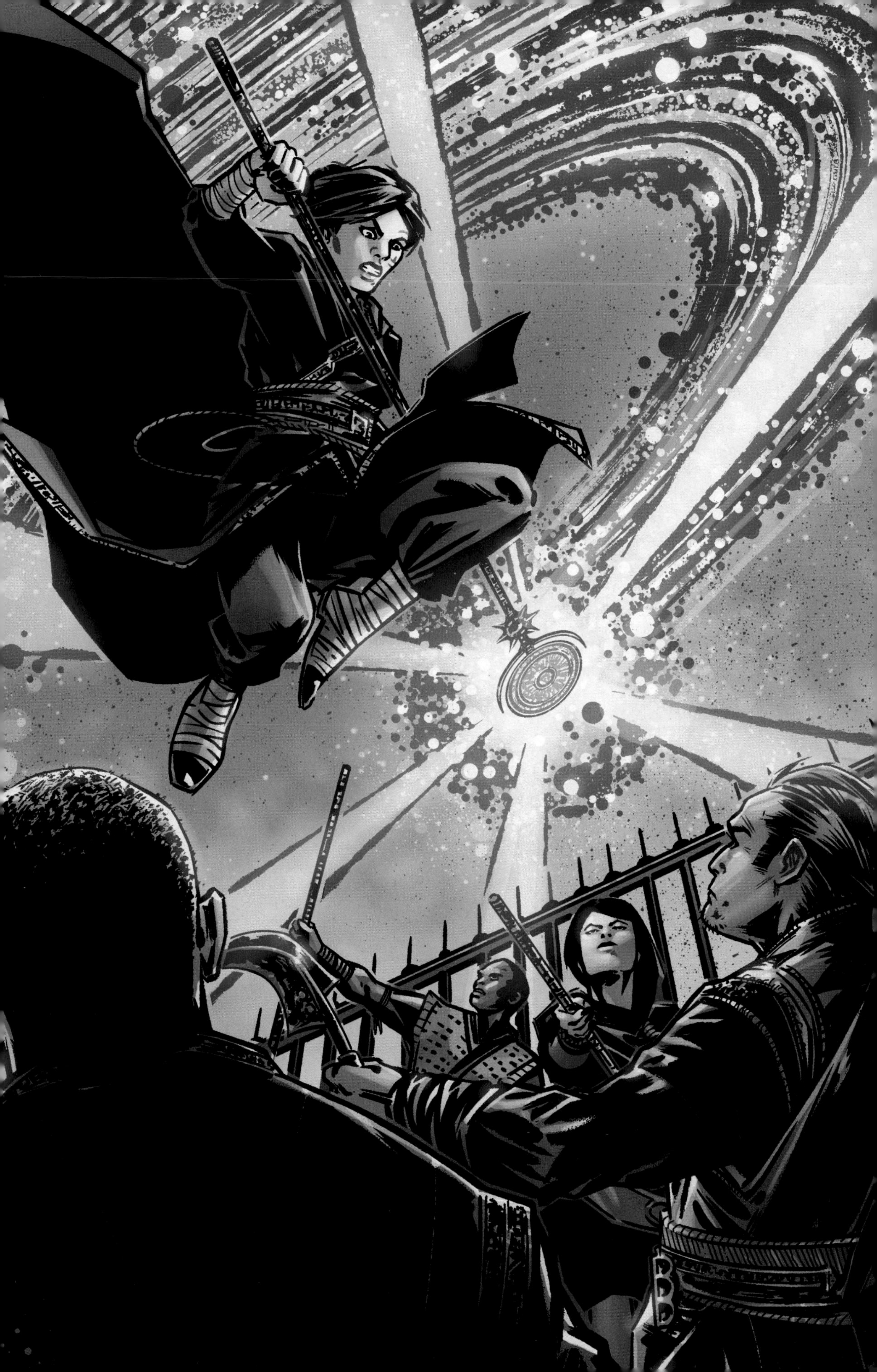

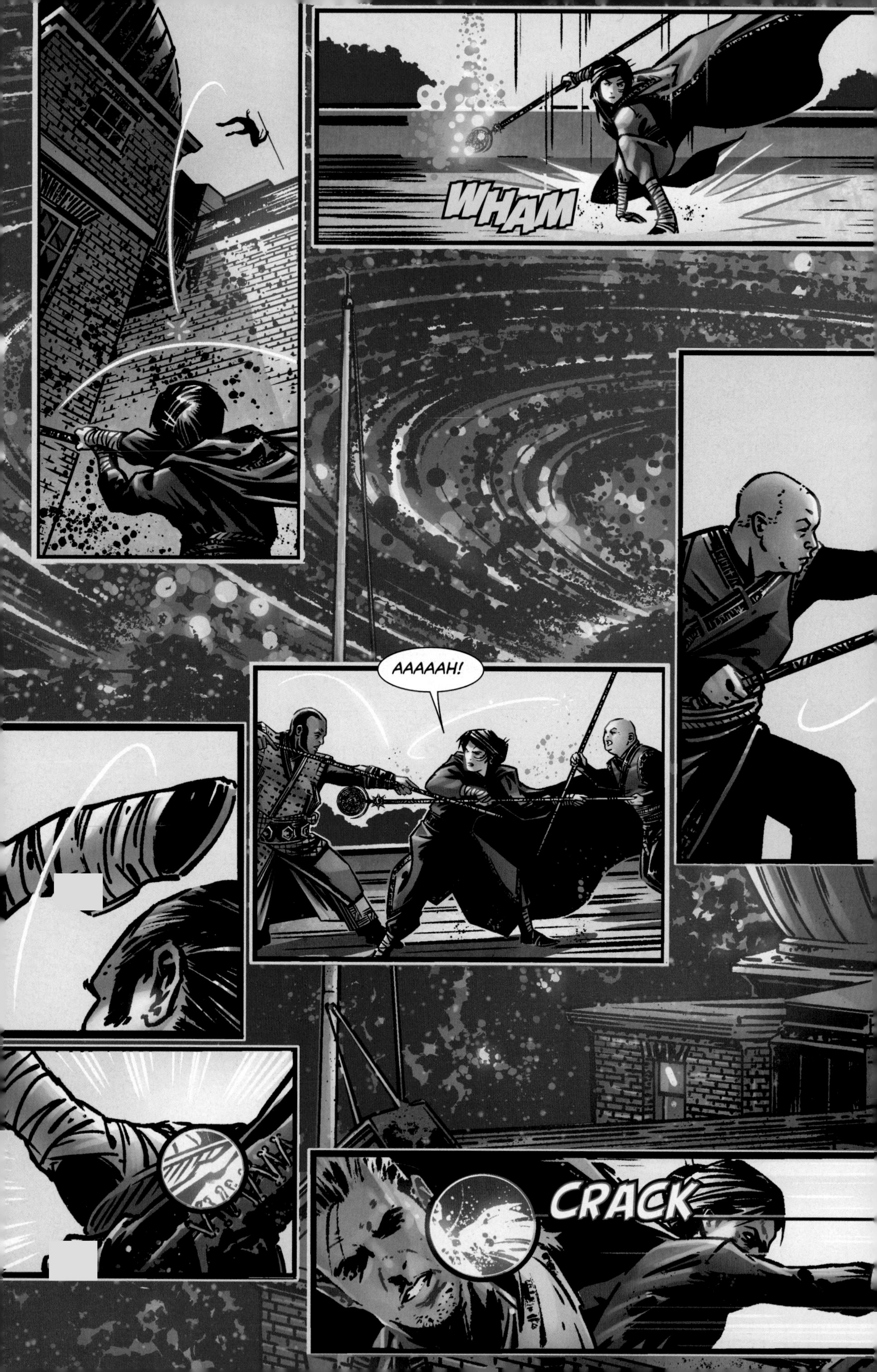
WHAM
AAAAAH!
CRACK

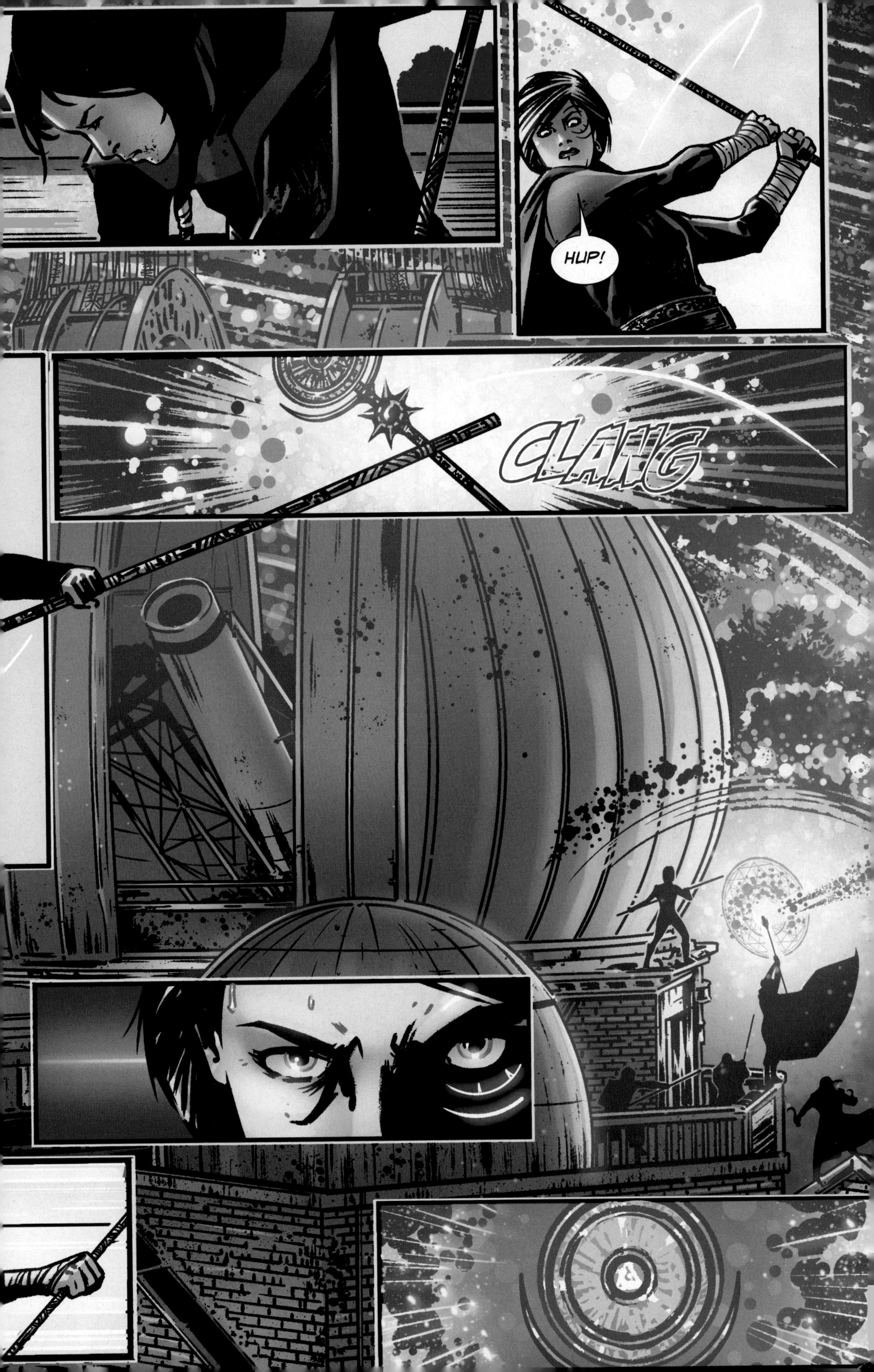
HUP!
CLANG

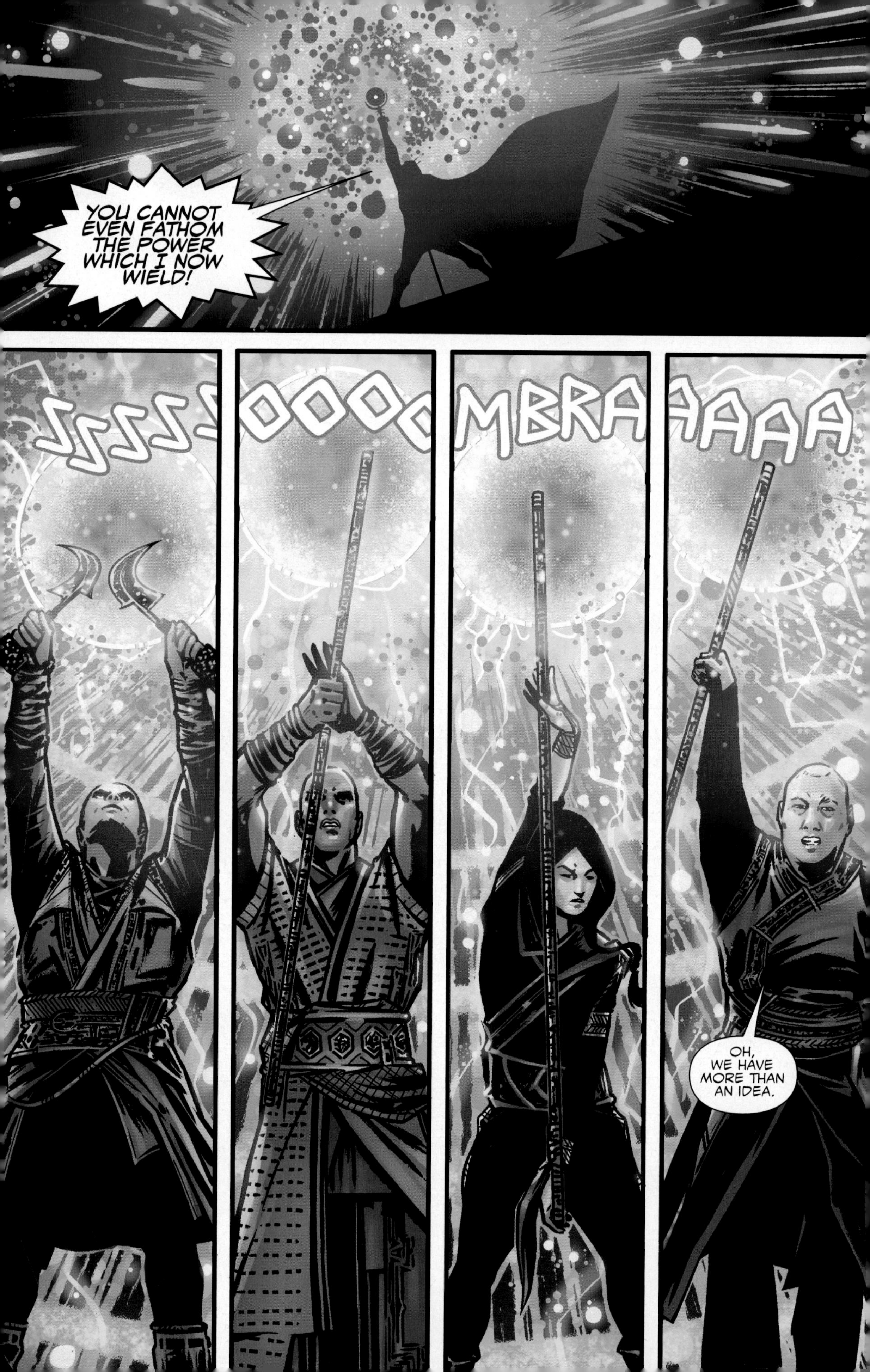
YOU CANNOT EVEN FATHOM THE POWER WHICH I NOW WIELD!
SSSSOOOOMBRAAAAA
OH, WE HAVE MORE THAN AN IDEA.

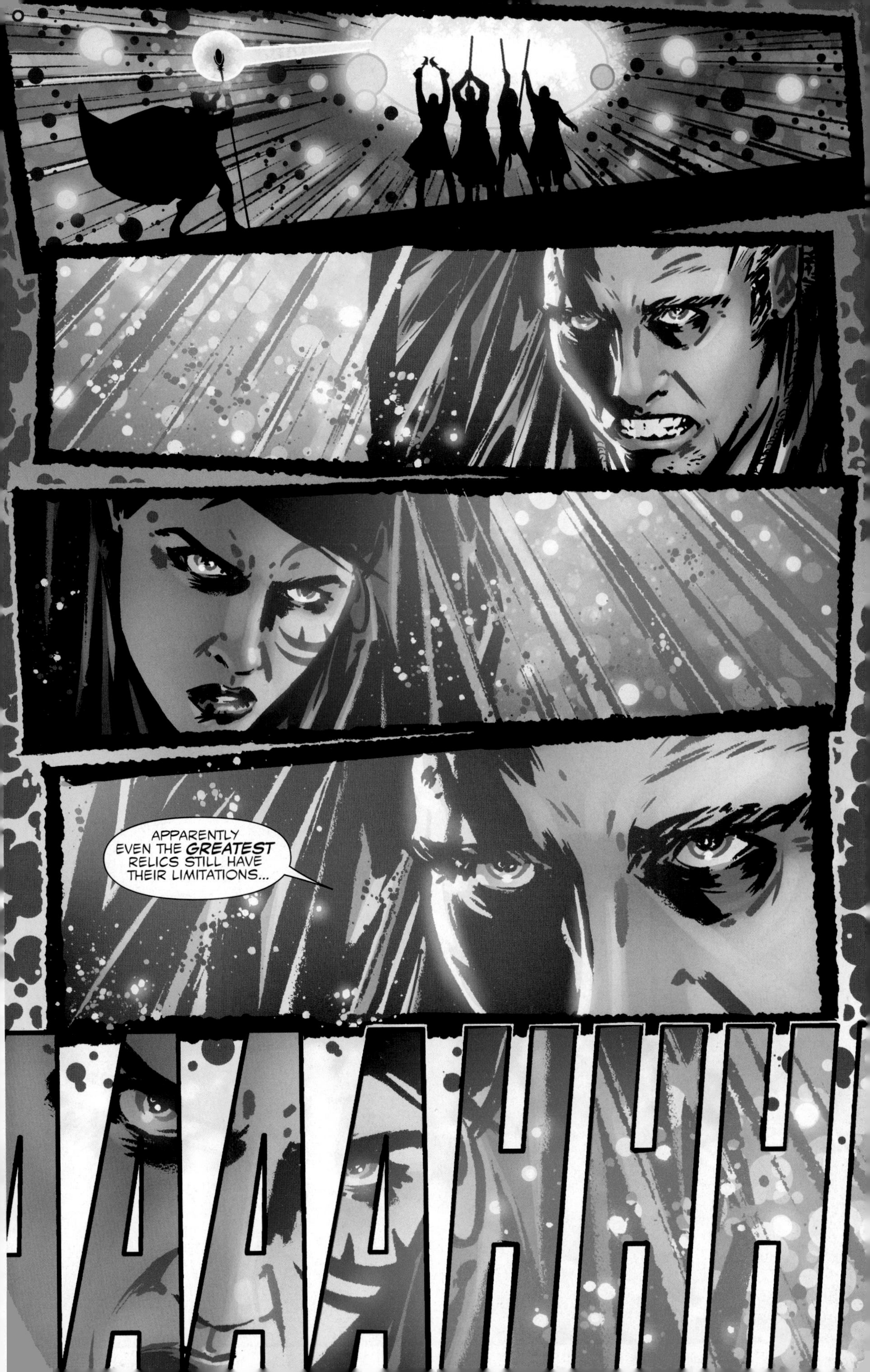
APPARENTLY EVEN THE GREATEST RELICS STILL HAVE THEIR LIMITATIONS...
AAAAHHHHH

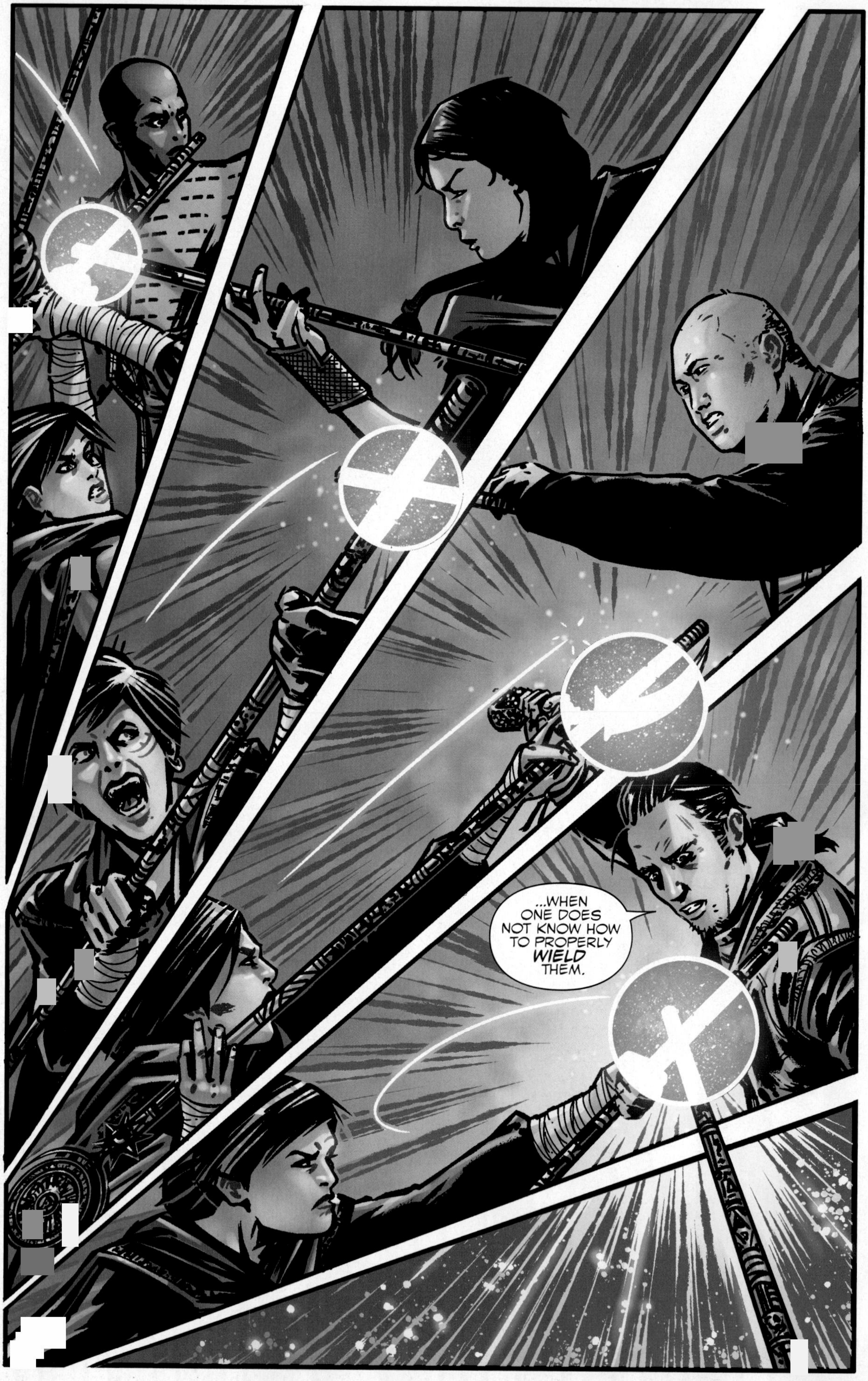
...WHEN ONE DOES NOT KNOW HOW TO PROPERLY **WIELD** THEM.

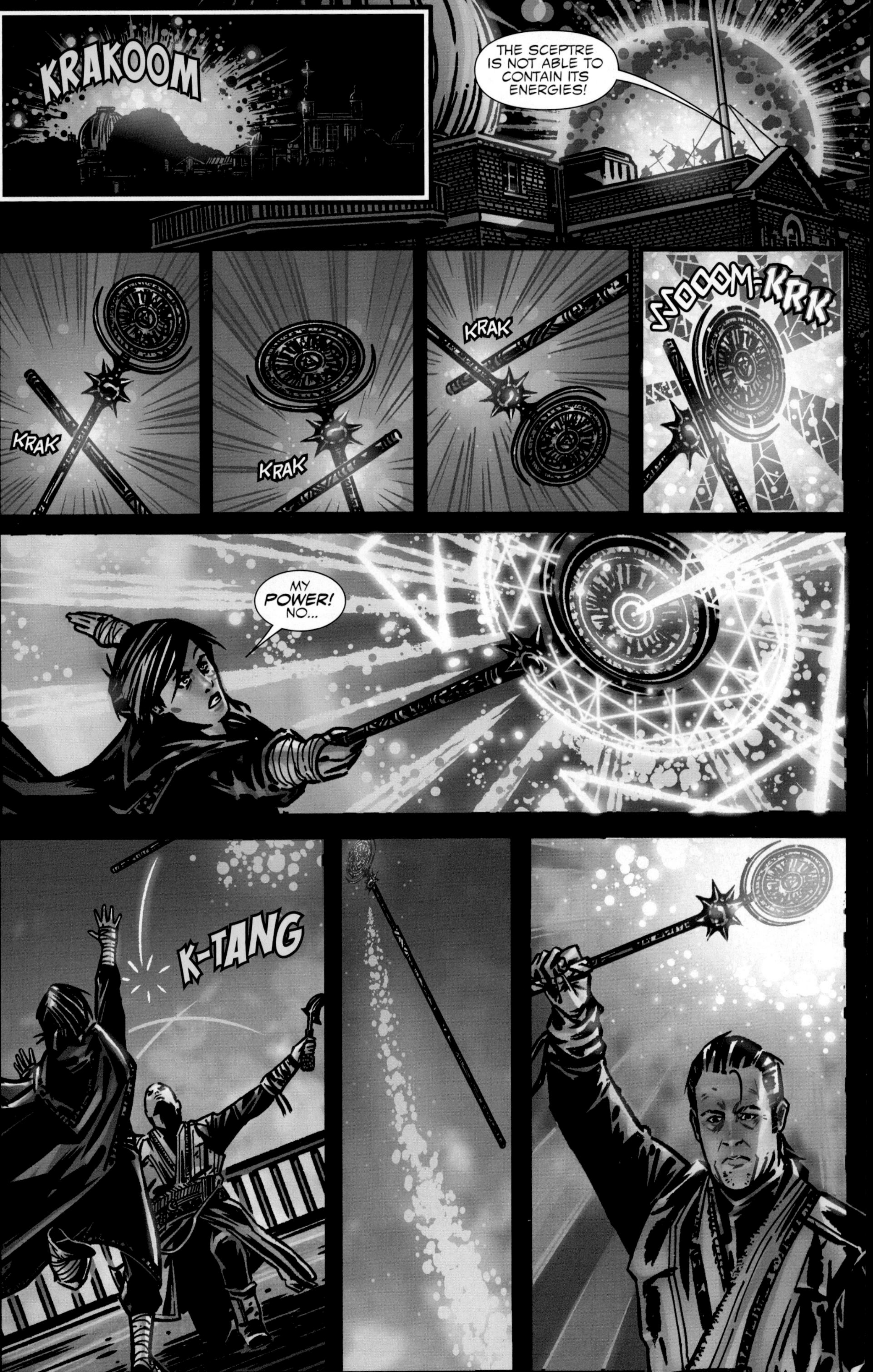
KRAKOOM
THE SCEPTRE IS NOT ABLE TO CONTAIN ITS ENERGIES!
KRAK
KRAK
KRAK
WOOOM-KRK
MY POWER! NO...
K-TANG

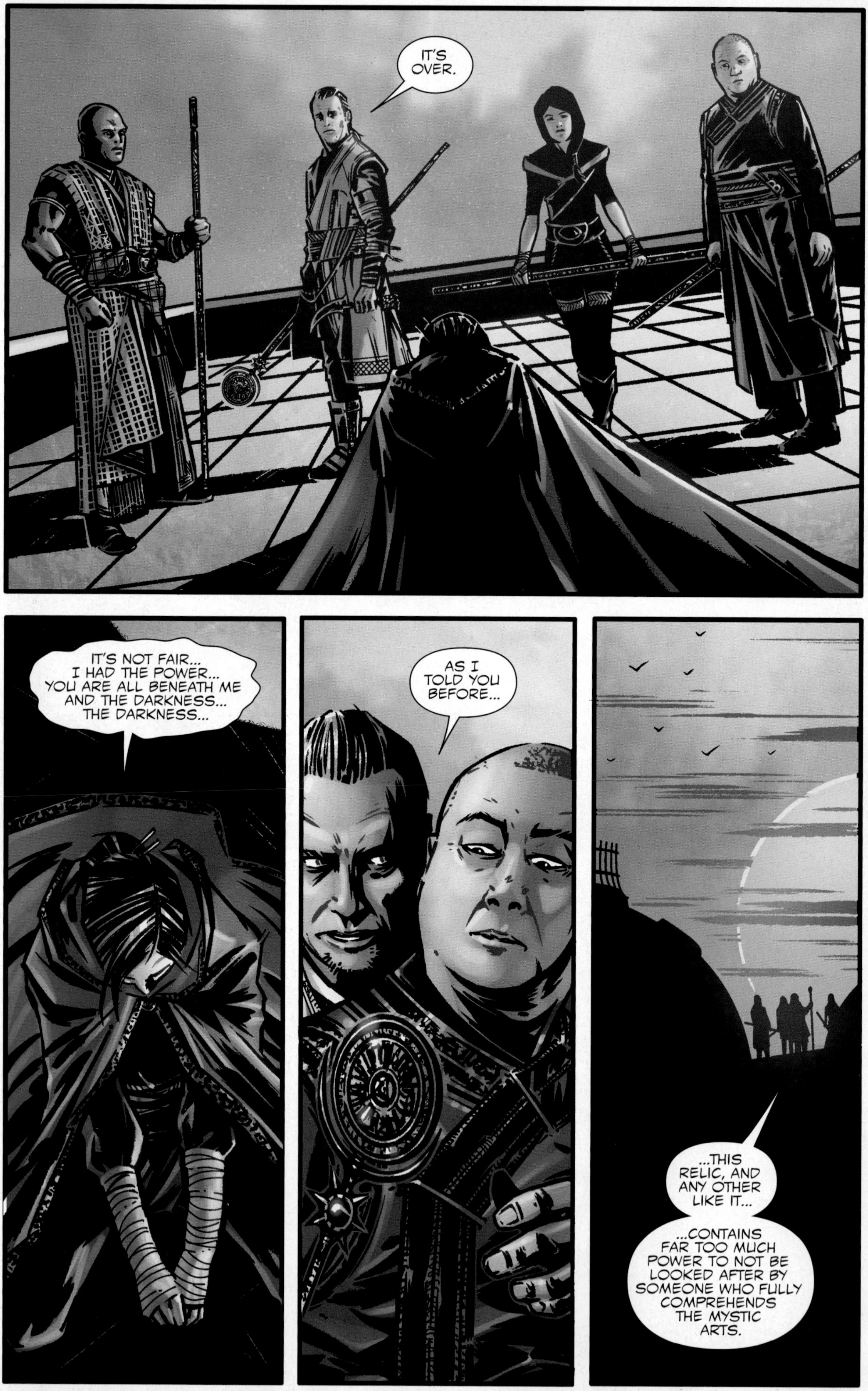

IT'S OVER.
IT'S NOT FAIR... I HAD THE POWER... YOU ARE ALL BENEATH ME AND THE DARKNESS... THE DARKNESS...
AS I TOLD YOU BEFORE...
...THIS RELIC, AND ANY OTHER LIKE IT...
...CONTAINS FAR TOO MUCH POWER TO NOT BE LOOKED AFTER BY SOMEONE WHO FULLY COMPREHENDS THE MYSTIC ARTS.

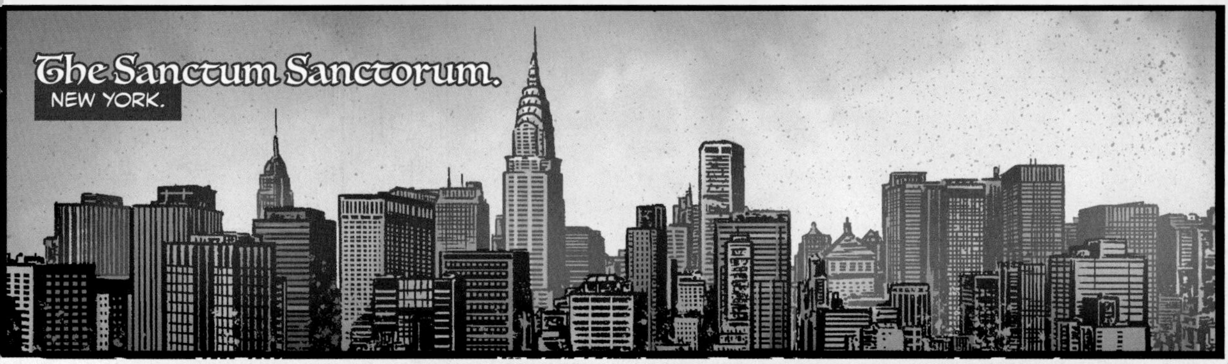
The Sanctum Sanctorum.
NEW YORK.

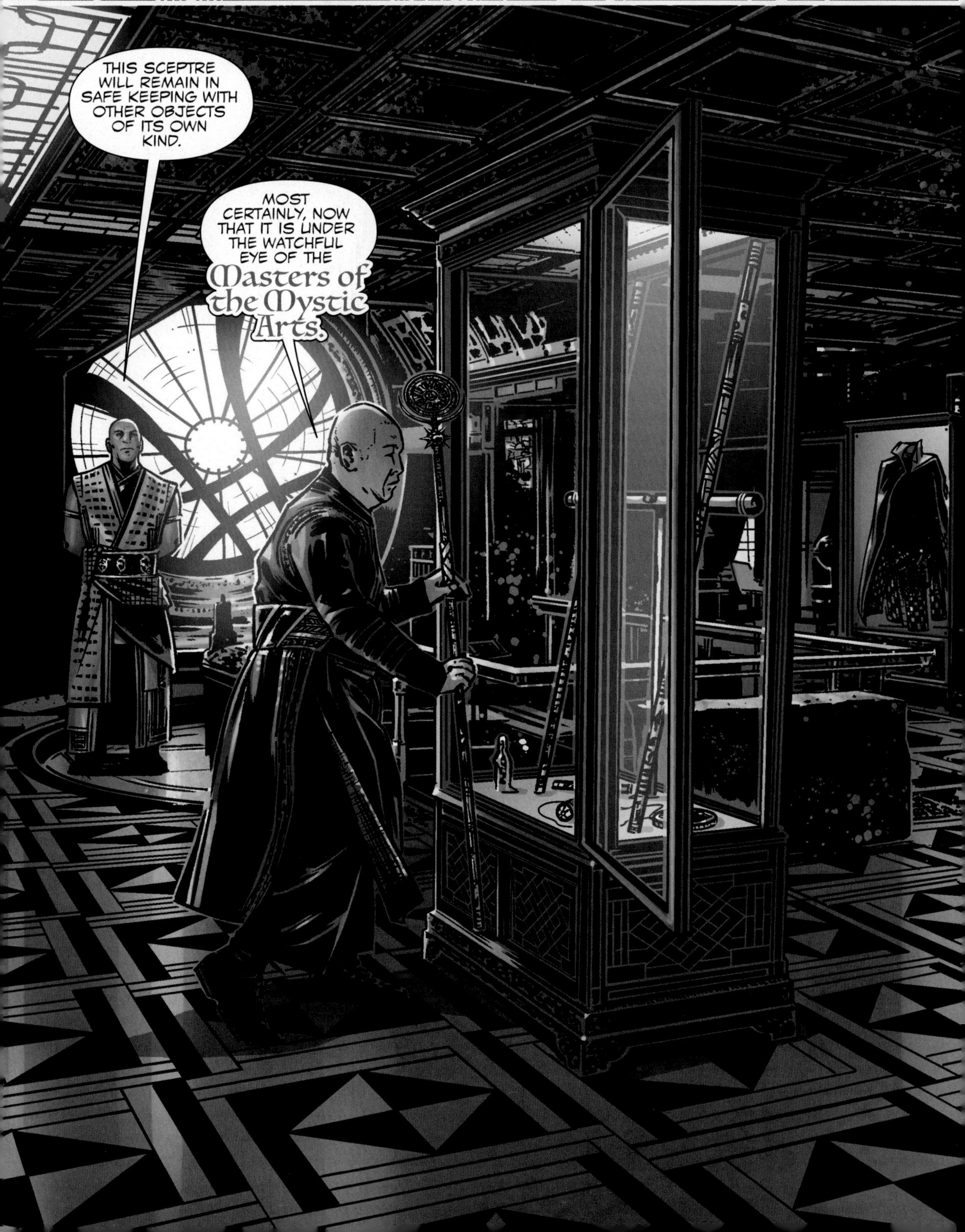
THIS SCEPTRE WILL REMAIN IN SAFE KEEPING WITH OTHER OBJECTS OF ITS OWN KIND.
MOST CERTAINLY, NOW THAT IT IS UNDER THE WATCHFUL EYE OF THE Masters of the Mystic Arts.

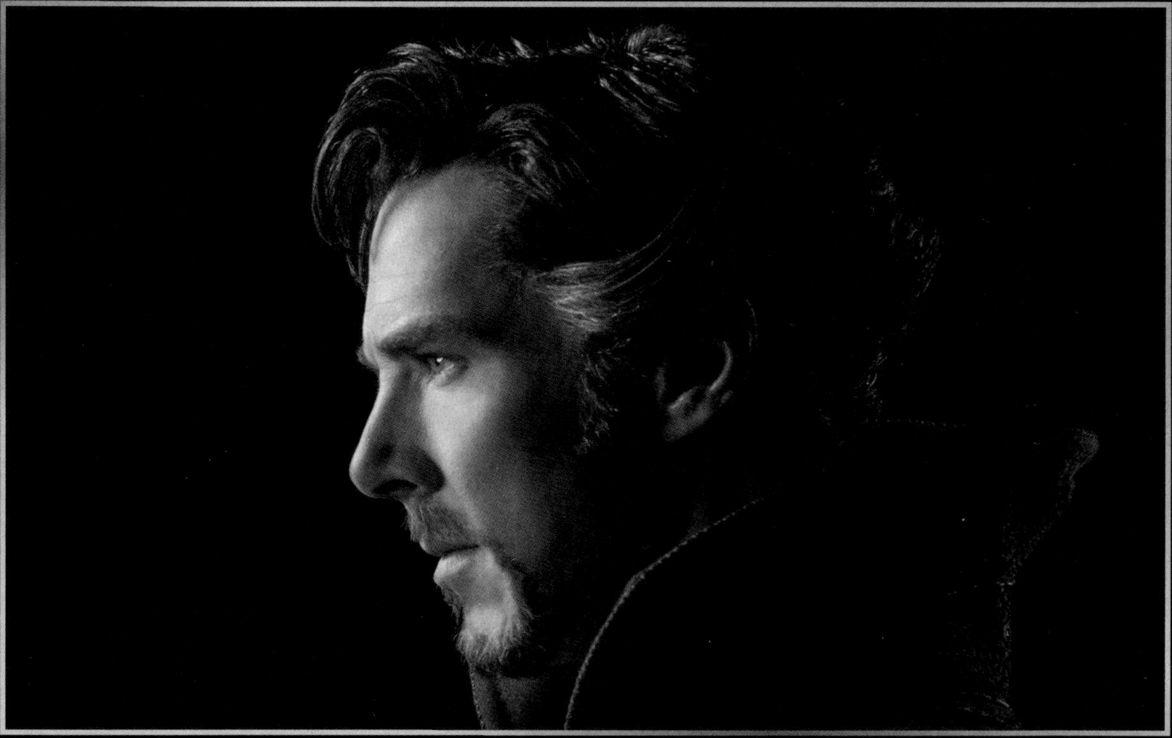

MARVEL'S DOCTOR STRANGE PRELUDE #2

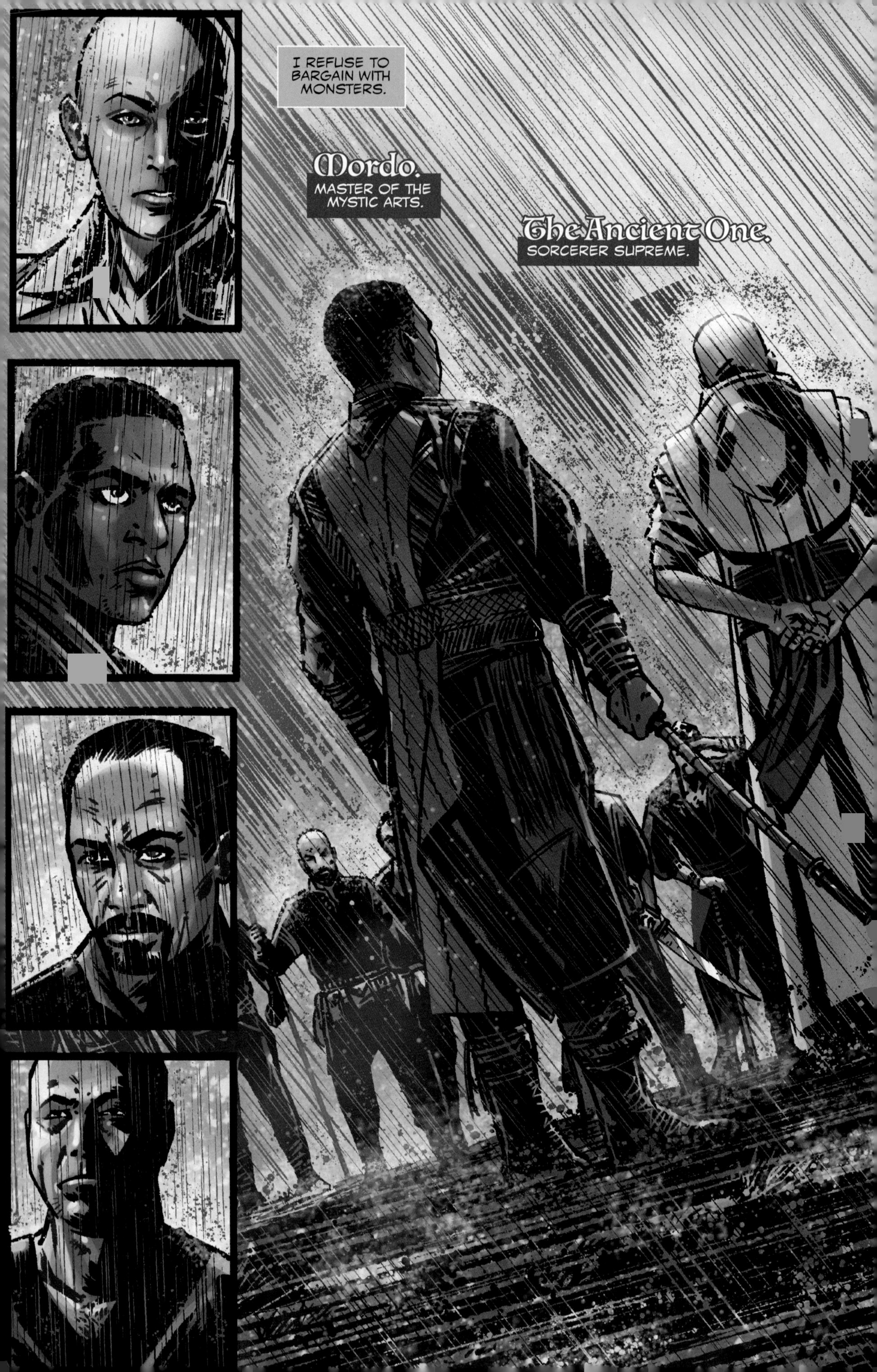
I REFUSE TO BARGAIN WITH MONSTERS.
Mordo.
MASTER OF THE MYSTIC ARTS.
The Ancient One.
SORCERER SUPREME.

Guizhou, China.

WHEN MORDO TOLD
ME THE ARROW OF
APOLLON HAD BEEN
DISCOVERED, I
SENSED HE KNEW
THE KIND OF MAN
WHO HAD FOUND IT.

Jiāo'ào Zhànshì.
LEADER OF THE DRAGON RAIDERS.

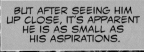

BUT AFTER SEEING HIM
UP CLOSE, IT'S APPARENT
HE IS AS SMALL AS
HIS ASPIRATIONS.

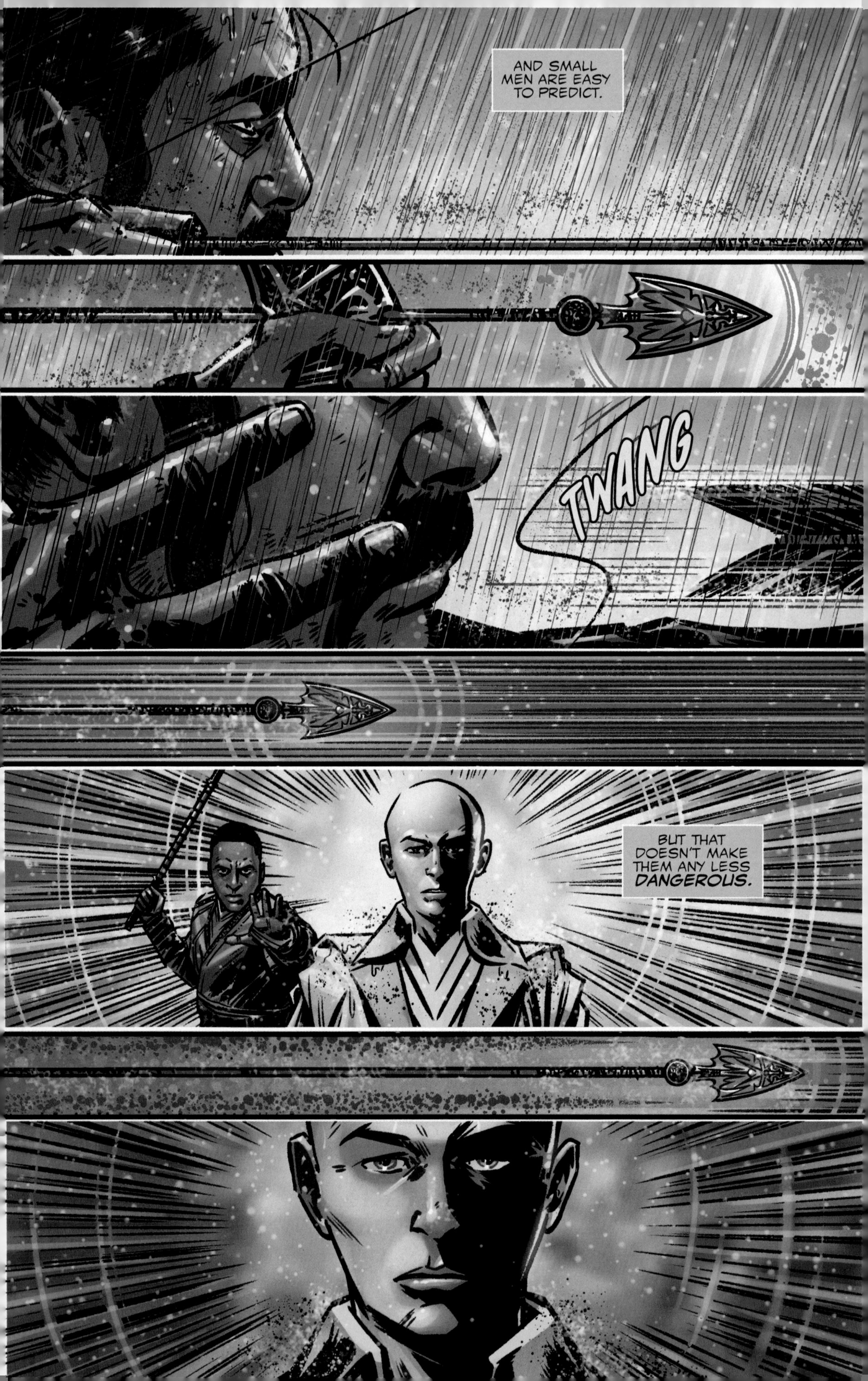
AND SMALL MEN ARE EASY TO PREDICT.
TWANG
BUT THAT DOESN'T MAKE THEM ANY LESS DANGEROUS.

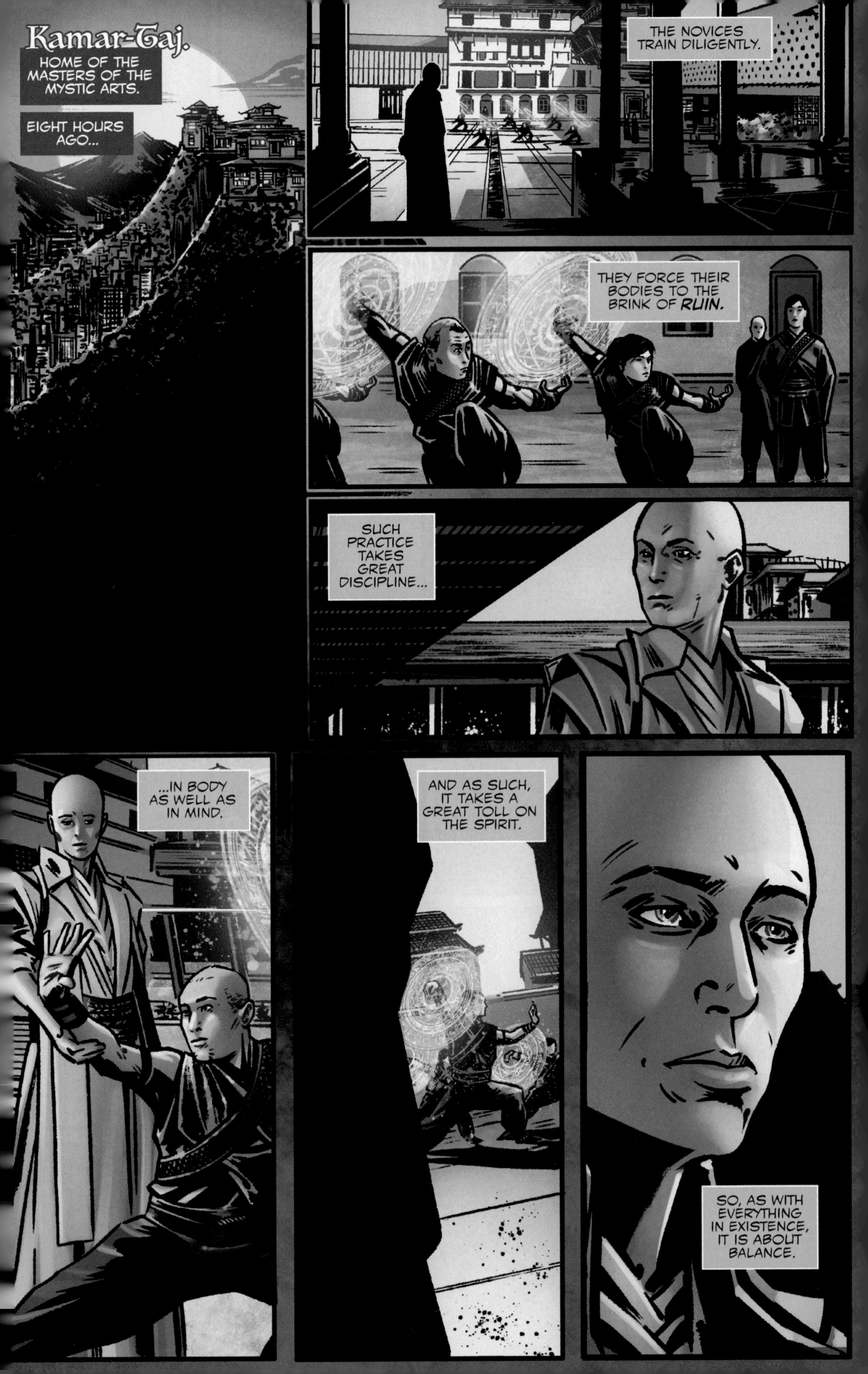
Kamar-Taj.
HOME OF THE MASTERS OF THE MYSTIC ARTS.
EIGHT HOURS AGO...
THE NOVICES TRAIN DILIGENTLY.
THEY FORCE THEIR BODIES TO THE BRINK OF RUIN.
SUCH PRACTICE TAKES GREAT DISCIPLINE...
...IN BODY AS WELL AS IN MIND.
AND AS SUCH, IT TAKES A GREAT TOLL ON THE SPIRIT.
SO, AS WITH EVERYTHING IN EXISTENCE, IT IS ABOUT BALANCE.

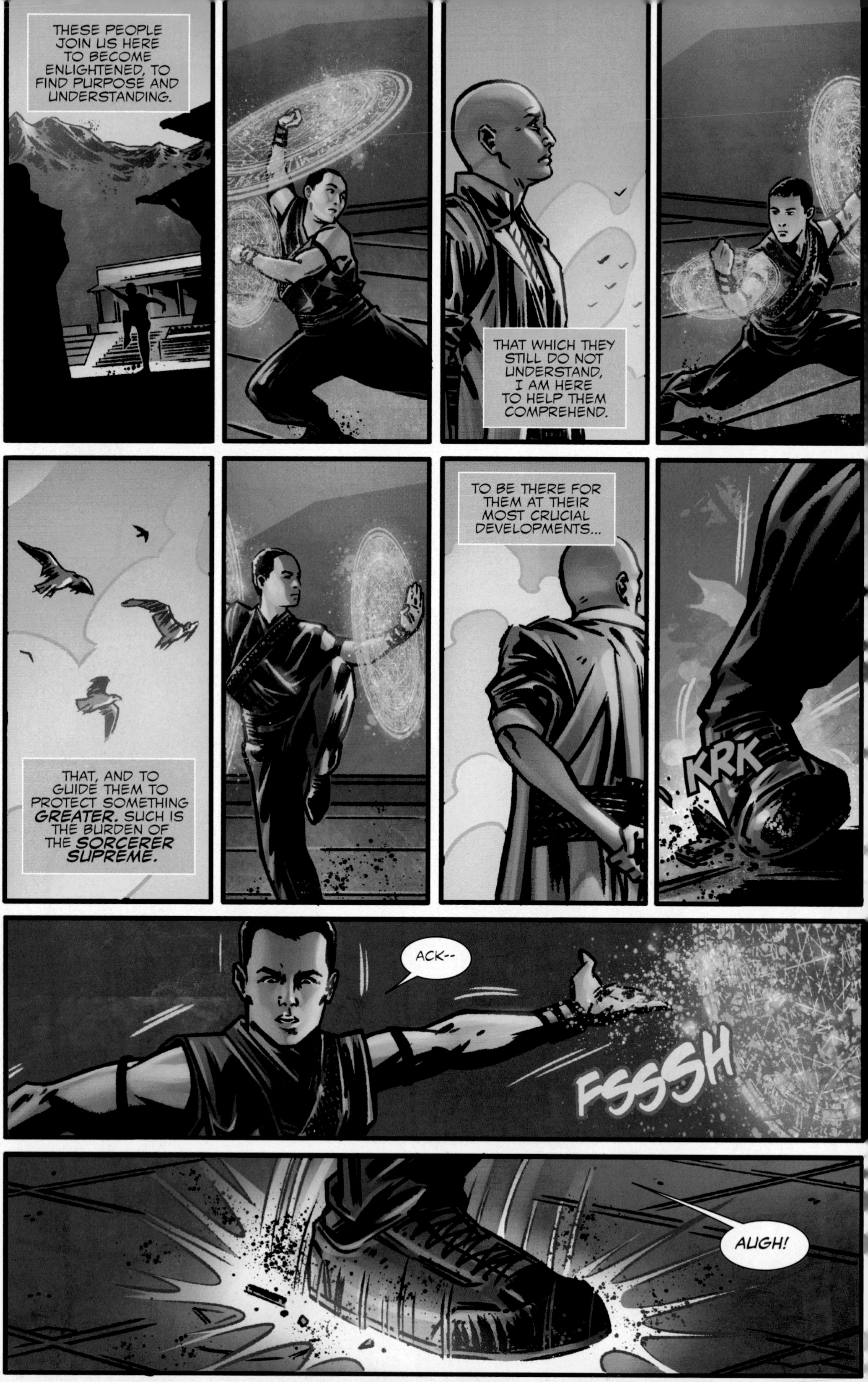

THESE PEOPLE JOIN US HERE TO BECOME ENLIGHTENED, TO FIND PURPOSE AND UNDERSTANDING.
THAT WHICH THEY STILL DO NOT UNDERSTAND, I AM HERE TO HELP THEM COMPREHEND.
THAT, AND TO GUIDE THEM TO PROTECT SOMETHING GREATER. SUCH IS THE BURDEN OF THE SORCERER SUPREME.
TO BE THERE FOR THEM AT THEIR MOST CRUCIAL DEVELOPMENTS...
KRK
ACK--
FSSSH
AUGH!

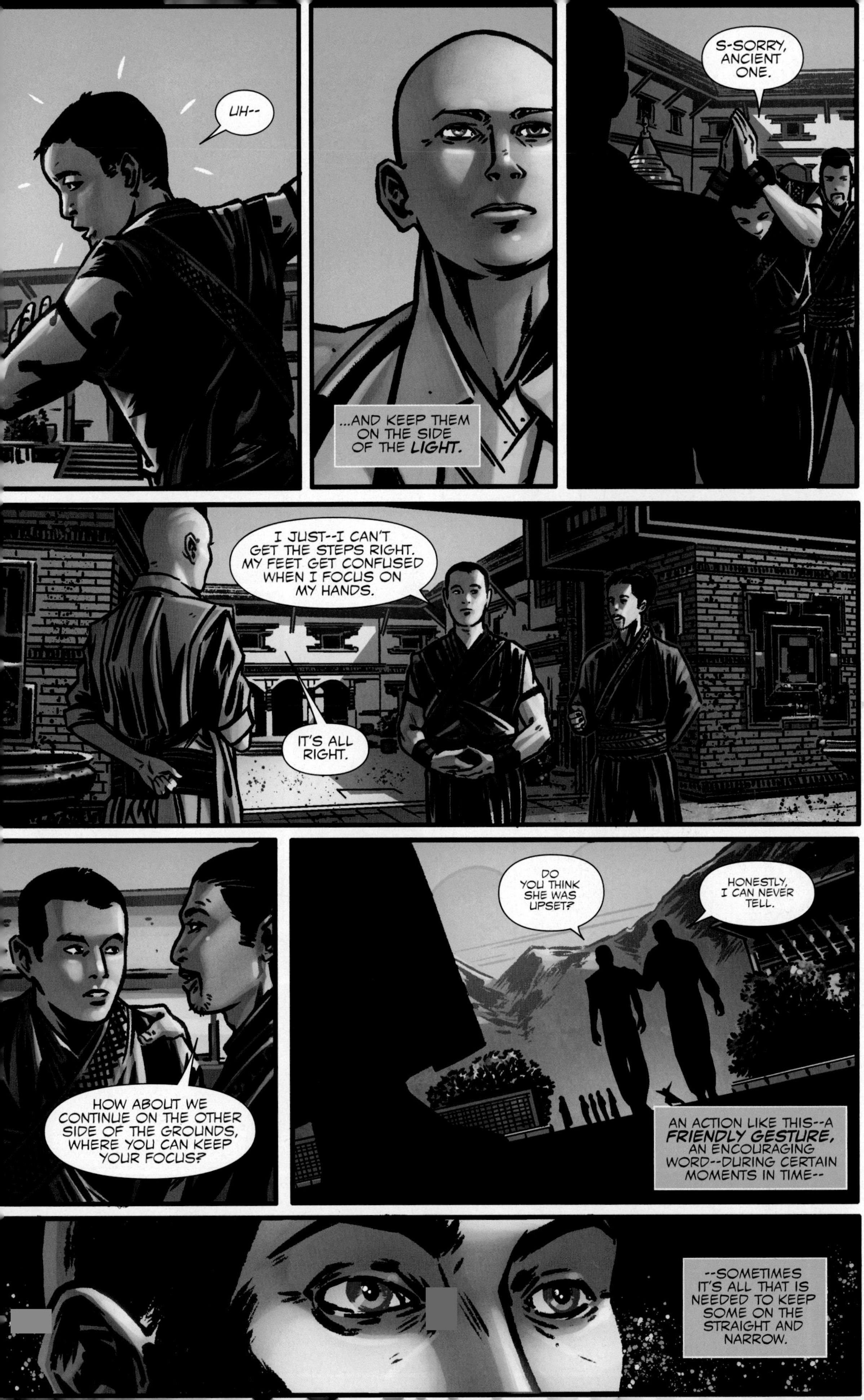
UH--
...AND KEEP THEM ON THE SIDE OF THE LIGHT.
S-SORRY, ANCIENT ONE.
I JUST--I CAN'T GET THE STEPS RIGHT. MY FEET GET CONFUSED WHEN I FOCUS ON MY HANDS.
IT'S ALL RIGHT.
HOW ABOUT WE CONTINUE ON THE OTHER SIDE OF THE GROUNDS, WHERE YOU CAN KEEP YOUR FOCUS?
DO YOU THINK SHE WAS UPSET?
HONESTLY, I CAN NEVER TELL.
AN ACTION LIKE THIS--A FRIENDLY GESTURE, AN ENCOURAGING WORD--DURING CERTAIN MOMENTS IN TIME--
--SOMETIMES IT'S ALL THAT IS NEEDED TO KEEP SOME ON THE STRAIGHT AND NARROW.

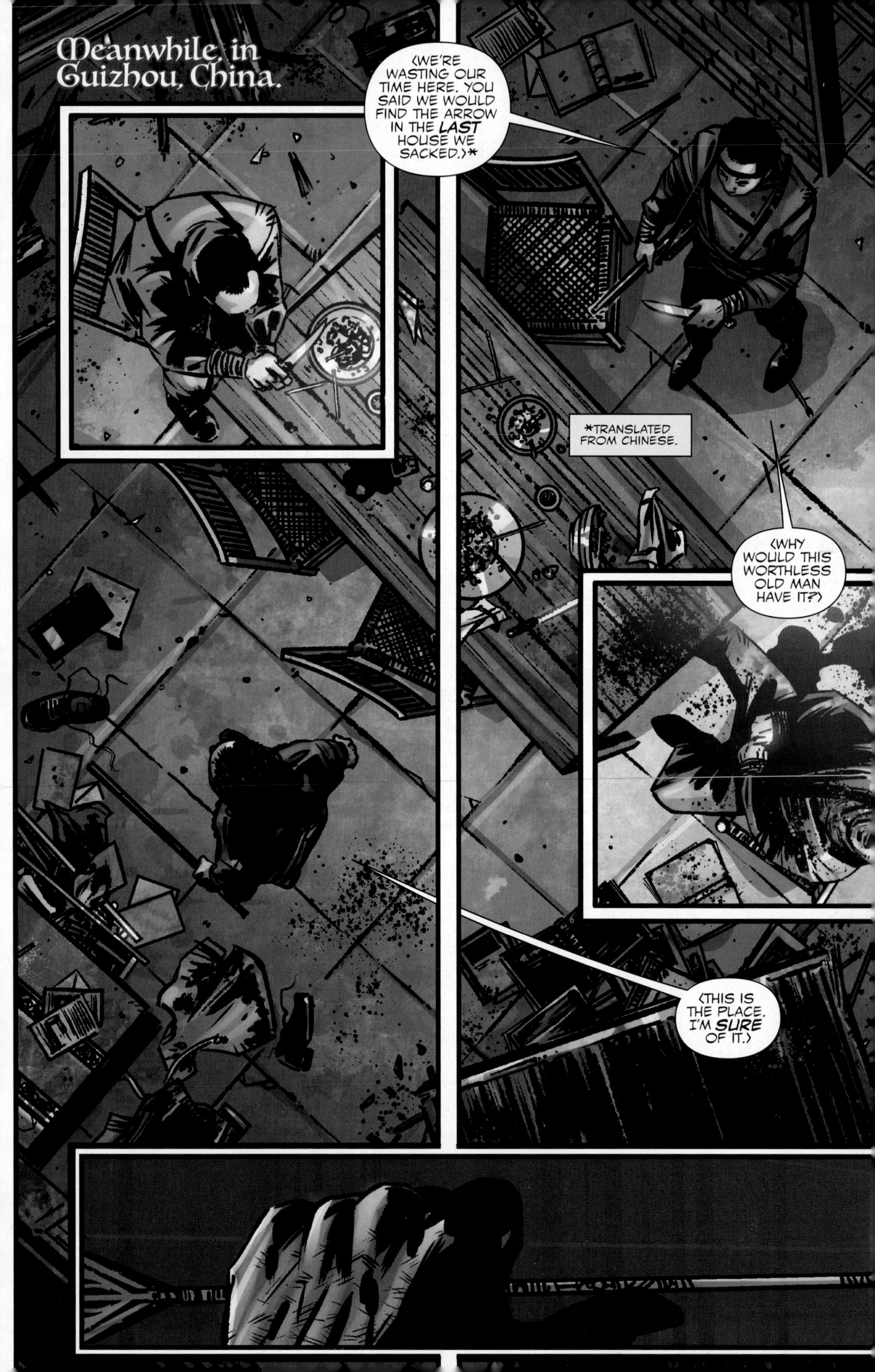
Meanwhile, in Guizhou, China.
<WE'RE WASTING OUR TIME HERE. YOU SAID WE WOULD FIND THE ARROW IN THE LAST HOUSE WE SACKED.>*
*TRANSLATED FROM CHINESE.
<WHY WOULD THIS WORTHLESS OLD MAN HAVE IT?>
<THIS IS THE PLACE. I'M SURE OF IT.>

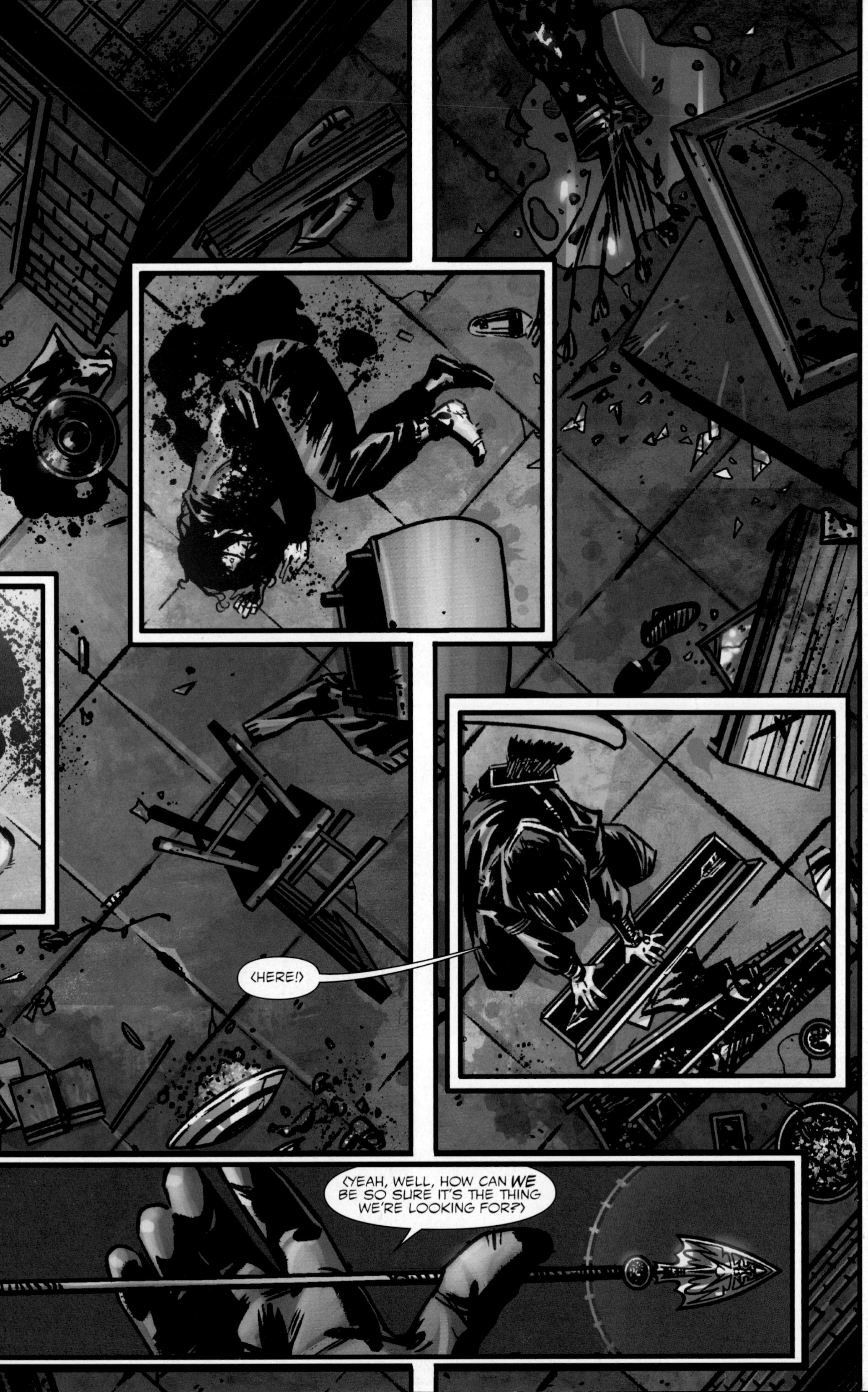
‹HERE!›
‹YEAH, WELL, HOW CAN WE BE SO SURE IT'S THE THING WE'RE LOOKING FOR?›

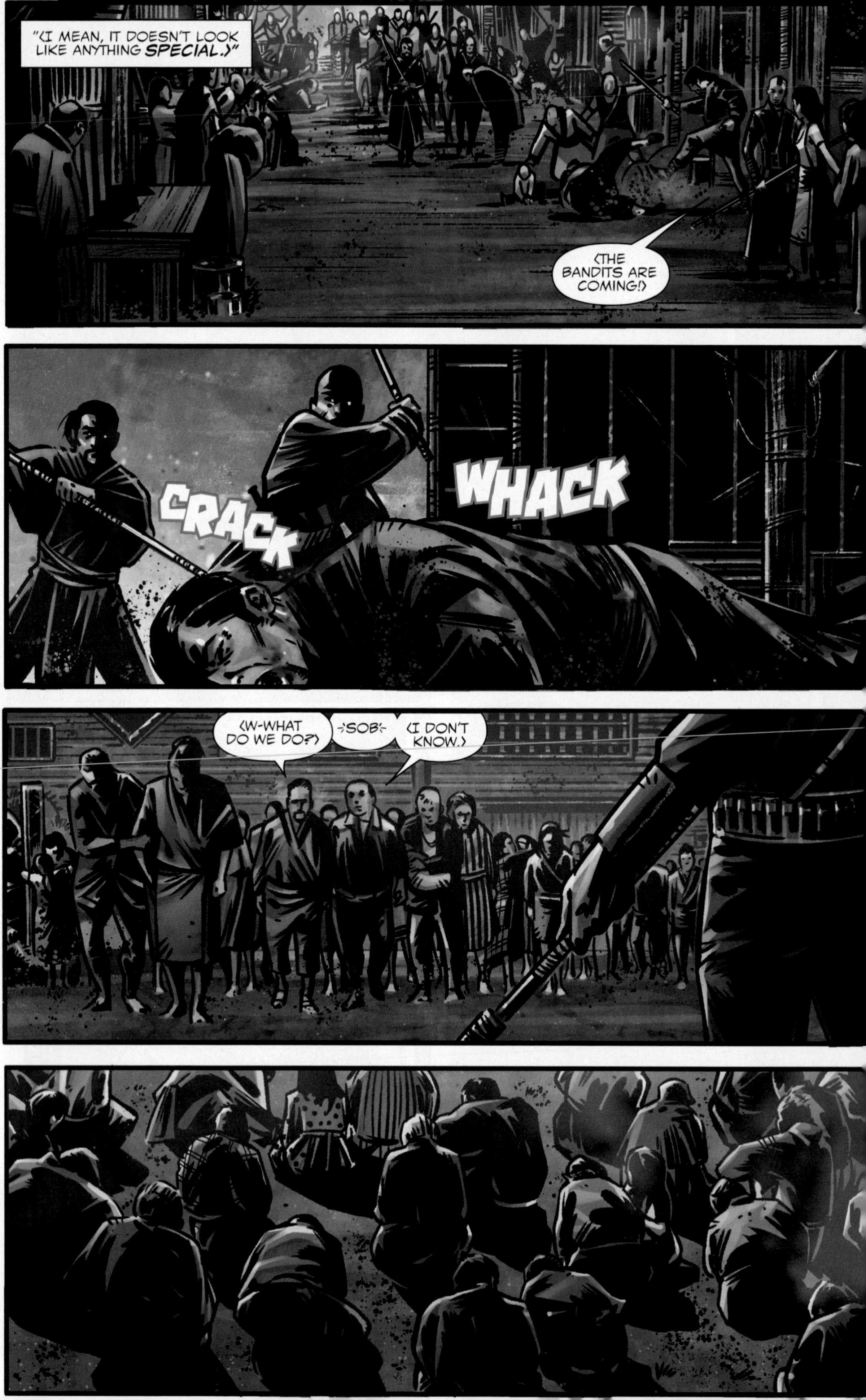
"‹I MEAN, IT DOESN'T LOOK LIKE ANYTHING SPECIAL.›"
‹THE BANDITS ARE COMING!›
CRACK
WHACK
‹W-WHAT DO WE DO?›
-SOB-
‹I DON'T KNOW.›

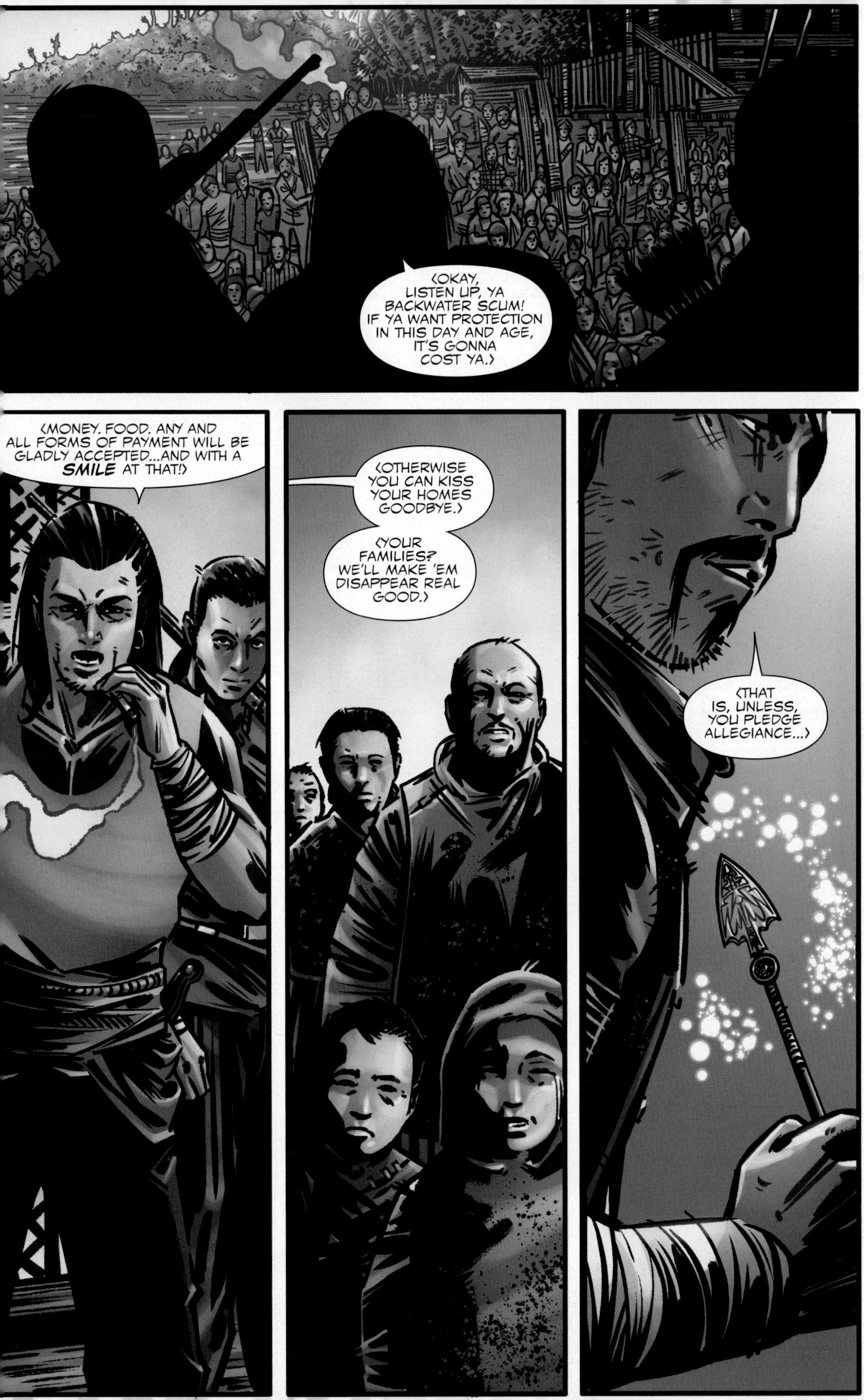

‹OKAY, LISTEN UP, YA BACKWATER SCUM! IF YA WANT PROTECTION IN THIS DAY AND AGE, IT'S GONNA COST YA.›
‹MONEY. FOOD. ANY AND ALL FORMS OF PAYMENT WILL BE GLADLY ACCEPTED...AND WITH A SMILE AT THAT!›
‹OTHERWISE YOU CAN KISS YOUR HOMES GOODBYE.›
‹YOUR FAMILIES? WE'LL MAKE 'EM DISAPPEAR REAL GOOD.›
‹THAT IS, UNLESS, YOU PLEDGE ALLEGIANCE...›

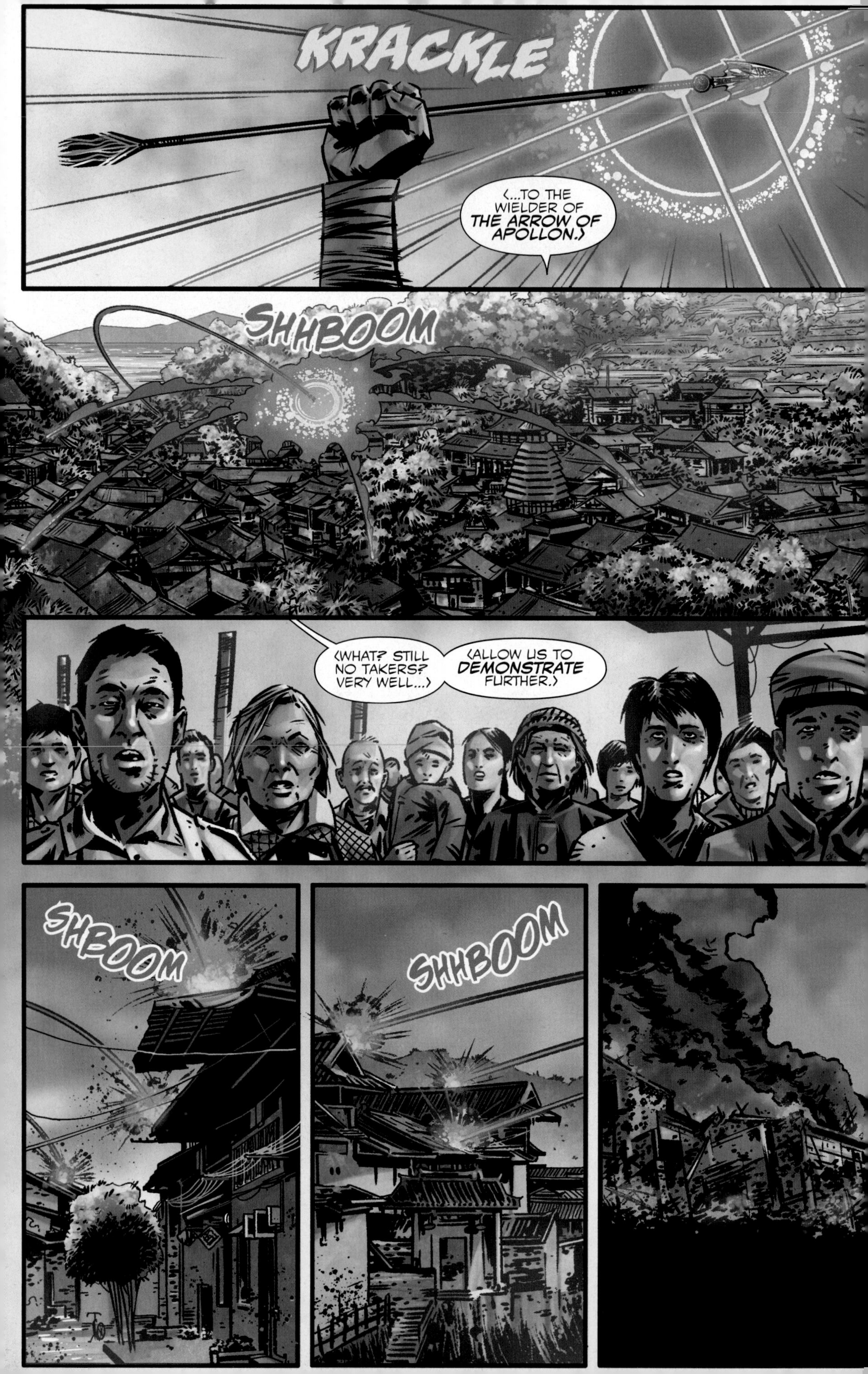
KRACKLE
<...TO THE WIELDER OF THE ARROW OF APOLLON.>
SHHBOOM
<WHAT? STILL NO TAKERS? VERY WELL...>
<ALLOW US TO DEMONSTRATE FURTHER.>
SHBOOM
SHHBOOM

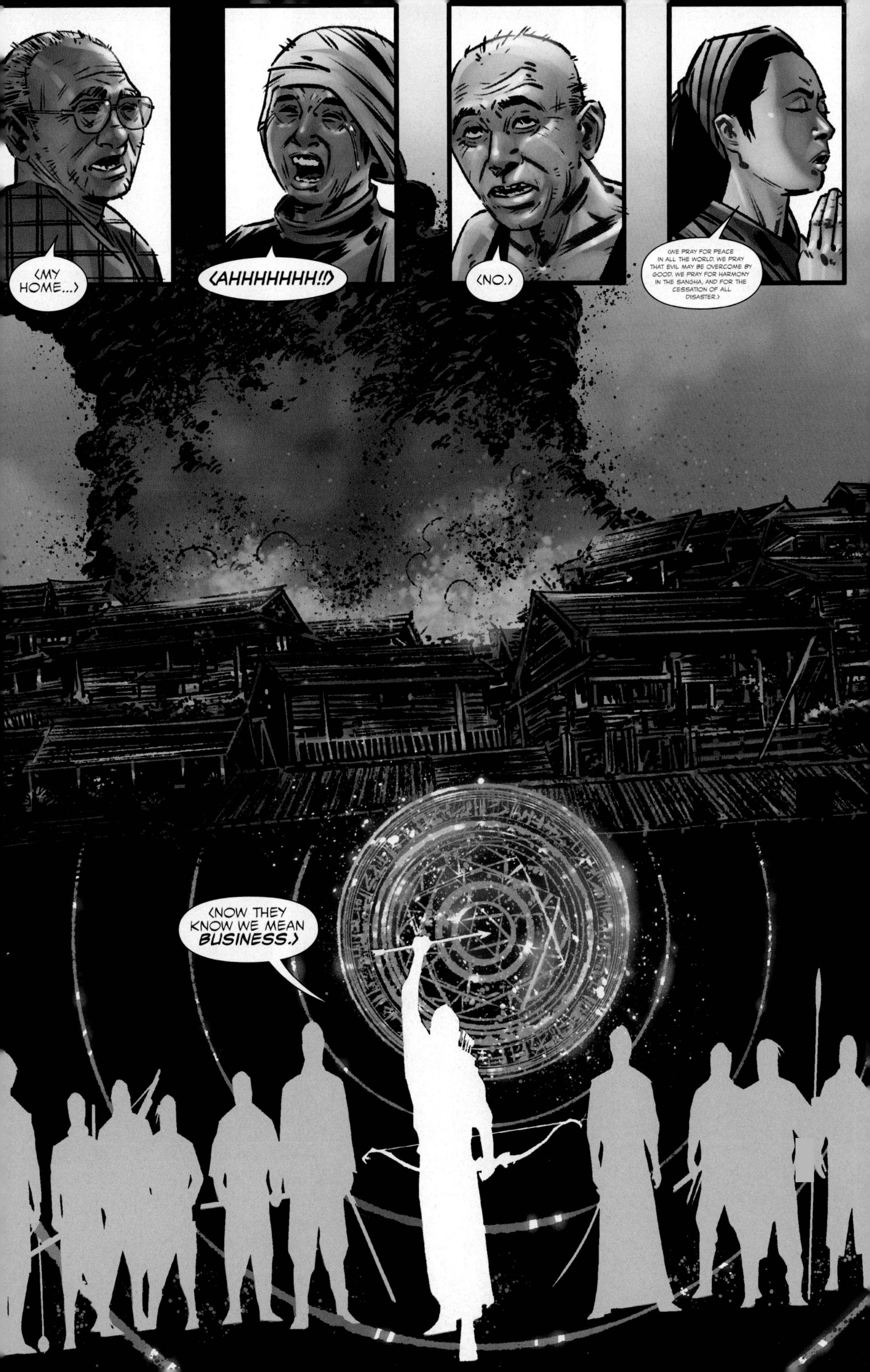
‹MY HOME...›
‹AHHHHHHH!!›
‹NO.›
‹WE PRAY FOR PEACE IN ALL THE WORLD. WE PRAY THAT EVIL MAY BE OVERCOME BY GOOD. WE PRAY FOR HARMONY IN THE SANGHA, AND FOR THE CESSATION OF ALL DISASTER.›
‹NOW THEY KNOW WE MEAN **BUSINESS**.›

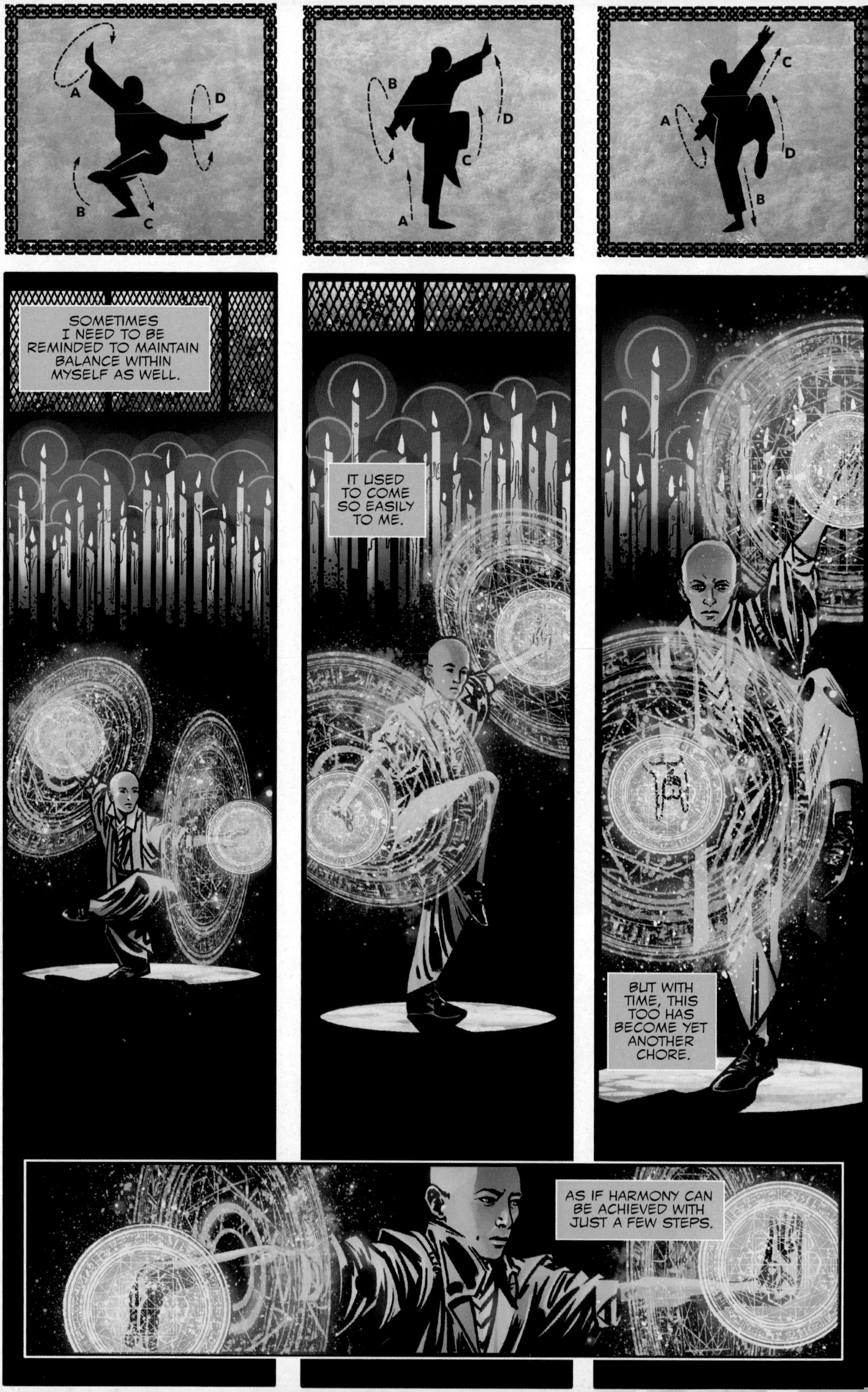
A
D
B
C
B
D
C
A
C
A
D
B
SOMETIMES I NEED TO BE REMINDED TO MAINTAIN BALANCE WITHIN MYSELF AS WELL.
IT USED TO COME SO EASILY TO ME.
BUT WITH TIME, THIS TOO HAS BECOME YET ANOTHER CHORE.
AS IF HARMONY CAN BE ACHIEVED WITH JUST A FEW STEPS.

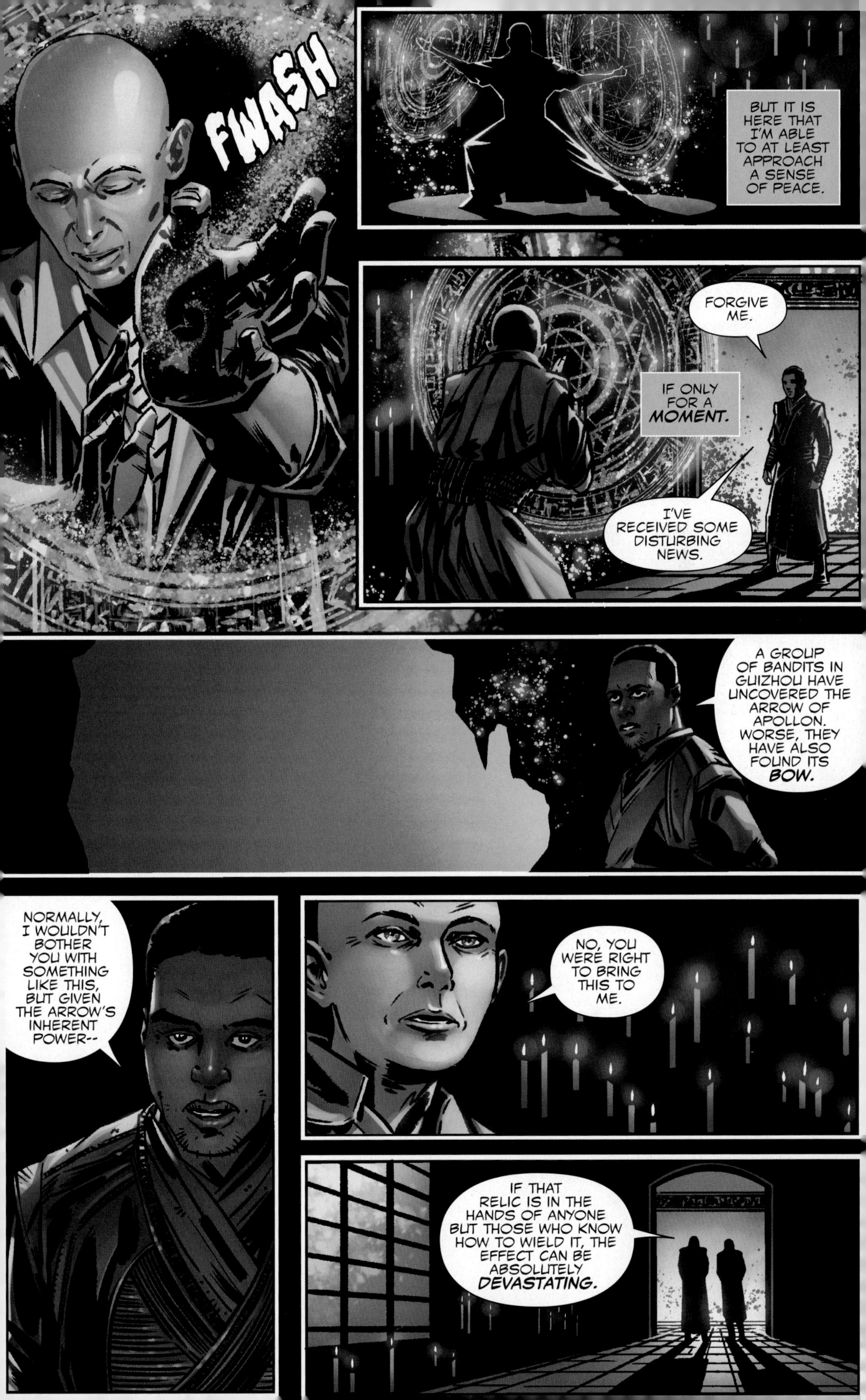
FWASH
BUT IT IS HERE THAT I'M ABLE TO AT LEAST APPROACH A SENSE OF PEACE.
FORGIVE ME.
IF ONLY FOR A MOMENT.
I'VE RECEIVED SOME DISTURBING NEWS.
A GROUP OF BANDITS IN GUIZHOU HAVE UNCOVERED THE ARROW OF APOLLON. WORSE, THEY HAVE ALSO FOUND ITS BOW.
NORMALLY, I WOULDN'T BOTHER YOU WITH SOMETHING LIKE THIS, BUT GIVEN THE ARROW'S INHERENT POWER--
NO, YOU WERE RIGHT TO BRING THIS TO ME.
IF THAT RELIC IS IN THE HANDS OF ANYONE BUT THOSE WHO KNOW HOW TO WIELD IT, THE EFFECT CAN BE ABSOLUTELY DEVASTATING.

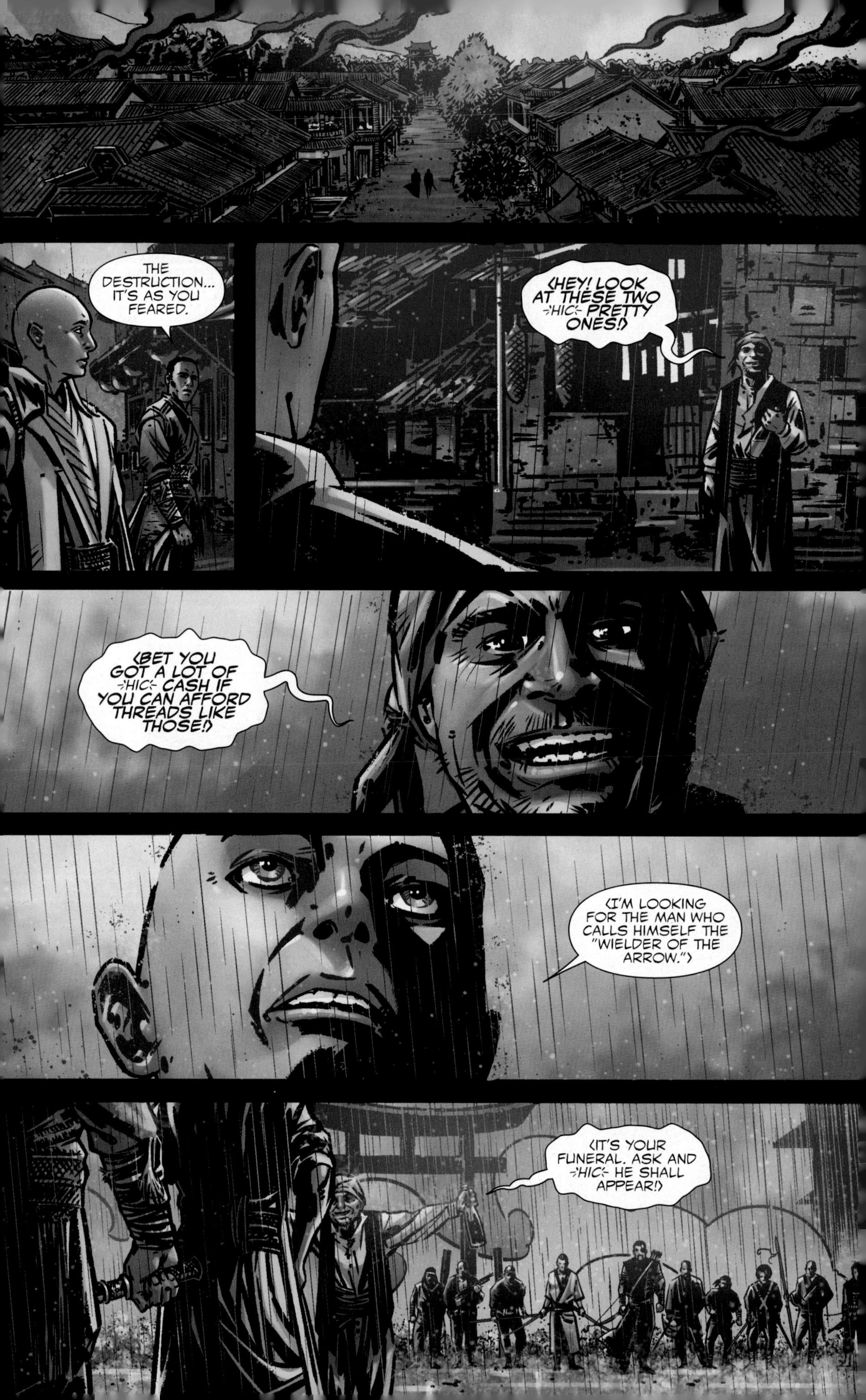
THE DESTRUCTION... IT'S AS YOU FEARED.
‹HEY! LOOK AT THESE TWO -HIC- PRETTY ONES!›
‹BET YOU GOT A LOT OF -HIC- CASH IF YOU CAN AFFORD THREADS LIKE THOSE!›
‹I'M LOOKING FOR THE MAN WHO CALLS HIMSELF THE "WIELDER OF THE ARROW."›
‹IT'S YOUR FUNERAL. ASK AND -HIC- HE SHALL APPEAR!›

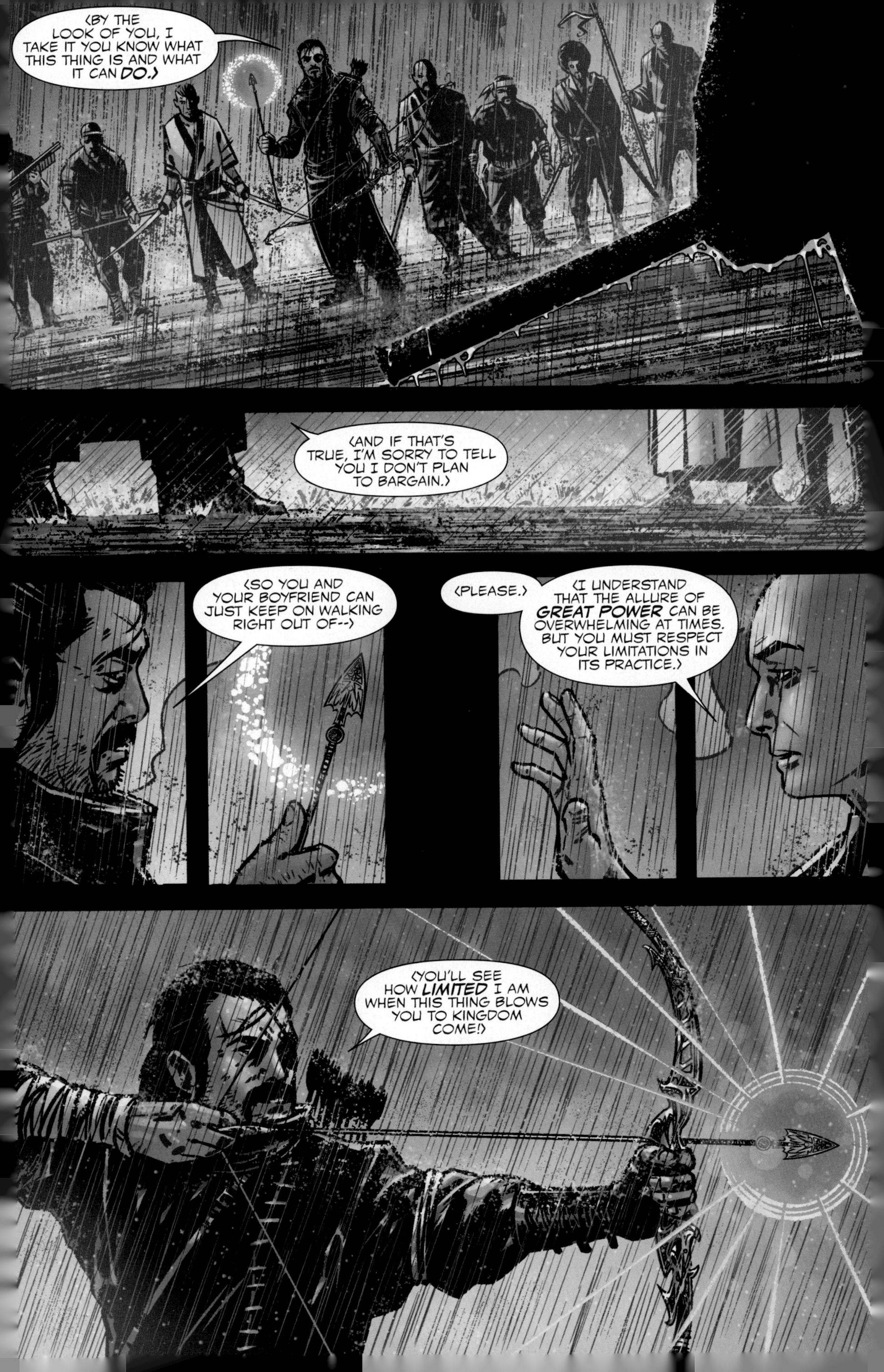

⟨BY THE LOOK OF YOU, I TAKE IT YOU KNOW WHAT THIS THING IS AND WHAT IT CAN **DO.**⟩
⟨AND IF THAT'S TRUE, I'M SORRY TO TELL YOU I DON'T PLAN TO BARGAIN.⟩
⟨SO YOU AND YOUR BOYFRIEND CAN JUST KEEP ON WALKING RIGHT OUT OF--⟩
⟨PLEASE.⟩
⟨I UNDERSTAND THAT THE ALLURE OF **GREAT POWER** CAN BE OVERWHELMING AT TIMES. BUT YOU MUST RESPECT YOUR LIMITATIONS IN ITS PRACTICE.⟩
⟨YOU'LL SEE HOW **LIMITED** I AM WHEN THIS THING BLOWS YOU TO KINGDOM COME!⟩

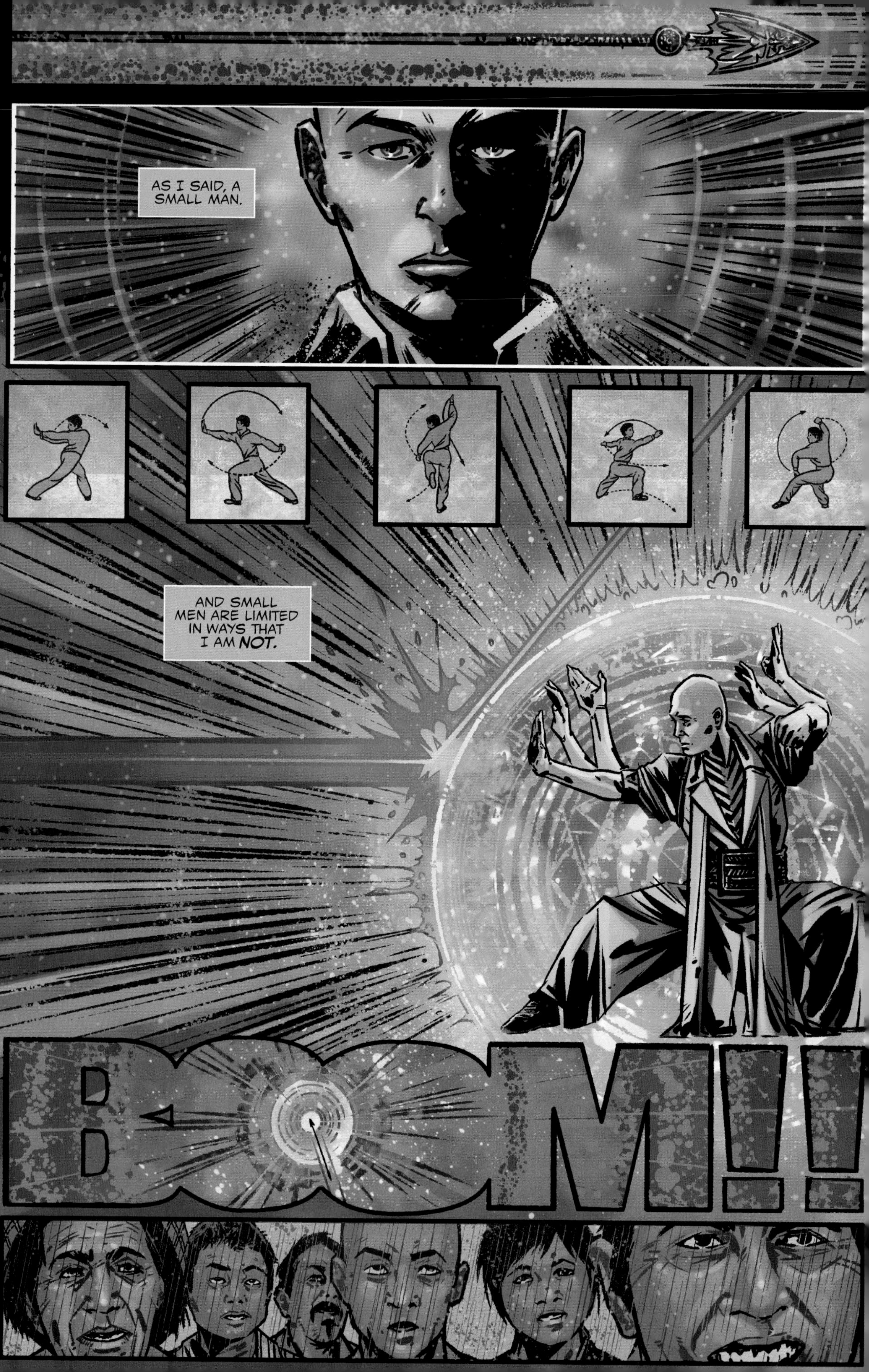
AS I SAID, A SMALL MAN.
AND SMALL MEN ARE LIMITED IN WAYS THAT I AM NOT.
BOOM!!

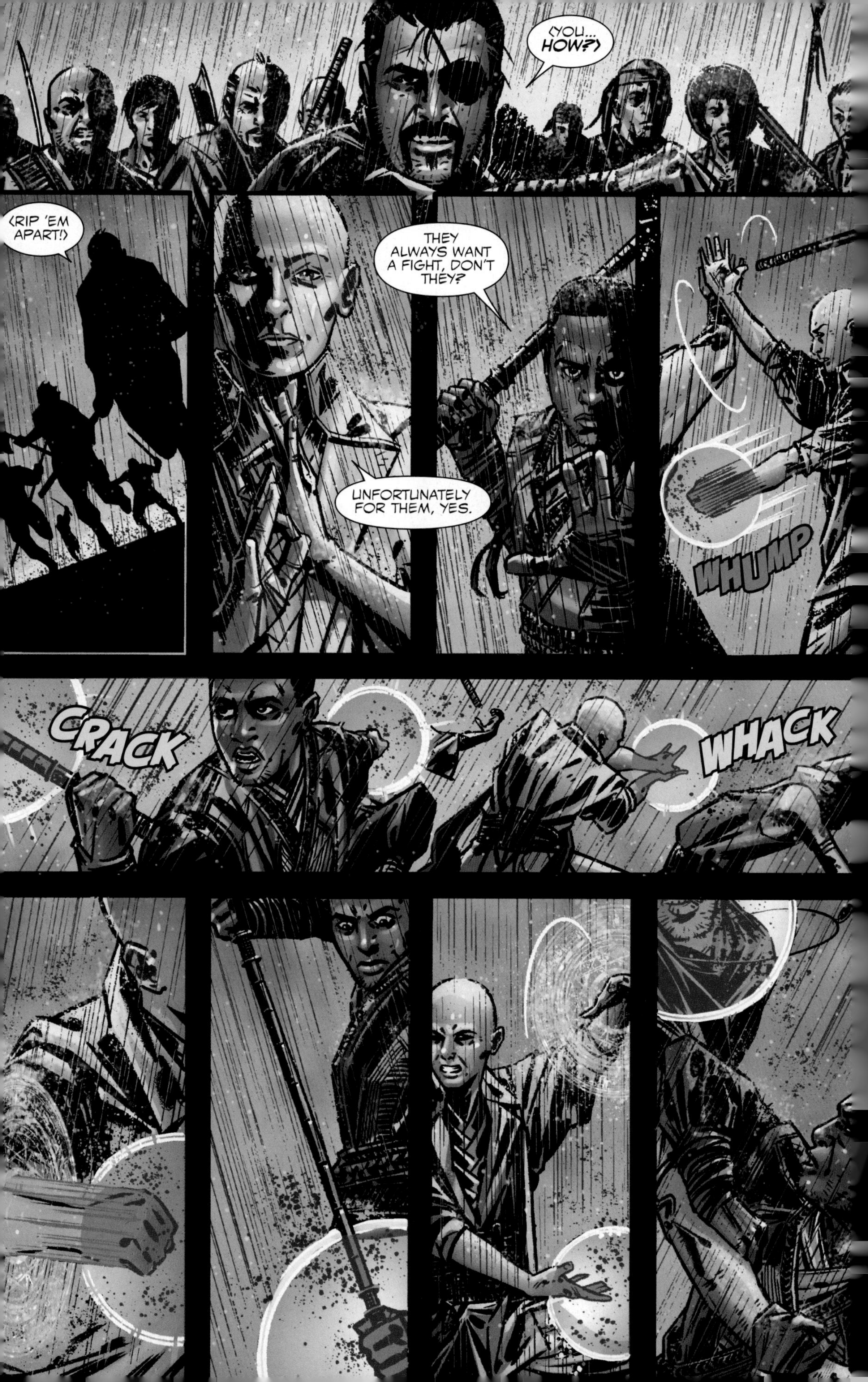
‹YOU... HOW?›
‹RIP 'EM APART!›
THEY ALWAYS WANT A FIGHT, DON'T THEY?
UNFORTUNATELY FOR THEM, YES.
WHUMP
CRACK
WHACK

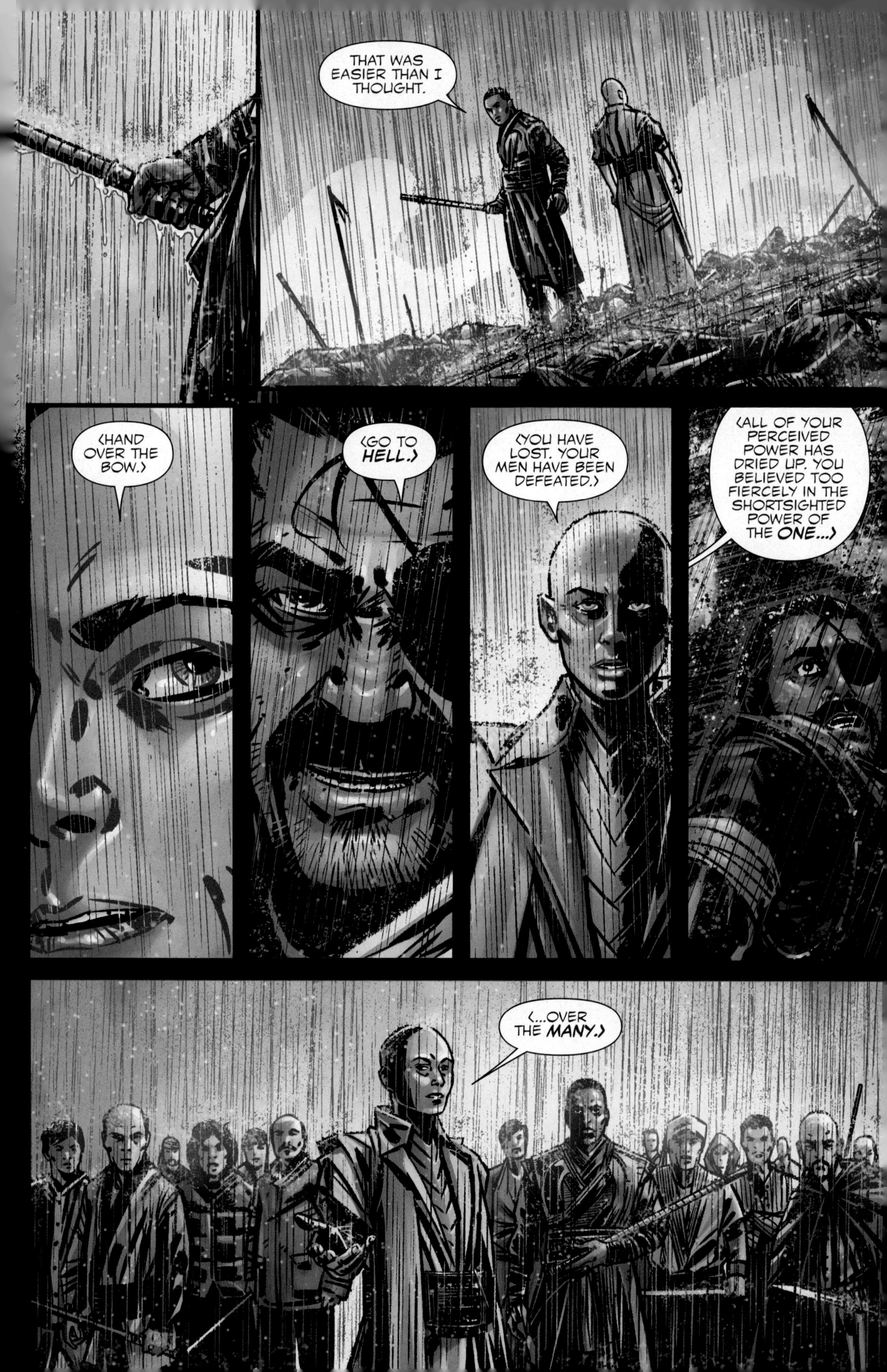
THAT WAS EASIER THAN I THOUGHT.
‹HAND OVER THE BOW.›
‹GO TO HELL.›
‹YOU HAVE LOST. YOUR MEN HAVE BEEN DEFEATED.›
‹ALL OF YOUR PERCEIVED POWER HAS DRIED UP. YOU BELIEVED TOO FIERCELY IN THE SHORTSIGHTED POWER OF THE ONE...›
‹...OVER THE MANY.›

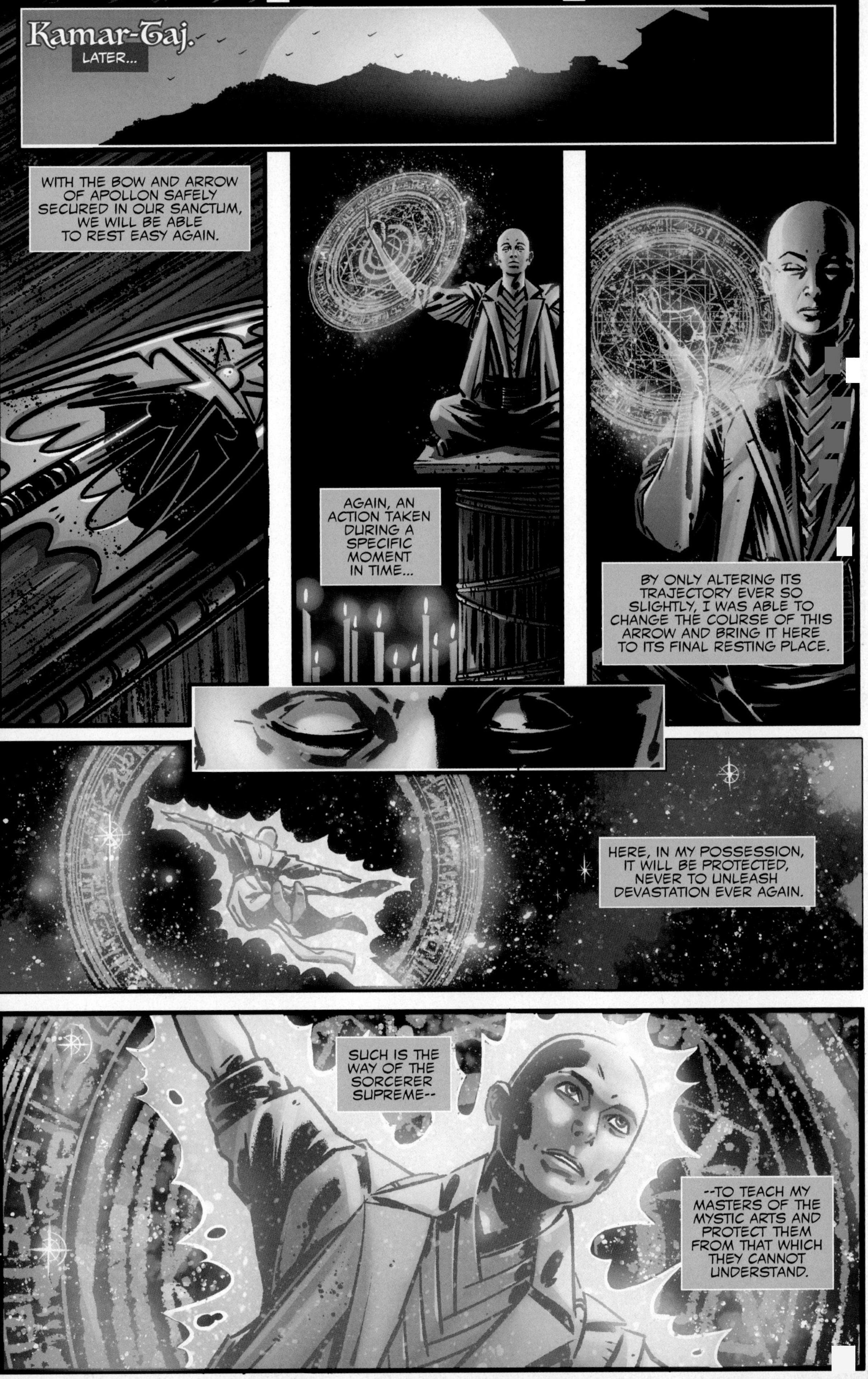

Kamar-Taj.
LATER...
WITH THE BOW AND ARROW OF APOLLON SAFELY SECURED IN OUR SANCTUM, WE WILL BE ABLE TO REST EASY AGAIN.
AGAIN, AN ACTION TAKEN DURING A SPECIFIC MOMENT IN TIME...
BY ONLY ALTERING ITS TRAJECTORY EVER SO SLIGHTLY, I WAS ABLE TO CHANGE THE COURSE OF THIS ARROW AND BRING IT HERE TO ITS FINAL RESTING PLACE.
HERE, IN MY POSSESSION, IT WILL BE PROTECTED, NEVER TO UNLEASH DEVASTATION EVER AGAIN.
SUCH IS THE WAY OF THE SORCERER SUPREME--
--TO TEACH MY MASTERS OF THE MYSTIC ARTS AND PROTECT THEM FROM THAT WHICH THEY CANNOT UNDERSTAND.

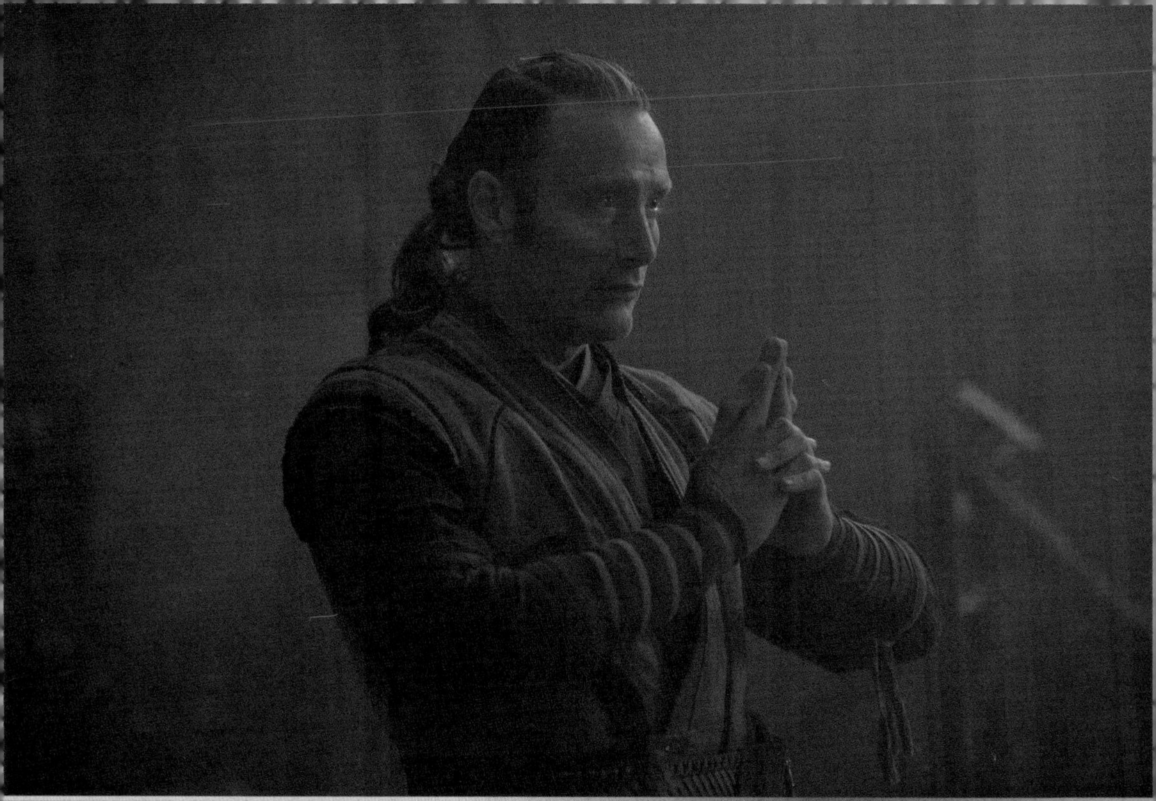

MARVEL'S DOCTOR STRANGE PRELUDE INFINITE COMIC #1

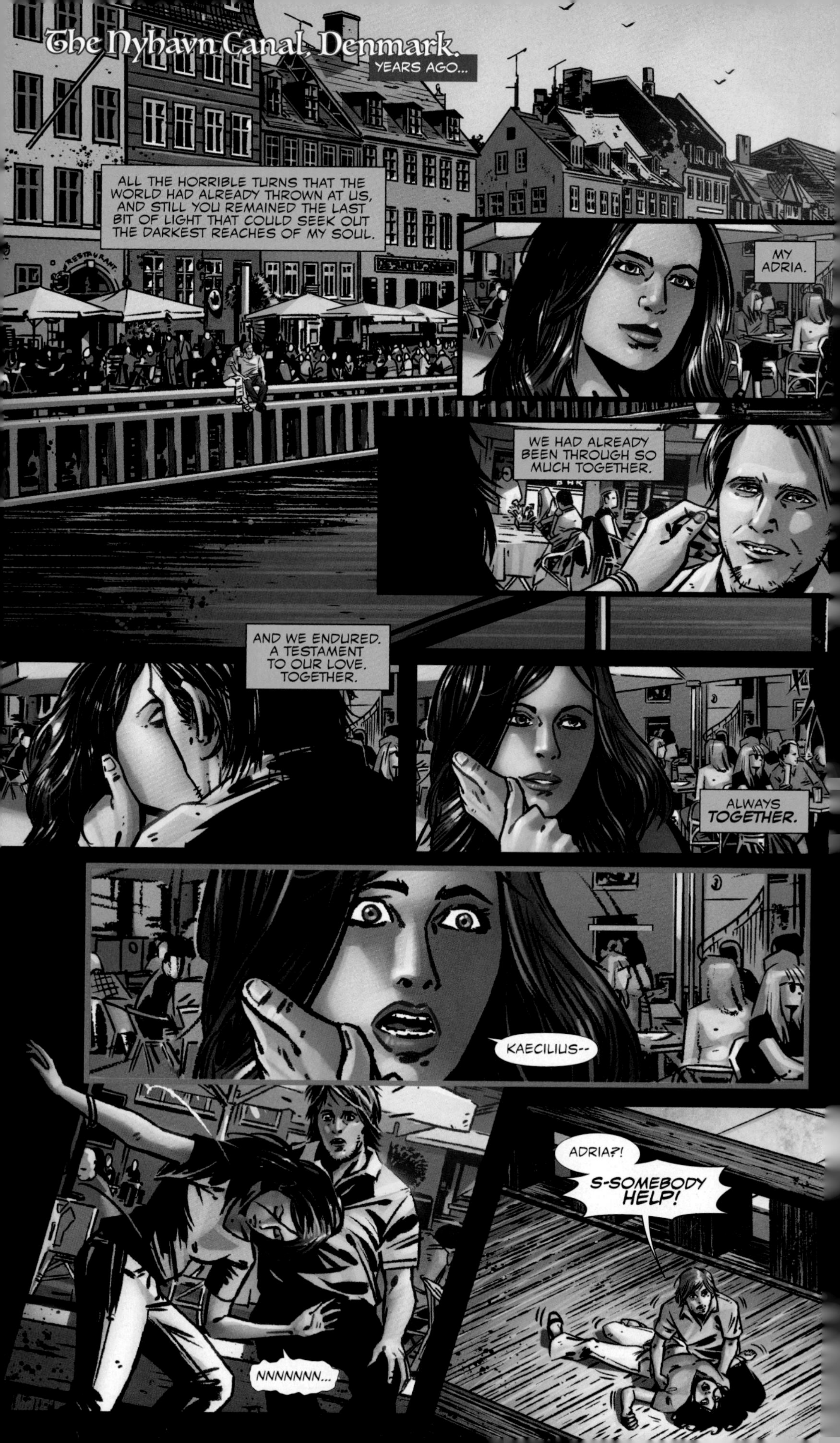
The Nyhavn Canal, Denmark.
YEARS AGO...
ALL THE HORRIBLE TURNS THAT THE WORLD HAD ALREADY THROWN AT US, AND STILL YOU REMAINED THE LAST BIT OF LIGHT THAT COULD SEEK OUT THE DARKEST REACHES OF MY SOUL.
MY ADRIA.
WE HAD ALREADY BEEN THROUGH SO MUCH TOGETHER.
AND WE ENDURED. A TESTAMENT TO OUR LOVE. TOGETHER.
ALWAYS TOGETHER.
KAECILIUS--
NNNNNNN...
ADRIA?!
S-SOMEBODY HELP!

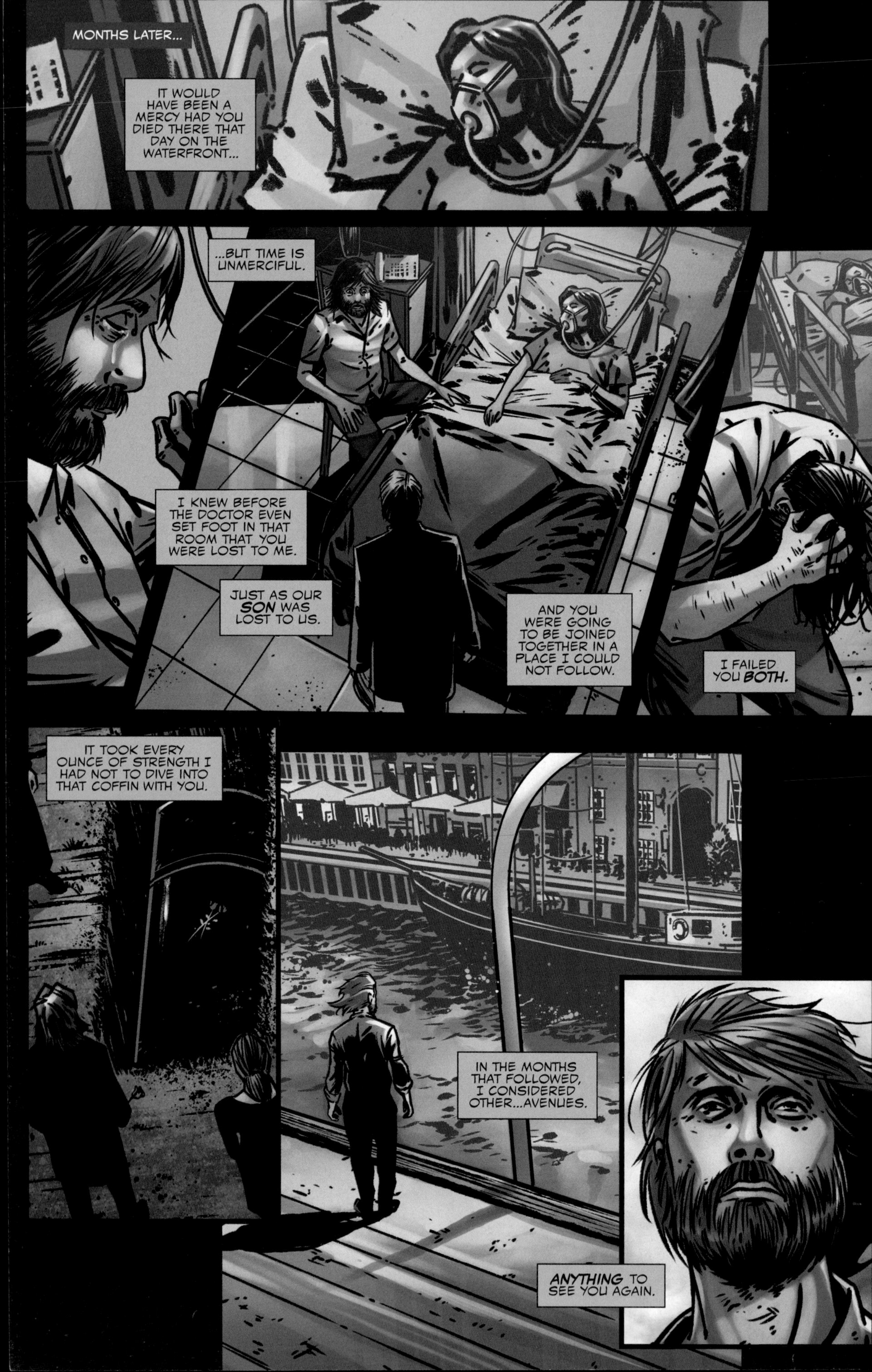
MONTHS LATER...
IT WOULD HAVE BEEN A MERCY HAD YOU DIED THERE THAT DAY ON THE WATERFRONT...
...BUT TIME IS UNMERCIFUL.
I KNEW BEFORE THE DOCTOR EVEN SET FOOT IN THAT ROOM THAT YOU WERE LOST TO ME.
JUST AS OUR SON WAS LOST TO US.
AND YOU WERE GOING TO BE JOINED TOGETHER IN A PLACE I COULD NOT FOLLOW.
I FAILED YOU BOTH.
IT TOOK EVERY OUNCE OF STRENGTH I HAD NOT TO DIVE INTO THAT COFFIN WITH YOU.
IN THE MONTHS THAT FOLLOWED, I CONSIDERED OTHER...AVENUES.
ANYTHING TO SEE YOU AGAIN.

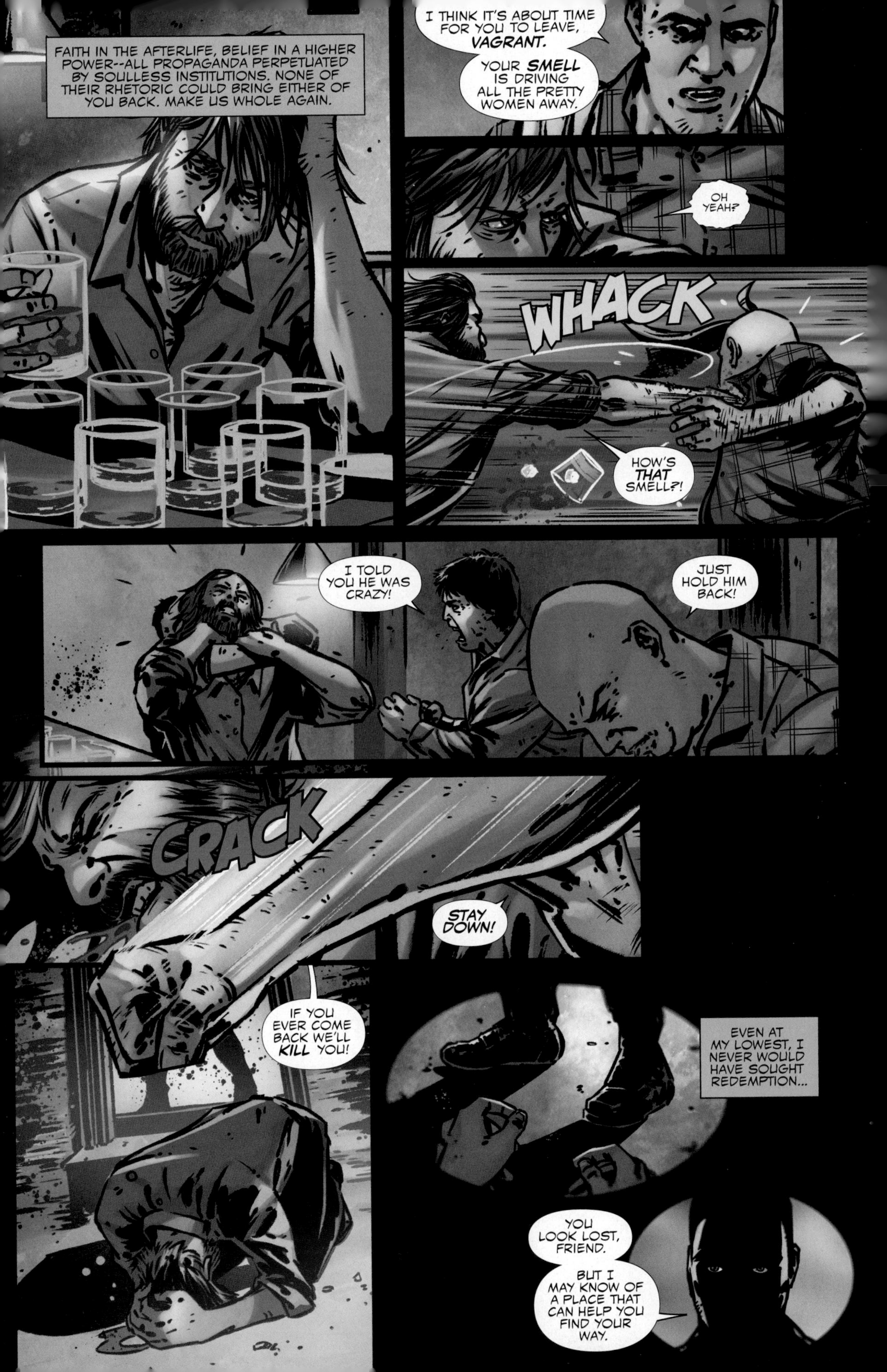
FAITH IN THE AFTERLIFE, BELIEF IN A HIGHER POWER--ALL PROPAGANDA PERPETUATED BY SOULLESS INSTITUTIONS. NONE OF THEIR RHETORIC COULD BRING EITHER OF YOU BACK. MAKE US WHOLE AGAIN.
I THINK IT'S ABOUT TIME FOR YOU TO LEAVE, VAGRANT.
YOUR SMELL IS DRIVING ALL THE PRETTY WOMEN AWAY.
OH YEAH?
WHACK
HOW'S THAT SMELL?!
I TOLD YOU HE WAS CRAZY!
JUST HOLD HIM BACK!
CRACK
STAY DOWN!
IF YOU EVER COME BACK WE'LL KILL YOU!
EVEN AT MY LOWEST, I NEVER WOULD HAVE SOUGHT REDEMPTION...
YOU LOOK LOST, FRIEND.
BUT I MAY KNOW OF A PLACE THAT CAN HELP YOU FIND YOUR WAY.

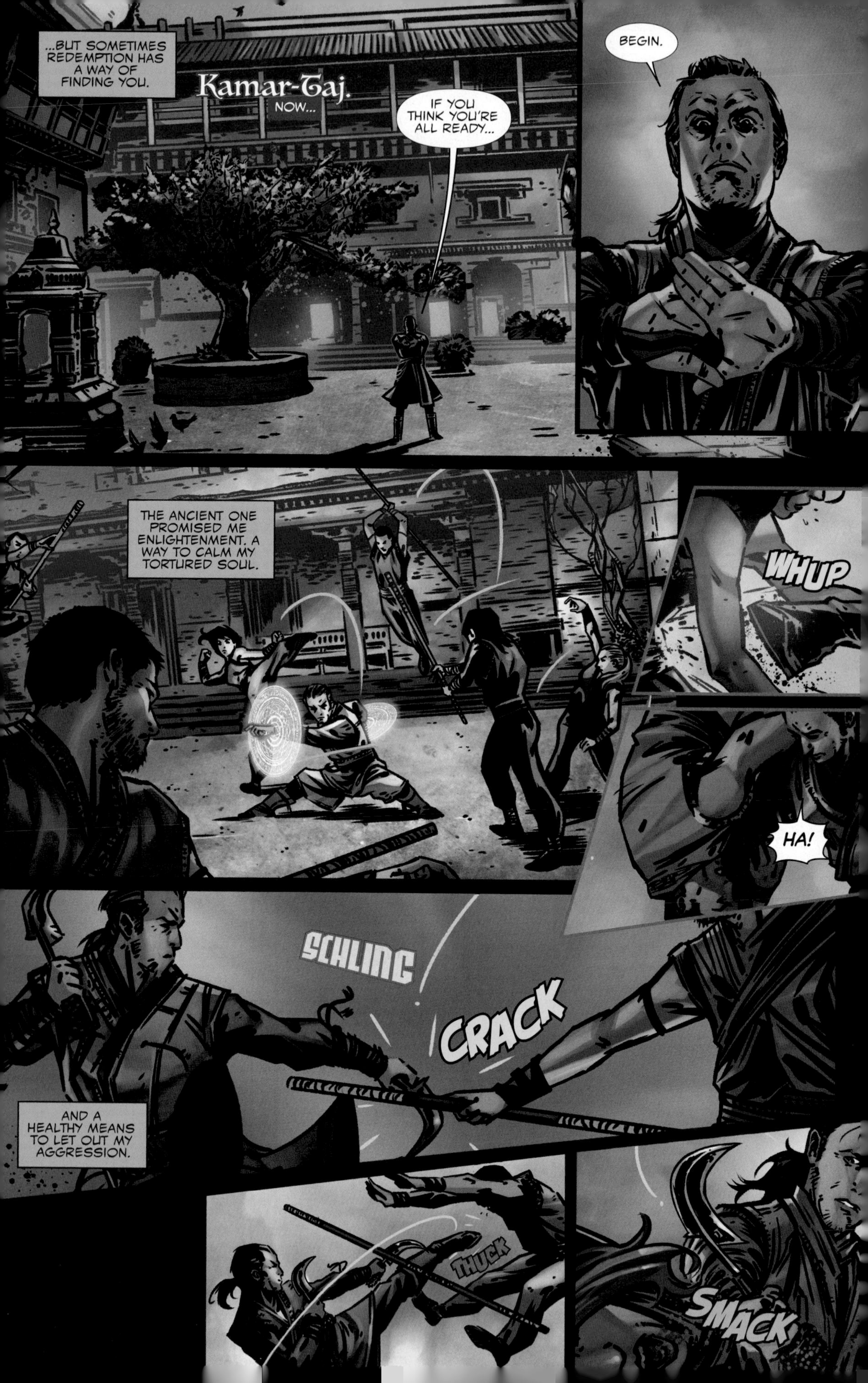
...BUT SOMETIMES REDEMPTION HAS A WAY OF FINDING YOU.
Kamar-Taj.
NOW...
IF YOU THINK YOU'RE ALL READY...
BEGIN.
THE ANCIENT ONE PROMISED ME ENLIGHTENMENT. A WAY TO CALM MY TORTURED SOUL.
WHUP
HA!
SCHLING
CRACK
AND A HEALTHY MEANS TO LET OUT MY AGGRESSION.
THUCK
SMACK

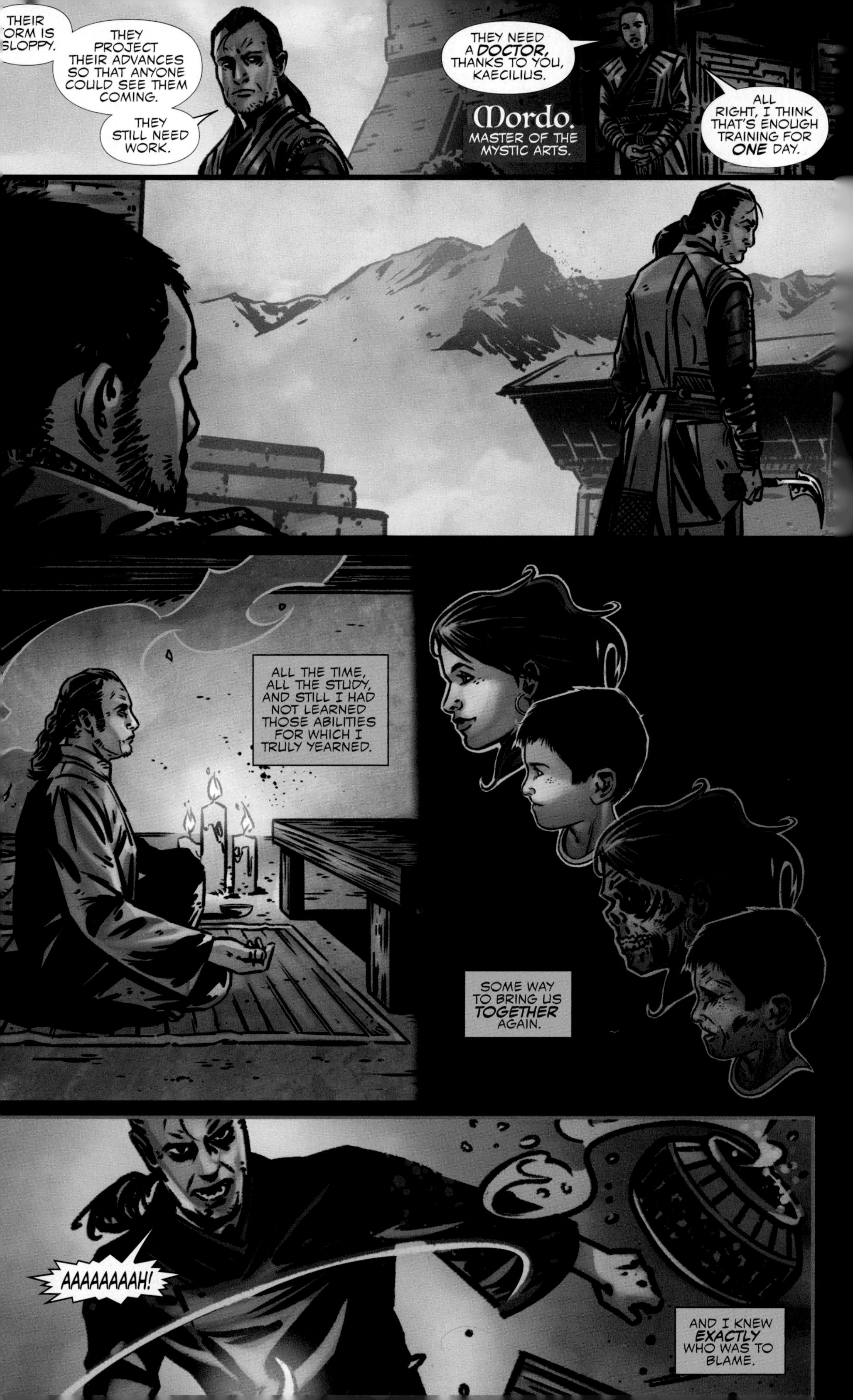
THEIR FORM IS SLOPPY.
THEY PROJECT THEIR ADVANCES SO THAT ANYONE COULD SEE THEM COMING.
THEY STILL NEED WORK.
THEY NEED A DOCTOR, THANKS TO YOU, KAECILIUS.
Mordo. MASTER OF THE MYSTIC ARTS.
ALL RIGHT, I THINK THAT'S ENOUGH TRAINING FOR ONE DAY.
ALL THE TIME, ALL THE STUDY, AND STILL I HAD NOT LEARNED THOSE ABILITIES FOR WHICH I TRULY YEARNED.
SOME WAY TO BRING US TOGETHER AGAIN.
AAAAAAAAH!
AND I KNEW EXACTLY WHO WAS TO BLAME.

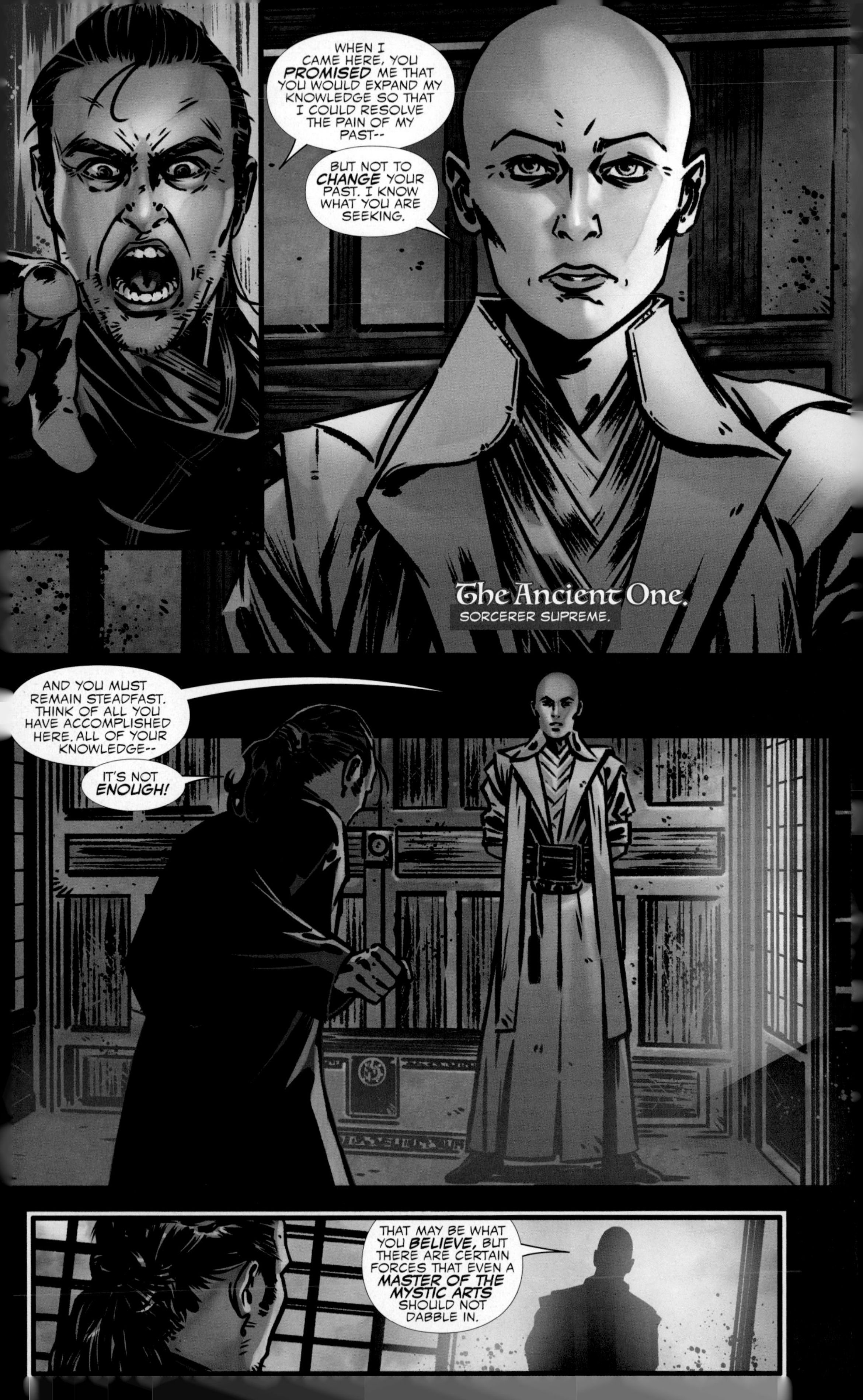
WHEN I CAME HERE, YOU PROMISED ME THAT YOU WOULD EXPAND MY KNOWLEDGE SO THAT I COULD RESOLVE THE PAIN OF MY PAST--
BUT NOT TO CHANGE YOUR PAST. I KNOW WHAT YOU ARE SEEKING.
The Ancient One.
SORCERER SUPREME.
AND YOU MUST REMAIN STEADFAST. THINK OF ALL YOU HAVE ACCOMPLISHED HERE. ALL OF YOUR KNOWLEDGE--
IT'S NOT ENOUGH!
THAT MAY BE WHAT YOU BELIEVE, BUT THERE ARE CERTAIN FORCES THAT EVEN A MASTER OF THE MYSTIC ARTS SHOULD NOT DABBLE IN.

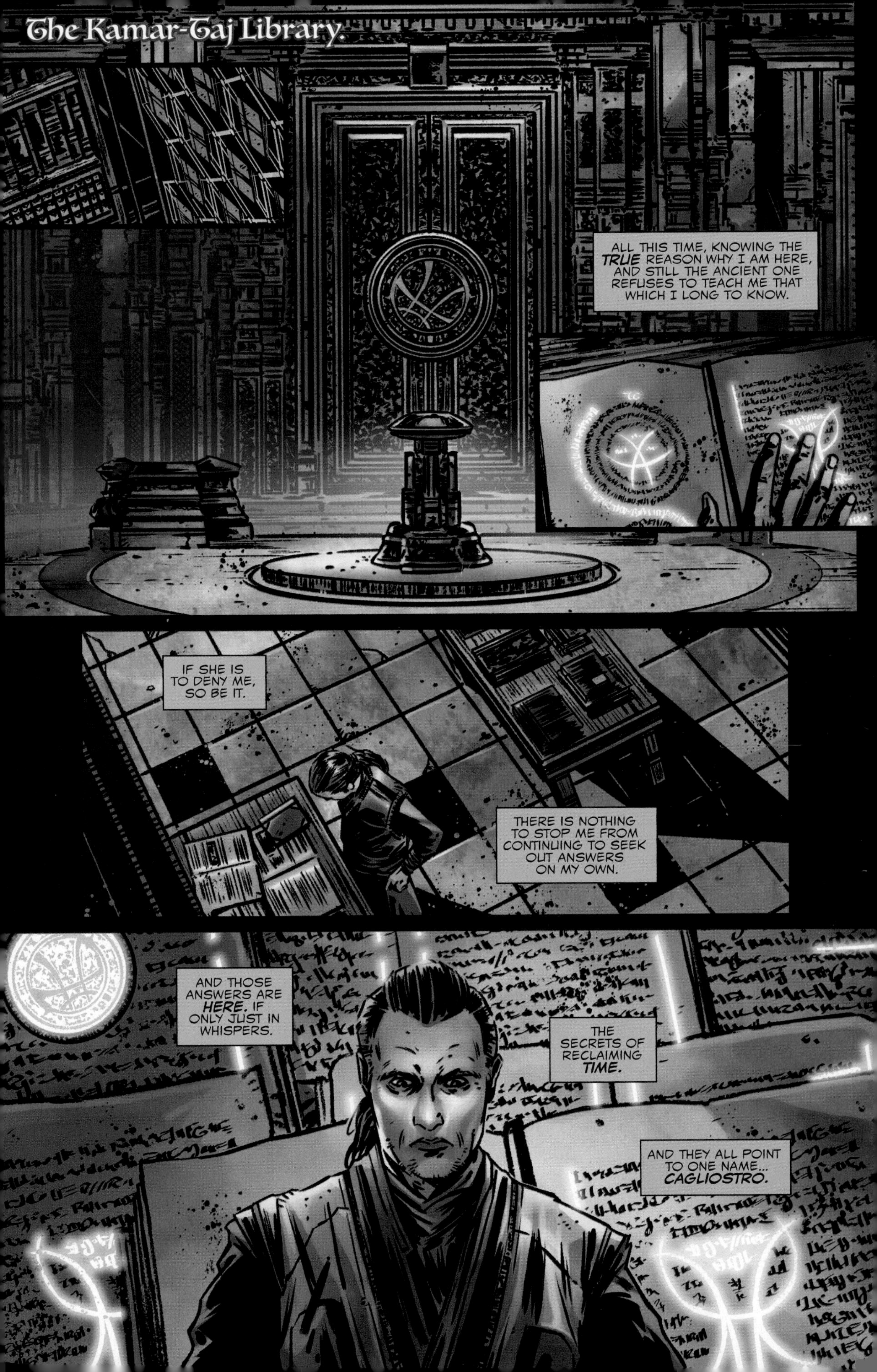
The Kamar-Taj Library.
ALL THIS TIME, KNOWING THE TRUE REASON WHY I AM HERE, AND STILL THE ANCIENT ONE REFUSES TO TEACH ME THAT WHICH I LONG TO KNOW.
IF SHE IS TO DENY ME, SO BE IT.
THERE IS NOTHING TO STOP ME FROM CONTINUING TO SEEK OUT ANSWERS ON MY OWN.
AND THOSE ANSWERS ARE HERE. IF ONLY JUST IN WHISPERS.
THE SECRETS OF RECLAIMING TIME.
AND THEY ALL POINT TO ONE NAME... CAGLIOSTRO.

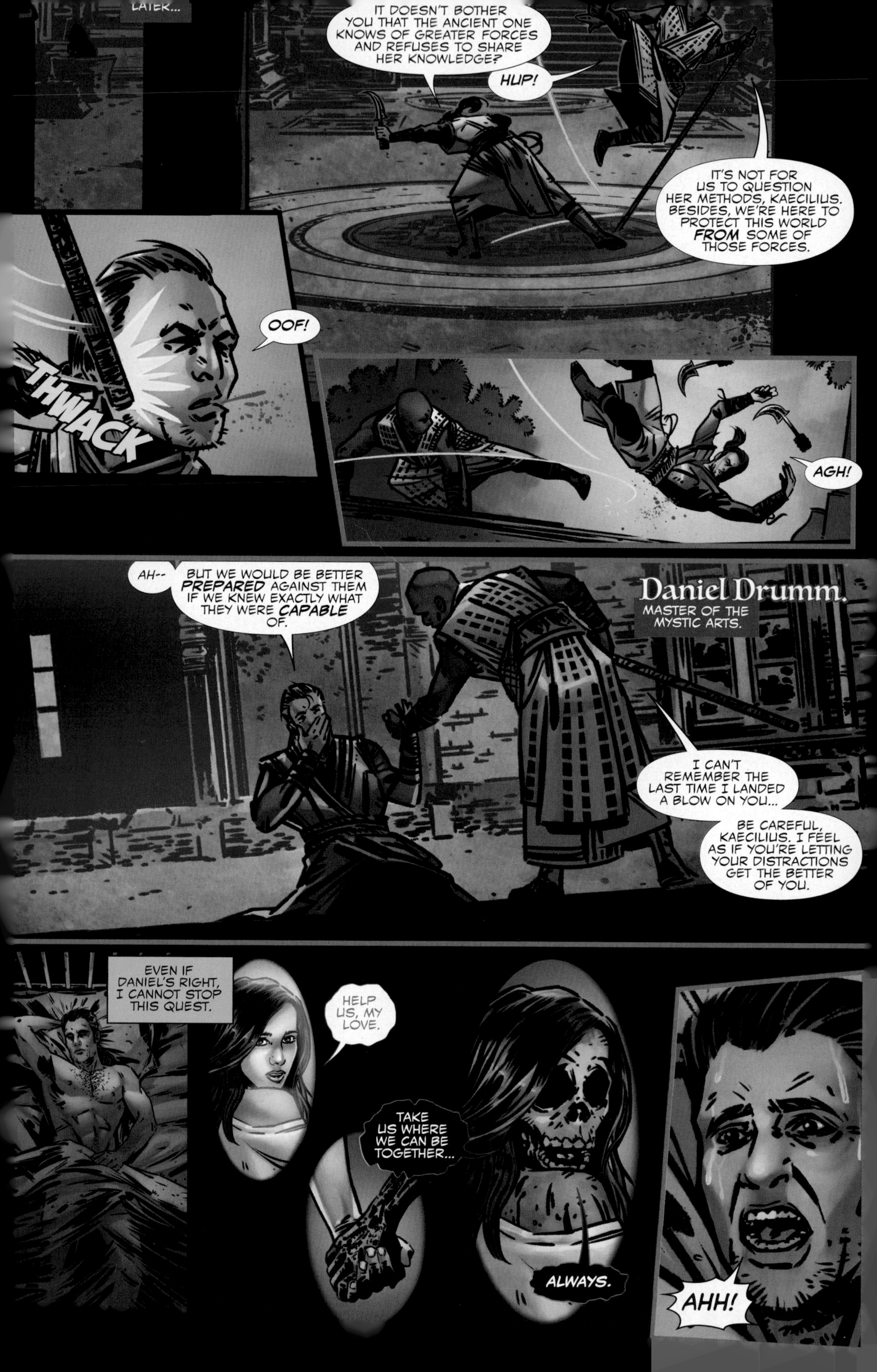
LATER...
IT DOESN'T BOTHER YOU THAT THE ANCIENT ONE KNOWS OF GREATER FORCES AND REFUSES TO SHARE HER KNOWLEDGE?
HUP!
IT'S NOT FOR US TO QUESTION HER METHODS, KAECILIUS. BESIDES, WE'RE HERE TO PROTECT THIS WORLD FROM SOME OF THOSE FORCES.
THWACK
OOF!
AGH!
AH--
BUT WE WOULD BE BETTER PREPARED AGAINST THEM IF WE KNEW EXACTLY WHAT THEY WERE CAPABLE OF.
Daniel Drumm.
MASTER OF THE MYSTIC ARTS.
I CAN'T REMEMBER THE LAST TIME I LANDED A BLOW ON YOU...
BE CAREFUL, KAECILIUS. I FEEL AS IF YOU'RE LETTING YOUR DISTRACTIONS GET THE BETTER OF YOU.
EVEN IF DANIEL'S RIGHT, I CANNOT STOP THIS QUEST.
HELP US, MY LOVE.
TAKE US WHERE WE CAN BE TOGETHER...
ALWAYS.
AHH!

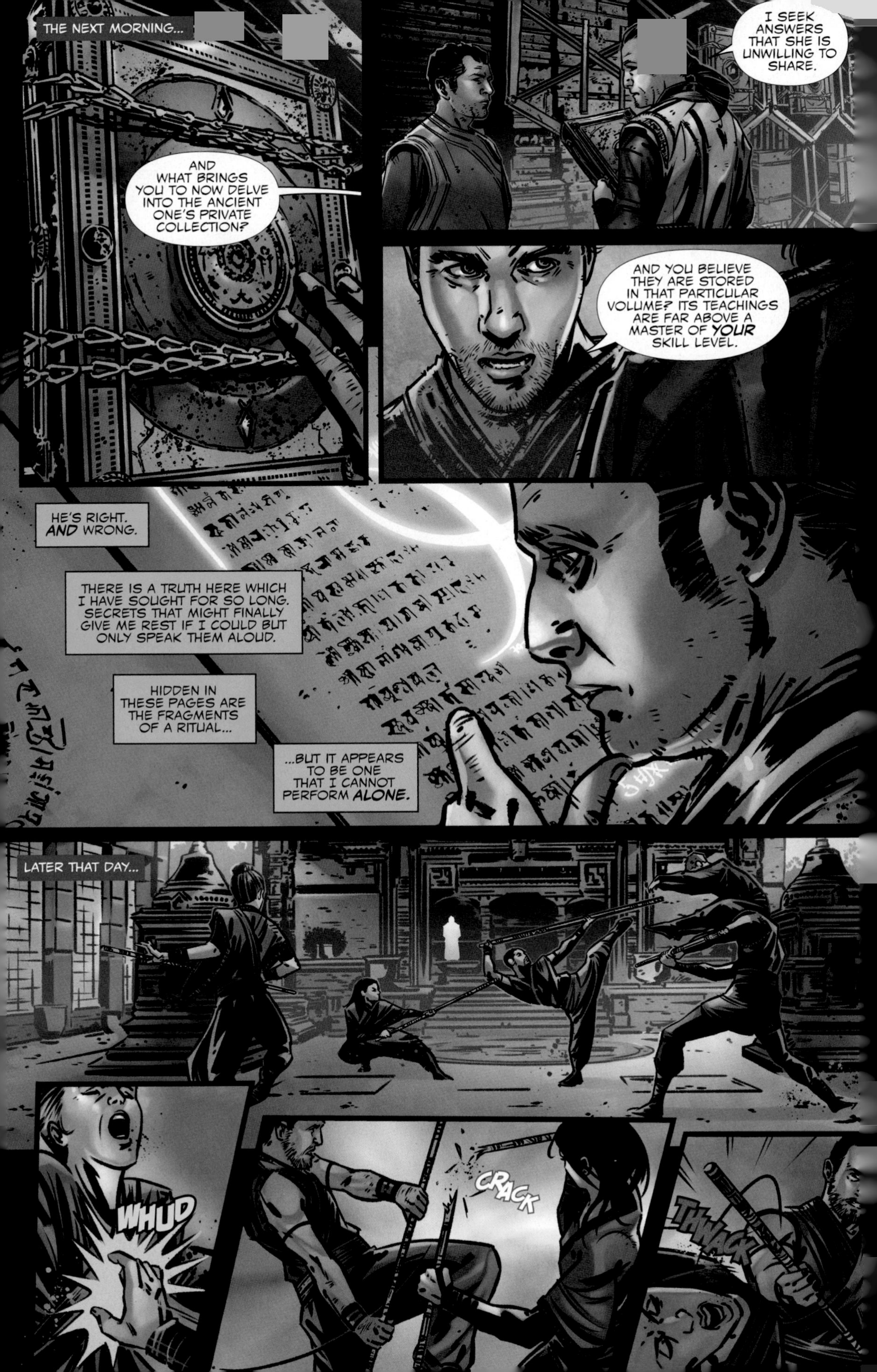
THE NEXT MORNING...
AND WHAT BRINGS YOU TO NOW DELVE INTO THE ANCIENT ONE'S PRIVATE COLLECTION?
I SEEK ANSWERS THAT SHE IS UNWILLING TO SHARE.
AND YOU BELIEVE THEY ARE STORED IN THAT PARTICULAR VOLUME? ITS TEACHINGS ARE FAR ABOVE A MASTER OF YOUR SKILL LEVEL.
HE'S RIGHT. AND WRONG.
THERE IS A TRUTH HERE WHICH I HAVE SOUGHT FOR SO LONG. SECRETS THAT MIGHT FINALLY GIVE ME REST IF I COULD BUT ONLY SPEAK THEM ALOUD.
HIDDEN IN THESE PAGES ARE THE FRAGMENTS OF A RITUAL...
...BUT IT APPEARS TO BE ONE THAT I CANNOT PERFORM ALONE.
LATER THAT DAY...
WHUD
CRACK
THWACK

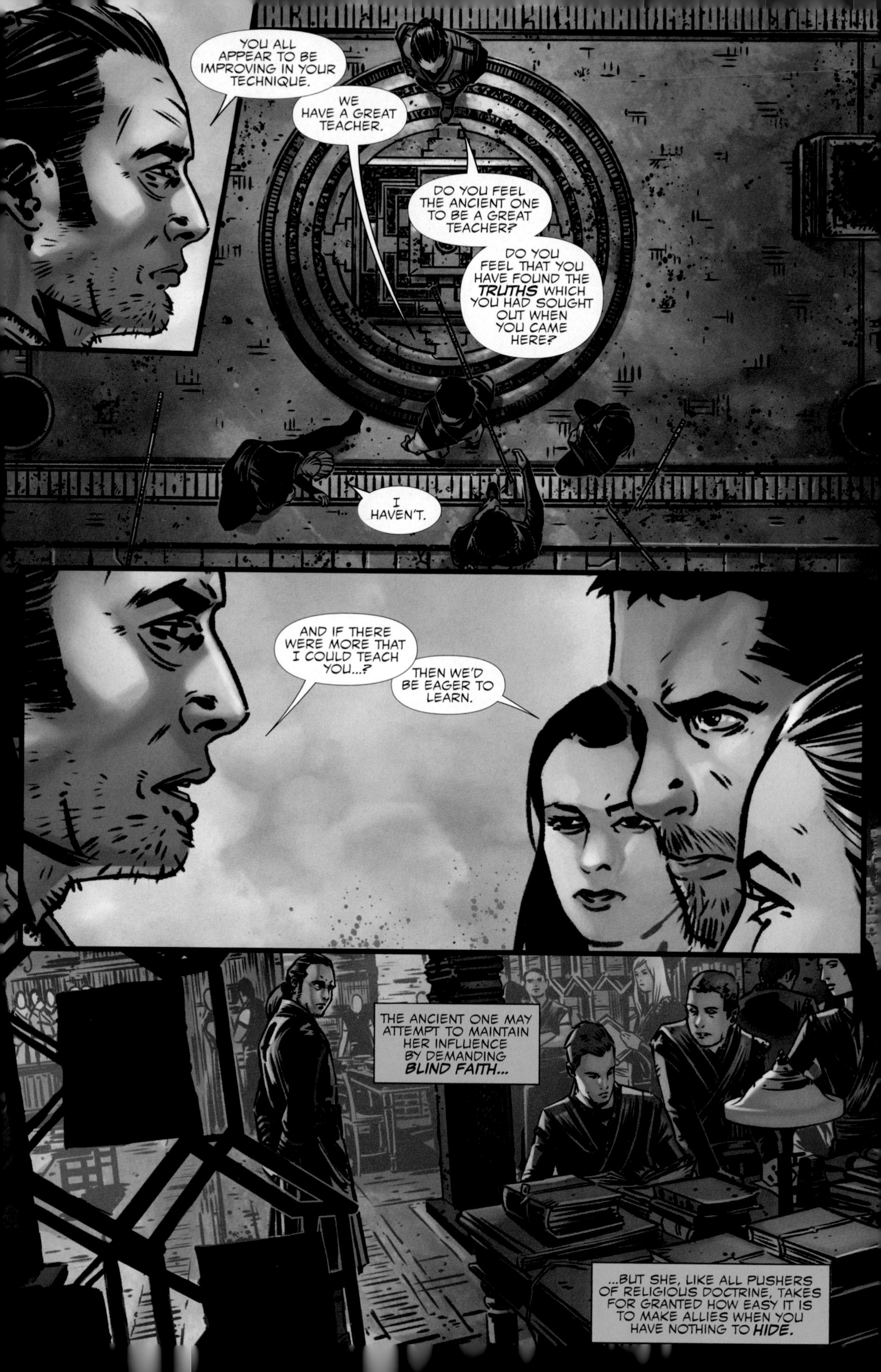
YOU ALL APPEAR TO BE IMPROVING IN YOUR TECHNIQUE.
WE HAVE A GREAT TEACHER.
DO YOU FEEL THE ANCIENT ONE TO BE A GREAT TEACHER?
DO YOU FEEL THAT YOU HAVE FOUND THE TRUTHS WHICH YOU HAD SOUGHT OUT WHEN YOU CAME HERE?
I HAVEN'T.
AND IF THERE WERE MORE THAT I COULD TEACH YOU...?
THEN WE'D BE EAGER TO LEARN.
THE ANCIENT ONE MAY ATTEMPT TO MAINTAIN HER INFLUENCE BY DEMANDING BLIND FAITH...
...BUT SHE, LIKE ALL PUSHERS OF RELIGIOUS DOCTRINE, TAKES FOR GRANTED HOW EASY IT IS TO MAKE ALLIES WHEN YOU HAVE NOTHING TO HIDE.

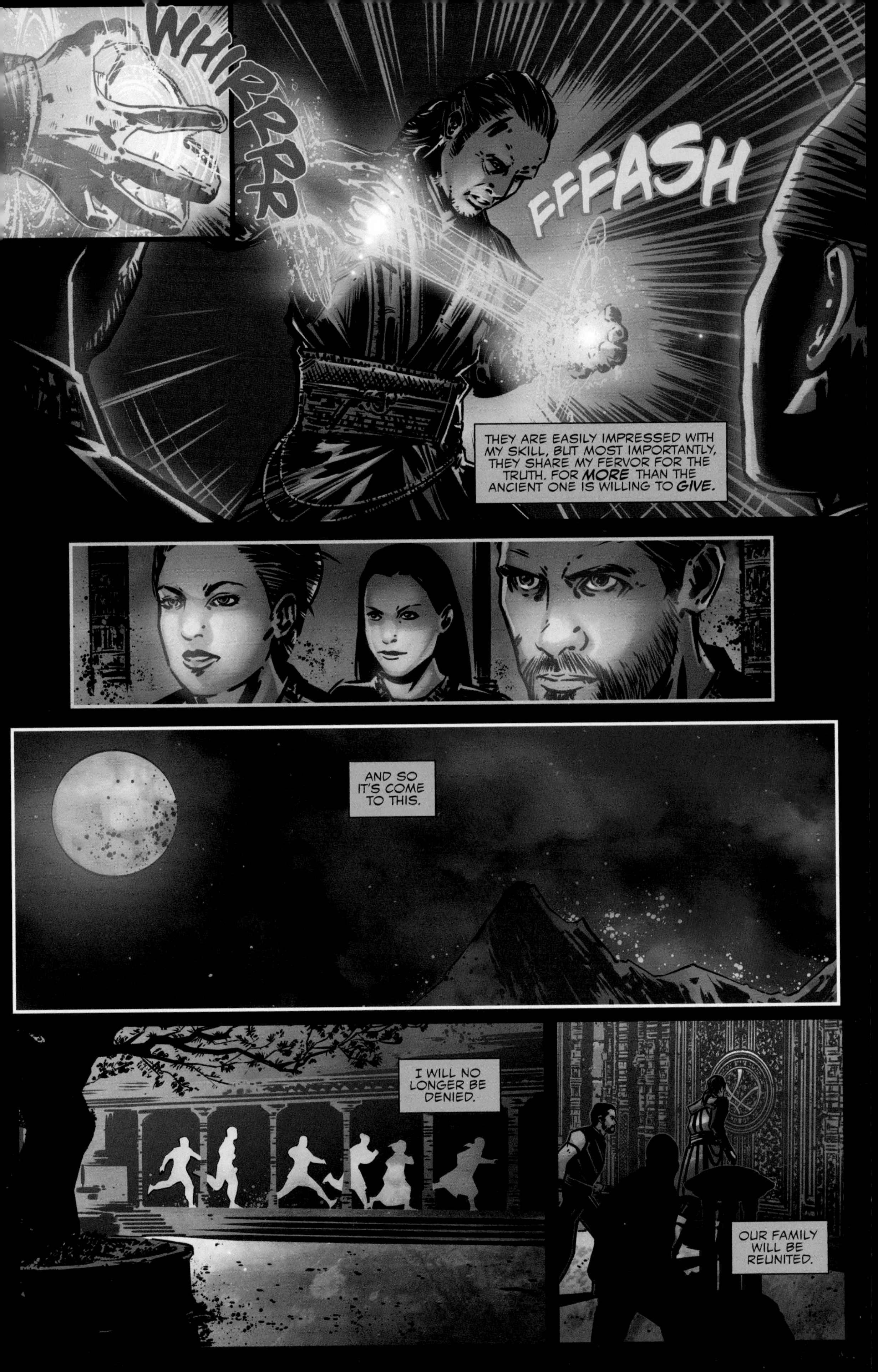
WHIRRR
FFFASH
THEY ARE EASILY IMPRESSED WITH MY SKILL, BUT MOST IMPORTANTLY, THEY SHARE MY FERVOR FOR THE TRUTH. FOR MORE THAN THE ANCIENT ONE IS WILLING TO GIVE.
AND SO IT'S COME TO THIS.
I WILL NO LONGER BE DENIED.
OUR FAMILY WILL BE REUNITED.

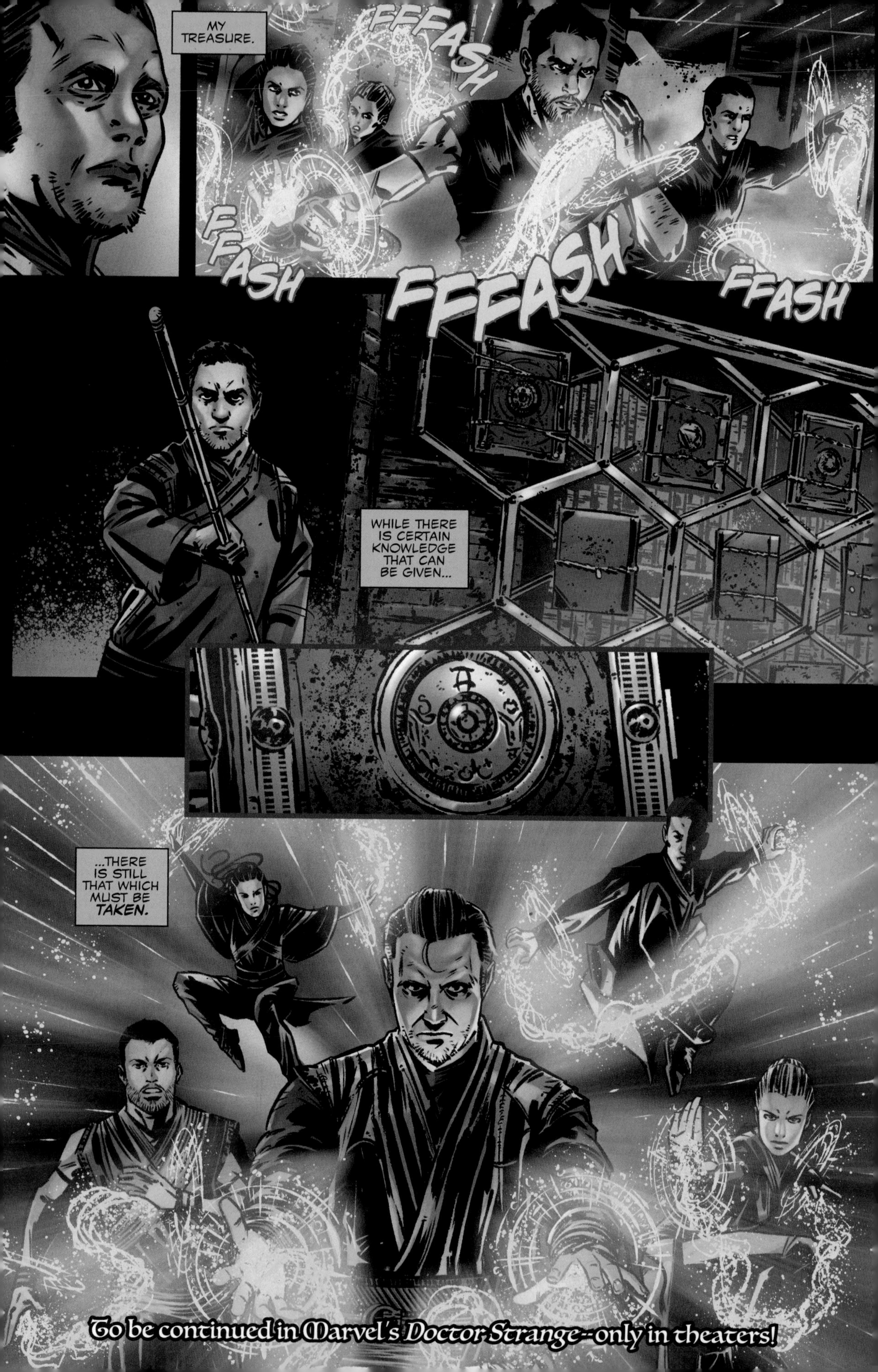
MY TREASURE.
FFFASH
FFASH
FFFASH
FFASH
WHILE THERE IS CERTAIN KNOWLEDGE THAT CAN BE GIVEN...
...THERE IS STILL THAT WHICH MUST BE TAKEN.
To be continued in Marvel's Doctor Strange--only in theaters!

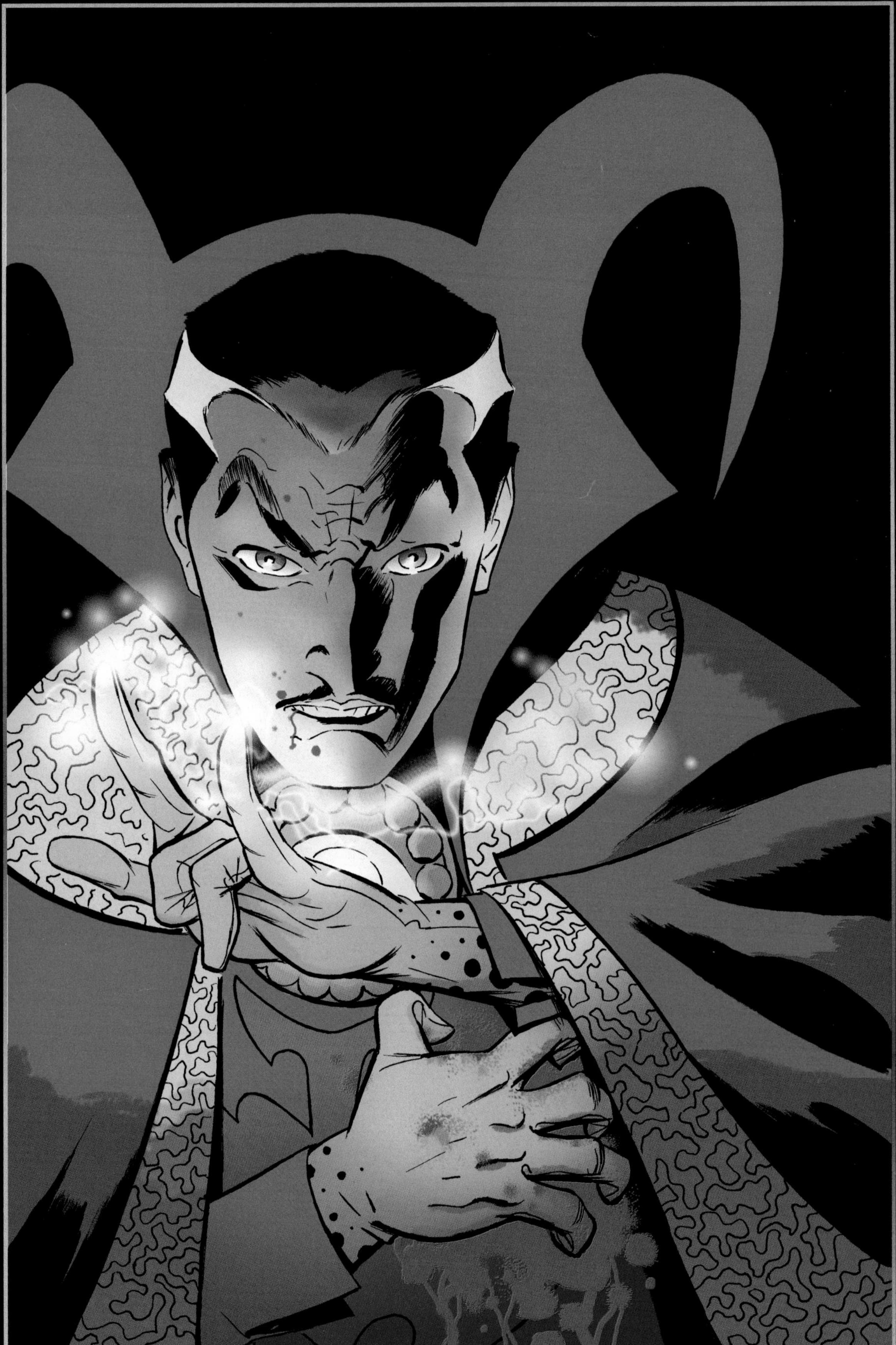

DOCTOR STRANGE: THE OATH #1

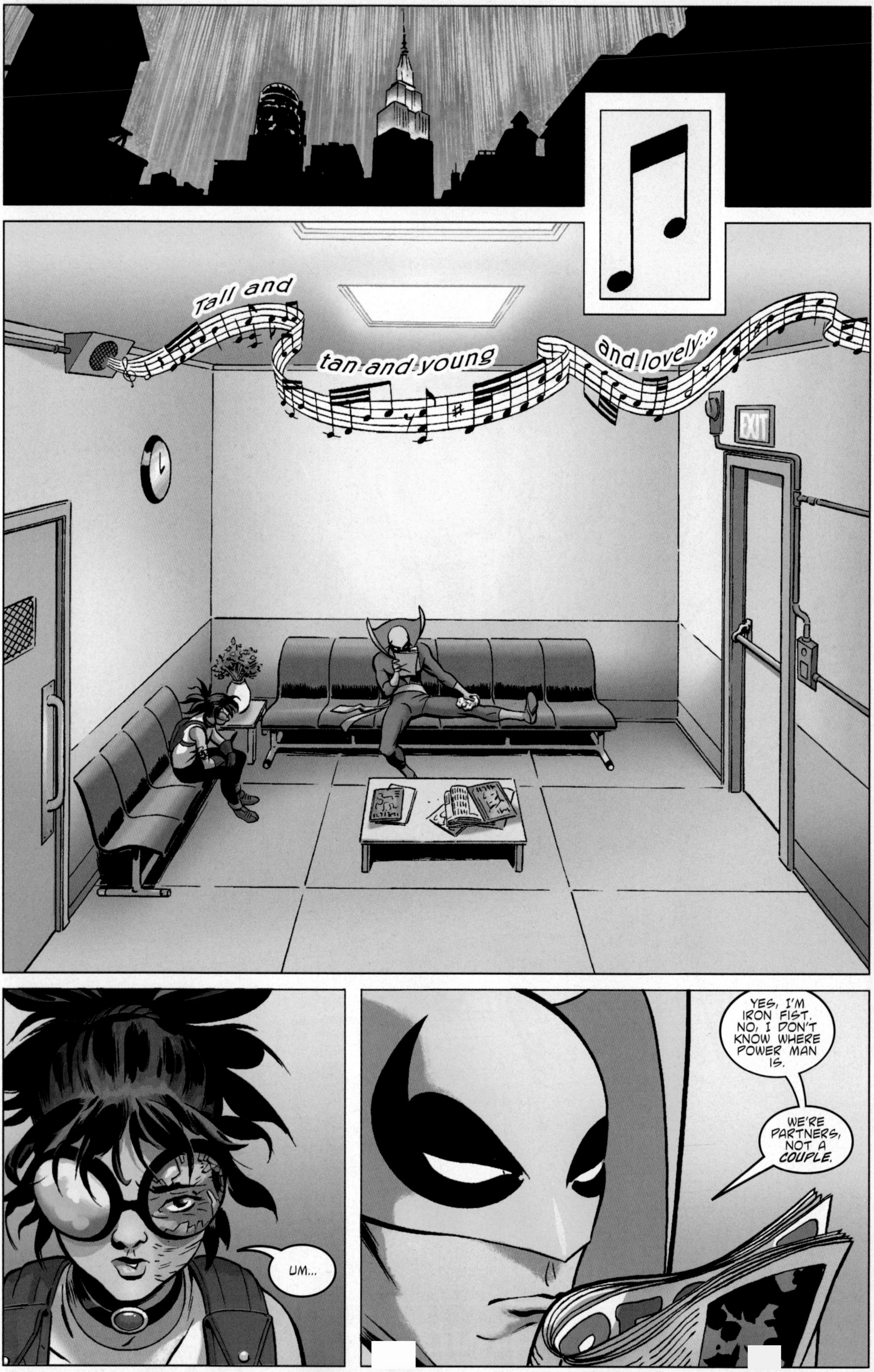
Tall and
tan and young
and lovely...
EXIT
UM...
YES, I'M IRON FIST. NO, I DON'T KNOW WHERE POWER MAN IS.
WE'RE PARTNERS, NOT A *COUPLE*.

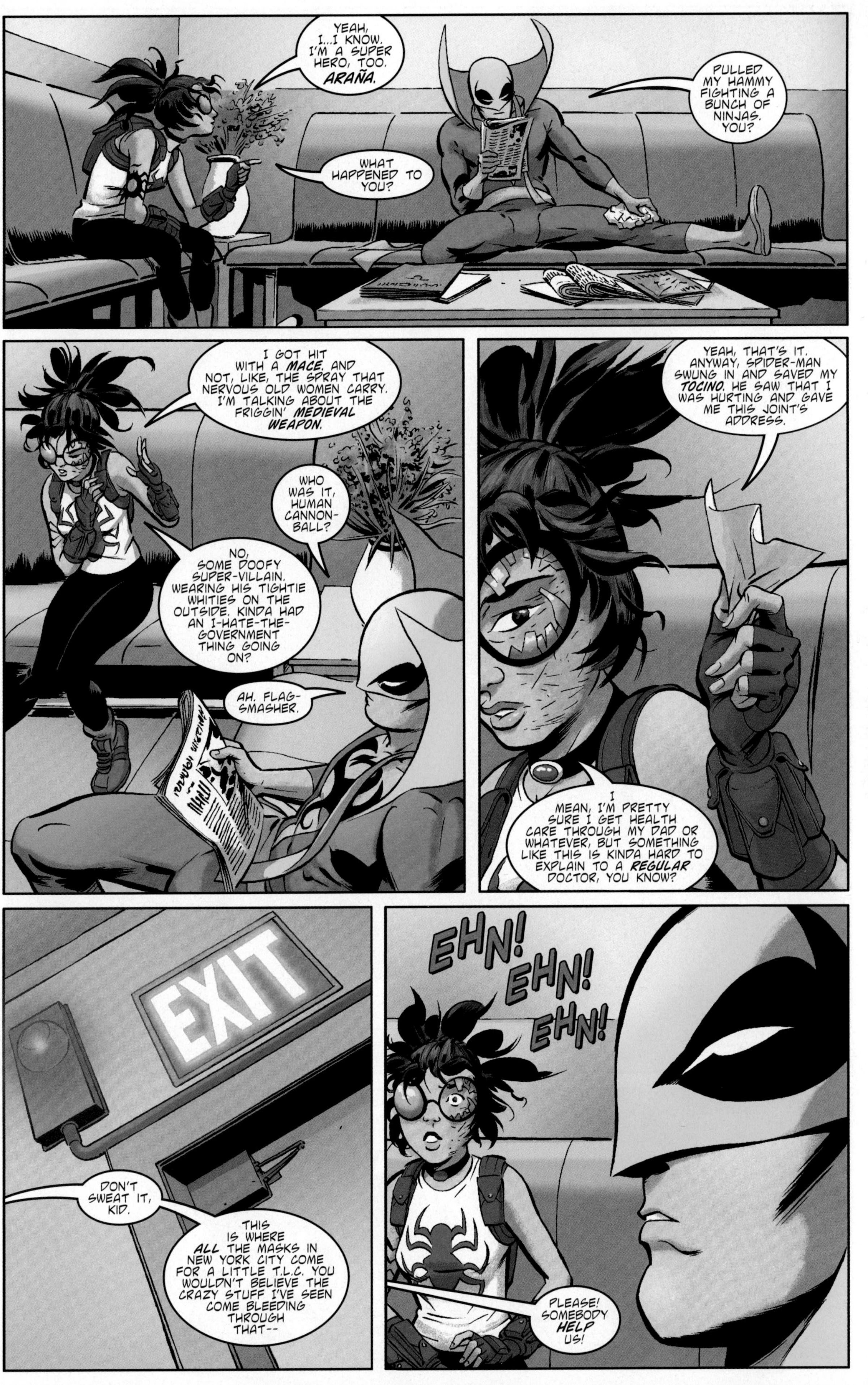
YEAH, I...I KNOW. I'M A SUPER HERO, TOO. ARAÑA.
PULLED MY HAMMY FIGHTING A BUNCH OF NINJAS. YOU?
WHAT HAPPENED TO YOU?
I GOT HIT WITH A MACE. AND NOT, LIKE, THE SPRAY THAT NERVOUS OLD WOMEN CARRY. I'M TALKING ABOUT THE FRIGGIN' MEDIEVAL WEAPON.
WHO WAS IT, HUMAN CANNON-BALL?
NO, SOME DOOFY SUPER-VILLAIN. WEARING HIS TIGHTIE WHITIES ON THE OUTSIDE. KINDA HAD AN I-HATE-THE-GOVERNMENT THING GOING ON?
AH. FLAG-SMASHER.
YEAH, THAT'S IT. ANYWAY, SPIDER-MAN SWUNG IN AND SAVED MY TOCINO. HE SAW THAT I WAS HURTING AND GAVE ME THIS JOINT'S ADDRESS.
I MEAN, I'M PRETTY SURE I GET HEALTH CARE THROUGH MY DAD OR WHATEVER, BUT SOMETHING LIKE THIS IS KINDA HARD TO EXPLAIN TO A REGULAR DOCTOR, YOU KNOW?
EXIT
DON'T SWEAT IT, KID.
THIS IS WHERE ALL THE MASKS IN NEW YORK CITY COME FOR A LITTLE T.L.C. YOU WOULDN'T BELIEVE THE CRAZY STUFF I'VE SEEN COME BLEEDING THROUGH THAT--
EHN! EHN! EHN!
PLEASE! SOMEBODY HELP US!

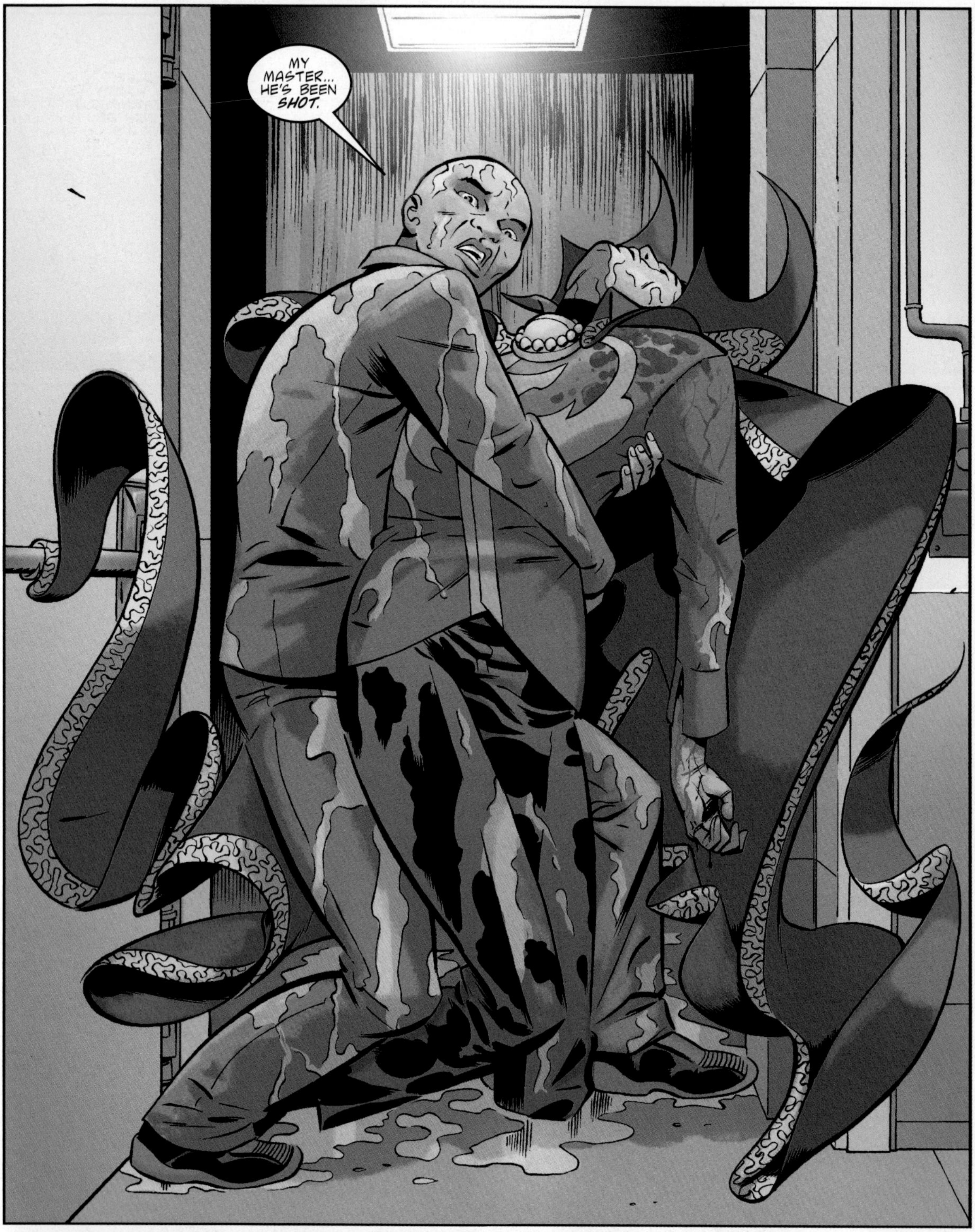
MY MASTER... HE'S BEEN SHOT.

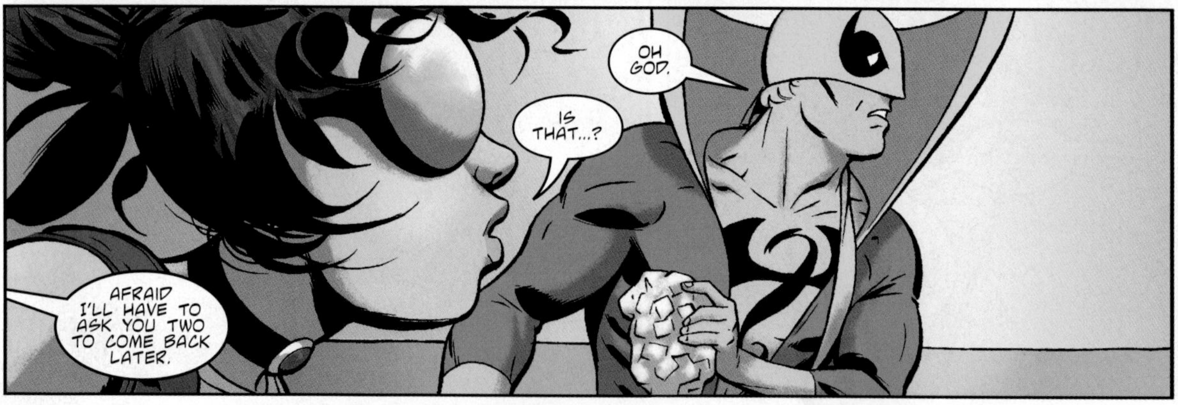
OH GOD.
IS THAT...?
AFRAID I'LL HAVE TO ASK YOU TWO TO COME BACK LATER.

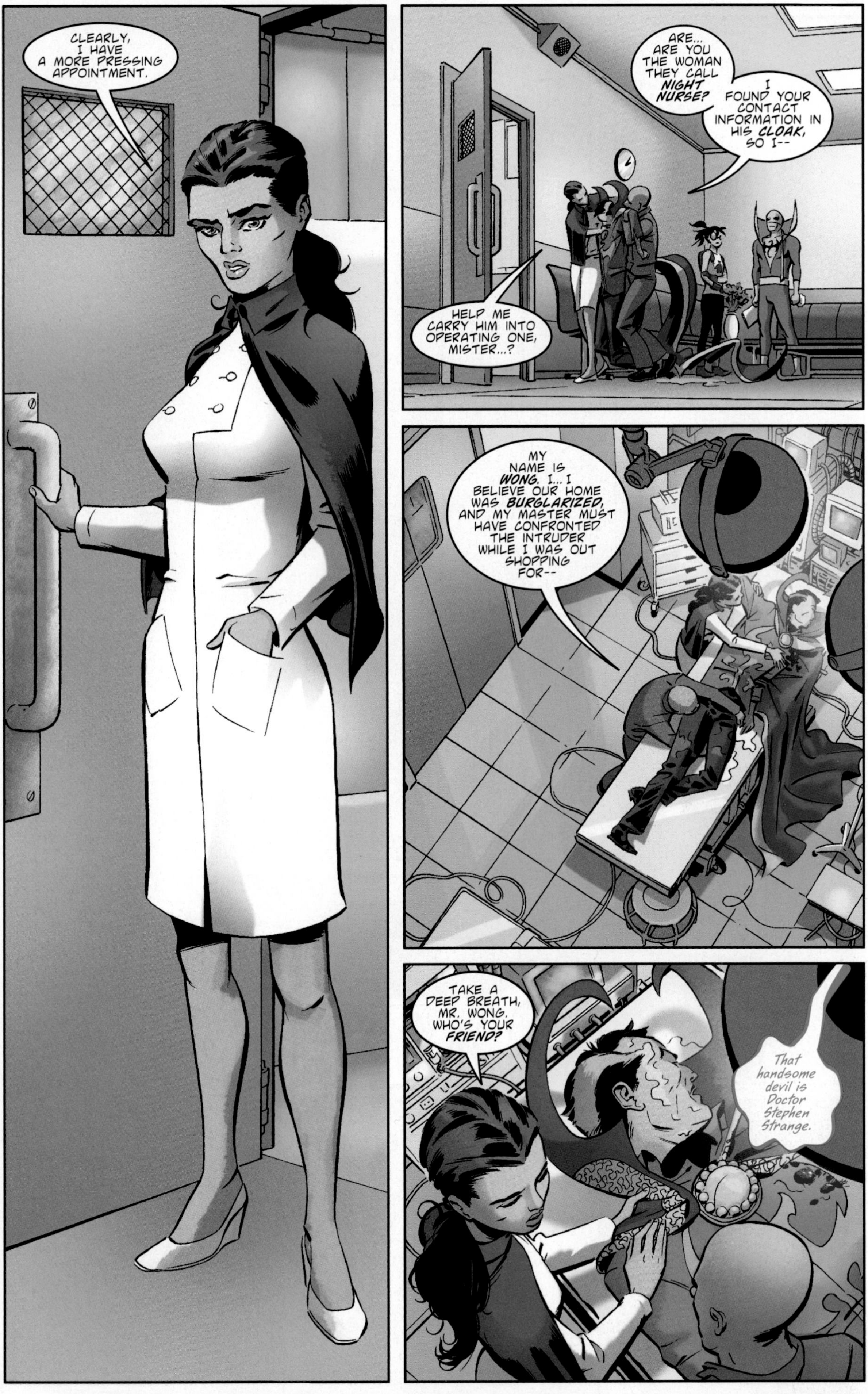
CLEARLY, I HAVE A MORE PRESSING APPOINTMENT.
ARE... ARE YOU THE WOMAN THEY CALL NIGHT NURSE?
I FOUND YOUR CONTACT INFORMATION IN HIS CLOAK, SO I--
HELP ME CARRY HIM INTO OPERATING ONE, MISTER...?
MY NAME IS WONG. I... I BELIEVE OUR HOME WAS BURGLARIZED, AND MY MASTER MUST HAVE CONFRONTED THE INTRUDER WHILE I WAS OUT SHOPPING FOR--
TAKE A DEEP BREATH, MR. WONG. WHO'S YOUR FRIEND?
That handsome devil is Doctor Stephen Strange.

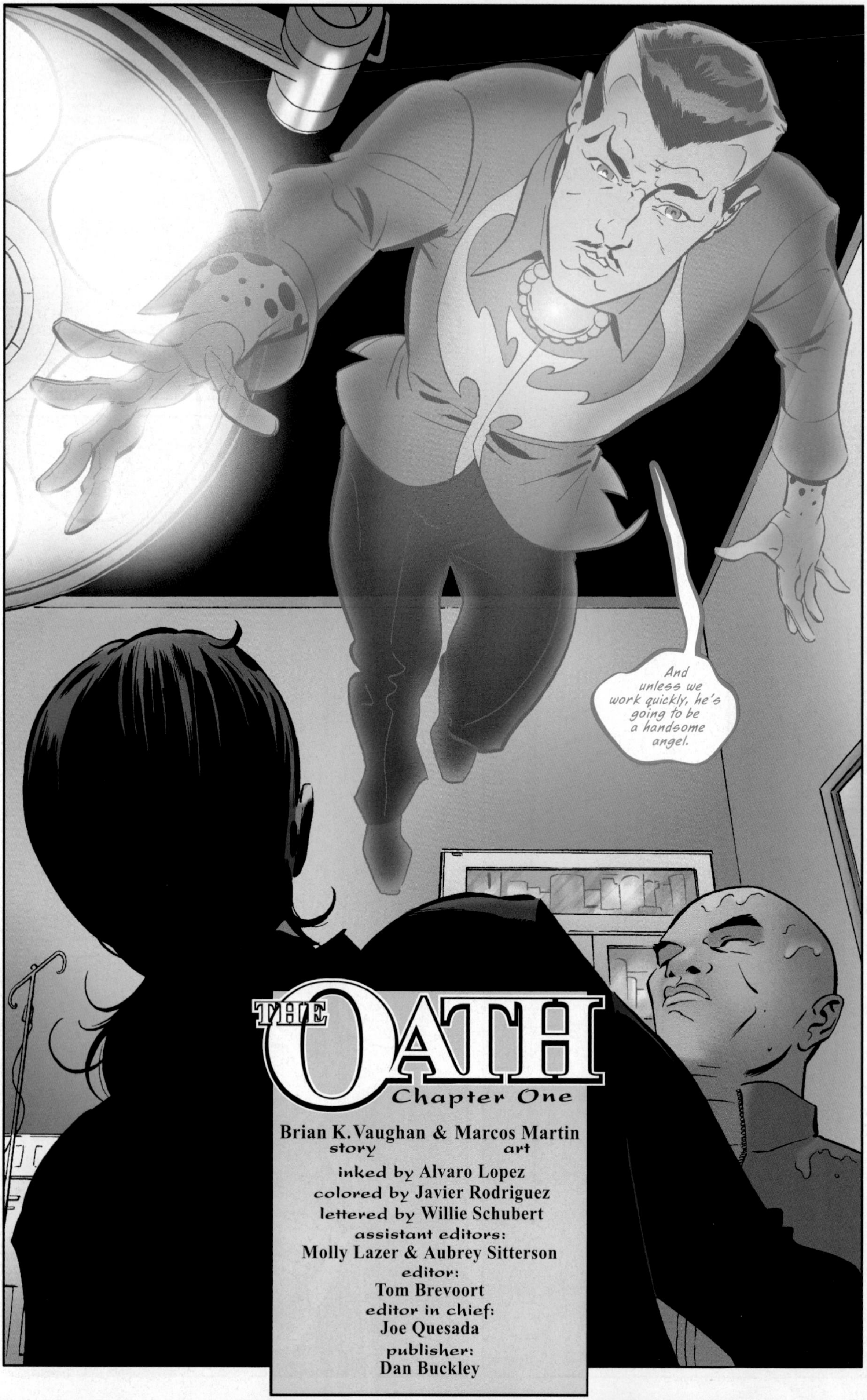
And unless we work quickly, he's going to be a handsome angel.
THE OATH
Chapter One
Brian K. Vaughan & Marcos Martin
story art
inked by Alvaro Lopez
colored by Javier Rodriguez
lettered by Willie Schubert
assistant editors:
Molly Lazer & Aubrey Sitterson
editor:
Tom Brevoort
editor in chief:
Joe Quesada
publisher:
Dan Buckley

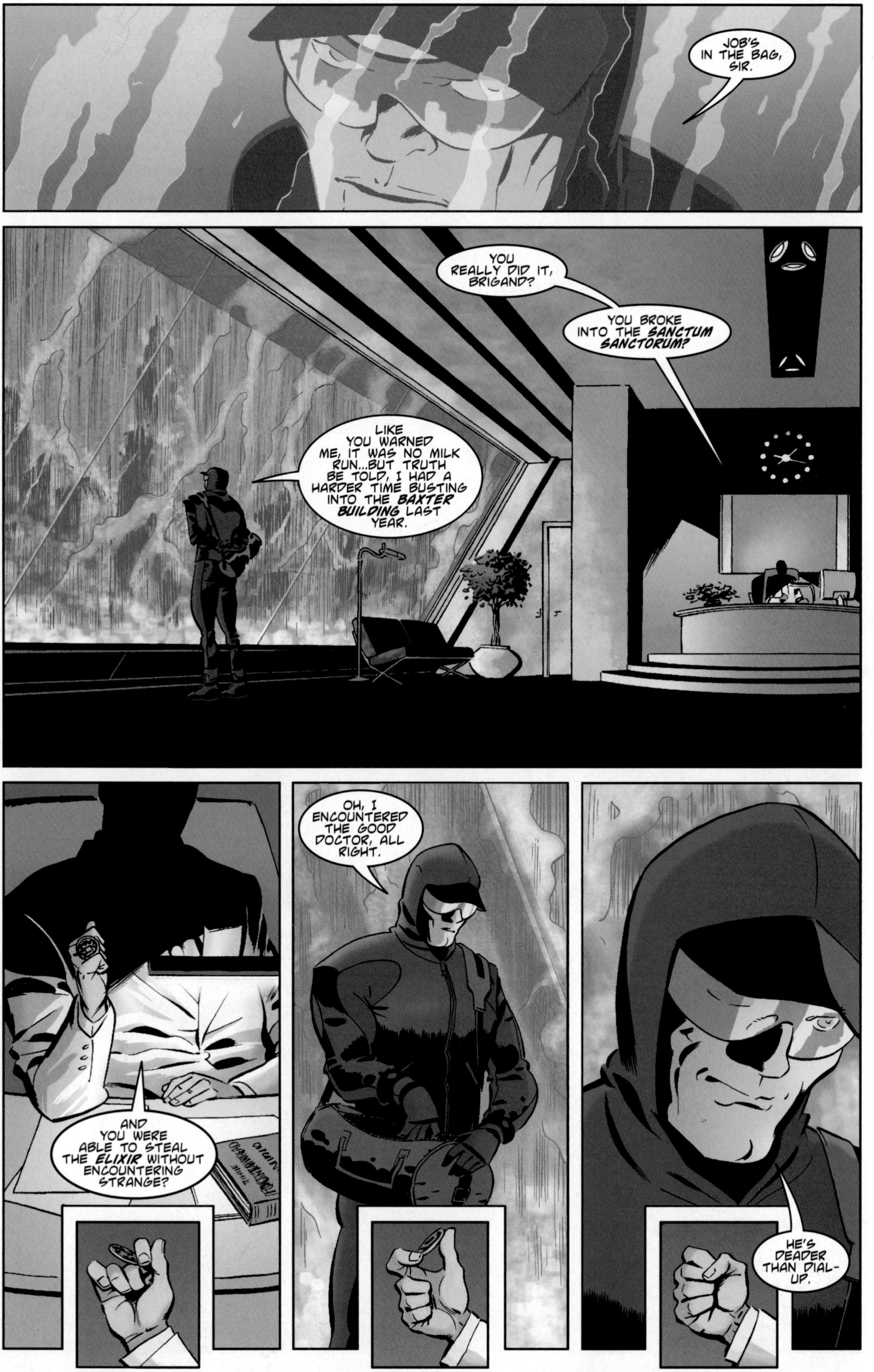
JOB'S IN THE BAG, SIR.
YOU REALLY DID IT, BRIGAND?
YOU BROKE INTO THE SANCTUM SANCTORUM?
LIKE YOU WARNED ME, IT WAS NO MILK RUN...BUT TRUTH BE TOLD, I HAD A HARDER TIME BUSTING INTO THE BAXTER BUILDING LAST YEAR.
AND YOU WERE ABLE TO STEAL THE ELIXIR WITHOUT ENCOUNTERING STRANGE?
OH, I ENCOUNTERED THE GOOD DOCTOR, ALL RIGHT.
HE'S DEADER THAN DIAL-UP.

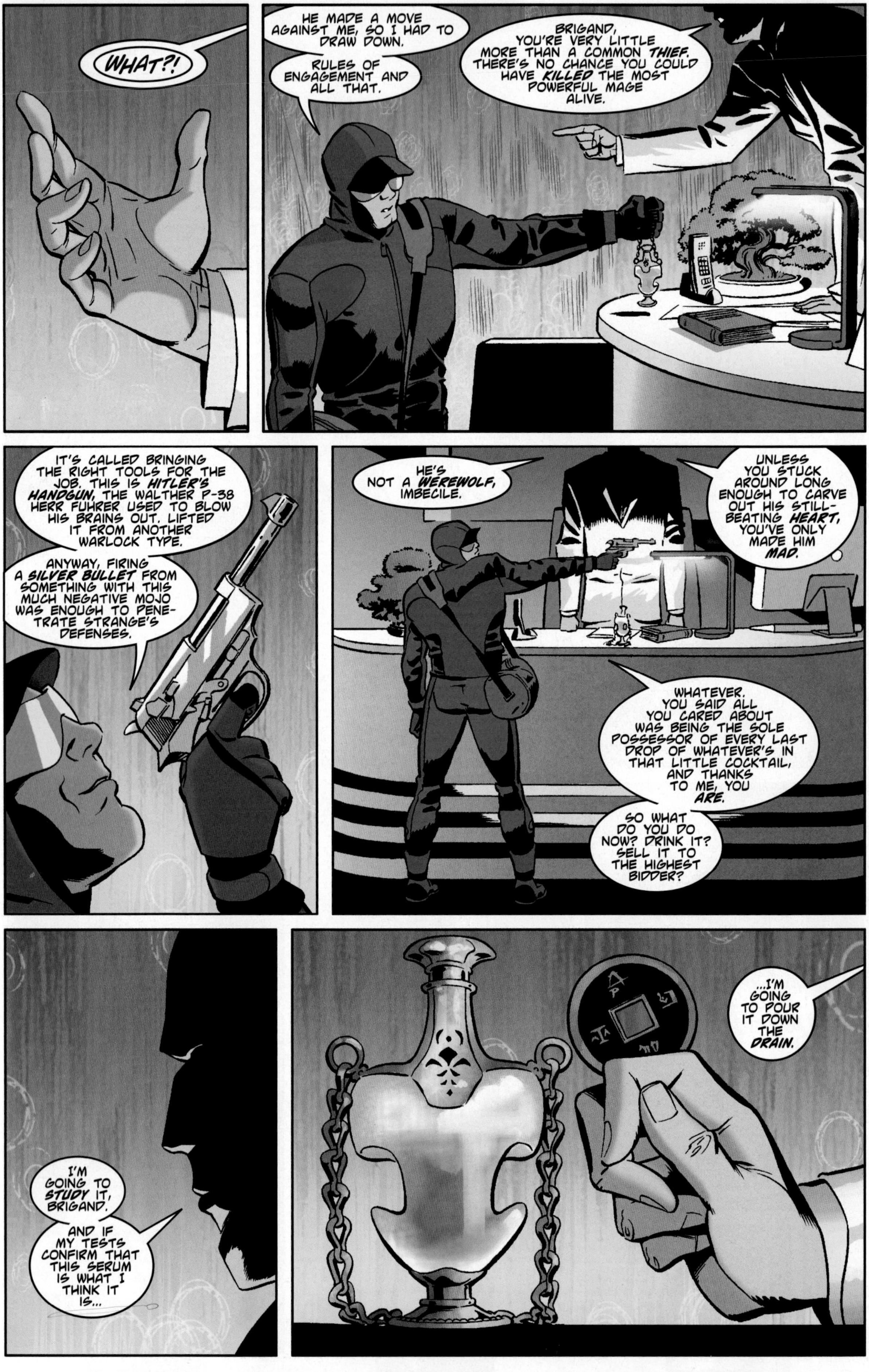
WHAT?!
HE MADE A MOVE AGAINST ME, SO I HAD TO DRAW DOWN.
RULES OF ENGAGEMENT AND ALL THAT.
BRIGAND, YOU'RE VERY LITTLE MORE THAN A COMMON THIEF. THERE'S NO CHANCE YOU COULD HAVE KILLED THE MOST POWERFUL MAGE ALIVE.
IT'S CALLED BRINGING THE RIGHT TOOLS FOR THE JOB. THIS IS HITLER'S HANDGUN, THE WALTHER P-38 HERR FUHRER USED TO BLOW HIS BRAINS OUT. LIFTED IT FROM ANOTHER WARLOCK TYPE.
ANYWAY, FIRING A SILVER BULLET FROM SOMETHING WITH THIS MUCH NEGATIVE MOJO WAS ENOUGH TO PENETRATE STRANGE'S DEFENSES.
HE'S NOT A WEREWOLF, IMBECILE.
UNLESS YOU STUCK AROUND LONG ENOUGH TO CARVE OUT HIS STILL-BEATING HEART, YOU'VE ONLY MADE HIM MAD.
WHATEVER. YOU SAID ALL YOU CARED ABOUT WAS BEING THE SOLE POSSESSOR OF EVERY LAST DROP OF WHATEVER'S IN THAT LITTLE COCKTAIL, AND THANKS TO ME, YOU ARE.
SO WHAT DO YOU DO NOW? DRINK IT? SELL IT TO THE HIGHEST BIDDER?
I'M GOING TO STUDY IT, BRIGAND.
AND IF MY TESTS CONFIRM THAT THIS SERUM IS WHAT I THINK IT IS...
...I'M GOING TO POUR IT DOWN THE DRAIN.

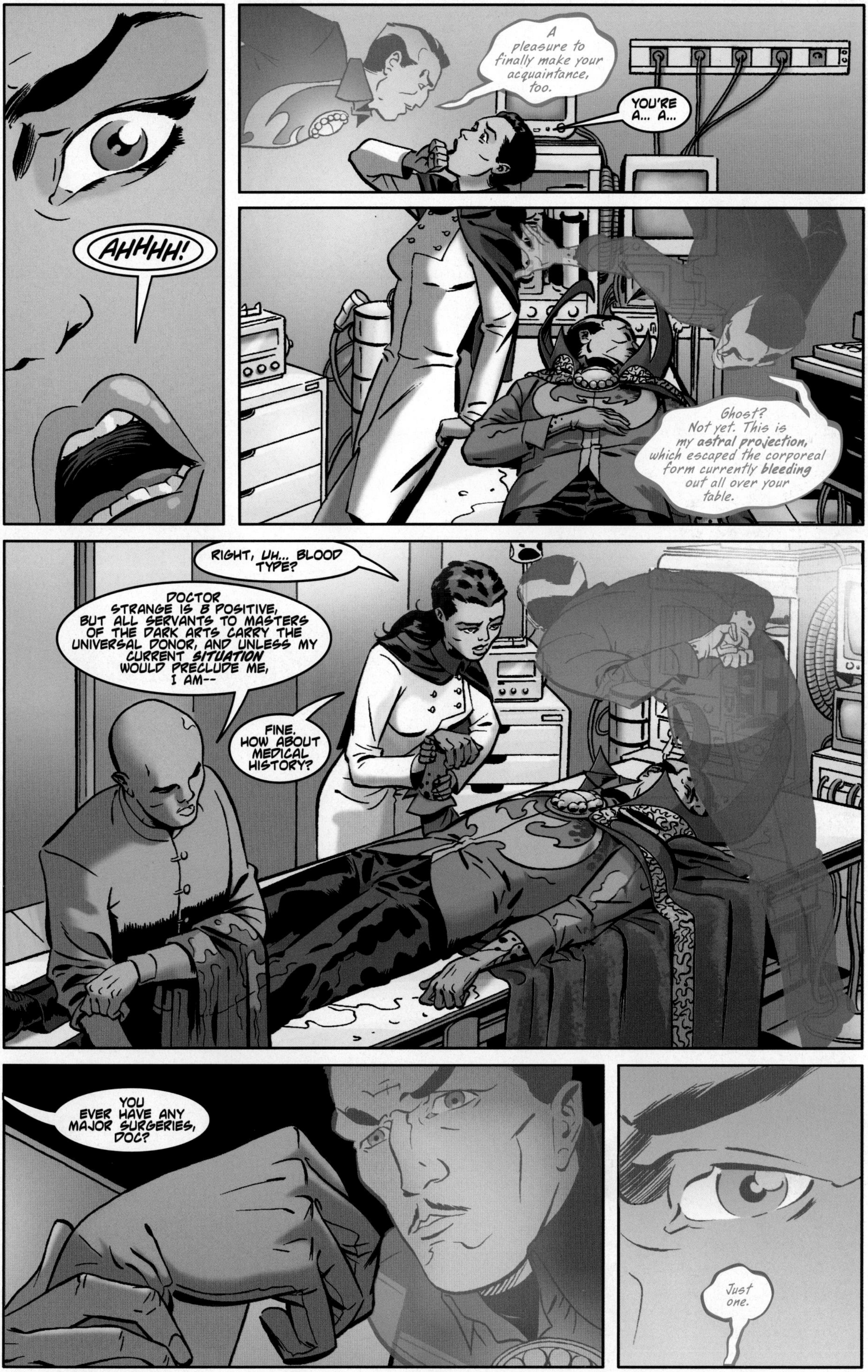
AHHHH!
A pleasure to finally make your acquaintance, too.
YOU'RE A... A...
Ghost? Not yet. This is my **astral projection**, which escaped the corporeal form currently **bleeding** out all over your table.
RIGHT, UH... BLOOD TYPE?
DOCTOR STRANGE IS B POSITIVE, BUT ALL SERVANTS TO MASTERS OF THE DARK ARTS CARRY THE UNIVERSAL DONOR, AND UNLESS MY CURRENT *SITUATION* WOULD PRECLUDE ME, I AM--
FINE. HOW ABOUT MEDICAL HISTORY?
YOU EVER HAVE ANY MAJOR SURGERIES, DOC?
Just one.

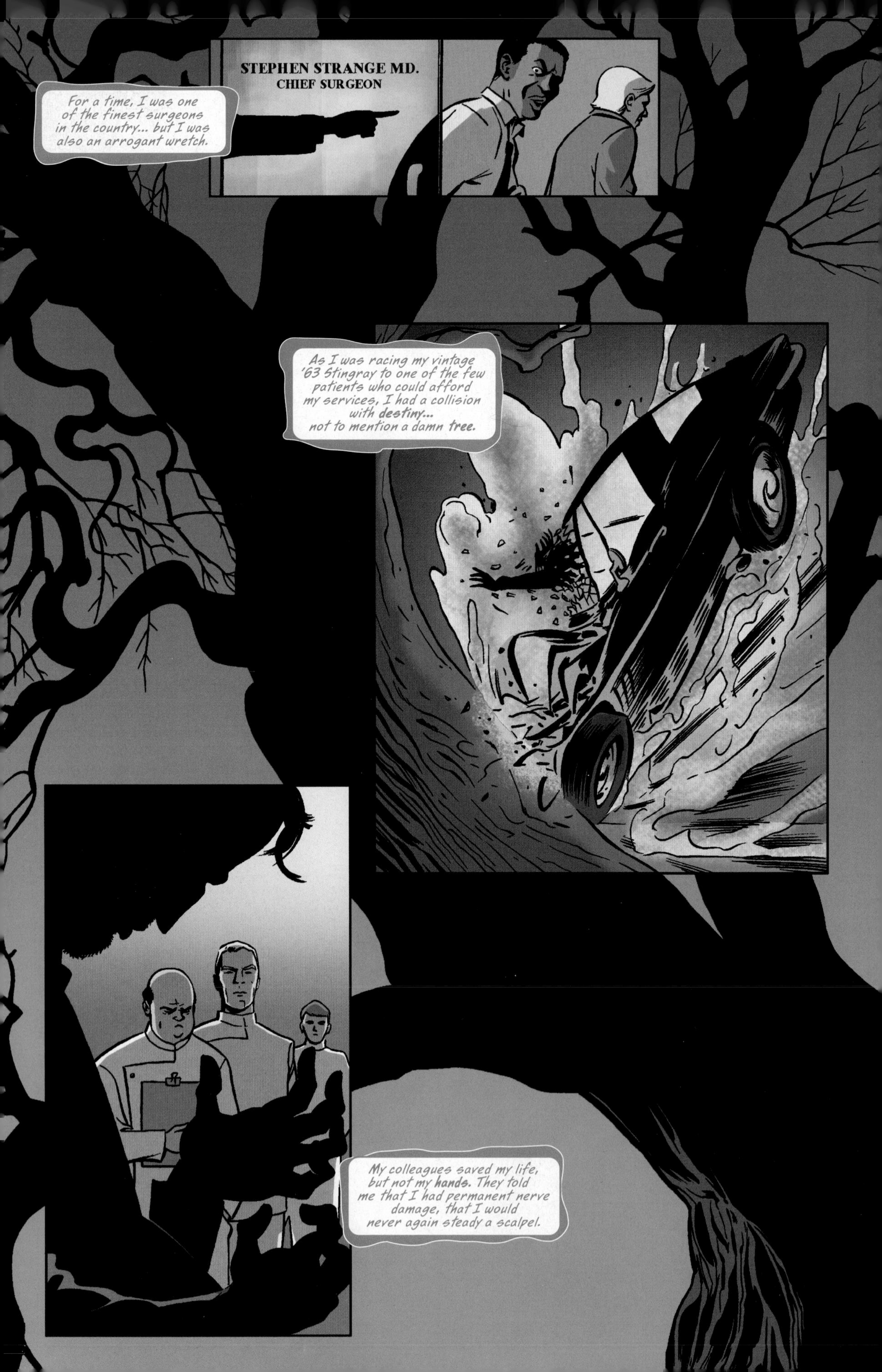

STEPHEN STRANGE MD.
CHIEF SURGEON
For a time, I was one of the finest surgeons in the country... but I was also an arrogant wretch.
As I was racing my vintage '63 Stingray to one of the few patients who could afford my services, I had a collision with destiny... not to mention a damn tree.
My colleagues saved my life, but not my hands. They told me that I had permanent nerve damage, that I would never again steady a scalpel.

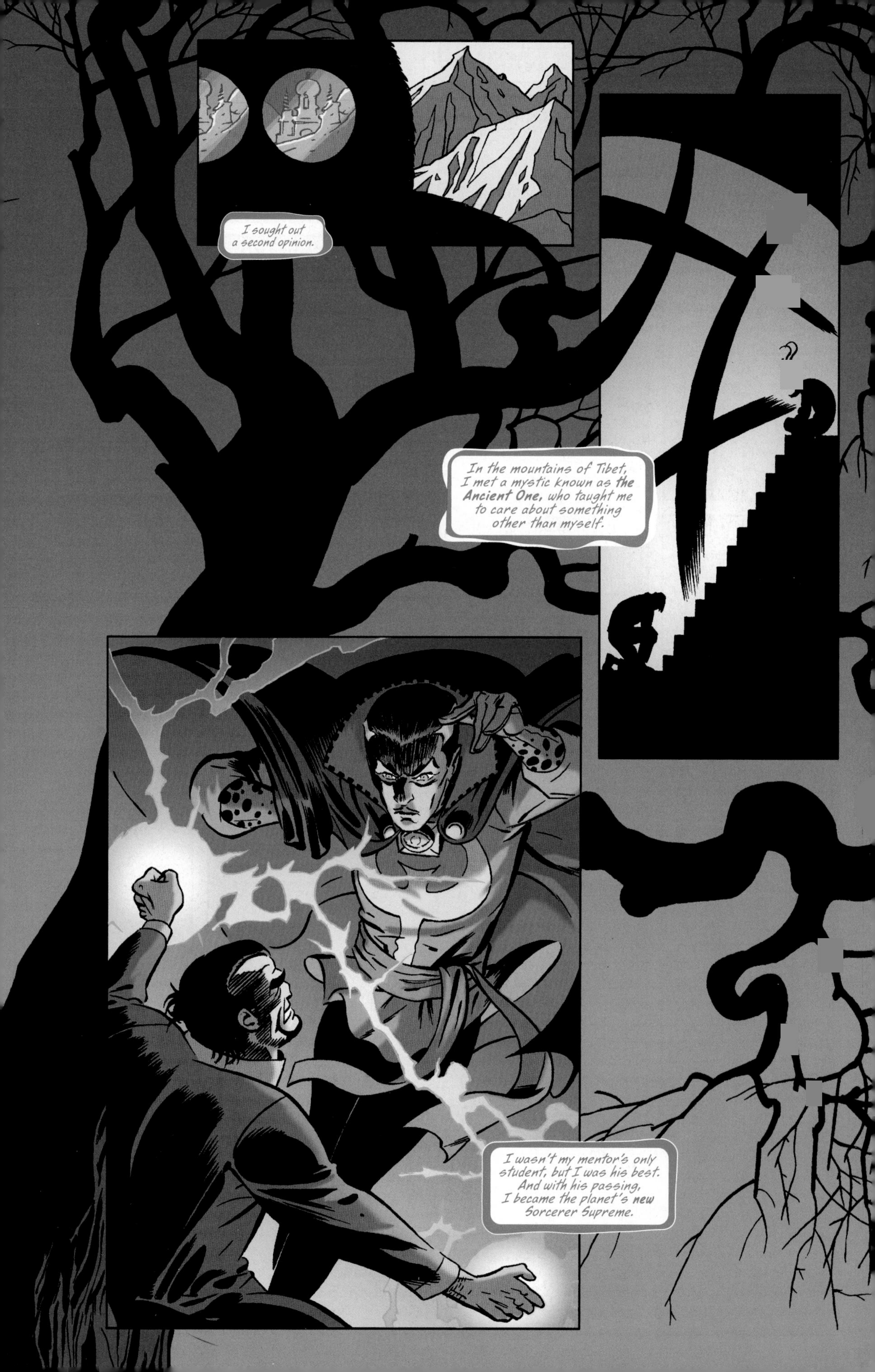
I sought out a second opinion.
In the mountains of Tibet, I met a mystic known as **the Ancient One,** who taught me to care about something other than myself.
I wasn't my mentor's only student, but I was his best. And with his passing, I became the planet's **new** Sorcerer Supreme.

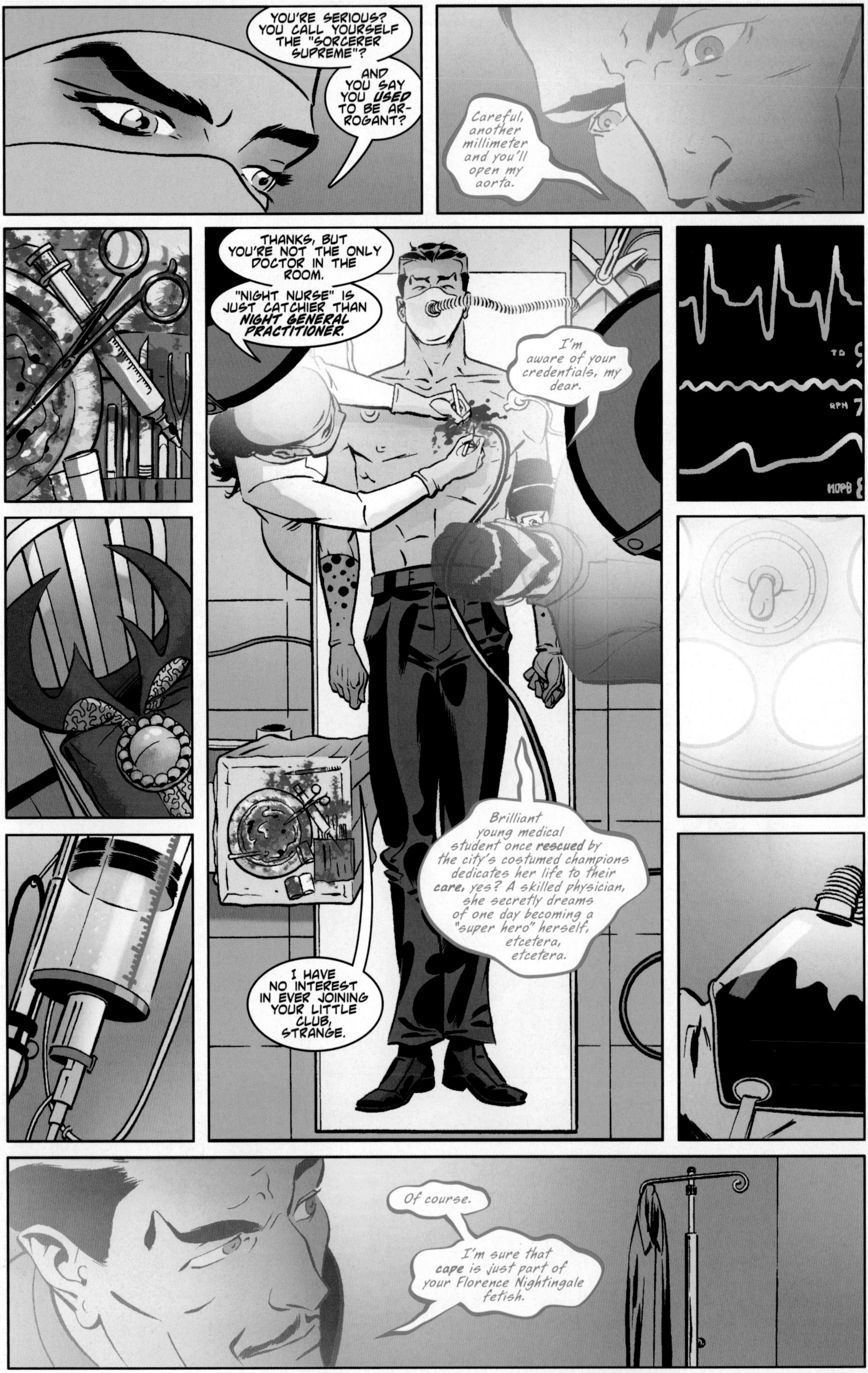
YOU'RE SERIOUS? YOU CALL YOURSELF THE "SORCERER SUPREME"?
AND YOU SAY YOU *USED* TO BE AR-ROGANT?
Careful, another millimeter and you'll open my aorta.
THANKS, BUT YOU'RE NOT THE ONLY DOCTOR IN THE ROOM.
"NIGHT NURSE" IS JUST CATCHIER THAN ***NIGHT GENERAL PRACTITIONER.***
I'm aware of your credentials, my dear.
Brilliant young medical student once **rescued** by the city's costumed champions dedicates her life to their **care**, yes? A skilled physician, she secretly dreams of one day becoming a "super hero" herself, etcetera, etcetera.
I HAVE NO INTEREST IN EVER JOINING YOUR LITTLE CLUB, STRANGE.
Of course.
I'm sure that **cape** is just part of your Florence Nightingale fetish.

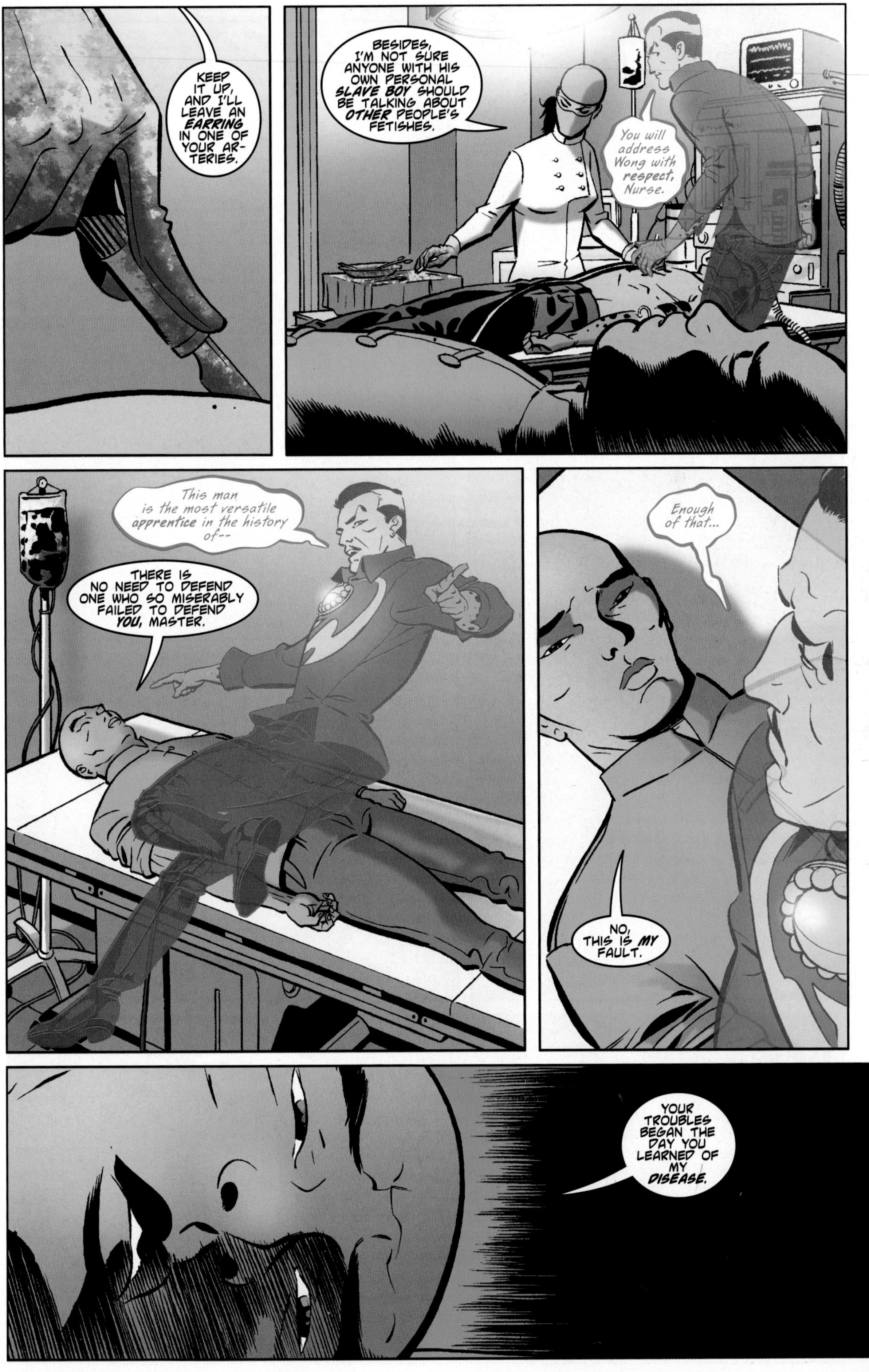
KEEP IT UP, AND I'LL LEAVE AN EARRING IN ONE OF YOUR ARTERIES.
BESIDES, I'M NOT SURE ANYONE WITH HIS OWN PERSONAL SLAVE BOY SHOULD BE TALKING ABOUT OTHER PEOPLE'S FETISHES.
You will address Wong with respect, Nurse.
This man is the most versatile apprentice in the history of--
THERE IS NO NEED TO DEFEND ONE WHO SO MISERABLY FAILED TO DEFEND YOU, MASTER.
Enough of that...
NO, THIS IS MY FAULT.
YOUR TROUBLES BEGAN THE DAY YOU LEARNED OF MY DISEASE.

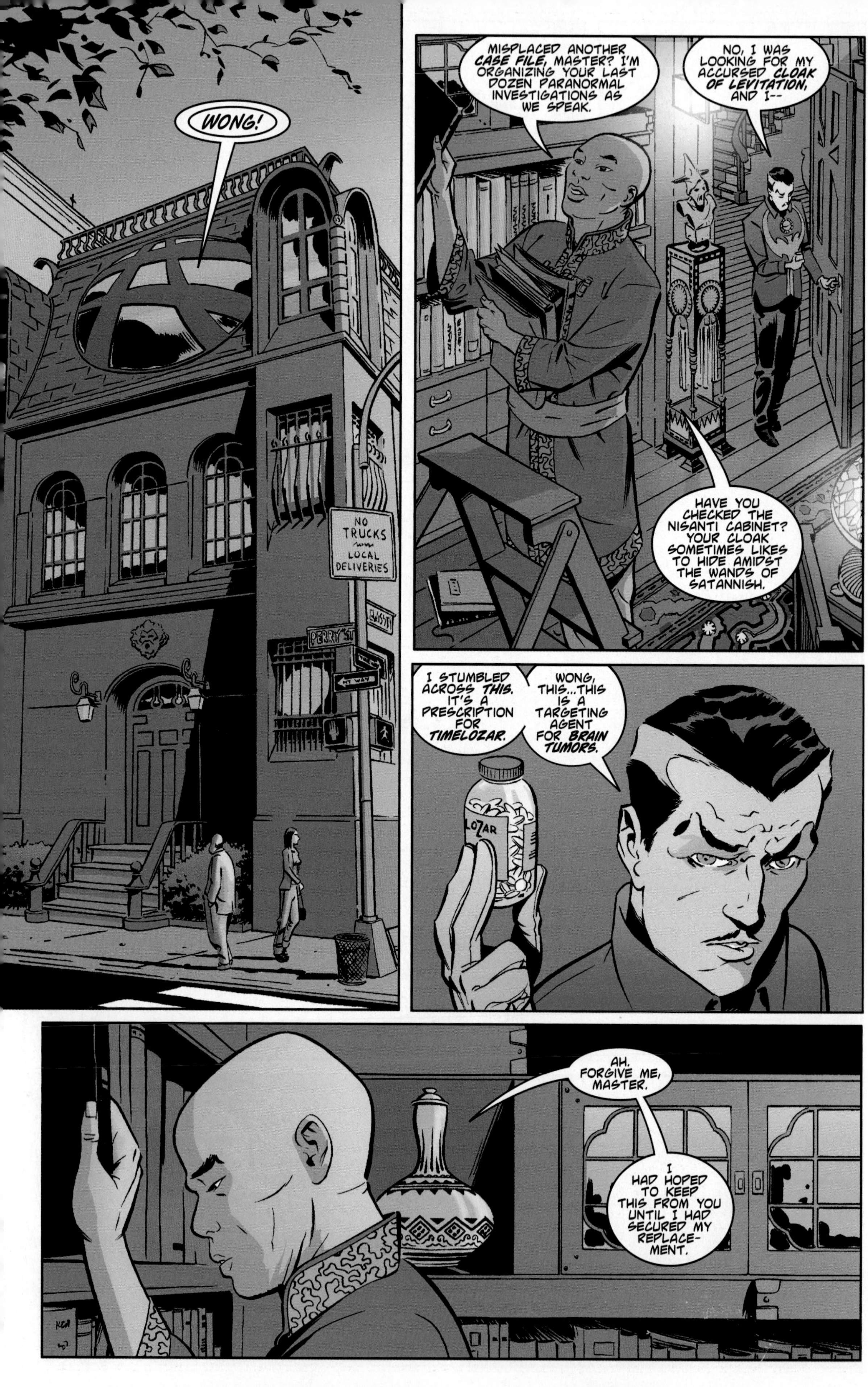
WONG!
NO TRUCKS
LOCAL DELIVERIES
PERRY ST
MISPLACED ANOTHER CASE FILE, MASTER? I'M ORGANIZING YOUR LAST DOZEN PARANORMAL INVESTIGATIONS AS WE SPEAK.
NO, I WAS LOOKING FOR MY ACCURSED CLOAK OF LEVITATION, AND I--
HAVE YOU CHECKED THE NISANTI CABINET? YOUR CLOAK SOMETIMES LIKES TO HIDE AMIDST THE WANDS OF SATANNISH.
I STUMBLED ACROSS THIS. IT'S A PRESCRIPTION FOR TIMELOZAR.
WONG, THIS...THIS IS A TARGETING AGENT FOR BRAIN TUMORS.
LOZAR
AH. FORGIVE ME, MASTER.
I HAD HOPED TO KEEP THIS FROM YOU UNTIL I HAD SECURED MY REPLACE-MENT.

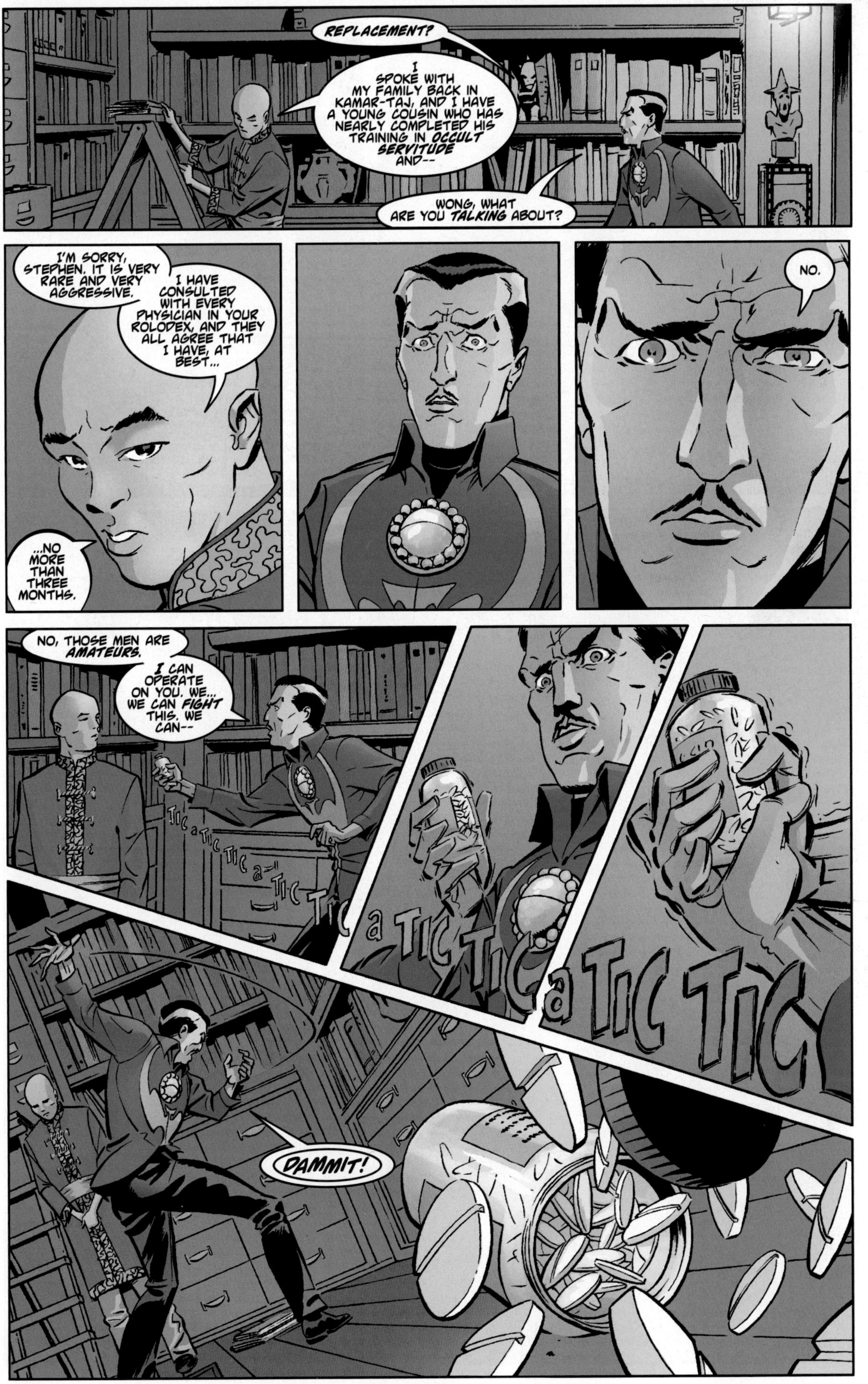
REPLACEMENT?
I SPOKE WITH MY FAMILY BACK IN KAMAR-TAJ, AND I HAVE A YOUNG COUSIN WHO HAS NEARLY COMPLETED HIS TRAINING IN OCCULT SERVITUDE AND--
WONG, WHAT ARE YOU TALKING ABOUT?
I'M SORRY, STEPHEN. IT IS VERY RARE AND VERY AGGRESSIVE.
I HAVE CONSULTED WITH EVERY PHYSICIAN IN YOUR ROLODEX, AND THEY ALL AGREE THAT I HAVE, AT BEST...
...NO MORE THAN THREE MONTHS.
NO.
NO, THOSE MEN ARE AMATEURS.
I CAN OPERATE ON YOU. WE... WE CAN FIGHT THIS. WE CAN--
TIC a TIC TIC a TIC TIC
TIC a TIC TIC a TIC TIC
DAMMIT!

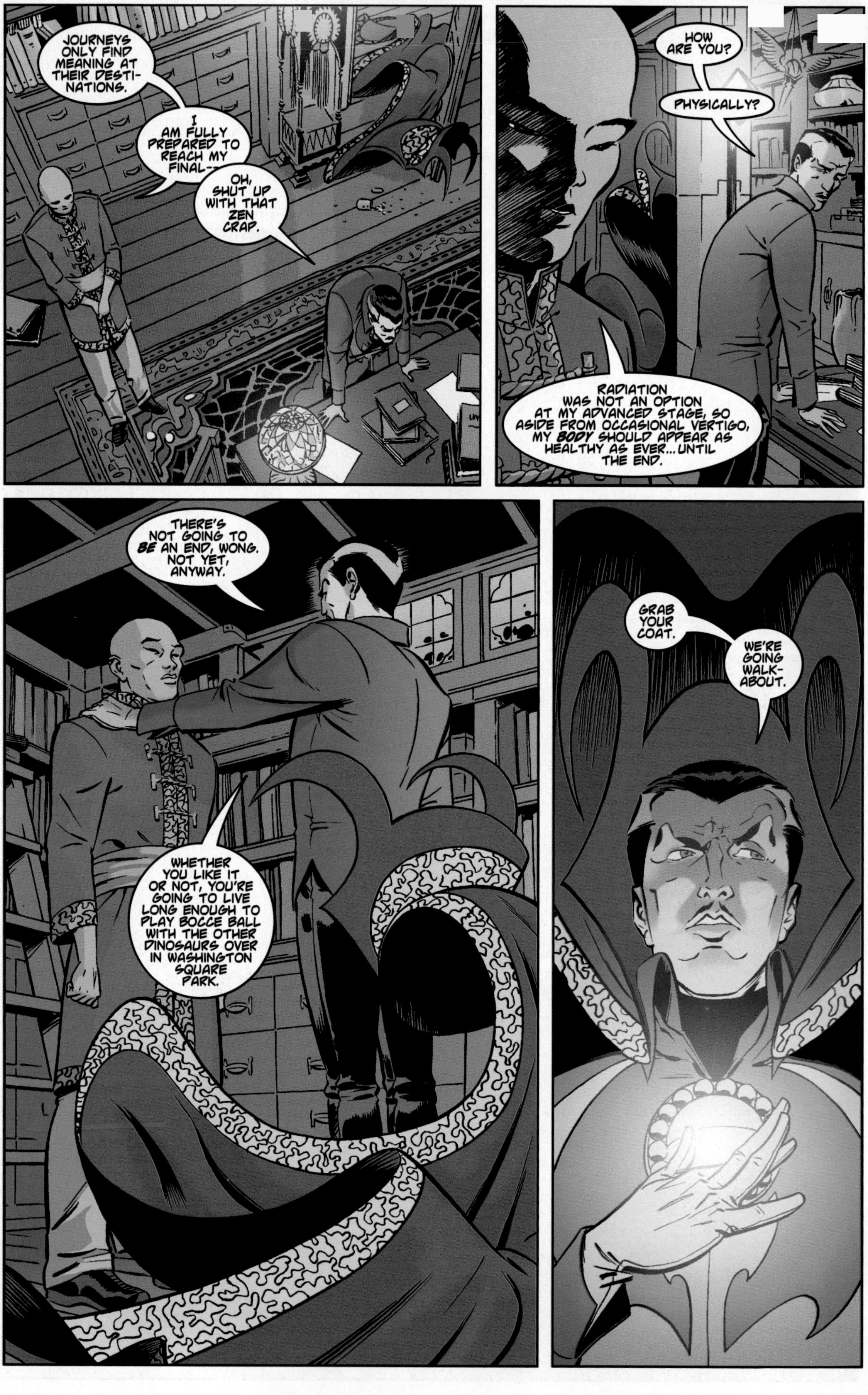
JOURNEYS ONLY FIND MEANING AT THEIR DESTI-NATIONS.
I AM FULLY PREPARED TO REACH MY FINAL--
OH, SHUT UP WITH THAT ZEN CRAP.
HOW ARE YOU?
PHYSICALLY?
RADIATION WAS NOT AN OPTION AT MY ADVANCED STAGE, SO ASIDE FROM OCCASIONAL VERTIGO, MY BODY SHOULD APPEAR AS HEALTHY AS EVER... UNTIL THE END.
THERE'S NOT GOING TO BE AN END, WONG. NOT YET, ANYWAY.
WHETHER YOU LIKE IT OR NOT, YOU'RE GOING TO LIVE LONG ENOUGH TO PLAY BOCCE BALL WITH THE OTHER DINOSAURS OVER IN WASHINGTON SQUARE PARK.
GRAB YOUR COAT.
WE'RE GOING WALK-ABOUT.

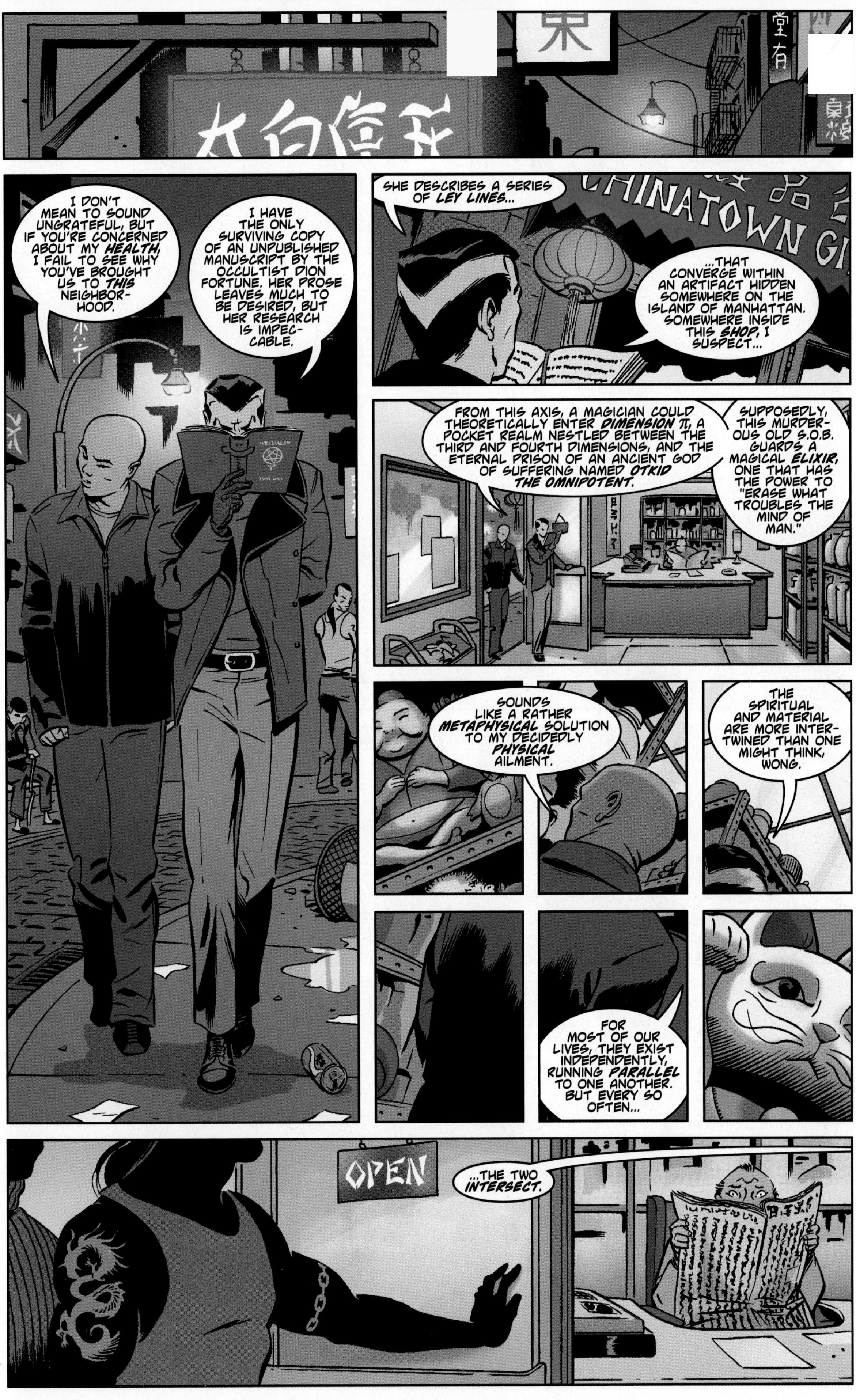

I DON'T MEAN TO SOUND UNGRATEFUL, BUT IF YOU'RE CONCERNED ABOUT MY *HEALTH*, I FAIL TO SEE WHY YOU'VE BROUGHT US TO *THIS* NEIGHBOR-HOOD.
I HAVE THE ONLY SURVIVING COPY OF AN UNPUBLISHED MANUSCRIPT BY THE OCCULTIST DION FORTUNE. HER PROSE LEAVES MUCH TO BE DESIRED, BUT HER RESEARCH IS IMPEC-CABLE.
SHE DESCRIBES A SERIES OF *LEY LINES*...
CHINATOWN GI
...THAT CONVERGE WITHIN AN ARTIFACT HIDDEN SOMEWHERE ON THE ISLAND OF MANHATTAN. SOMEWHERE INSIDE THIS *SHOP*, I SUSPECT...
FROM THIS AXIS, A MAGICIAN COULD THEORETICALLY ENTER *DIMENSION π*, A POCKET REALM NESTLED BETWEEN THE THIRD AND FOURTH DIMENSIONS, AND THE ETERNAL PRISON OF AN ANCIENT GOD OF SUFFERING NAMED *OTKID THE OMNIPOTENT*.
SUPPOSEDLY, THIS MURDER-OUS OLD S.O.B. GUARDS A MAGICAL *ELIXIR*, ONE THAT HAS THE POWER TO "ERASE WHAT TROUBLES THE MIND OF MAN."
SOUNDS LIKE A RATHER *METAPHYSICAL* SOLUTION TO MY DECIDEDLY *PHYSICAL* AILMENT.
THE SPIRITUAL AND MATERIAL ARE MORE INTER-TWINED THAN ONE MIGHT THINK, WONG.
FOR MOST OF OUR LIVES, THEY EXIST INDEPENDENTLY, RUNNING *PARALLEL* TO ONE ANOTHER. BUT EVERY SO OFTEN...
OPEN
...THE TWO *INTERSECT*.

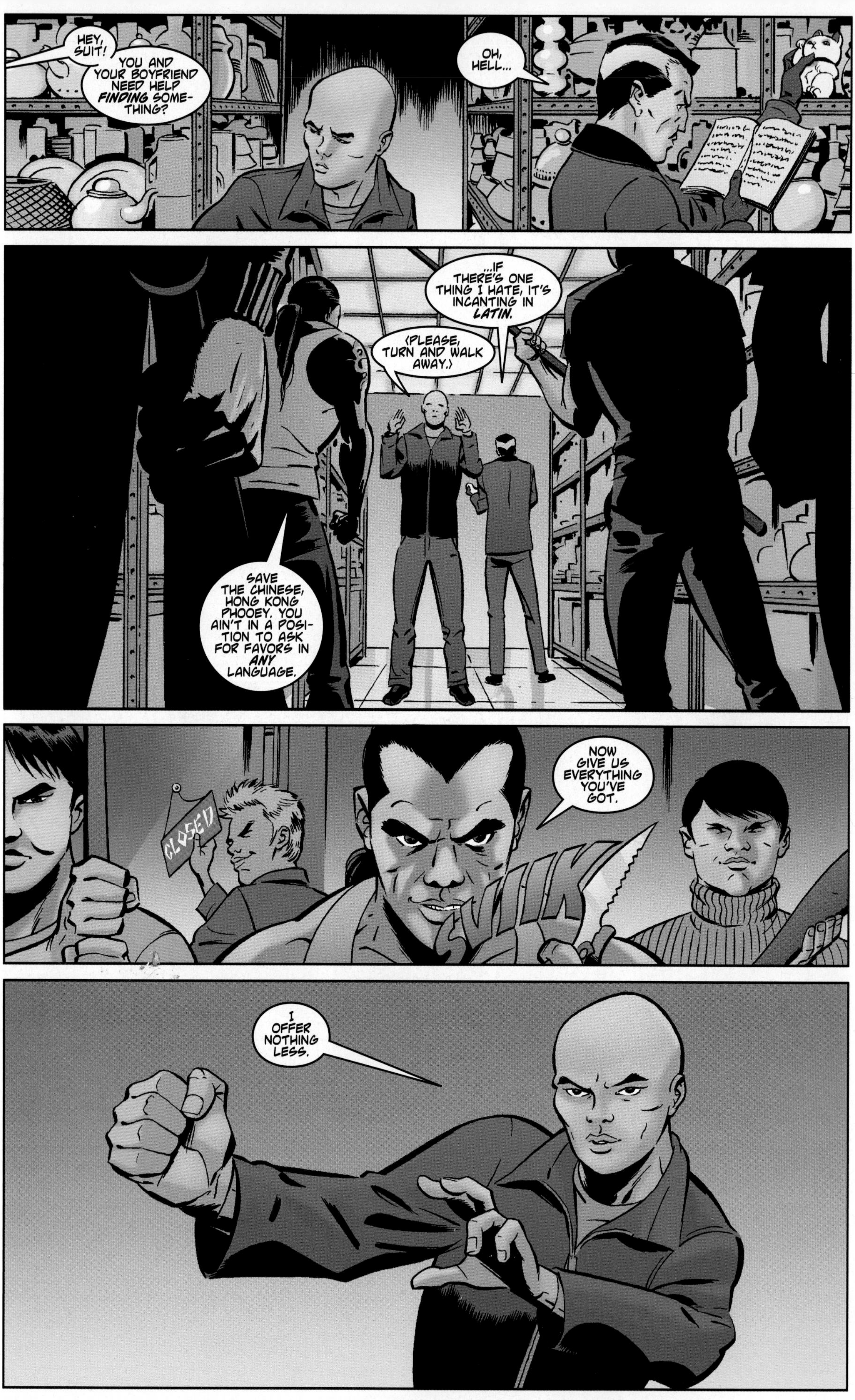

HEY, SUIT!
YOU AND YOUR BOYFRIEND NEED HELP FINDING SOME-THING?
OH, HELL...
...IF THERE'S ONE THING I HATE, IT'S INCANTING IN LATIN.
(PLEASE, TURN AND WALK AWAY.)
SAVE THE CHINESE, HONG KONG PHOOEY. YOU AIN'T IN A POSI-TION TO ASK FOR FAVORS IN ANY LANGUAGE.
CLOSED
NOW GIVE US EVERYTHING YOU'VE GOT.
SVLIK!
I OFFER NOTHING LESS.

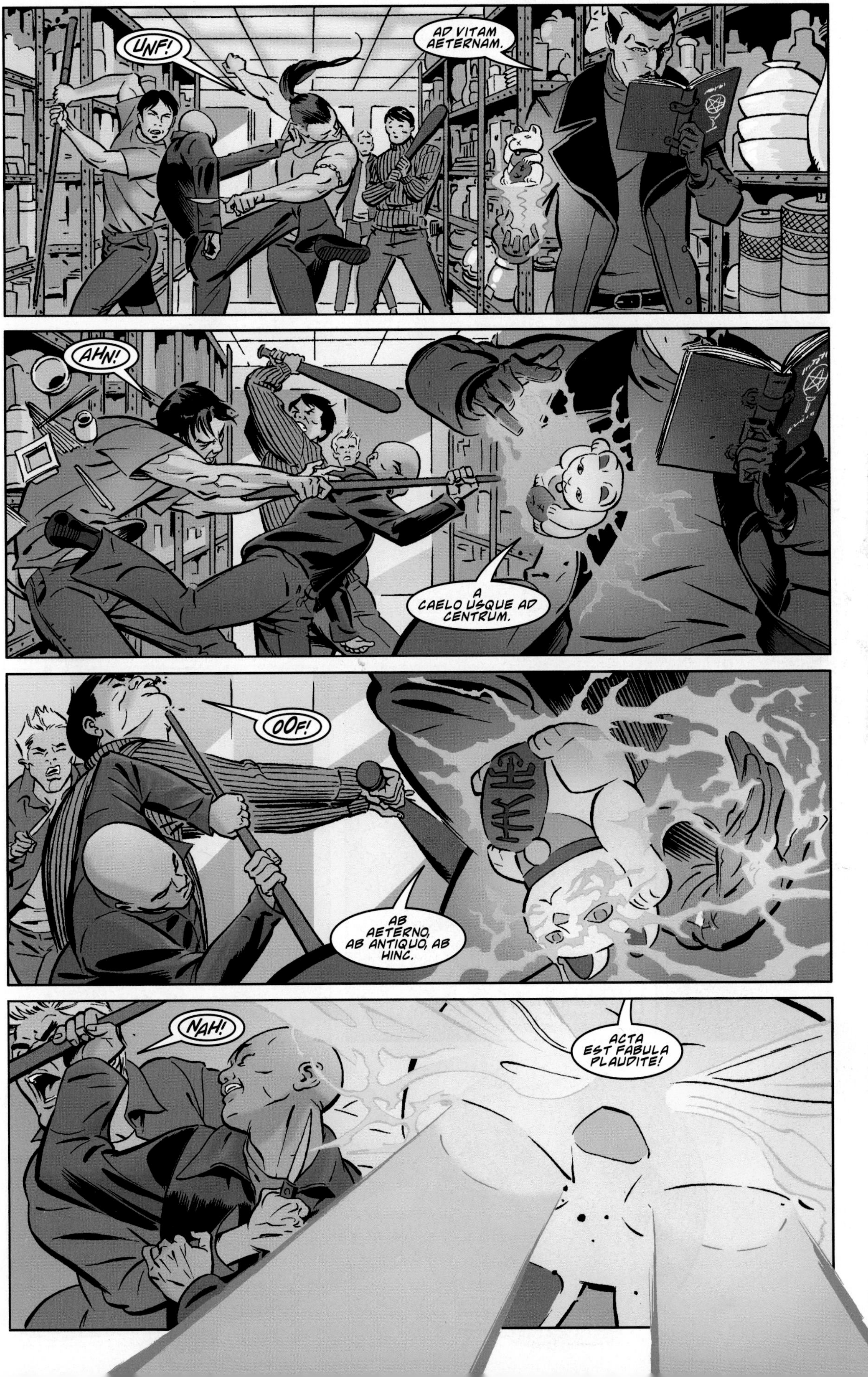
UNF!
AD VITAM AETERNAM.
AHN!
A CAELO USQUE AD CENTRUM.
OOF!
AB AETERNO, AB ANTIQUO, AB HINC.
NAH!
ACTA EST FABULA PLAUDITE!

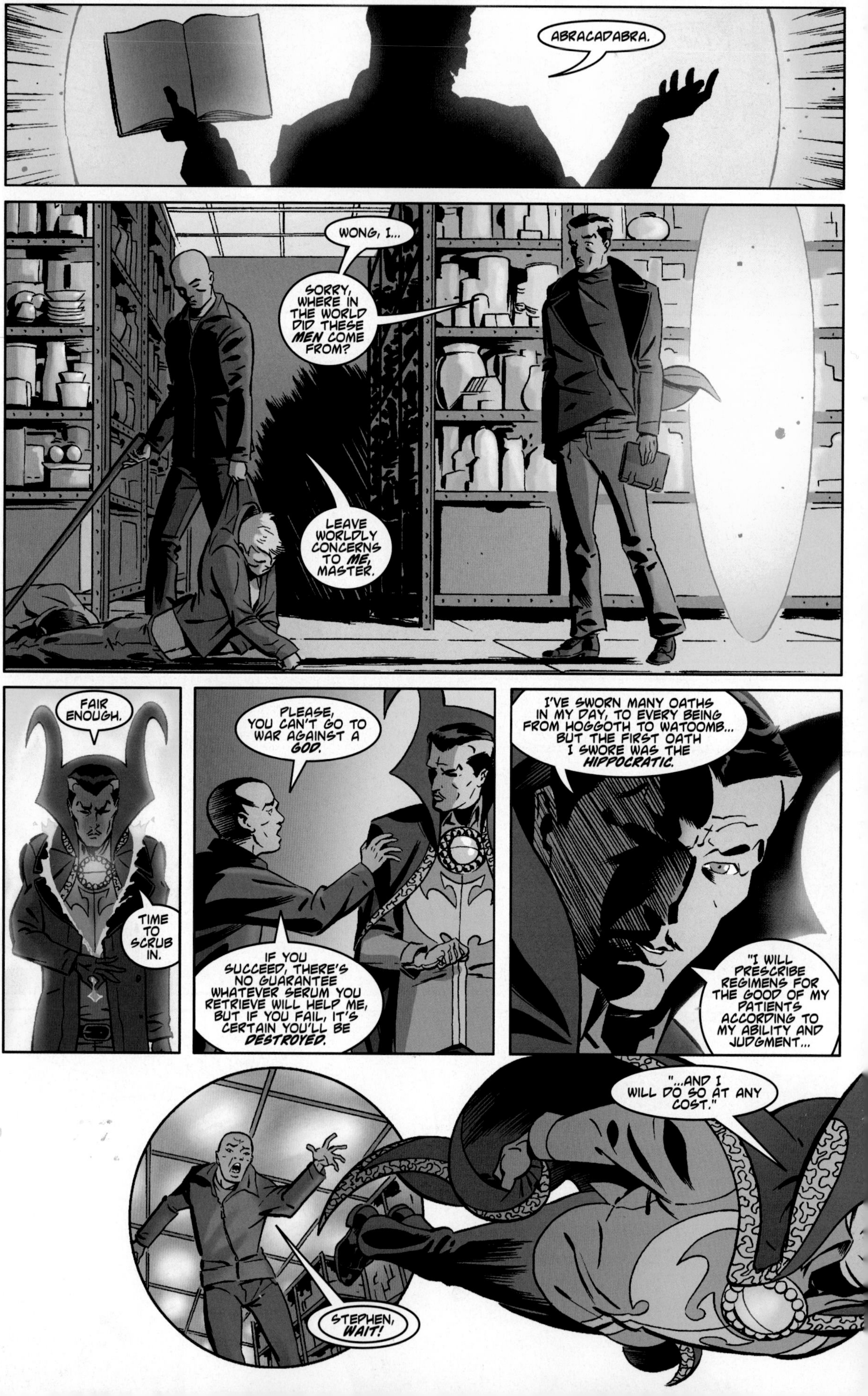

ABRACADABRA.
WONG, I...
SORRY, WHERE IN THE WORLD DID THESE MEN COME FROM?
LEAVE WORLDLY CONCERNS TO ME, MASTER.
FAIR ENOUGH.
TIME TO SCRUB IN.
PLEASE, YOU CAN'T GO TO WAR AGAINST A GOD.
IF YOU SUCCEED, THERE'S NO GUARANTEE WHATEVER SERUM YOU RETRIEVE WILL HELP ME, BUT IF YOU FAIL, IT'S CERTAIN YOU'LL BE DESTROYED.
I'VE SWORN MANY OATHS IN MY DAY, TO EVERY BEING FROM HOGGOTH TO WATOOMB... BUT THE FIRST OATH I SWORE WAS THE HIPPOCRATIC.
"I WILL PRESCRIBE REGIMENS FOR THE GOOD OF MY PATIENTS ACCORDING TO MY ABILITY AND JUDGMENT...
"...AND I WILL DO SO AT ANY COST."
STEPHEN, WAIT!

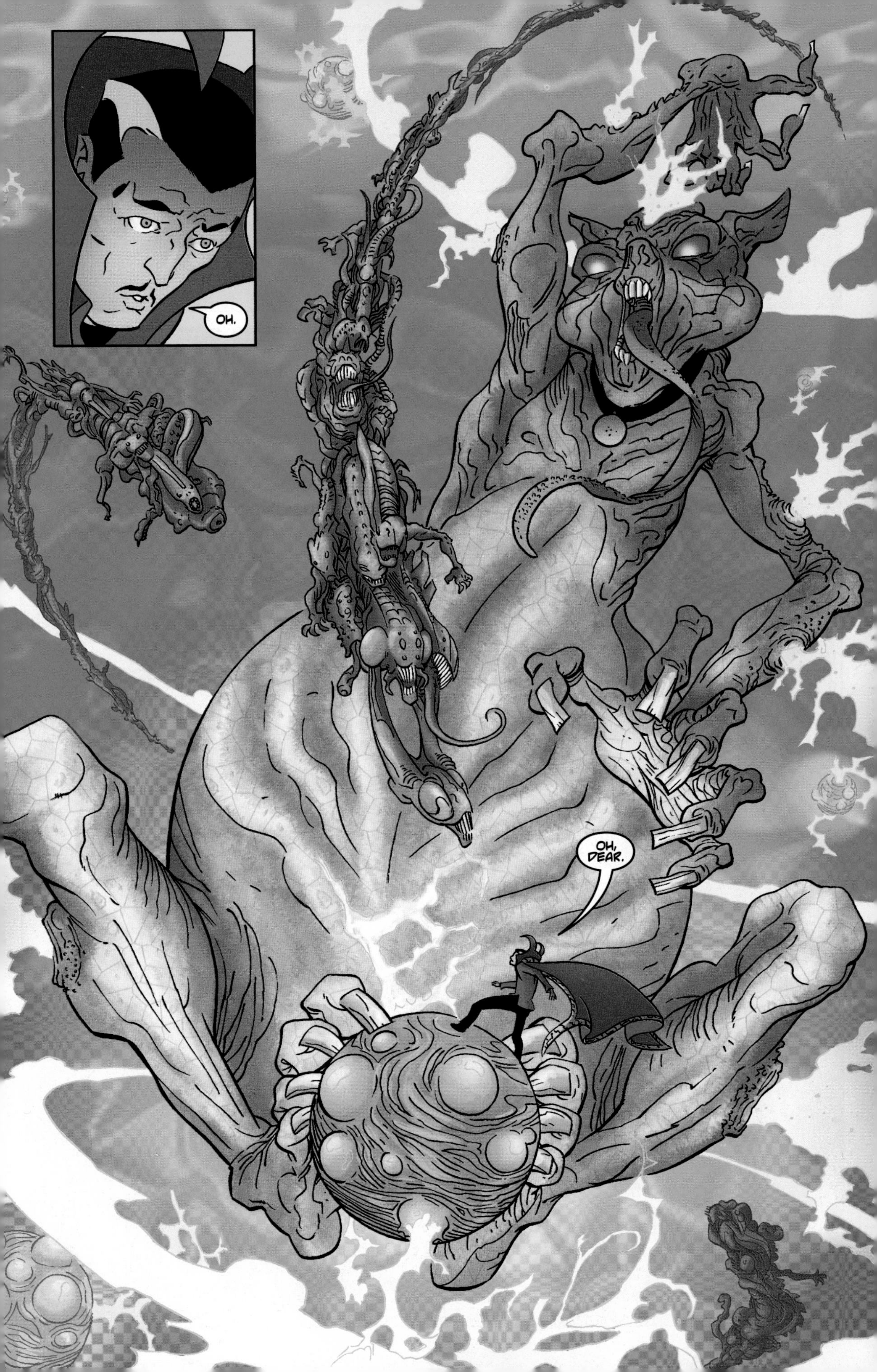
OH.
OH, DEAR.

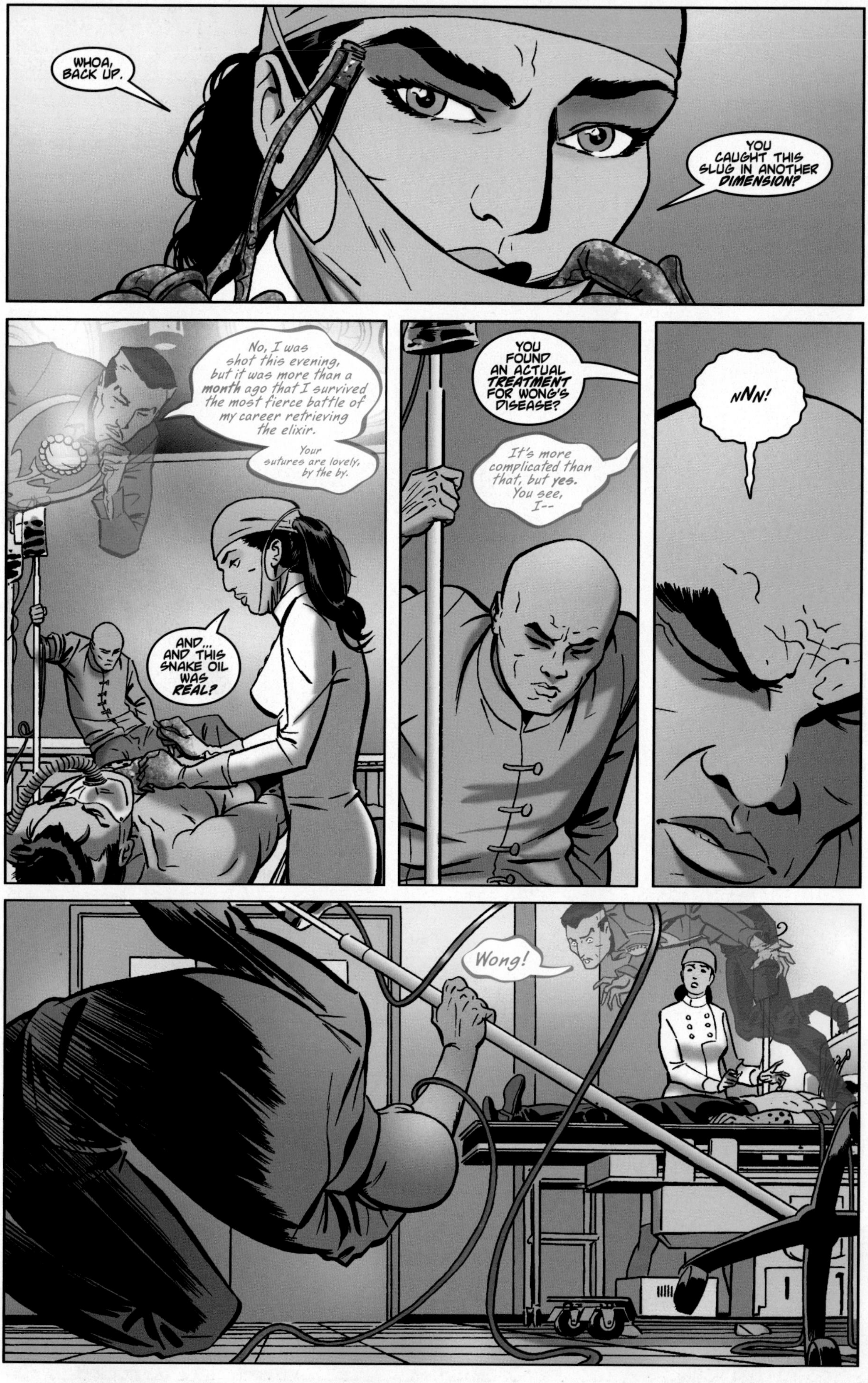
WHOA, BACK UP.
YOU CAUGHT THIS SLUG IN ANOTHER DIMENSION?
No, I was shot this evening, but it was more than a month ago that I survived the most fierce battle of my career retrieving the elixir.
Your sutures are lovely, by the by.
AND... AND THIS SNAKE OIL WAS REAL?
YOU FOUND AN ACTUAL TREATMENT FOR WONG'S DISEASE?
It's more complicated than that, but yes. You see, I--
NNN!
Wong!

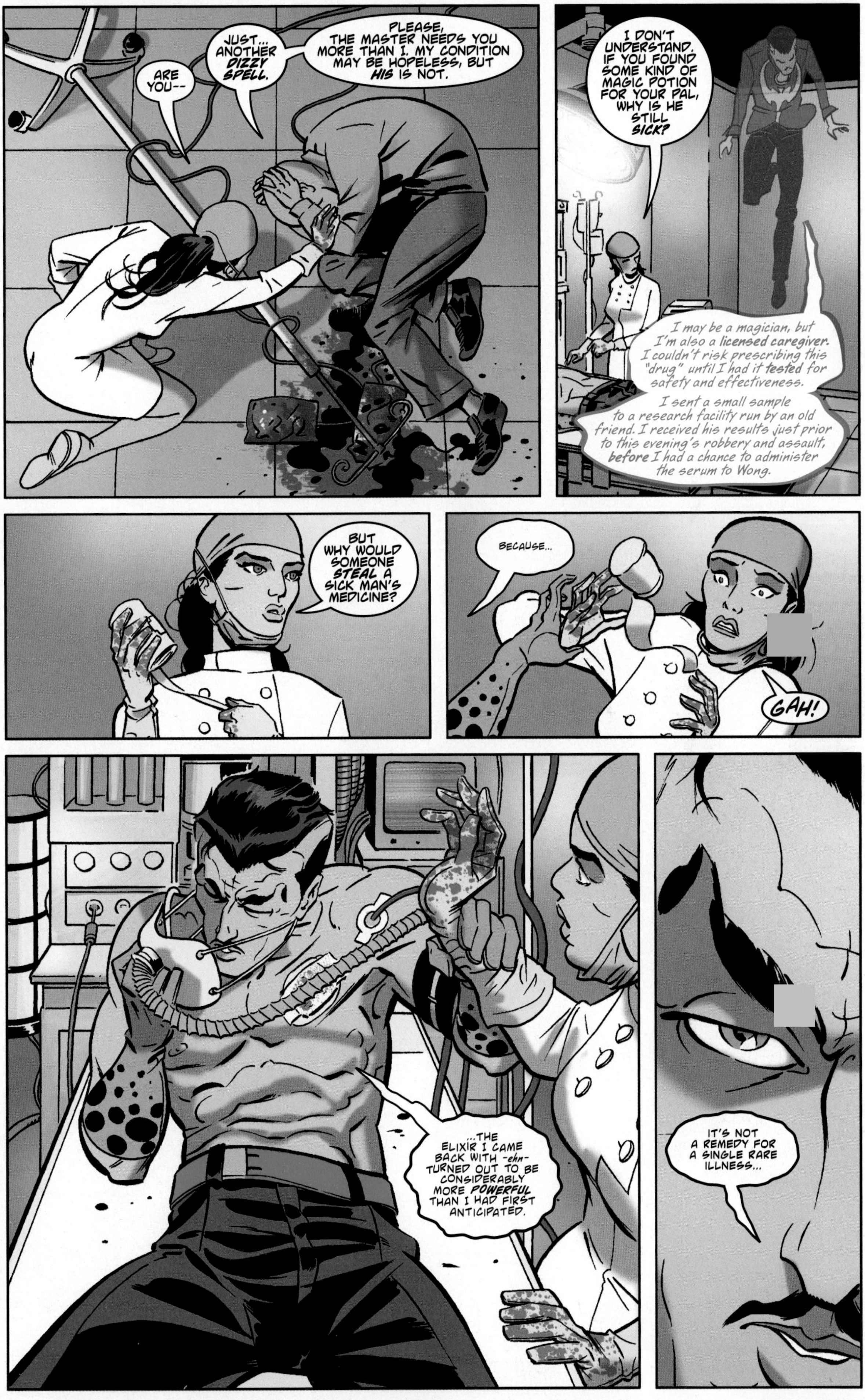
ARE YOU--
JUST... ANOTHER DIZZY SPELL.
PLEASE, THE MASTER NEEDS YOU MORE THAN I. MY CONDITION MAY BE HOPELESS, BUT HIS IS NOT.
I DON'T UNDERSTAND. IF YOU FOUND SOME KIND OF MAGIC POTION FOR YOUR PAL, WHY IS HE STILL SICK?
I may be a magician, but I'm also a licensed caregiver. I couldn't risk prescribing this "drug" until I had it tested for safety and effectiveness.
I sent a small sample to a research facility run by an old friend. I received his results just prior to this evening's robbery and assault, before I had a chance to administer the serum to Wong.
BUT WHY WOULD SOMEONE STEAL A SICK MAN'S MEDICINE?
BECAUSE...
GAH!
...THE ELIXIR I CAME BACK WITH -ehn- TURNED OUT TO BE CONSIDERABLY MORE POWERFUL THAN I HAD FIRST ANTICIPATED.
IT'S NOT A REMEDY FOR A SINGLE RARE ILLNESS...

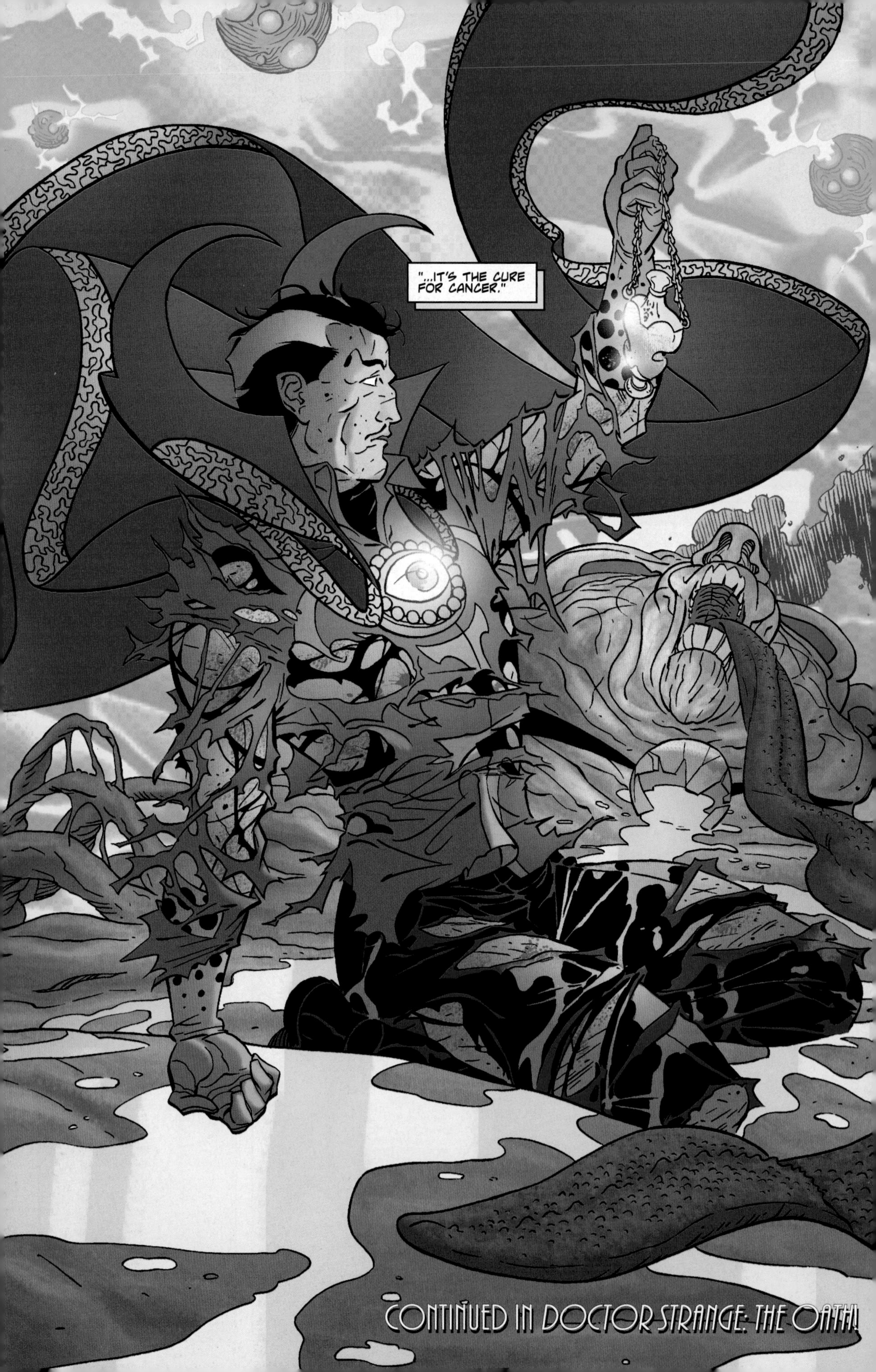
"...IT'S THE CURE FOR CANCER."
CONTINUED IN DOCTOR STRANGE: THE OATH!

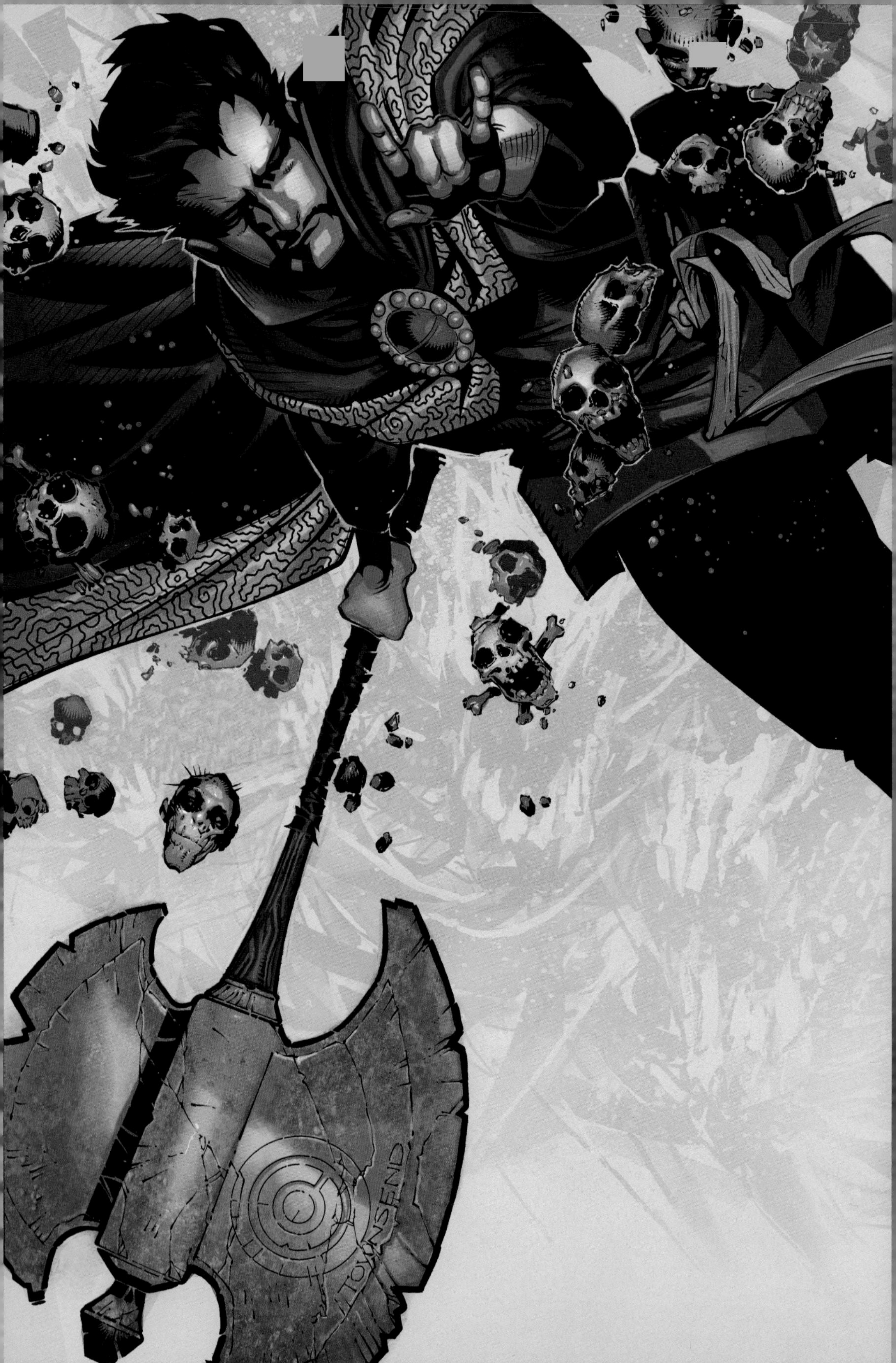
TOWNSEND

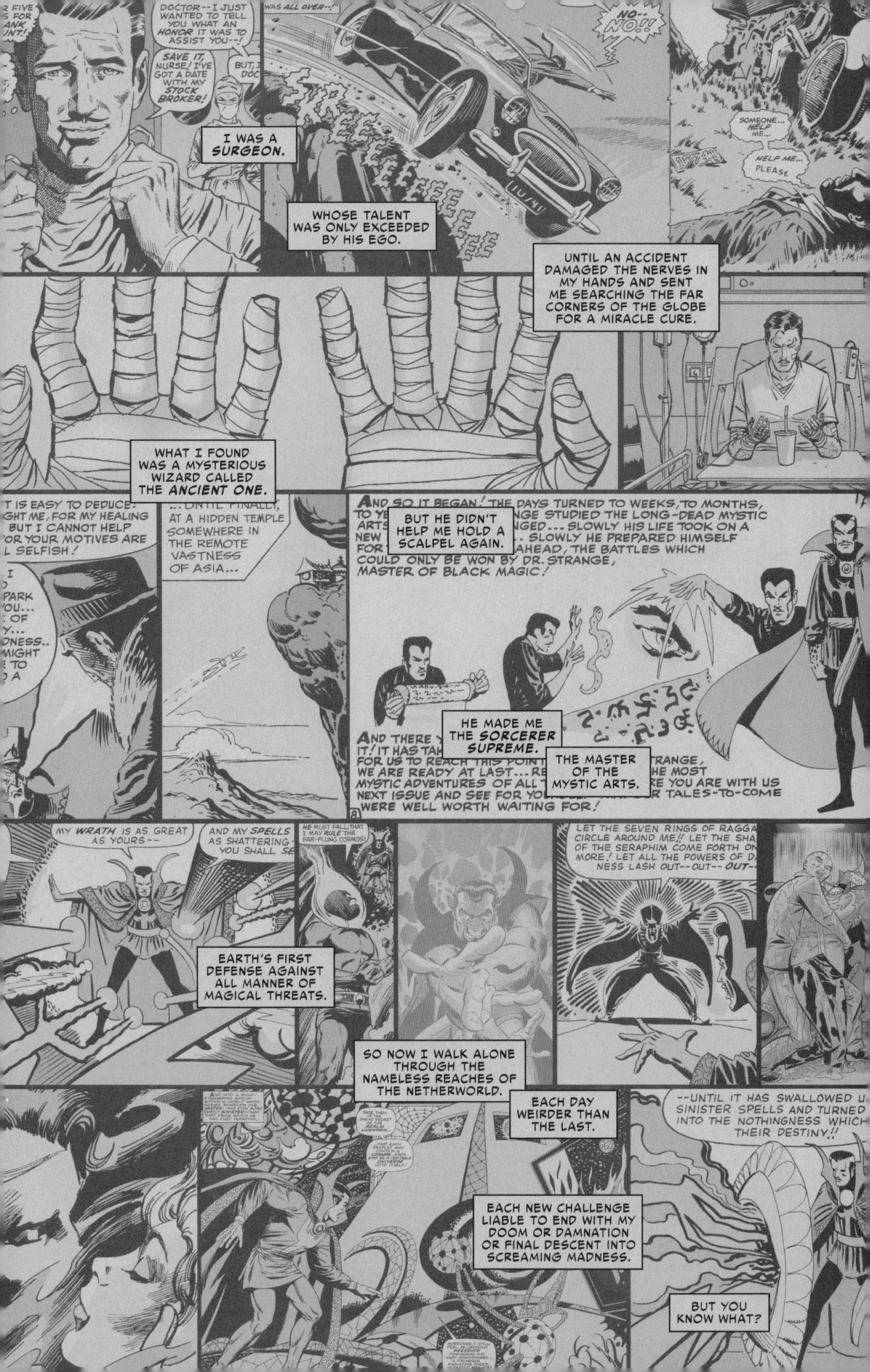

DOCTOR--I JUST WANTED TO TELL YOU WHAT AN HONOR IT WAS TO ASSIST YOU--!
SAVE IT, NURSE! I'VE GOT A DATE WITH MY STOCK BROKER!
I WAS A SURGEON.
NO-- NO!!
SOMEONE... HELP ME...
HELP ME... PLEASE
WHOSE TALENT WAS ONLY EXCEEDED BY HIS EGO.
UNTIL AN ACCIDENT DAMAGED THE NERVES IN MY HANDS AND SENT ME SEARCHING THE FAR CORNERS OF THE GLOBE FOR A MIRACLE CURE.
WHAT I FOUND WAS A MYSTERIOUS WIZARD CALLED THE ANCIENT ONE.
BUT I CANNOT HELP
SELFISH!
AT A HIDDEN TEMPLE SOMEWHERE IN THE REMOTE VASTNESS OF ASIA...
BUT HE DIDN'T HELP ME HOLD A SCALPEL AGAIN.
COULD ONLY BE WON BY DR. STRANGE, MASTER OF BLACK MAGIC!
HE MADE ME THE SORCERER SUPREME.
THE MASTER OF THE MYSTIC ARTS.
WE ARE READY AT LAST...
MYSTIC ADVENTURES OF ALL
NEXT ISSUE AND SEE FOR YOU
WERE WELL WORTH WAITING FOR!
MY WRATH IS AS GREAT AS YOURS--
AND MY SPELLS AS SHATTERING--
HE MUST FALL, THAT I MAY RULE THE FAR-FLUNG COSMOS!
CIRCLE AROUND ME!! LET THE SHA
OF THE SERAPHIM COME FORTH ON
MORE! LET ALL THE POWERS OF D
NESS LASH OUT--OUT--
EARTH'S FIRST DEFENSE AGAINST ALL MANNER OF MAGICAL THREATS.
SO NOW I WALK ALONE THROUGH THE NAMELESS REACHES OF THE NETHERWORLD.
EACH DAY WEIRDER THAN THE LAST.
--UNTIL IT HAS SWALLOWED U
SINISTER SPELLS AND TURNED
INTO THE NOTHINGNESS WHICH
THEIR DESTINY!!
EACH NEW CHALLENGE LIABLE TO END WITH MY DOOM OR DAMNATION OR FINAL DESCENT INTO SCREAMING MADNESS.
BUT YOU KNOW WHAT?

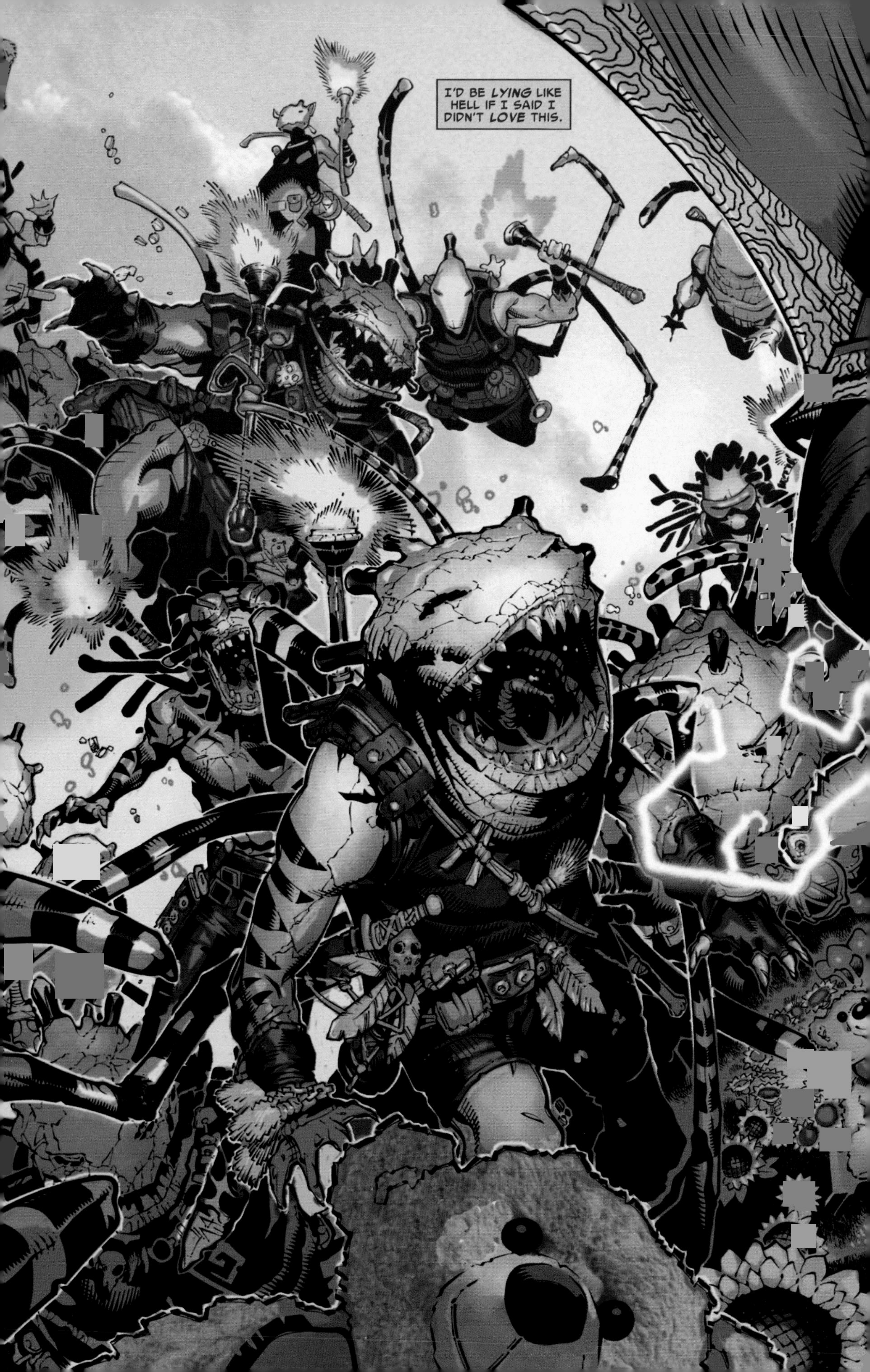
I'D BE LYING LIKE HELL IF I SAID I DIDN'T LOVE THIS.

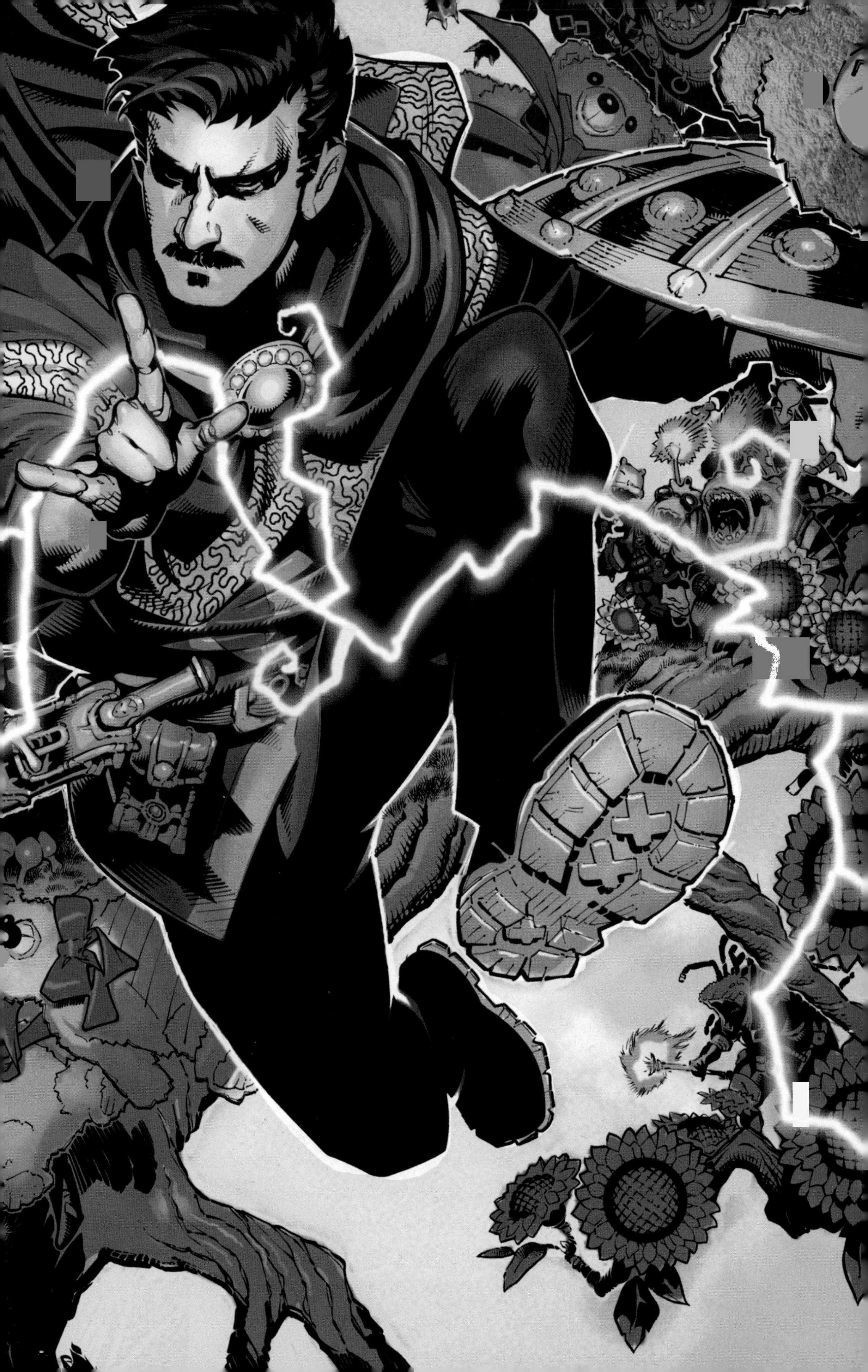

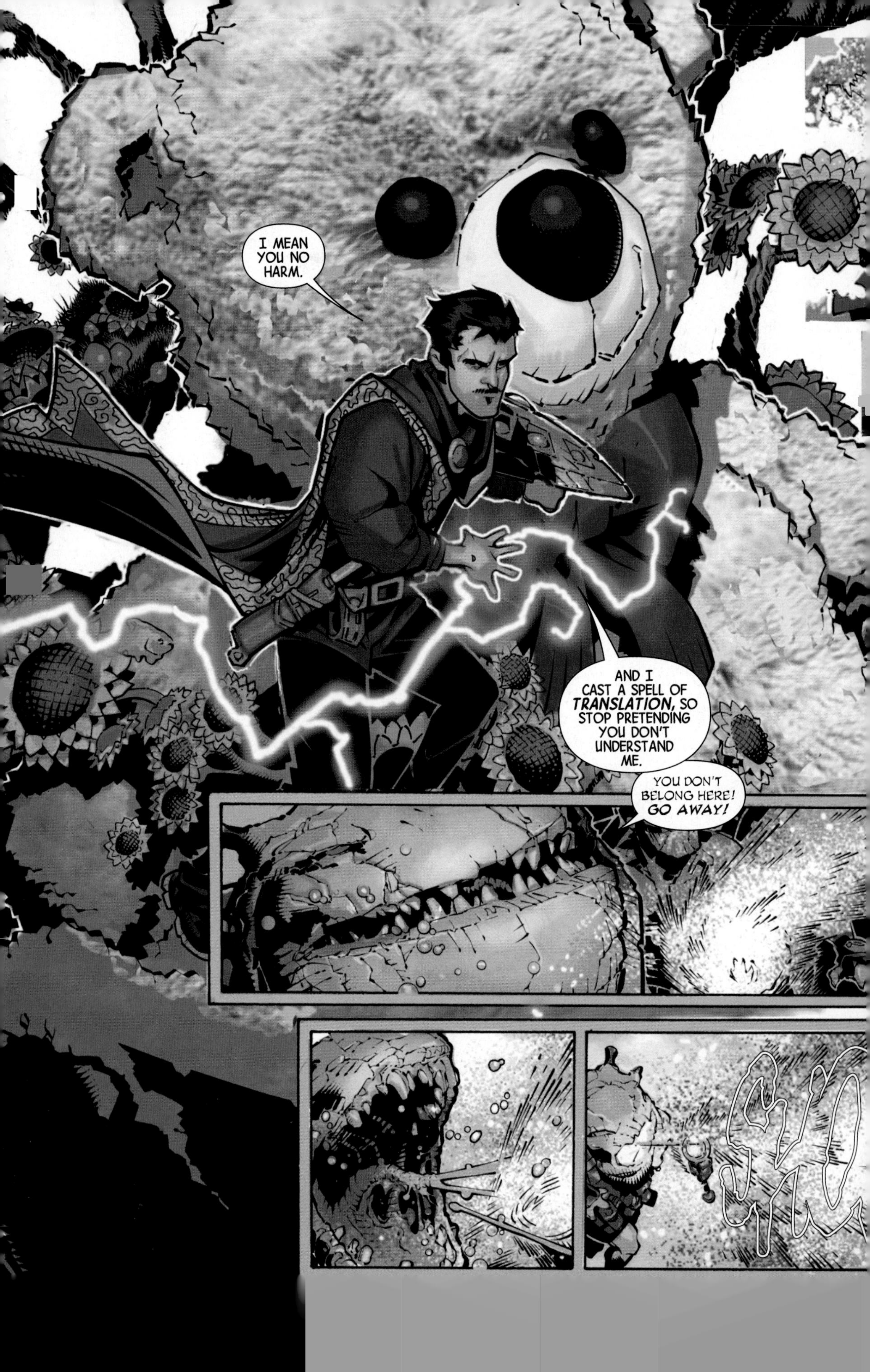
I MEAN YOU NO HARM.
AND I CAST A SPELL OF *TRANSLATION*, SO STOP PRETENDING YOU DON'T UNDERSTAND ME.
YOU DON'T BELONG HERE! **GO AWAY!**

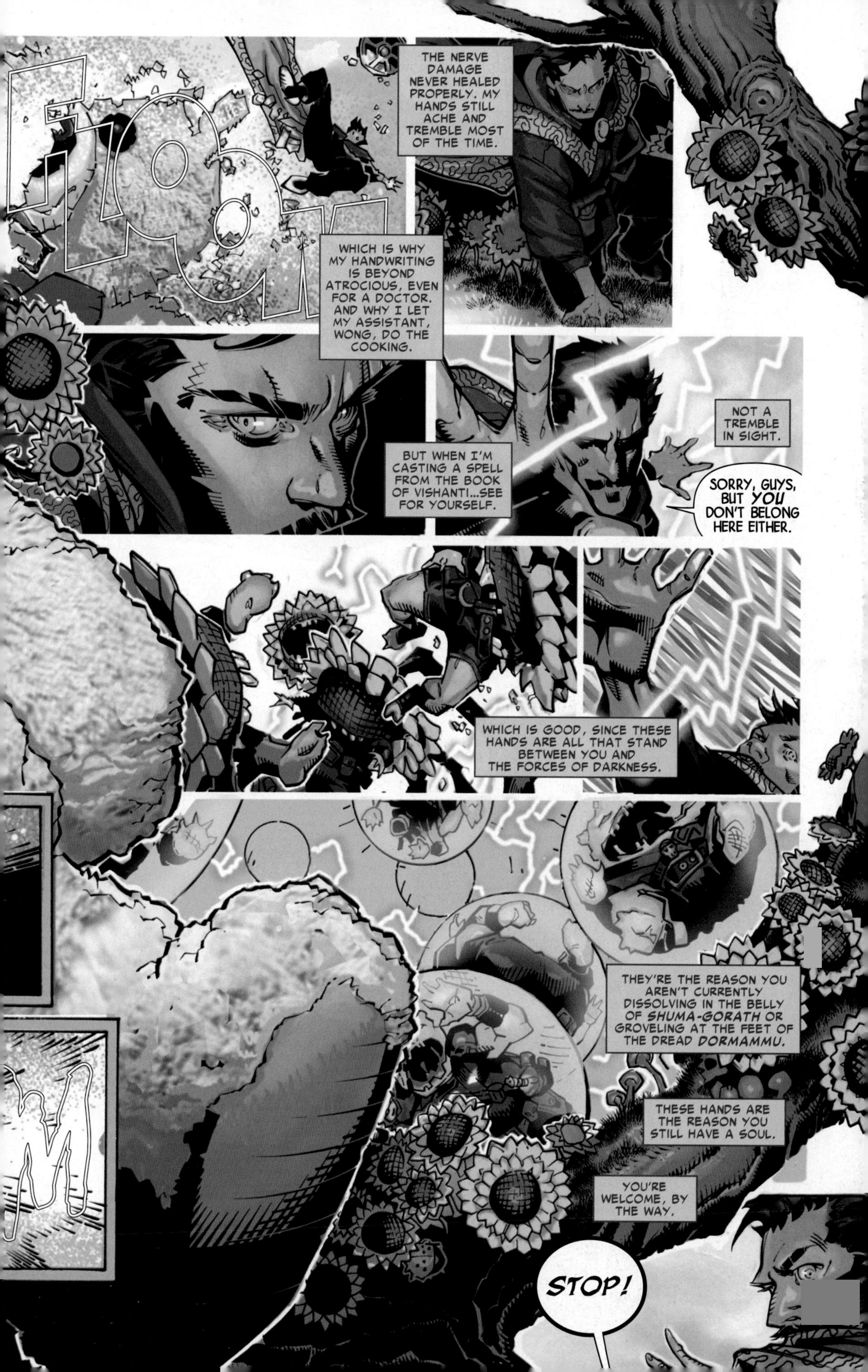
FZOOM
THE NERVE DAMAGE NEVER HEALED PROPERLY. MY HANDS STILL ACHE AND TREMBLE MOST OF THE TIME.
WHICH IS WHY MY HANDWRITING IS BEYOND ATROCIOUS, EVEN FOR A DOCTOR. AND WHY I LET MY ASSISTANT, WONG, DO THE COOKING.
BUT WHEN I'M CASTING A SPELL FROM THE BOOK OF VISHANTI...SEE FOR YOURSELF.
NOT A TREMBLE IN SIGHT.
SORRY, GUYS, BUT YOU DON'T BELONG HERE EITHER.
WHICH IS GOOD, SINCE THESE HANDS ARE ALL THAT STAND BETWEEN YOU AND THE FORCES OF DARKNESS.
THEY'RE THE REASON YOU AREN'T CURRENTLY DISSOLVING IN THE BELLY OF SHUMA-GORATH OR GROVELING AT THE FEET OF THE DREAD DORMAMMU.
THESE HANDS ARE THE REASON YOU STILL HAVE A SOUL.
YOU'RE WELCOME, BY THE WAY.
STOP!

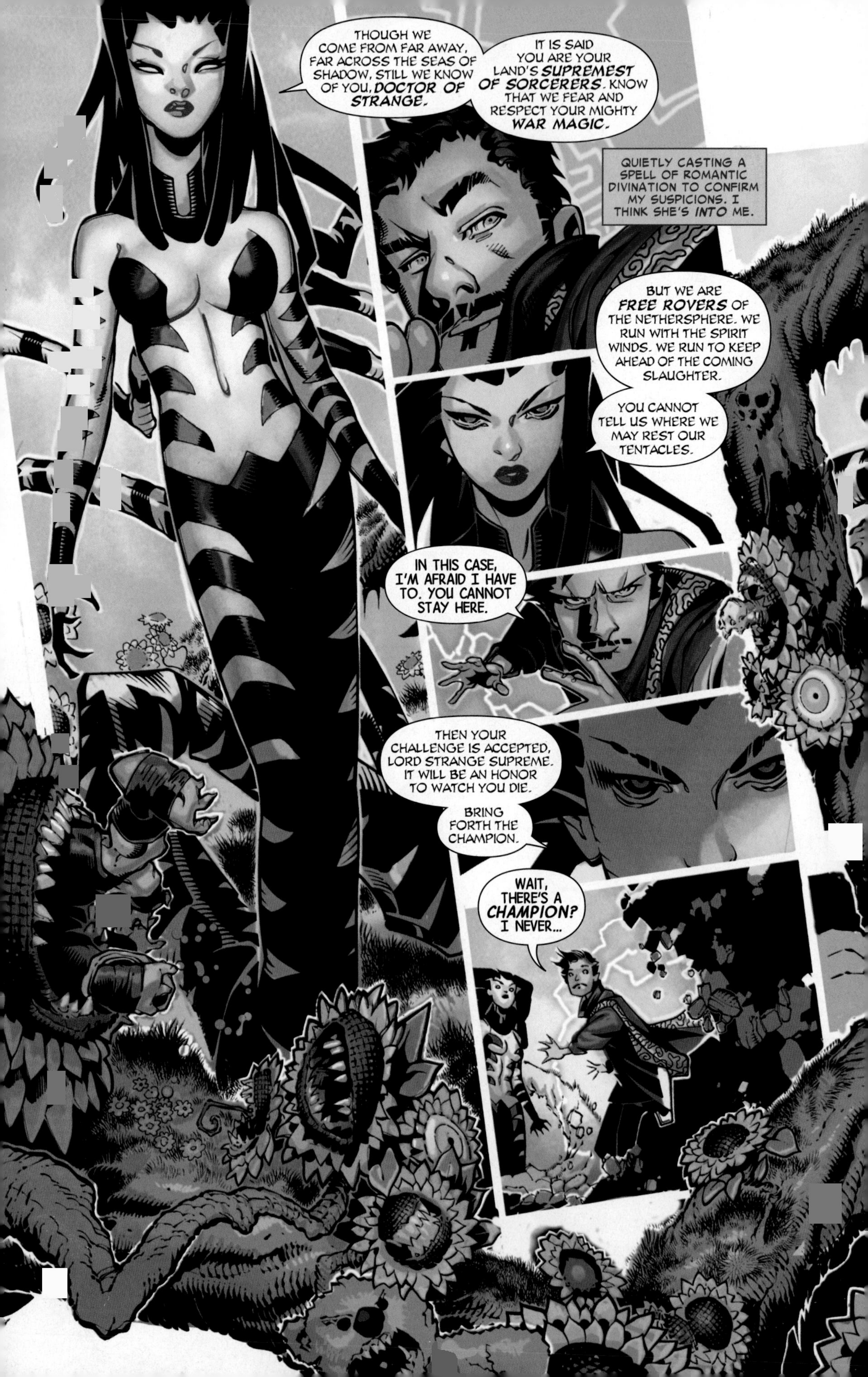
THOUGH WE COME FROM FAR AWAY, FAR ACROSS THE SEAS OF SHADOW, STILL WE KNOW OF YOU, DOCTOR OF STRANGE.
IT IS SAID YOU ARE YOUR LAND'S SUPREMEST OF SORCERERS. KNOW THAT WE FEAR AND RESPECT YOUR MIGHTY WAR MAGIC.
QUIETLY CASTING A SPELL OF ROMANTIC DIVINATION TO CONFIRM MY SUSPICIONS. I THINK SHE'S INTO ME.
BUT WE ARE FREE ROVERS OF THE NETHERSPHERE. WE RUN WITH THE SPIRIT WINDS. WE RUN TO KEEP AHEAD OF THE COMING SLAUGHTER.
YOU CANNOT TELL US WHERE WE MAY REST OUR TENTACLES.
IN THIS CASE, I'M AFRAID I HAVE TO. YOU CANNOT STAY HERE.
THEN YOUR CHALLENGE IS ACCEPTED, LORD STRANGE SUPREME. IT WILL BE AN HONOR TO WATCH YOU DIE.
BRING FORTH THE CHAMPION.
WAIT, THERE'S A CHAMPION? I NEVER...

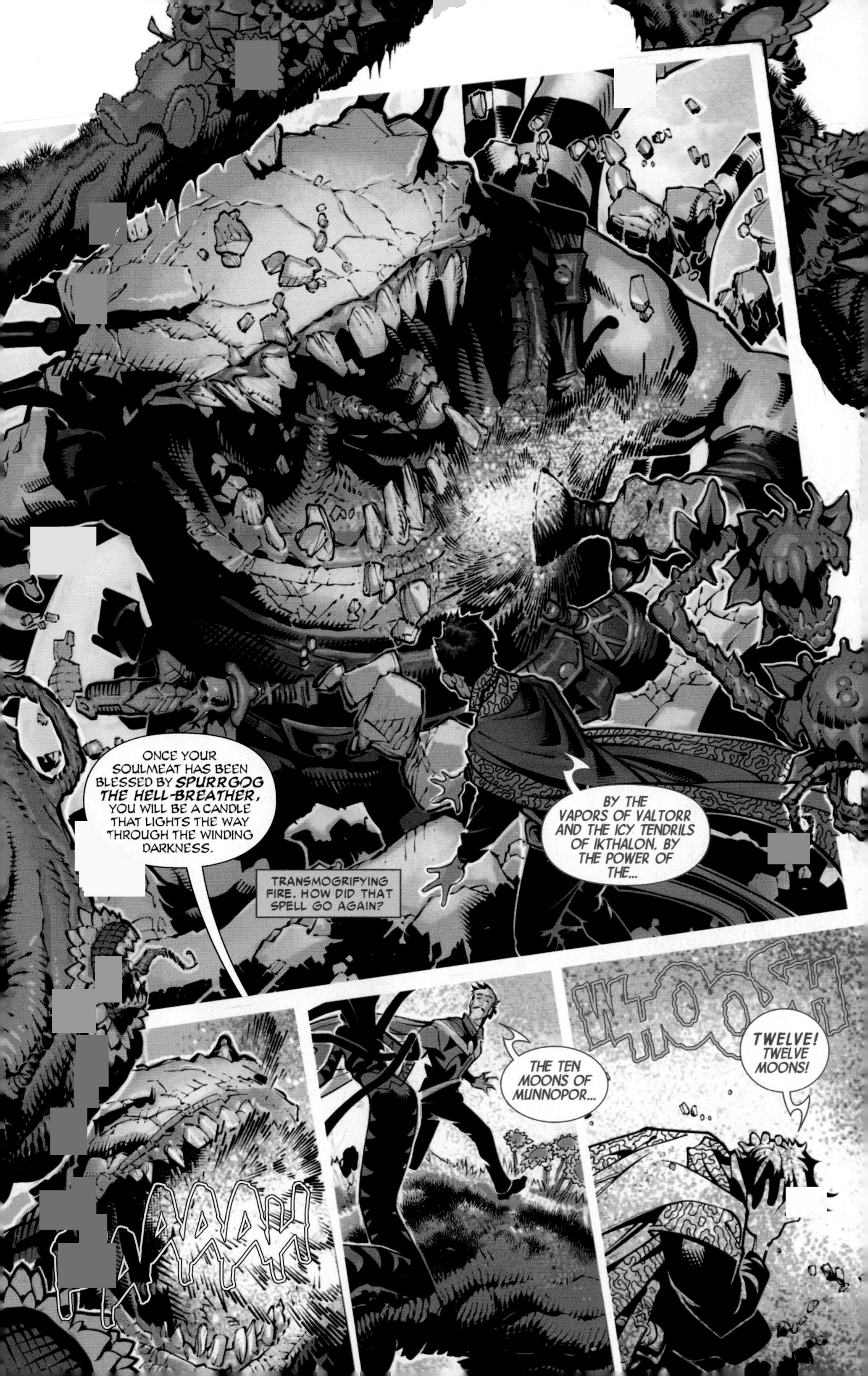
ONCE YOUR SOULMEAT HAS BEEN BLESSED BY SPURRGOG THE HELL-BREATHER, YOU WILL BE A CANDLE THAT LIGHTS THE WAY THROUGH THE WINDING DARKNESS.
TRANSMOGRIFYING FIRE. HOW DID THAT SPELL GO AGAIN?
BY THE VAPORS OF VALTORR AND THE ICY TENDRILS OF IKTHALON. BY THE POWER OF THE...
THE TEN MOONS OF MUNNOPOR...
WHOOSH
TWELVE! TWELVE MOONS!

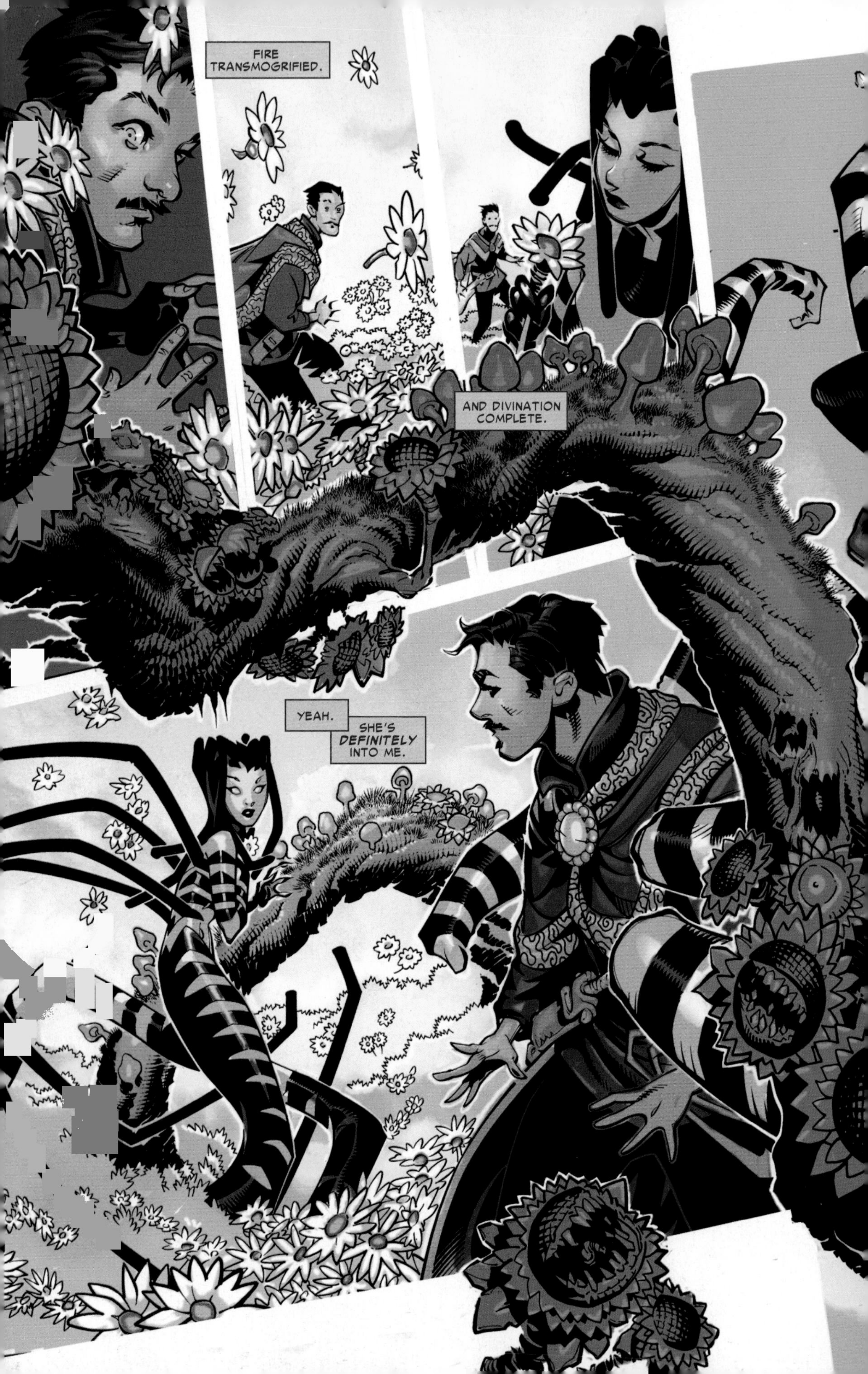
FIRE TRANSMOGRIFIED.
AND DIVINATION COMPLETE.
YEAH.
SHE'S *DEFINITELY* INTO ME.

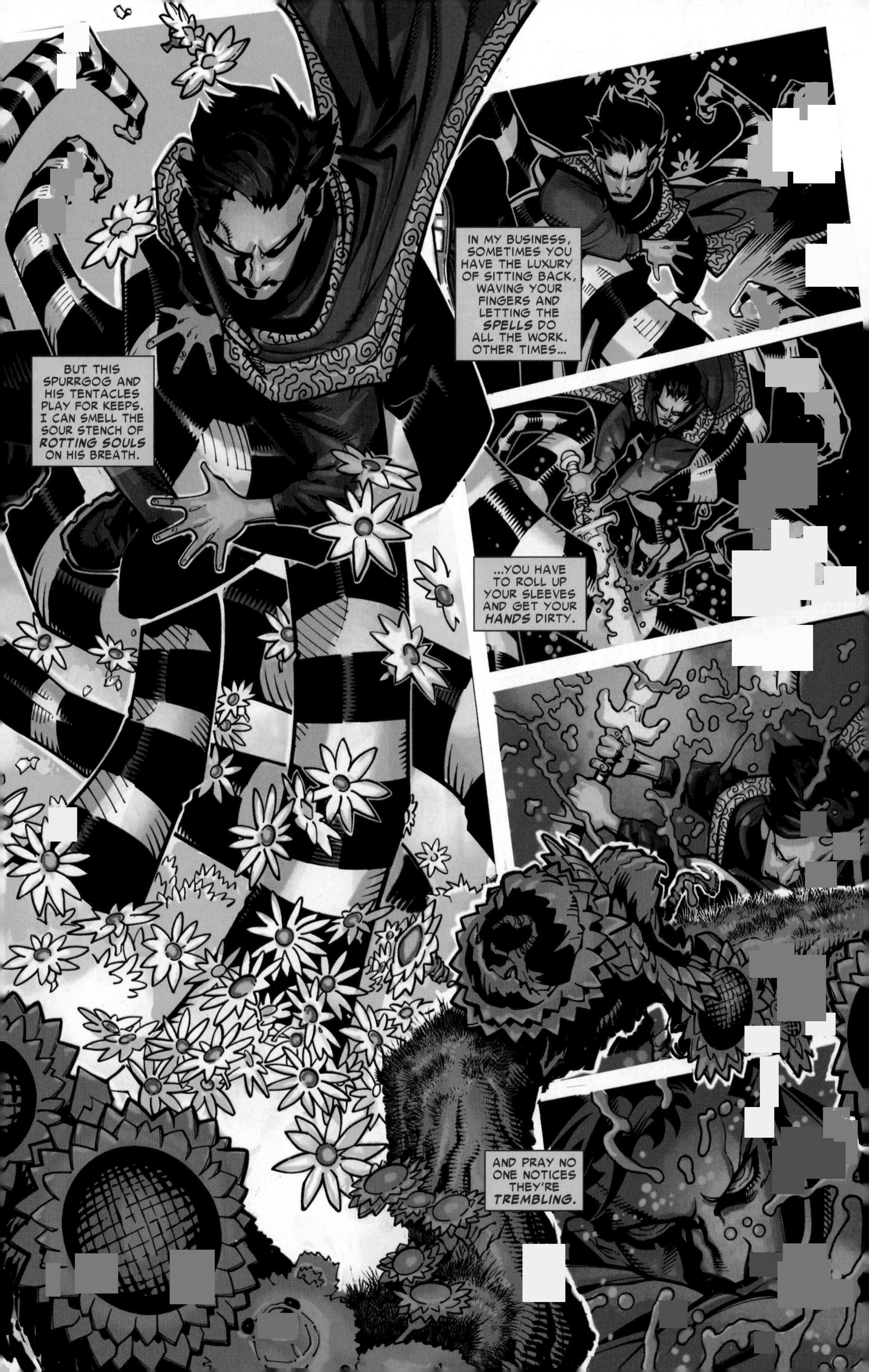
BUT THIS SPURRGOG AND HIS TENTACLES PLAY FOR KEEPS. I CAN SMELL THE SOUR STENCH OF ROTTING SOULS ON HIS BREATH.
IN MY BUSINESS, SOMETIMES YOU HAVE THE LUXURY OF SITTING BACK, WAVING YOUR FINGERS AND LETTING THE SPELLS DO ALL THE WORK. OTHER TIMES...
...YOU HAVE TO ROLL UP YOUR SLEEVES AND GET YOUR HANDS DIRTY.
AND PRAY NO ONE NOTICES THEY'RE TREMBLING.

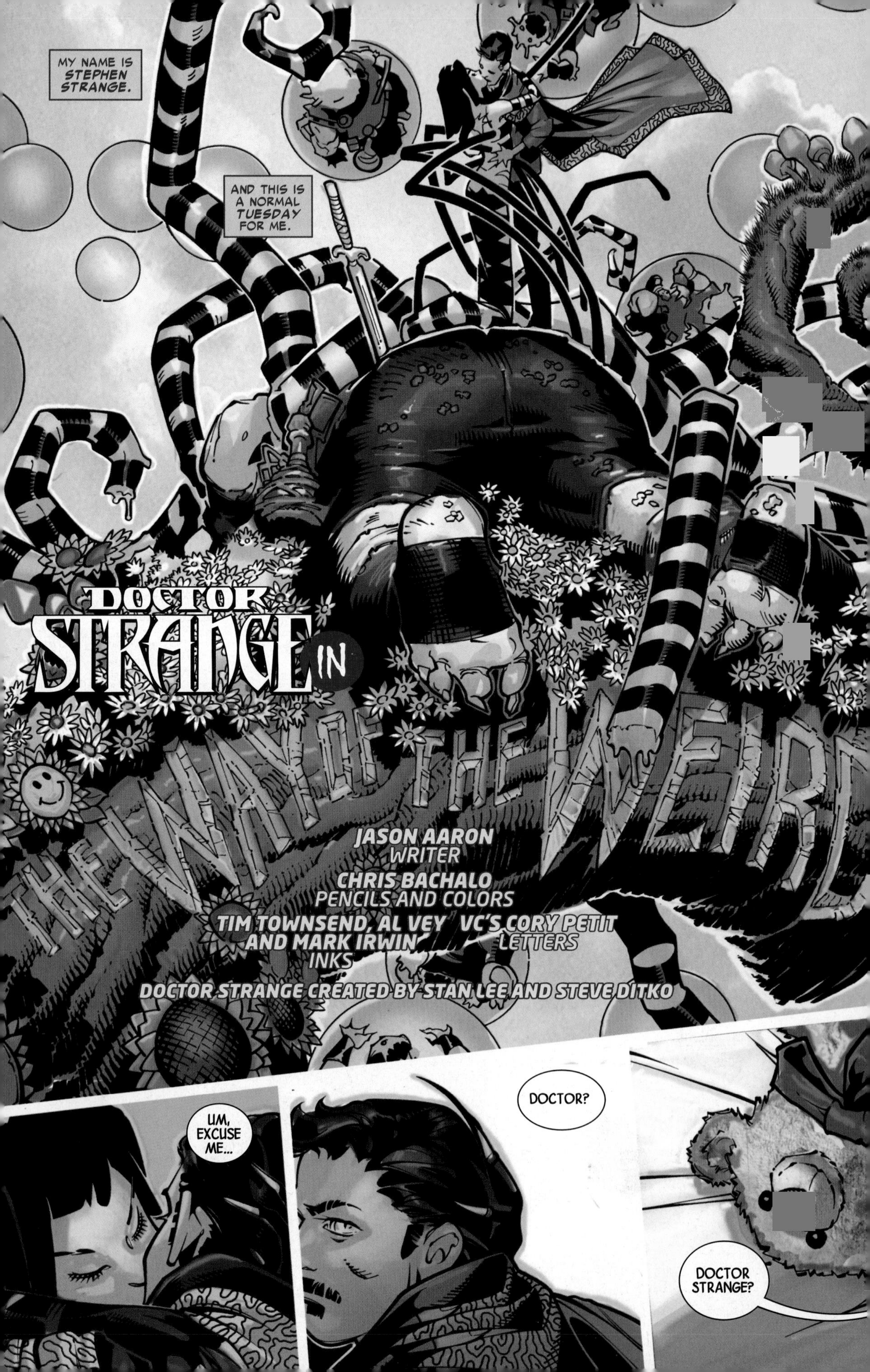
MY NAME IS STEPHEN STRANGE.
AND THIS IS A NORMAL TUESDAY FOR ME.
DOCTOR STRANGE IN
THE WAY OF THE WEIRD
JASON AARON WRITER
CHRIS BACHALO PENCILS AND COLORS
TIM TOWNSEND, AL VEY AND MARK IRWIN INKS
VC'S CORY PETIT LETTERS
DOCTOR STRANGE CREATED BY STAN LEE AND STEVE DITKO
UM, EXCUSE ME...
DOCTOR?
DOCTOR STRANGE?

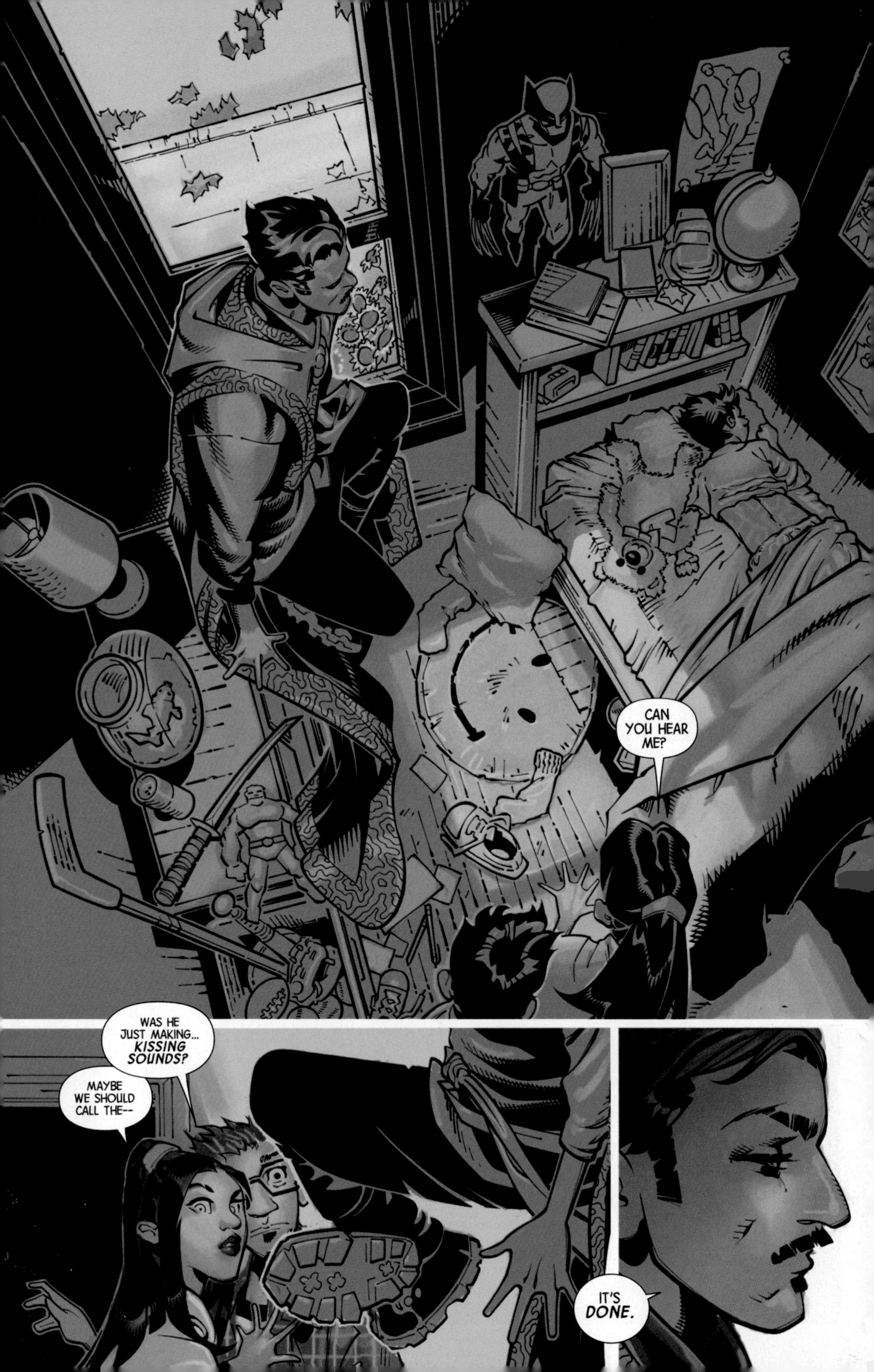
CAN YOU HEAR ME?
WAS HE JUST MAKING... KISSING SOUNDS?
MAYBE WE SHOULD CALL THE--
IT'S DONE.

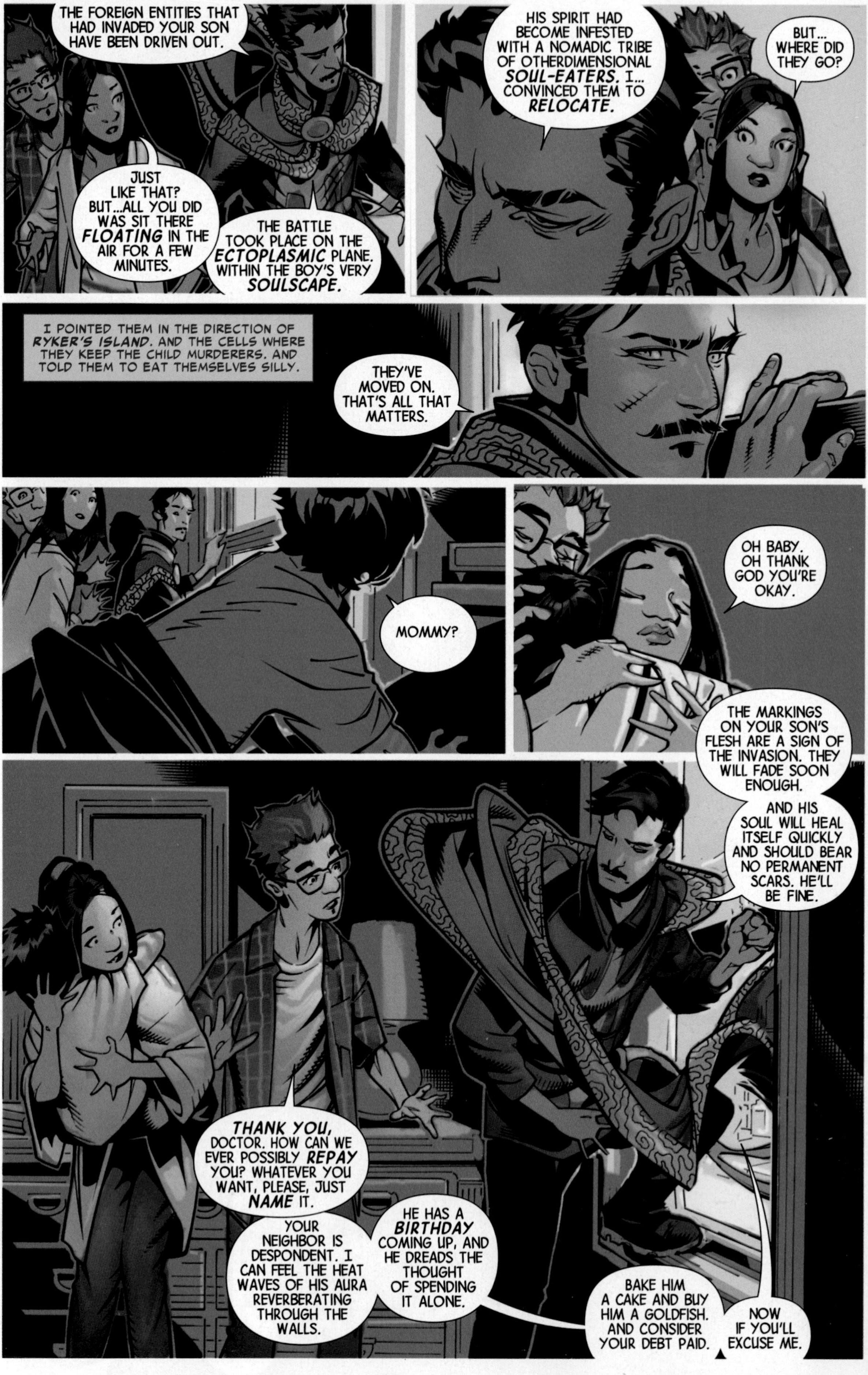
THE FOREIGN ENTITIES THAT HAD INVADED YOUR SON HAVE BEEN DRIVEN OUT.
JUST LIKE THAT? BUT...ALL YOU DID WAS SIT THERE FLOATING IN THE AIR FOR A FEW MINUTES.
THE BATTLE TOOK PLACE ON THE ECTOPLASMIC PLANE. WITHIN THE BOY'S VERY SOULSCAPE.
HIS SPIRIT HAD BECOME INFESTED WITH A NOMADIC TRIBE OF OTHERDIMENSIONAL SOUL-EATERS. I... CONVINCED THEM TO RELOCATE.
BUT... WHERE DID THEY GO?
I POINTED THEM IN THE DIRECTION OF RYKER'S ISLAND. AND THE CELLS WHERE THEY KEEP THE CHILD MURDERERS. AND TOLD THEM TO EAT THEMSELVES SILLY.
THEY'VE MOVED ON. THAT'S ALL THAT MATTERS.
MOMMY?
OH BABY. OH THANK GOD YOU'RE OKAY.
THE MARKINGS ON YOUR SON'S FLESH ARE A SIGN OF THE INVASION. THEY WILL FADE SOON ENOUGH.
AND HIS SOUL WILL HEAL ITSELF QUICKLY AND SHOULD BEAR NO PERMANENT SCARS. HE'LL BE FINE.
THANK YOU, DOCTOR. HOW CAN WE EVER POSSIBLY REPAY YOU? WHATEVER YOU WANT, PLEASE, JUST NAME IT.
YOUR NEIGHBOR IS DESPONDENT. I CAN FEEL THE HEAT WAVES OF HIS AURA REVERBERATING THROUGH THE WALLS.
HE HAS A BIRTHDAY COMING UP, AND HE DREADS THE THOUGHT OF SPENDING IT ALONE.
BAKE HIM A CAKE AND BUY HIM A GOLDFISH. AND CONSIDER YOUR DEBT PAID.
NOW IF YOU'LL EXCUSE ME.

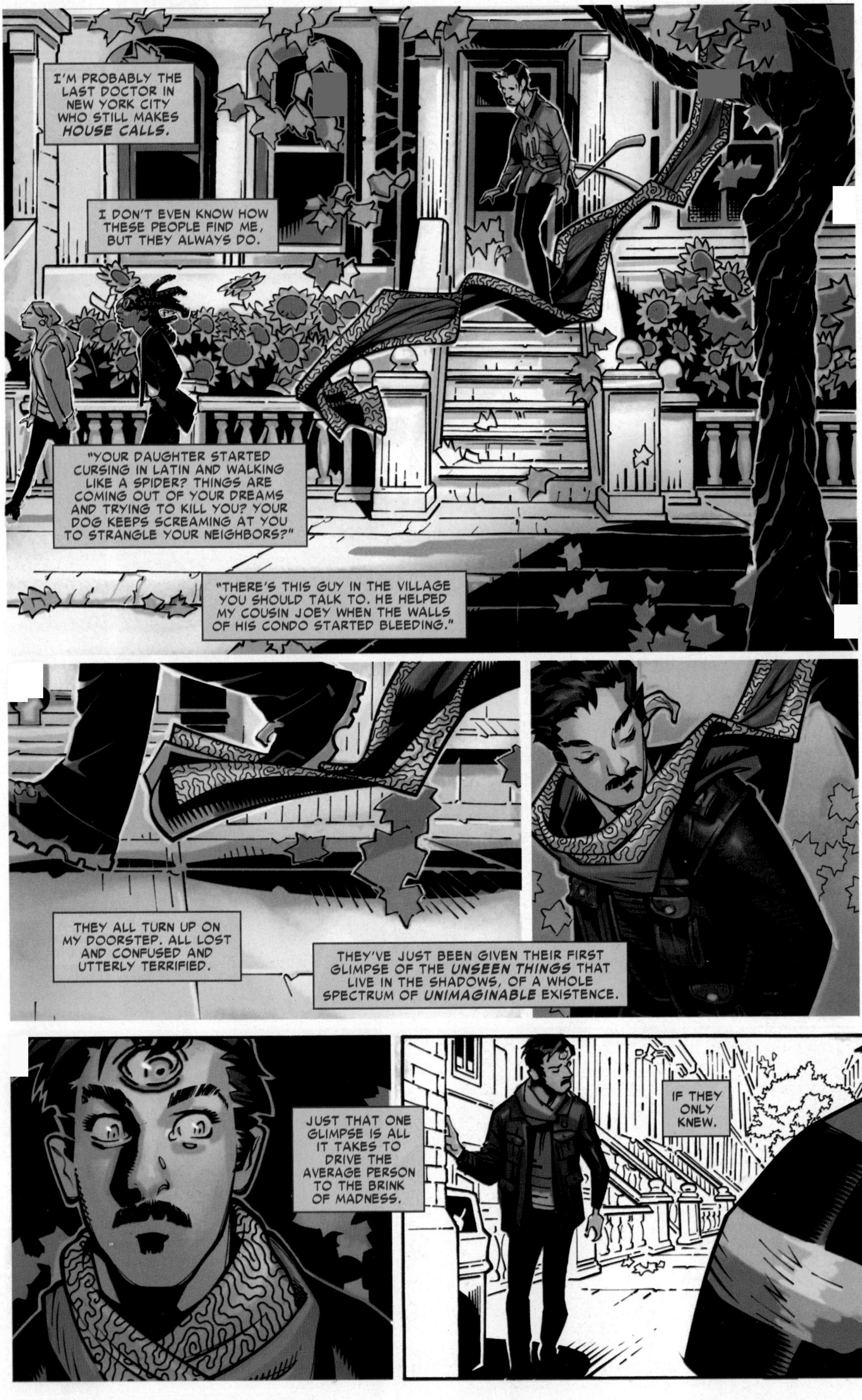
I'M PROBABLY THE LAST DOCTOR IN NEW YORK CITY WHO STILL MAKES HOUSE CALLS.
I DON'T EVEN KNOW HOW THESE PEOPLE FIND ME, BUT THEY ALWAYS DO.
"YOUR DAUGHTER STARTED CURSING IN LATIN AND WALKING LIKE A SPIDER? THINGS ARE COMING OUT OF YOUR DREAMS AND TRYING TO KILL YOU? YOUR DOG KEEPS SCREAMING AT YOU TO STRANGLE YOUR NEIGHBORS?"
"THERE'S THIS GUY IN THE VILLAGE YOU SHOULD TALK TO. HE HELPED MY COUSIN JOEY WHEN THE WALLS OF HIS CONDO STARTED BLEEDING."
THEY ALL TURN UP ON MY DOORSTEP. ALL LOST AND CONFUSED AND UTTERLY TERRIFIED.
THEY'VE JUST BEEN GIVEN THEIR FIRST GLIMPSE OF THE UNSEEN THINGS THAT LIVE IN THE SHADOWS, OF A WHOLE SPECTRUM OF UNIMAGINABLE EXISTENCE.
JUST THAT ONE GLIMPSE IS ALL IT TAKES TO DRIVE THE AVERAGE PERSON TO THE BRINK OF MADNESS.
IF THEY ONLY KNEW.

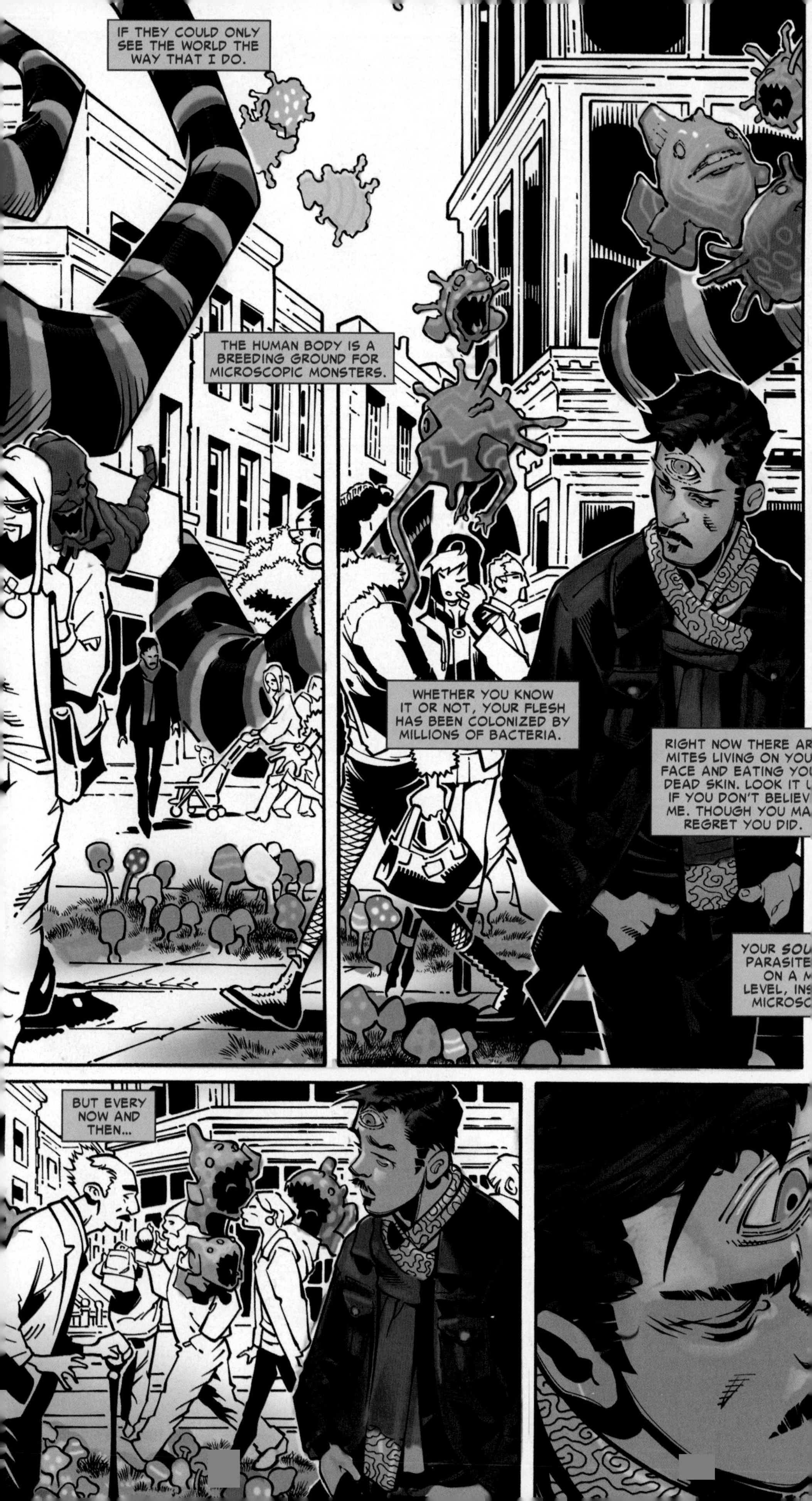
IF THEY COULD ONLY SEE THE WORLD THE WAY THAT I DO.
THE HUMAN BODY IS A BREEDING GROUND FOR MICROSCOPIC MONSTERS.
WHETHER YOU KNOW IT OR NOT, YOUR FLESH HAS BEEN COLONIZED BY MILLIONS OF BACTERIA.
RIGHT NOW THERE AR
MITES LIVING ON YOU
FACE AND EATING YOU
DEAD SKIN. LOOK IT U
IF YOU DON'T BELIEV
ME. THOUGH YOU MA
REGRET YOU DID.
YOUR SOU
PARASITE
ON A M
LEVEL, INS
MICROSC
BUT EVERY NOW AND THEN...

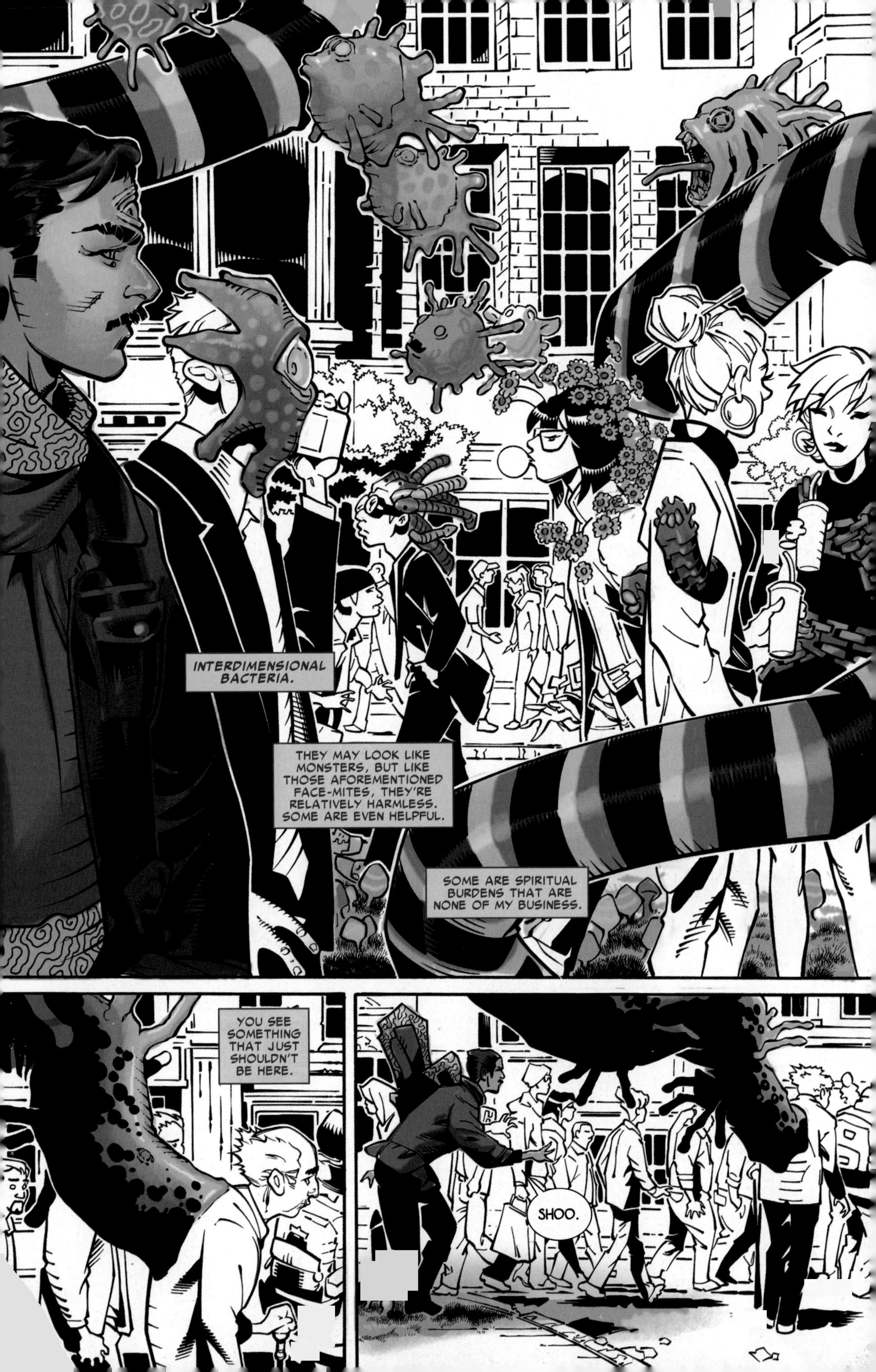
INTERDIMENSIONAL BACTERIA.
THEY MAY LOOK LIKE MONSTERS, BUT LIKE THOSE AFOREMENTIONED FACE-MITES, THEY'RE RELATIVELY HARMLESS. SOME ARE EVEN HELPFUL.
SOME ARE SPIRITUAL BURDENS THAT ARE NONE OF MY BUSINESS.
YOU SEE SOMETHING THAT JUST SHOULDN'T BE HERE.
SHOO.

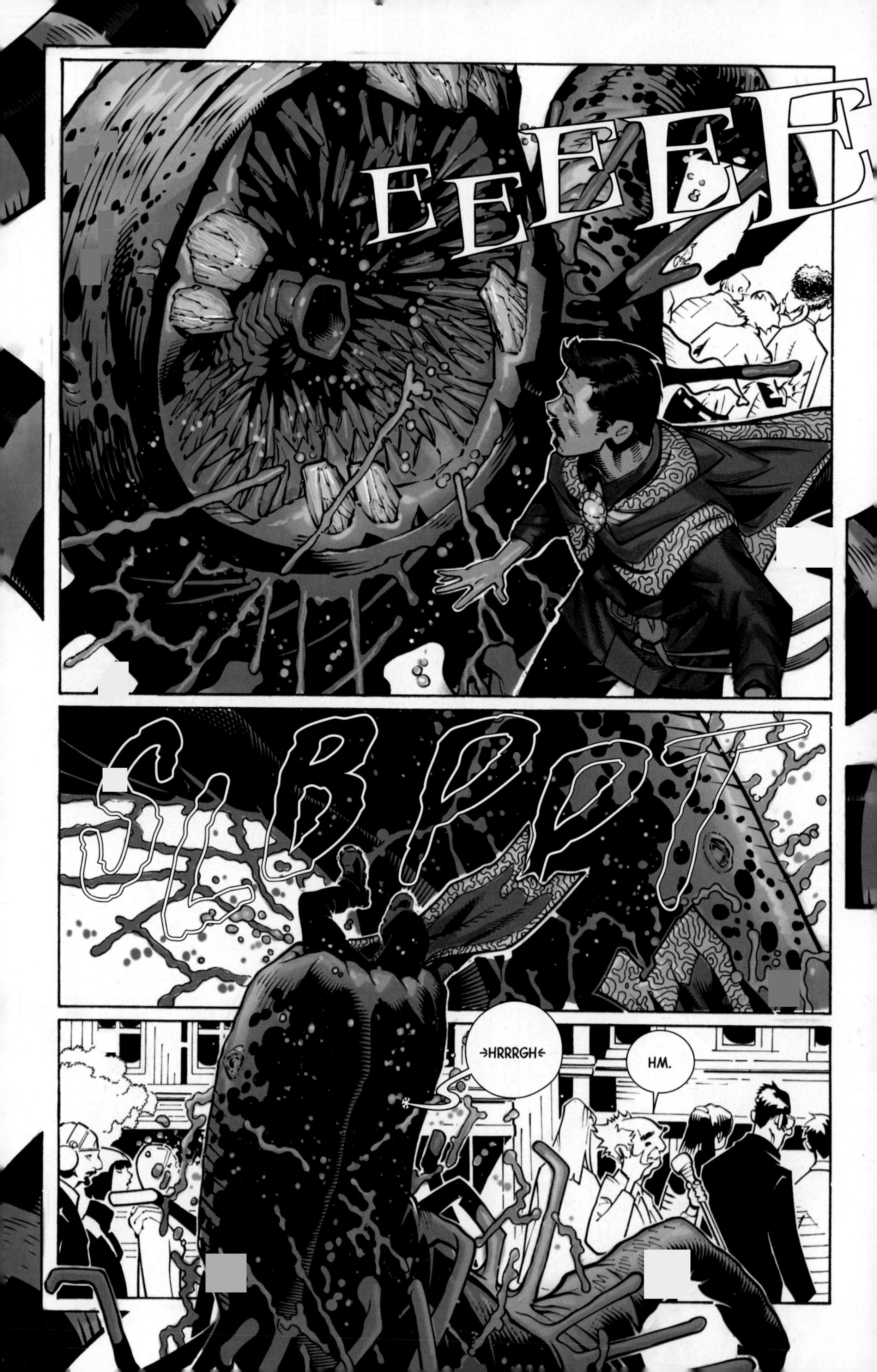
EEEEEE
SLRPPT
HRRRGH
HM.

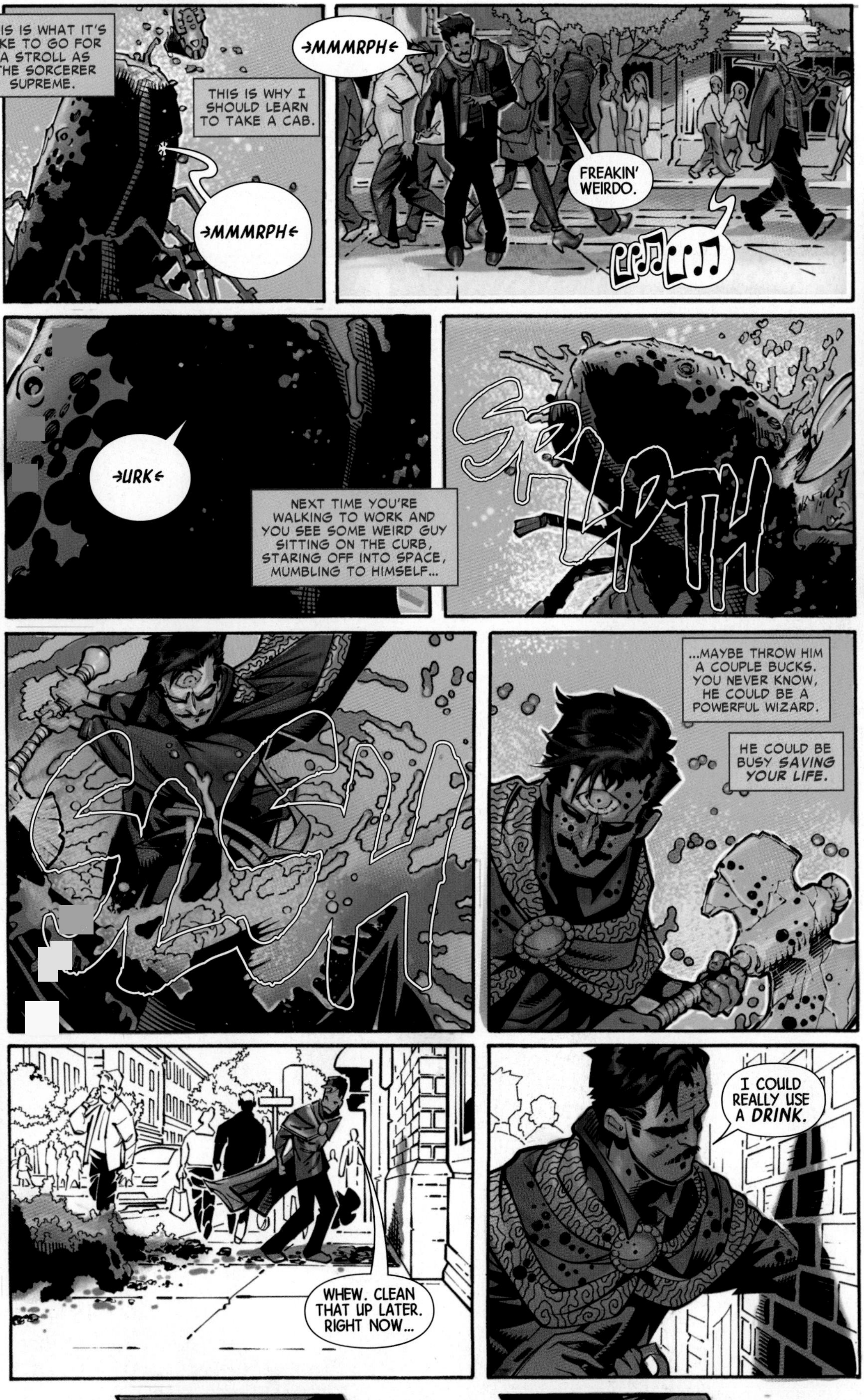

THIS IS WHAT IT'S LIKE TO GO FOR A STROLL AS THE SORCERER SUPREME.
THIS IS WHY I SHOULD LEARN TO TAKE A CAB.
MMMRPH
MMMRPH
FREAKIN' WEIRDO.
URK
NEXT TIME YOU'RE WALKING TO WORK AND YOU SEE SOME WEIRD GUY SITTING ON THE CURB, STARING OFF INTO SPACE, MUMBLING TO HIMSELF...
SPLPTH
SLSH
...MAYBE THROW HIM A COUPLE BUCKS. YOU NEVER KNOW, HE COULD BE A POWERFUL WIZARD.
HE COULD BE BUSY SAVING YOUR LIFE.
WHEW. CLEAN THAT UP LATER. RIGHT NOW...
I COULD REALLY USE A DRINK.

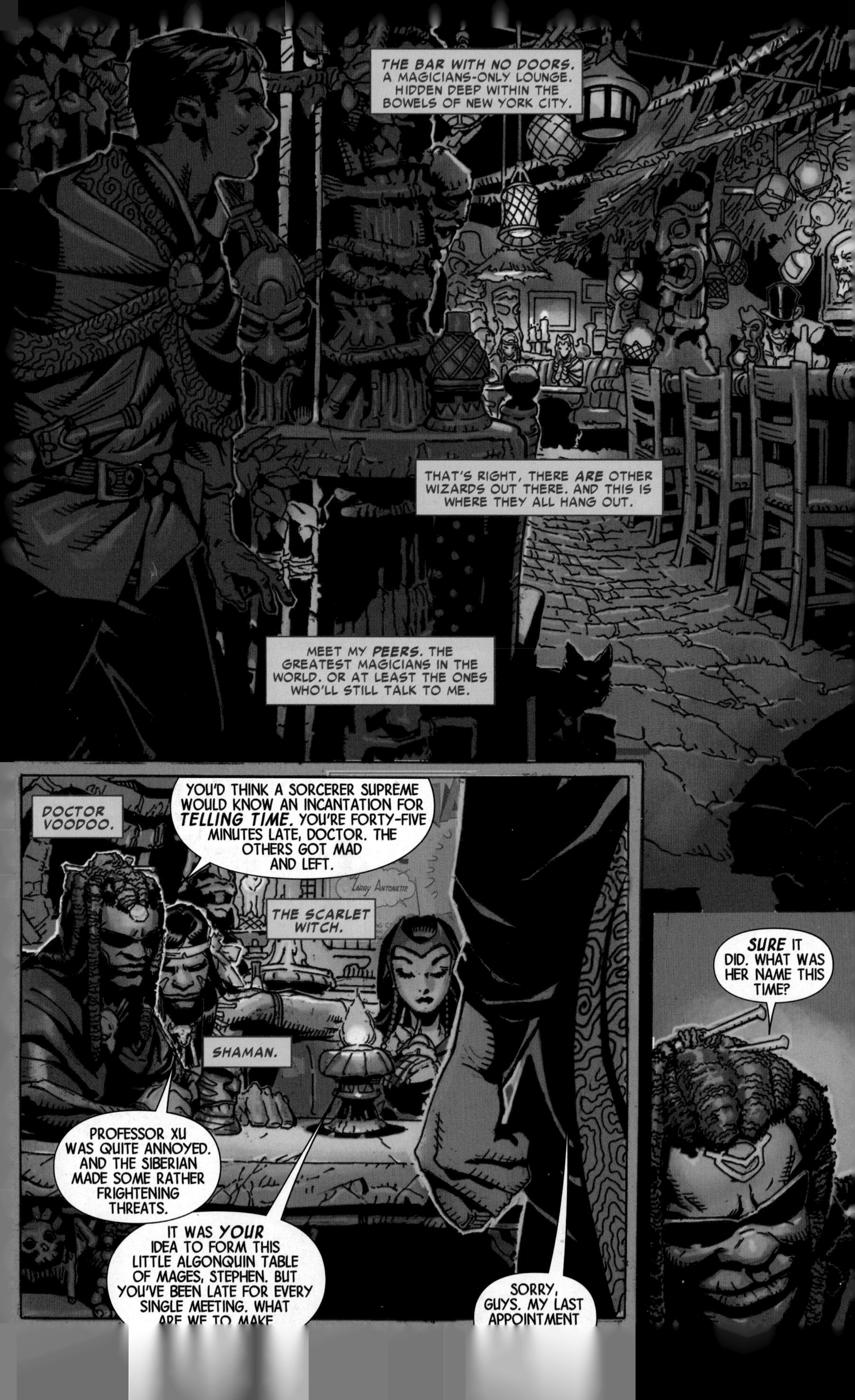
THE BAR WITH NO DOORS. A MAGICIANS-ONLY LOUNGE. HIDDEN DEEP WITHIN THE BOWELS OF NEW YORK CITY.
THAT'S RIGHT, THERE ARE OTHER WIZARDS OUT THERE. AND THIS IS WHERE THEY ALL HANG OUT.
MEET MY PEERS. THE GREATEST MAGICIANS IN THE WORLD. OR AT LEAST THE ONES WHO'LL STILL TALK TO ME.
DOCTOR VOODOO.
YOU'D THINK A SORCERER SUPREME WOULD KNOW AN INCANTATION FOR TELLING TIME. YOU'RE FORTY-FIVE MINUTES LATE, DOCTOR. THE OTHERS GOT MAD AND LEFT.
THE SCARLET WITCH.
SHAMAN.
PROFESSOR XU WAS QUITE ANNOYED. AND THE SIBERIAN MADE SOME RATHER FRIGHTENING THREATS.
IT WAS YOUR IDEA TO FORM THIS LITTLE ALGONQUIN TABLE OF MAGES, STEPHEN. BUT YOU'VE BEEN LATE FOR EVERY SINGLE MEETING. WHAT ARE WE TO MAKE
SORRY, GUYS. MY LAST APPOINTMENT
SURE IT DID. WHAT WAS HER NAME THIS TIME?

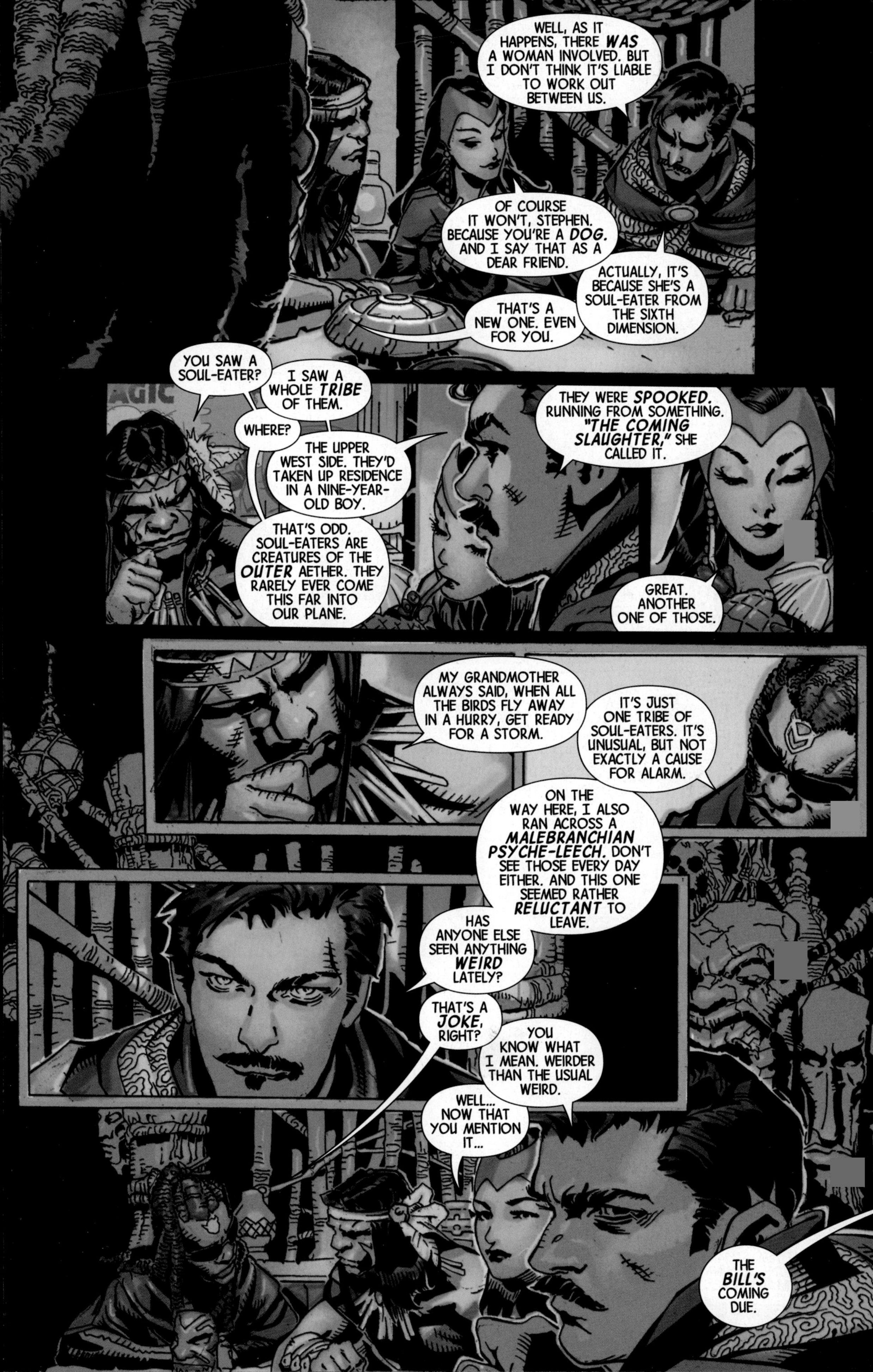
WELL, AS IT HAPPENS, THERE WAS A WOMAN INVOLVED. BUT I DON'T THINK IT'S LIABLE TO WORK OUT BETWEEN US.
OF COURSE IT WON'T, STEPHEN. BECAUSE YOU'RE A DOG. AND I SAY THAT AS A DEAR FRIEND.
ACTUALLY, IT'S BECAUSE SHE'S A SOUL-EATER FROM THE SIXTH DIMENSION.
THAT'S A NEW ONE. EVEN FOR YOU.
YOU SAW A SOUL-EATER?
I SAW A WHOLE TRIBE OF THEM.
WHERE?
THE UPPER WEST SIDE. THEY'D TAKEN UP RESIDENCE IN A NINE-YEAR-OLD BOY.
THEY WERE SPOOKED. RUNNING FROM SOMETHING. "THE COMING SLAUGHTER," SHE CALLED IT.
THAT'S ODD. SOUL-EATERS ARE CREATURES OF THE OUTER AETHER. THEY RARELY EVER COME THIS FAR INTO OUR PLANE.
GREAT. ANOTHER ONE OF THOSE.
MY GRANDMOTHER ALWAYS SAID, WHEN ALL THE BIRDS FLY AWAY IN A HURRY, GET READY FOR A STORM.
IT'S JUST ONE TRIBE OF SOUL-EATERS. IT'S UNUSUAL, BUT NOT EXACTLY A CAUSE FOR ALARM.
ON THE WAY HERE, I ALSO RAN ACROSS A MALEBRANCHIAN PSYCHE-LEECH. DON'T SEE THOSE EVERY DAY EITHER. AND THIS ONE SEEMED RATHER RELUCTANT TO LEAVE.
HAS ANYONE ELSE SEEN ANYTHING WEIRD LATELY?
THAT'S A JOKE, RIGHT?
YOU KNOW WHAT I MEAN. WEIRDER THAN THE USUAL WEIRD.
WELL... NOW THAT YOU MENTION IT...
THE BILL'S COMING DUE.

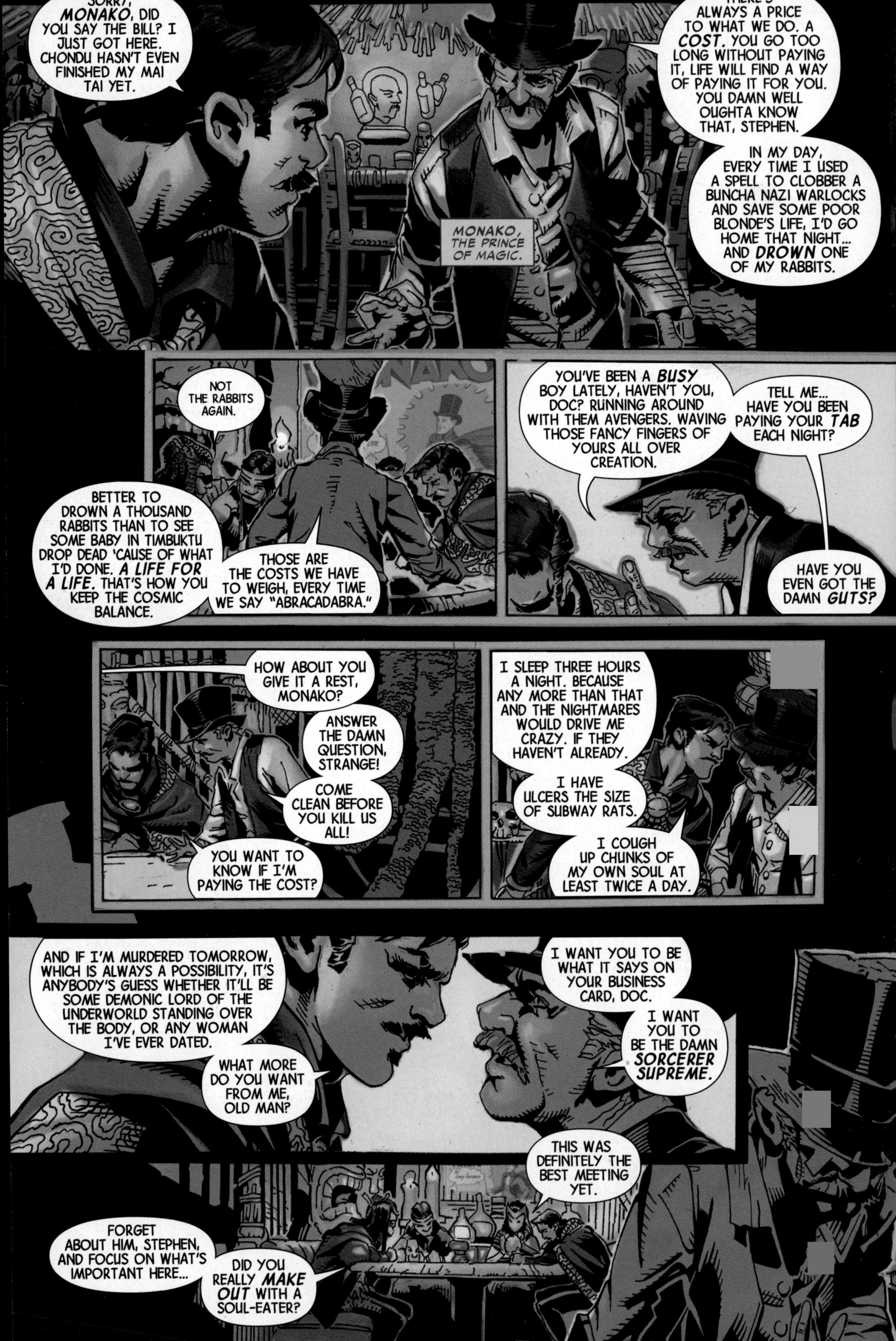

SORRY, MONAKO, DID YOU SAY THE BILL? I JUST GOT HERE. CHONDU HASN'T EVEN FINISHED MY MAI TAI YET.
MONAKO, THE PRINCE OF MAGIC.
THERE'S ALWAYS A PRICE TO WHAT WE DO. A COST. YOU GO TOO LONG WITHOUT PAYING IT, LIFE WILL FIND A WAY OF PAYING IT FOR YOU. YOU DAMN WELL OUGHTA KNOW THAT, STEPHEN.
IN MY DAY, EVERY TIME I USED A SPELL TO CLOBBER A BUNCHA NAZI WARLOCKS AND SAVE SOME POOR BLONDE'S LIFE, I'D GO HOME THAT NIGHT... AND DROWN ONE OF MY RABBITS.
NOT THE RABBITS AGAIN.
BETTER TO DROWN A THOUSAND RABBITS THAN TO SEE SOME BABY IN TIMBUKTU DROP DEAD 'CAUSE OF WHAT I'D DONE. A LIFE FOR A LIFE. THAT'S HOW YOU KEEP THE COSMIC BALANCE.
THOSE ARE THE COSTS WE HAVE TO WEIGH, EVERY TIME WE SAY "ABRACADABRA."
YOU'VE BEEN A BUSY BOY LATELY, HAVEN'T YOU, DOC? RUNNING AROUND WITH THEM AVENGERS. WAVING THOSE FANCY FINGERS OF YOURS ALL OVER CREATION.
TELL ME... HAVE YOU BEEN PAYING YOUR TAB EACH NIGHT?
HAVE YOU EVEN GOT THE DAMN GUTS?
HOW ABOUT YOU GIVE IT A REST, MONAKO?
ANSWER THE DAMN QUESTION, STRANGE!
COME CLEAN BEFORE YOU KILL US ALL!
YOU WANT TO KNOW IF I'M PAYING THE COST?
I SLEEP THREE HOURS A NIGHT. BECAUSE ANY MORE THAN THAT AND THE NIGHTMARES WOULD DRIVE ME CRAZY. IF THEY HAVEN'T ALREADY.
I HAVE ULCERS THE SIZE OF SUBWAY RATS.
I COUGH UP CHUNKS OF MY OWN SOUL AT LEAST TWICE A DAY.
AND IF I'M MURDERED TOMORROW, WHICH IS ALWAYS A POSSIBILITY, IT'S ANYBODY'S GUESS WHETHER IT'LL BE SOME DEMONIC LORD OF THE UNDERWORLD STANDING OVER THE BODY, OR ANY WOMAN I'VE EVER DATED.
WHAT MORE DO YOU WANT FROM ME, OLD MAN?
I WANT YOU TO BE WHAT IT SAYS ON YOUR BUSINESS CARD, DOC.
I WANT YOU TO BE THE DAMN SORCERER SUPREME.
THIS WAS DEFINITELY THE BEST MEETING YET.
FORGET ABOUT HIM, STEPHEN, AND FOCUS ON WHAT'S IMPORTANT HERE...
DID YOU REALLY MAKE OUT WITH A SOUL-EATER?

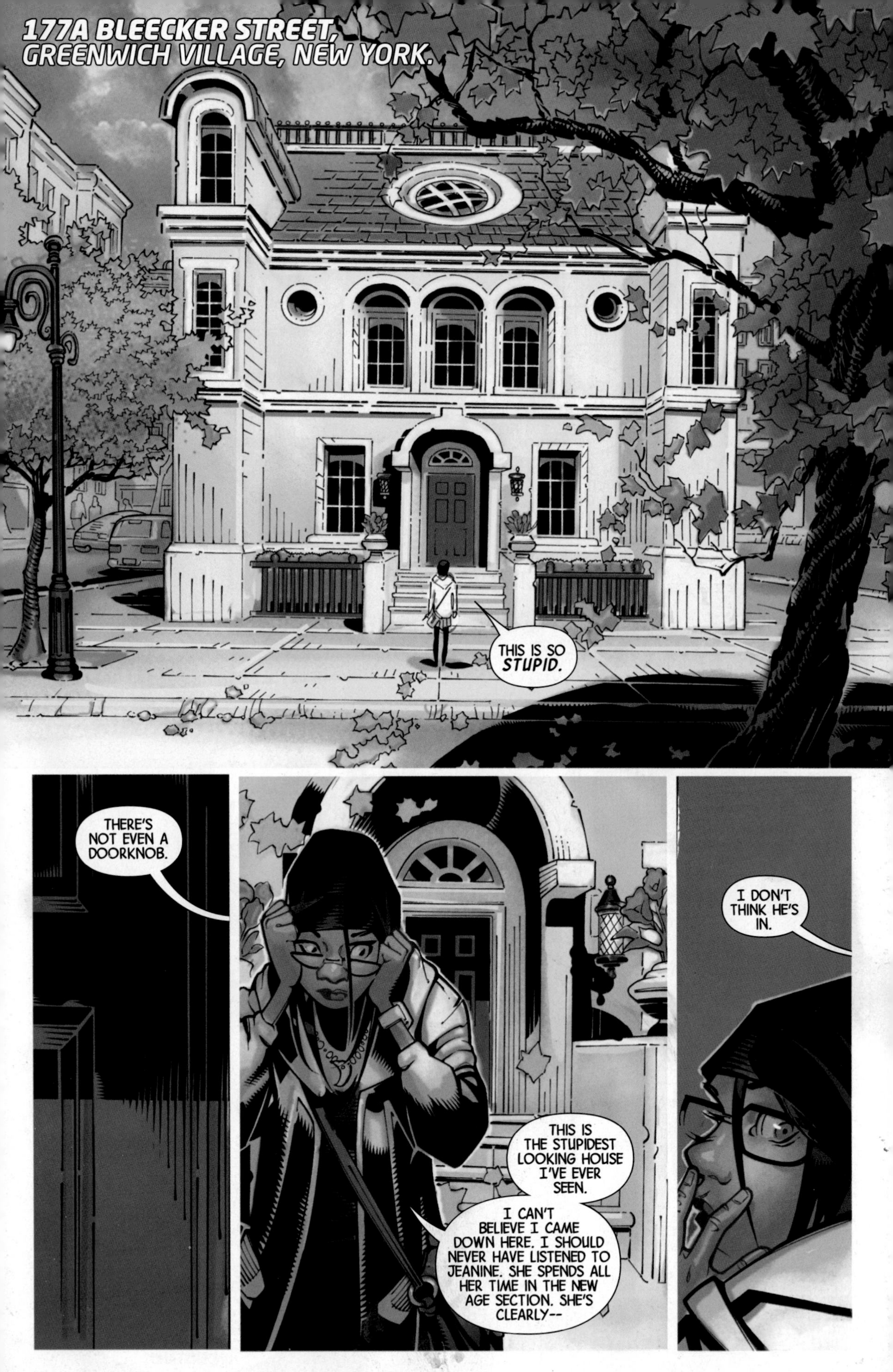

177A BLEECKER STREET,
GREENWICH VILLAGE, NEW YORK.
THIS IS SO STUPID.
THERE'S NOT EVEN A DOORKNOB.
THIS IS THE STUPIDEST LOOKING HOUSE I'VE EVER SEEN.
I CAN'T BELIEVE I CAME DOWN HERE. I SHOULD NEVER HAVE LISTENED TO JEANINE. SHE SPENDS ALL HER TIME IN THE NEW AGE SECTION. SHE'S CLEARLY--
I DON'T THINK HE'S IN.

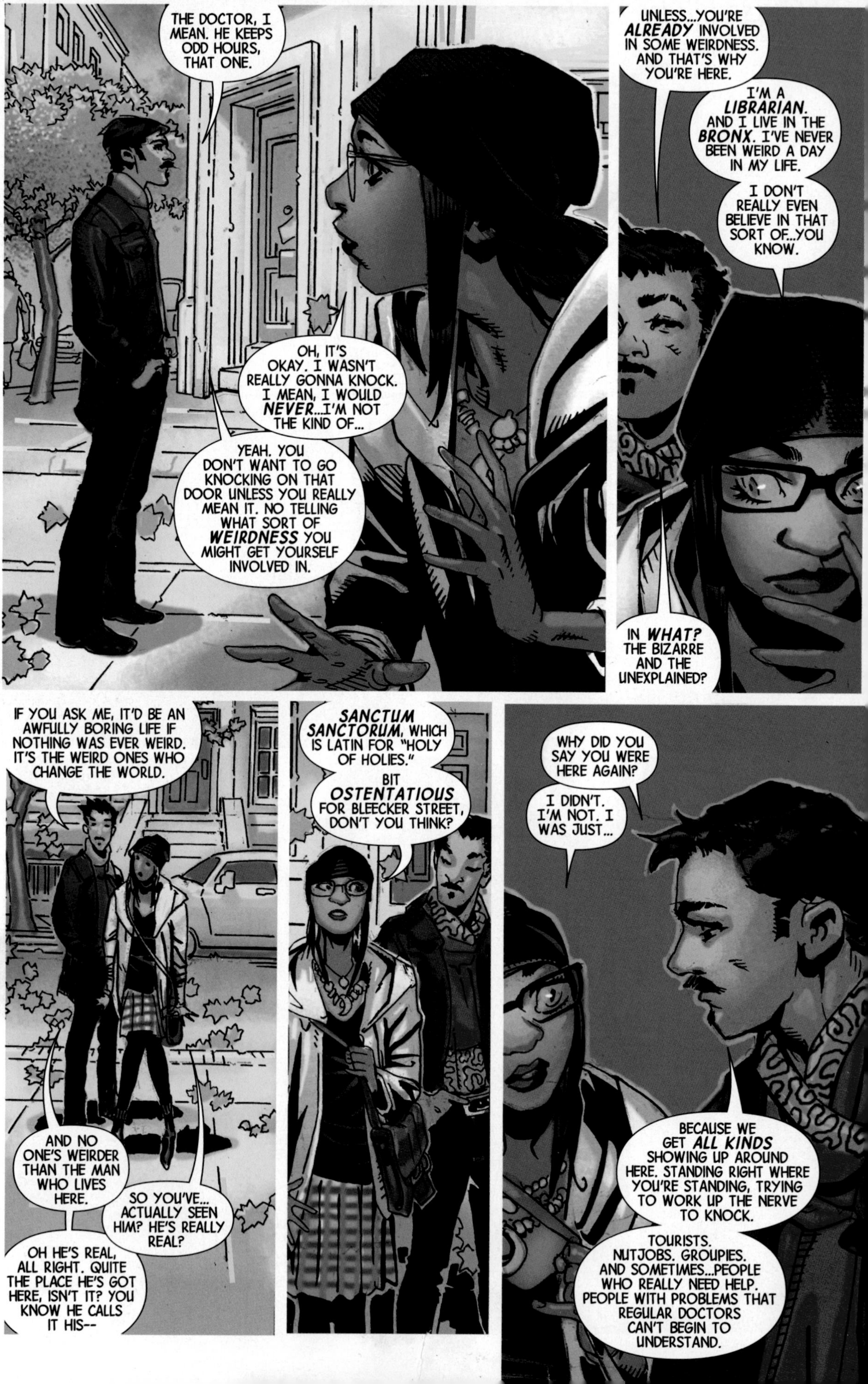
THE DOCTOR, I MEAN. HE KEEPS ODD HOURS, THAT ONE.
OH, IT'S OKAY. I WASN'T REALLY GONNA KNOCK. I MEAN, I WOULD NEVER...I'M NOT THE KIND OF...
YEAH. YOU DON'T WANT TO GO KNOCKING ON THAT DOOR UNLESS YOU REALLY MEAN IT. NO TELLING WHAT SORT OF WEIRDNESS YOU MIGHT GET YOURSELF INVOLVED IN.
UNLESS...YOU'RE ALREADY INVOLVED IN SOME WEIRDNESS. AND THAT'S WHY YOU'RE HERE.
I'M A LIBRARIAN. AND I LIVE IN THE BRONX. I'VE NEVER BEEN WEIRD A DAY IN MY LIFE.
I DON'T REALLY EVEN BELIEVE IN THAT SORT OF...YOU KNOW.
IN WHAT? THE BIZARRE AND THE UNEXPLAINED?
IF YOU ASK ME, IT'D BE AN AWFULLY BORING LIFE IF NOTHING WAS EVER WEIRD. IT'S THE WEIRD ONES WHO CHANGE THE WORLD.
AND NO ONE'S WEIRDER THAN THE MAN WHO LIVES HERE.
SO YOU'VE... ACTUALLY SEEN HIM? HE'S REALLY REAL?
OH HE'S REAL, ALL RIGHT. QUITE THE PLACE HE'S GOT HERE, ISN'T IT? YOU KNOW HE CALLS IT HIS--
SANCTUM SANCTORUM, WHICH IS LATIN FOR "HOLY OF HOLIES."
BIT OSTENTATIOUS FOR BLEECKER STREET, DON'T YOU THINK?
WHY DID YOU SAY YOU WERE HERE AGAIN?
I DIDN'T. I'M NOT. I WAS JUST...
BECAUSE WE GET ALL KINDS SHOWING UP AROUND HERE. STANDING RIGHT WHERE YOU'RE STANDING, TRYING TO WORK UP THE NERVE TO KNOCK.
TOURISTS. NUTJOBS. GROUPIES. AND SOMETIMES...PEOPLE WHO REALLY NEED HELP. PEOPLE WITH PROBLEMS THAT REGULAR DOCTORS CAN'T BEGIN TO UNDERSTAND.

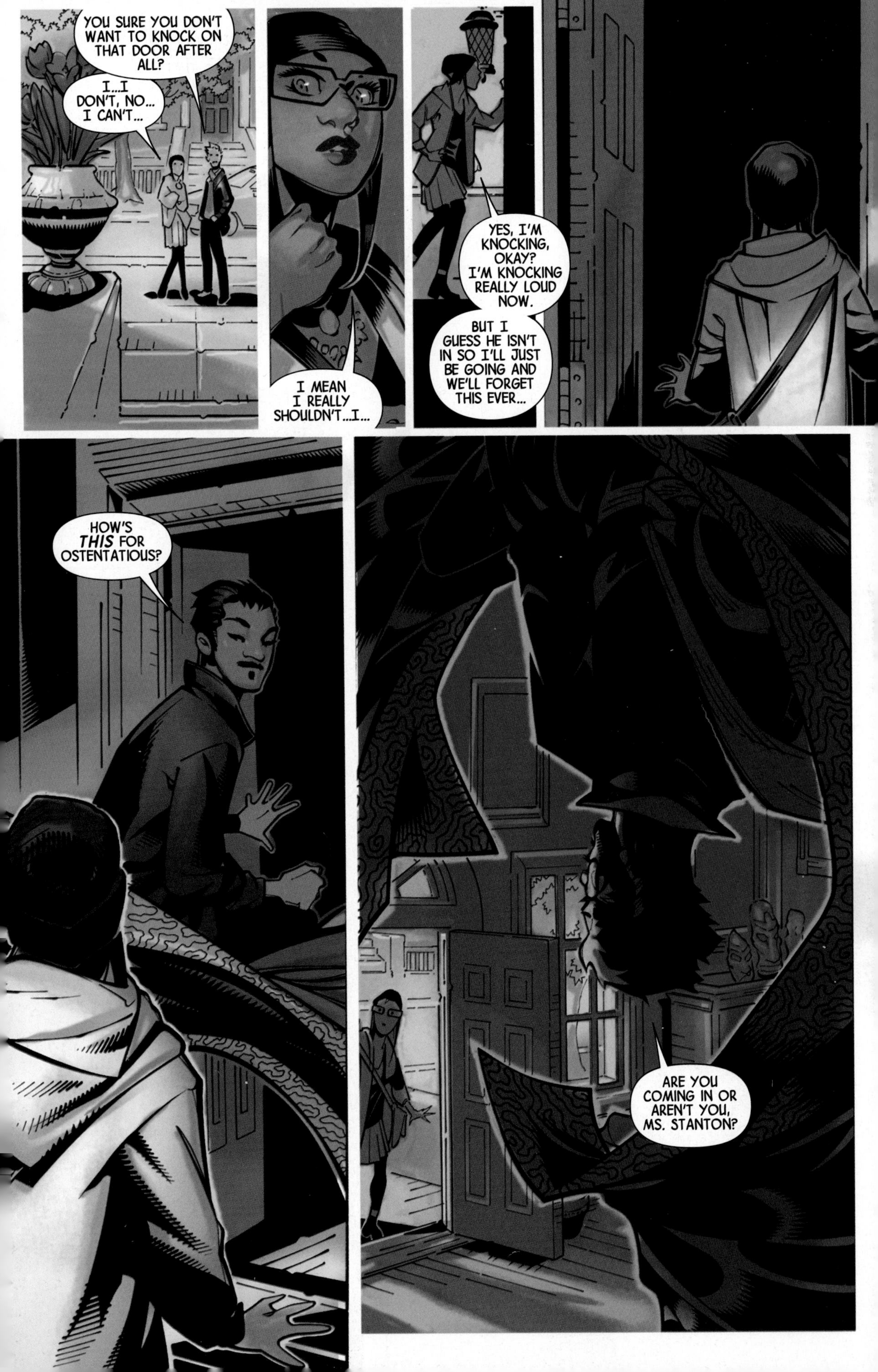
YOU SURE YOU DON'T WANT TO KNOCK ON THAT DOOR AFTER ALL?
I...I DON'T, NO... I CAN'T...
I MEAN I REALLY SHOULDN'T...I...
YES, I'M KNOCKING, OKAY? I'M KNOCKING REALLY LOUD NOW.
BUT I GUESS HE ISN'T IN SO I'LL JUST BE GOING AND WE'LL FORGET THIS EVER...
HOW'S THIS FOR OSTENTATIOUS?
ARE YOU COMING IN OR AREN'T YOU, MS. STANTON?

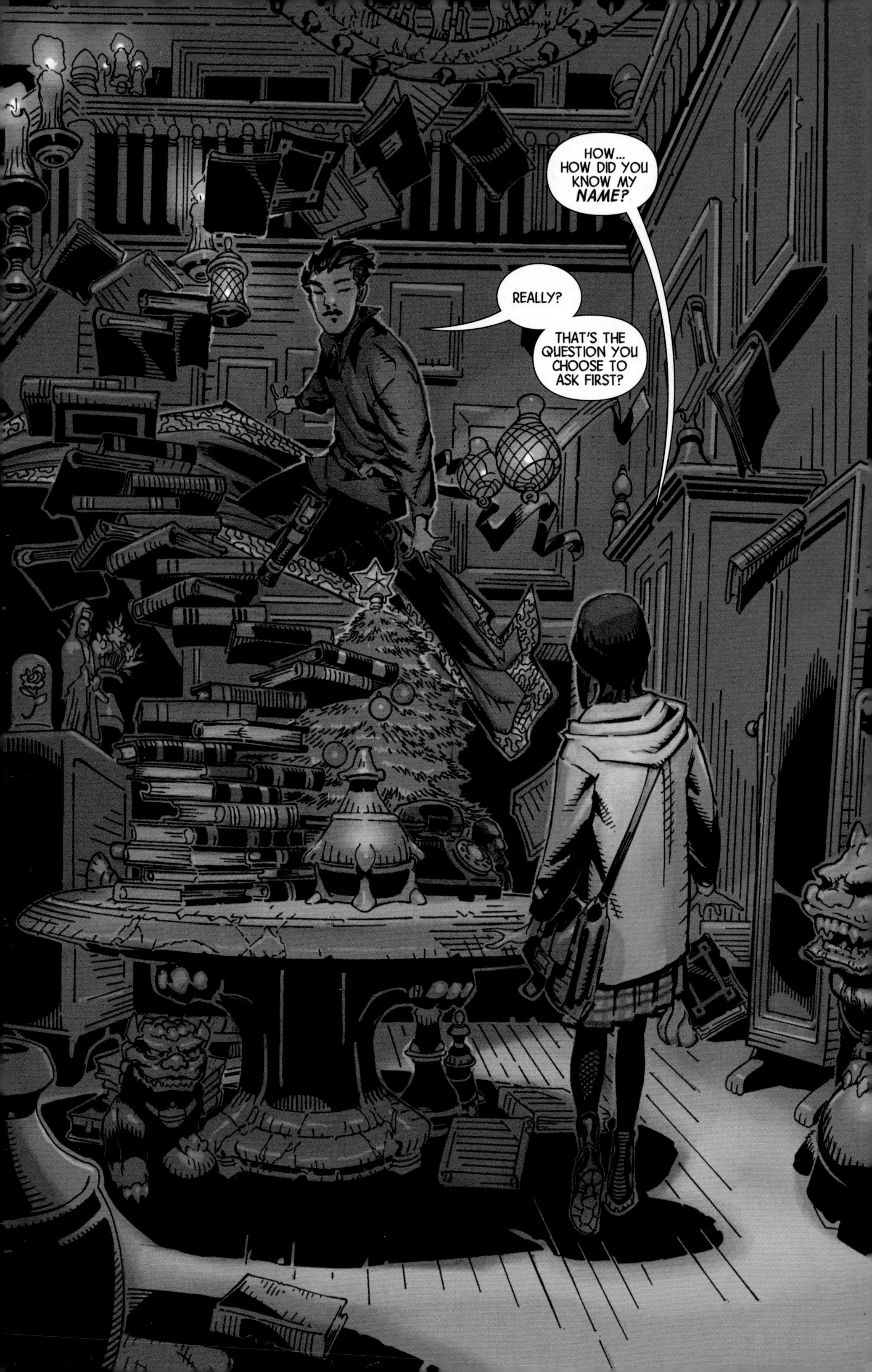
HOW... HOW DID YOU KNOW MY NAME?
REALLY?
THAT'S THE QUESTION YOU CHOOSE TO ASK FIRST?

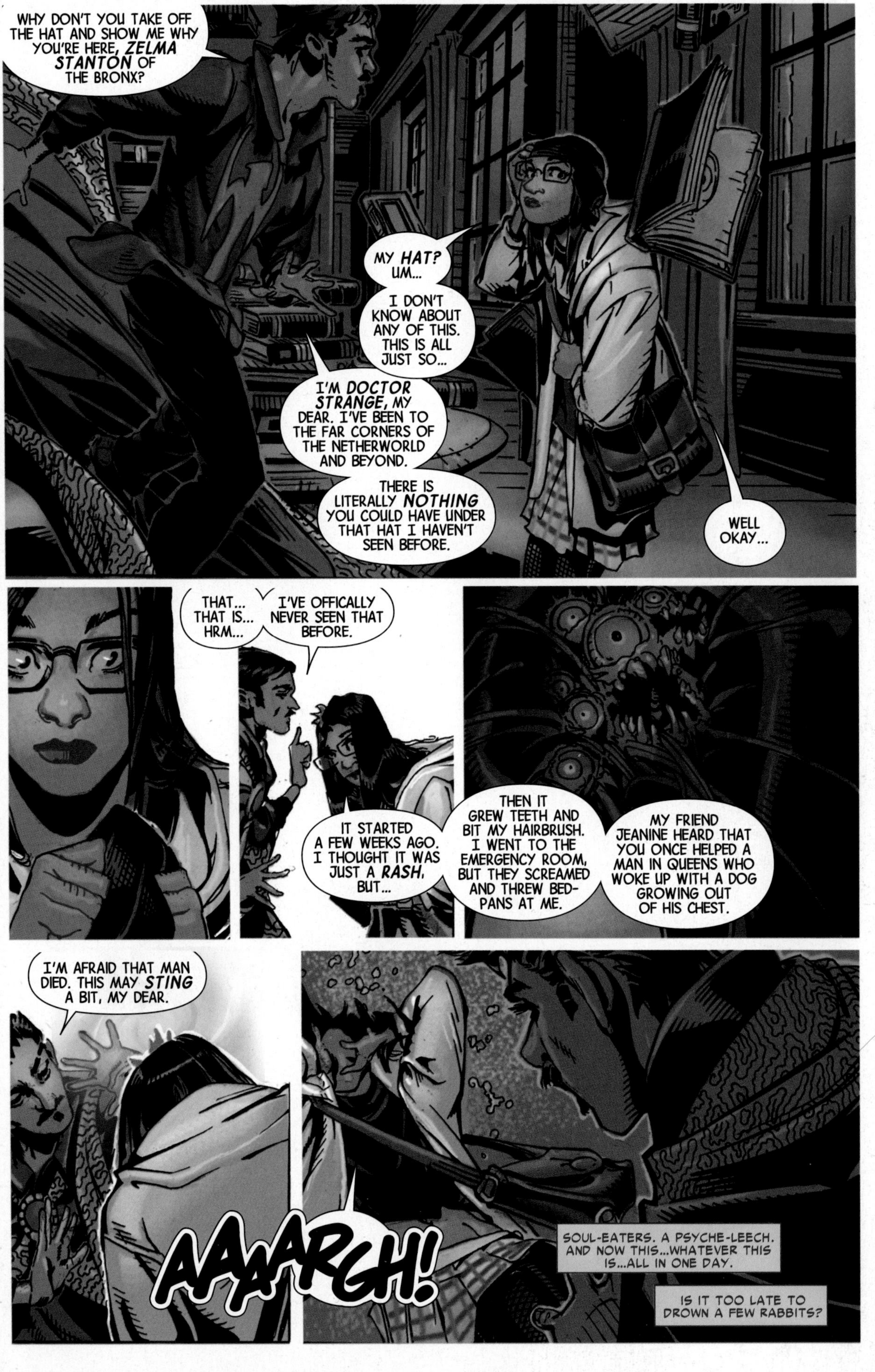
WHY DON'T YOU TAKE OFF THE HAT AND SHOW ME WHY YOU'RE HERE, ZELMA STANTON OF THE BRONX?
MY HAT? UM...
I DON'T KNOW ABOUT ANY OF THIS. THIS IS ALL JUST SO...
I'M DOCTOR STRANGE, MY DEAR. I'VE BEEN TO THE FAR CORNERS OF THE NETHERWORLD AND BEYOND.
THERE IS LITERALLY NOTHING YOU COULD HAVE UNDER THAT HAT I HAVEN'T SEEN BEFORE.
WELL OKAY...
THAT... THAT IS... HRM...
I'VE OFFICALLY NEVER SEEN THAT BEFORE.
IT STARTED A FEW WEEKS AGO. I THOUGHT IT WAS JUST A RASH, BUT...
THEN IT GREW TEETH AND BIT MY HAIRBRUSH. I WENT TO THE EMERGENCY ROOM, BUT THEY SCREAMED AND THREW BED-PANS AT ME.
MY FRIEND JEANINE HEARD THAT YOU ONCE HELPED A MAN IN QUEENS WHO WOKE UP WITH A DOG GROWING OUT OF HIS CHEST.
I'M AFRAID THAT MAN DIED. THIS MAY STING A BIT, MY DEAR.
AAAARGH!
SOUL-EATERS. A PSYCHE-LEECH. AND NOW THIS...WHATEVER THIS IS...ALL IN ONE DAY.
IS IT TOO LATE TO DROWN A FEW RABBITS?

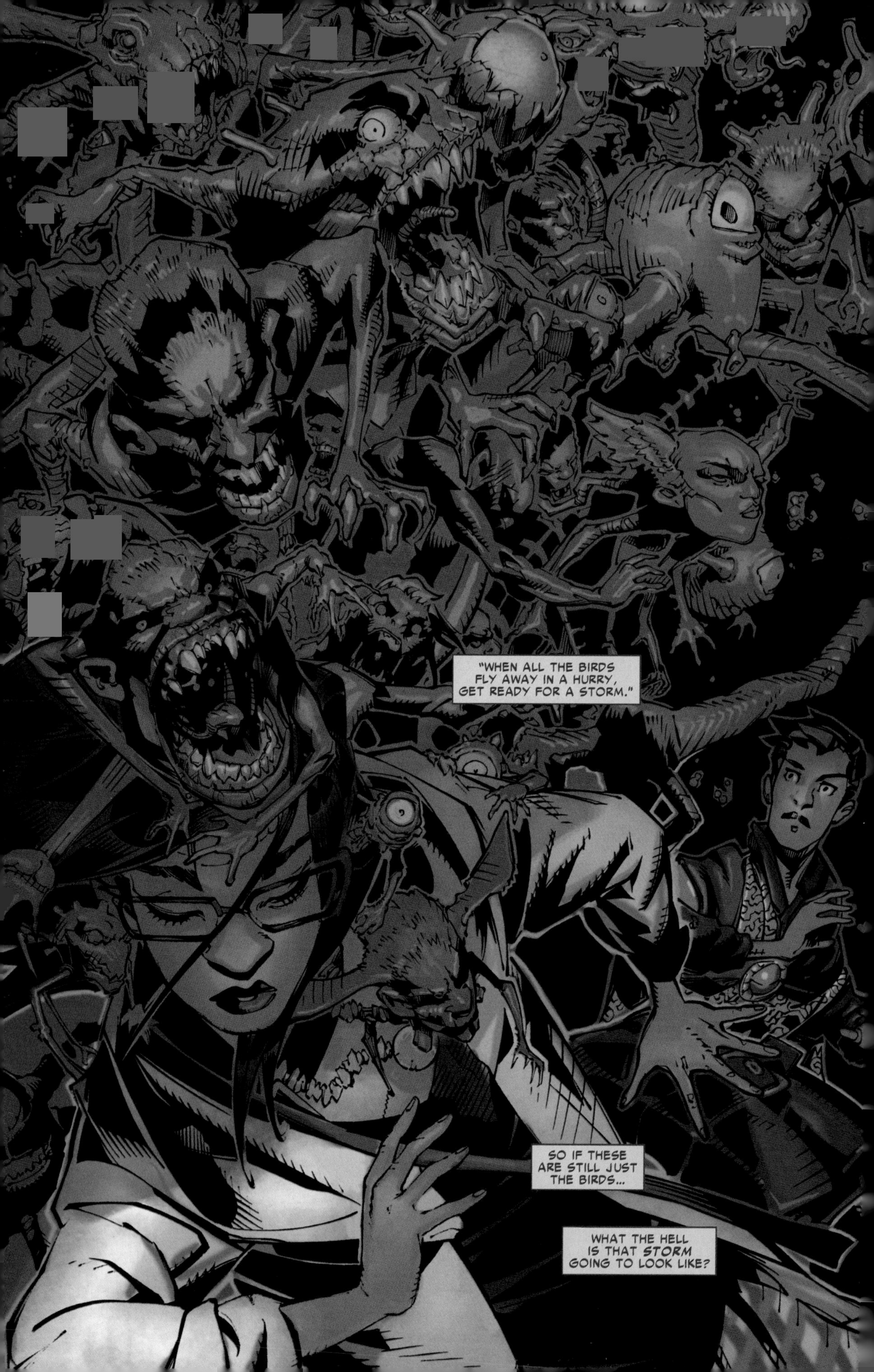
"WHEN ALL THE BIRDS FLY AWAY IN A HURRY, GET READY FOR A STORM."
SO IF THESE ARE STILL JUST THE BIRDS...
WHAT THE HELL IS THAT *STORM* GOING TO LOOK LIKE?

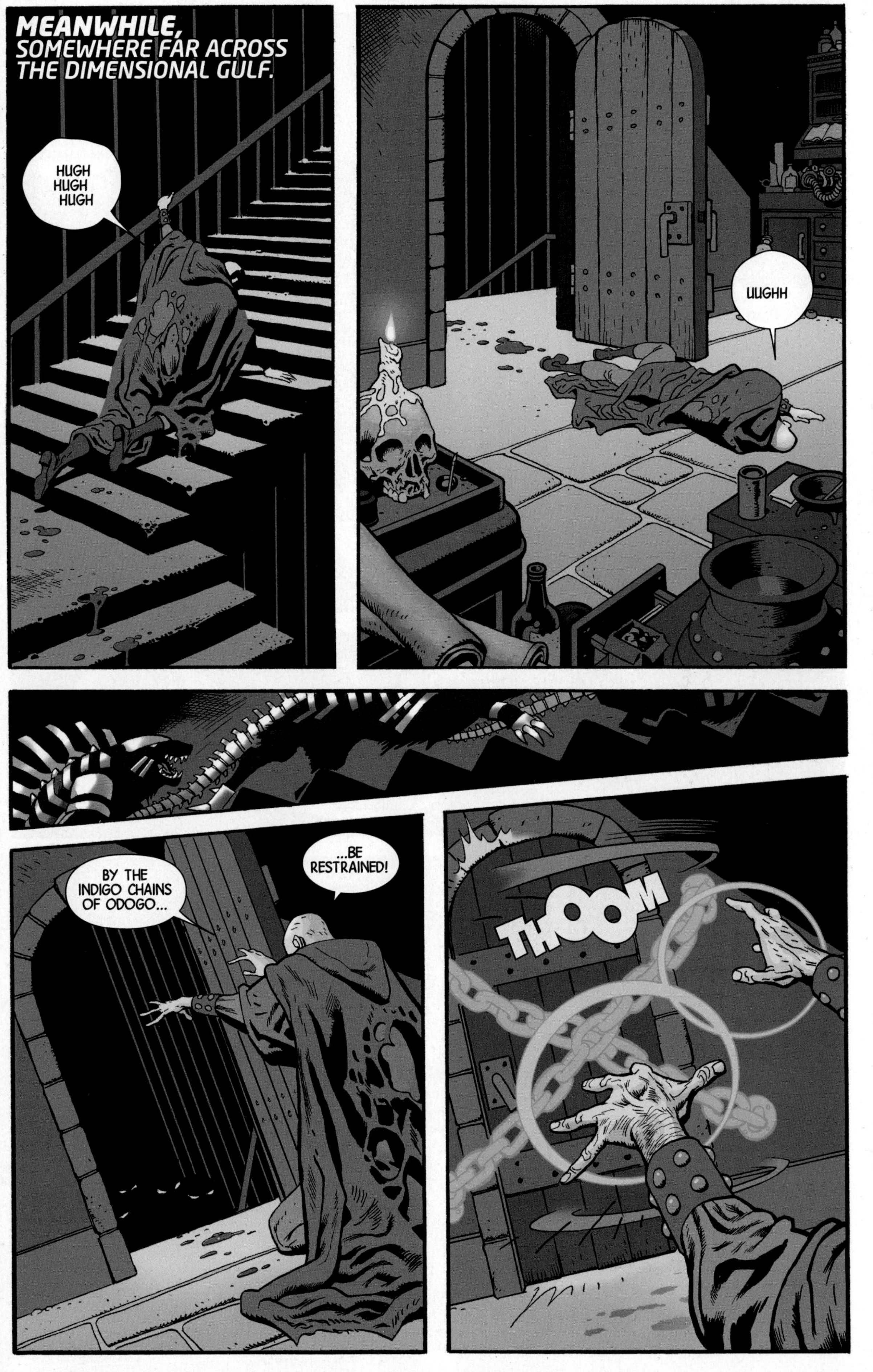
MEANWHILE, SOMEWHERE FAR ACROSS THE DIMENSIONAL GULF.
HUGH HUGH HUGH
UUGHH
BY THE INDIGO CHAINS OF ODOGO...
...BE RESTRAINED!
THOOM

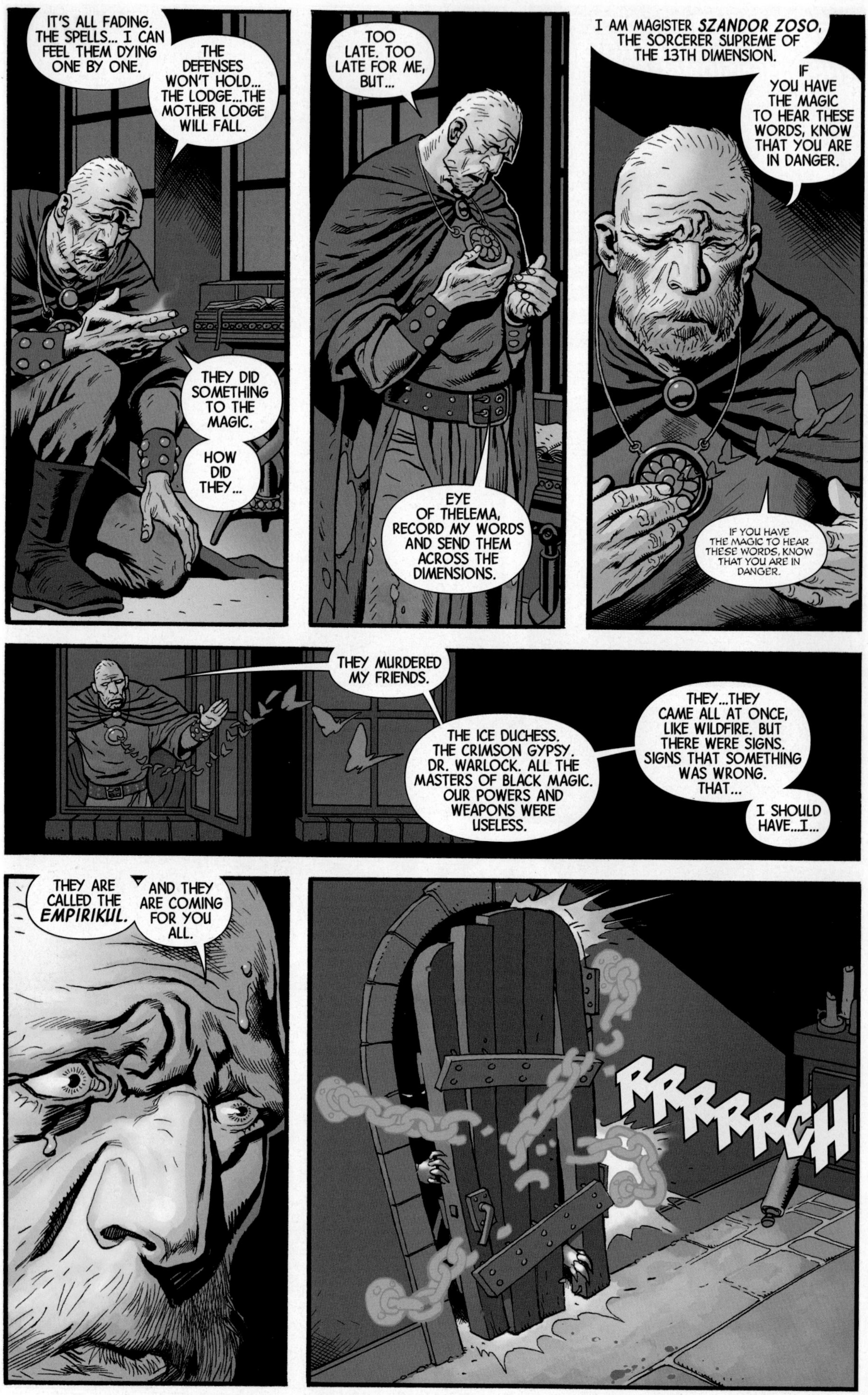
IT'S ALL FADING. THE SPELLS... I CAN FEEL THEM DYING ONE BY ONE.
THE DEFENSES WON'T HOLD... THE LODGE...THE MOTHER LODGE WILL FALL.
THEY DID SOMETHING TO THE MAGIC.
HOW DID THEY...
TOO LATE. TOO LATE FOR ME, BUT...
EYE OF THELEMA, RECORD MY WORDS AND SEND THEM ACROSS THE DIMENSIONS.
I AM MAGISTER SZANDOR ZOSO, THE SORCERER SUPREME OF THE 13TH DIMENSION.
IF YOU HAVE THE MAGIC TO HEAR THESE WORDS, KNOW THAT YOU ARE IN DANGER.
IF YOU HAVE THE MAGIC TO HEAR THESE WORDS, KNOW THAT YOU ARE IN DANGER.
THEY MURDERED MY FRIENDS.
THE ICE DUCHESS. THE CRIMSON GYPSY. DR. WARLOCK. ALL THE MASTERS OF BLACK MAGIC. OUR POWERS AND WEAPONS WERE USELESS.
THEY...THEY CAME ALL AT ONCE, LIKE WILDFIRE. BUT THERE WERE SIGNS. SIGNS THAT SOMETHING WAS WRONG. THAT...
I SHOULD HAVE...I...
THEY ARE CALLED THE EMPIRIKUL.
AND THEY ARE COMING FOR YOU ALL.
RRRRRCH

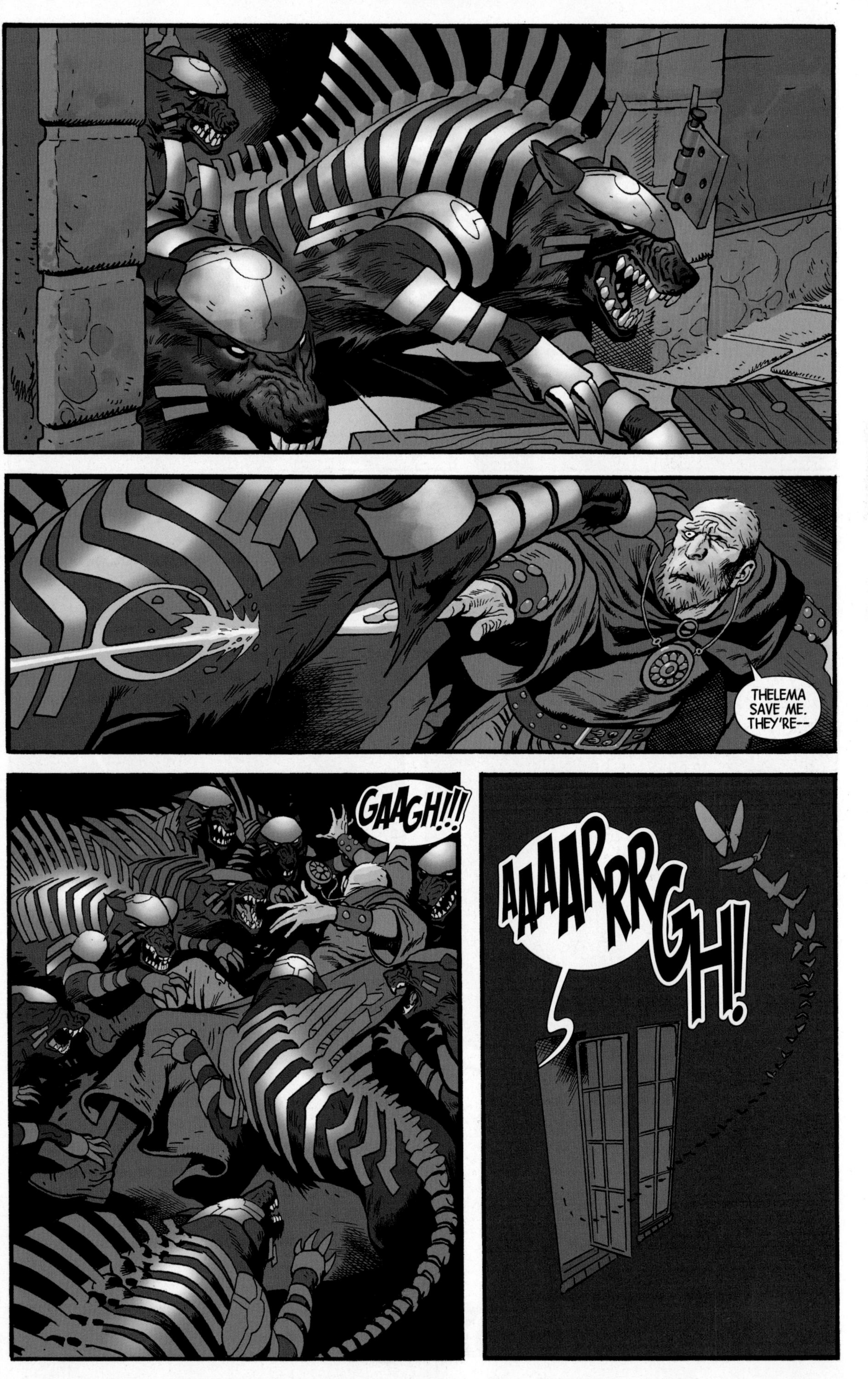
THELEMA SAVE ME. THEY'RE--
GAAGH!!!
AAAARRRGH!

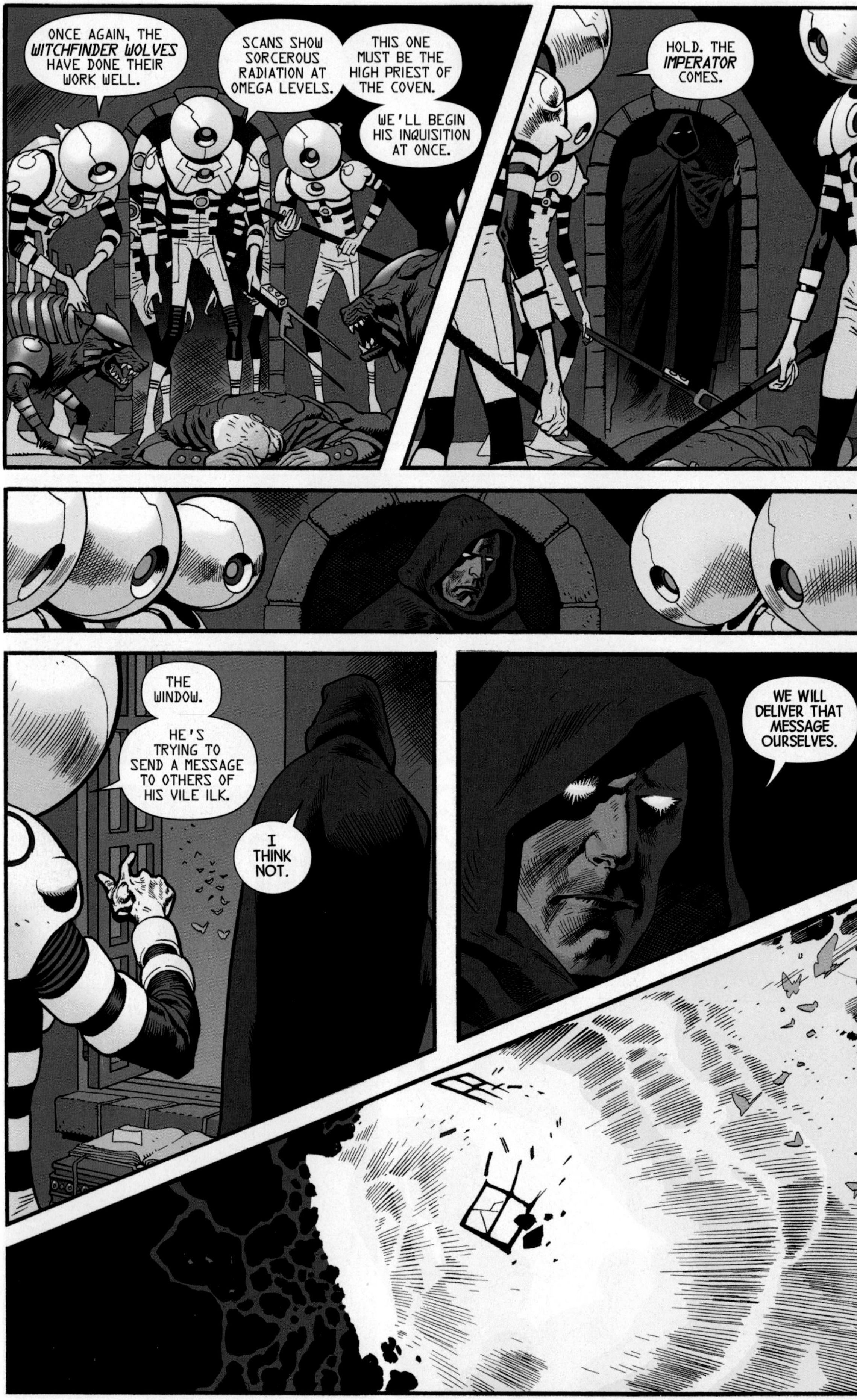
ONCE AGAIN, THE WITCHFINDER WOLVES HAVE DONE THEIR WORK WELL.
SCANS SHOW SORCEROUS RADIATION AT OMEGA LEVELS.
THIS ONE MUST BE THE HIGH PRIEST OF THE COVEN.
WE'LL BEGIN HIS INQUISITION AT ONCE.
HOLD. THE IMPERATOR COMES.
THE WINDOW.
HE'S TRYING TO SEND A MESSAGE TO OTHERS OF HIS VILE ILK.
I THINK NOT.
WE WILL DELIVER THAT MESSAGE OURSELVES.

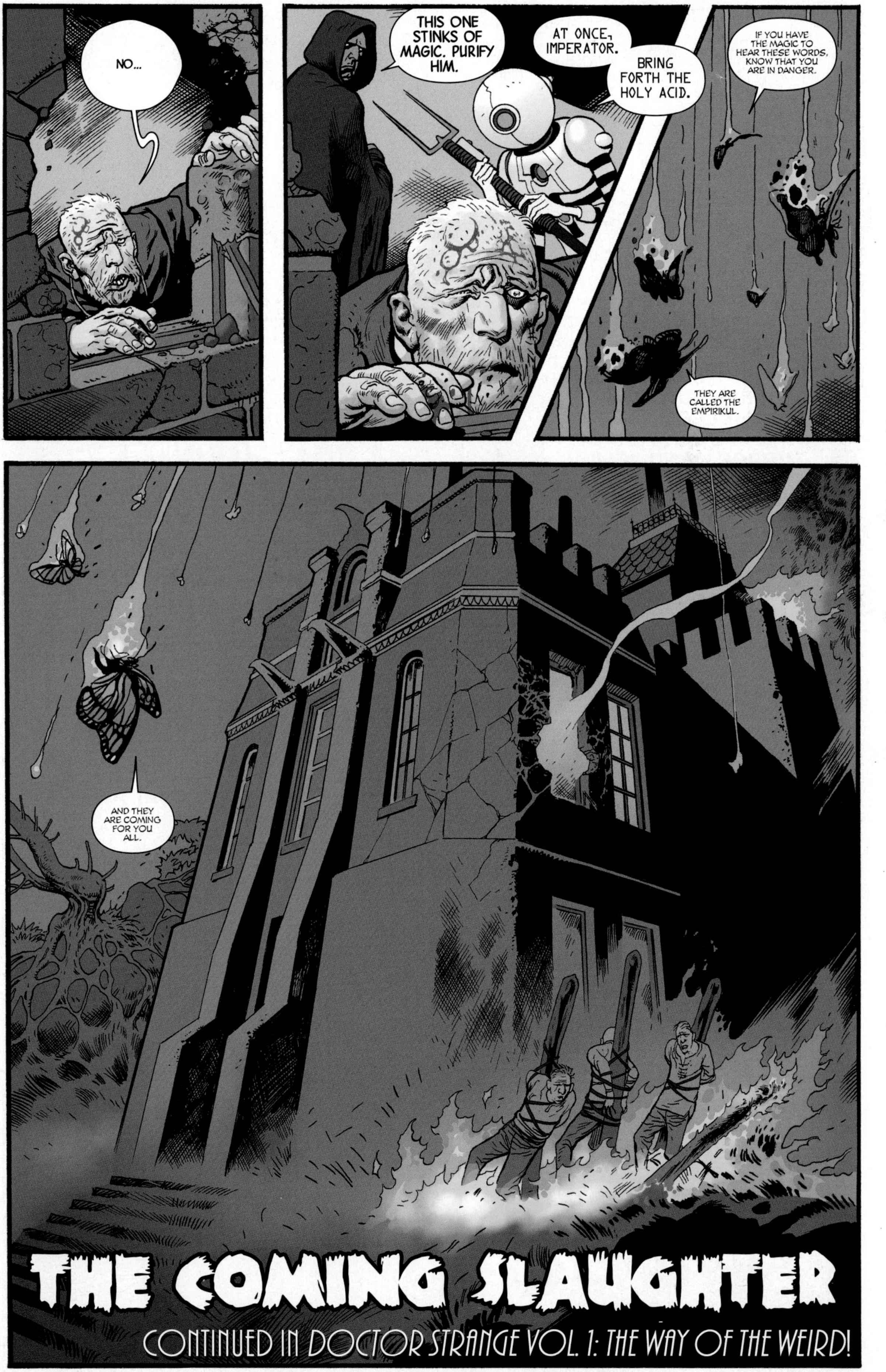

NO...
THIS ONE STINKS OF MAGIC. PURIFY HIM.
AT ONCE, IMPERATOR.
BRING FORTH THE HOLY ACID.
IF YOU HAVE THE MAGIC TO HEAR THESE WORDS, KNOW THAT YOU ARE IN DANGER.
THEY ARE CALLED THE EMPIRIKUL.
AND THEY ARE COMING FOR YOU ALL.
THE COMING SLAUGHTER

CONTINUED IN *DOCTOR STRANGE* VOL. 1: THE WAY OF THE WEIRD!

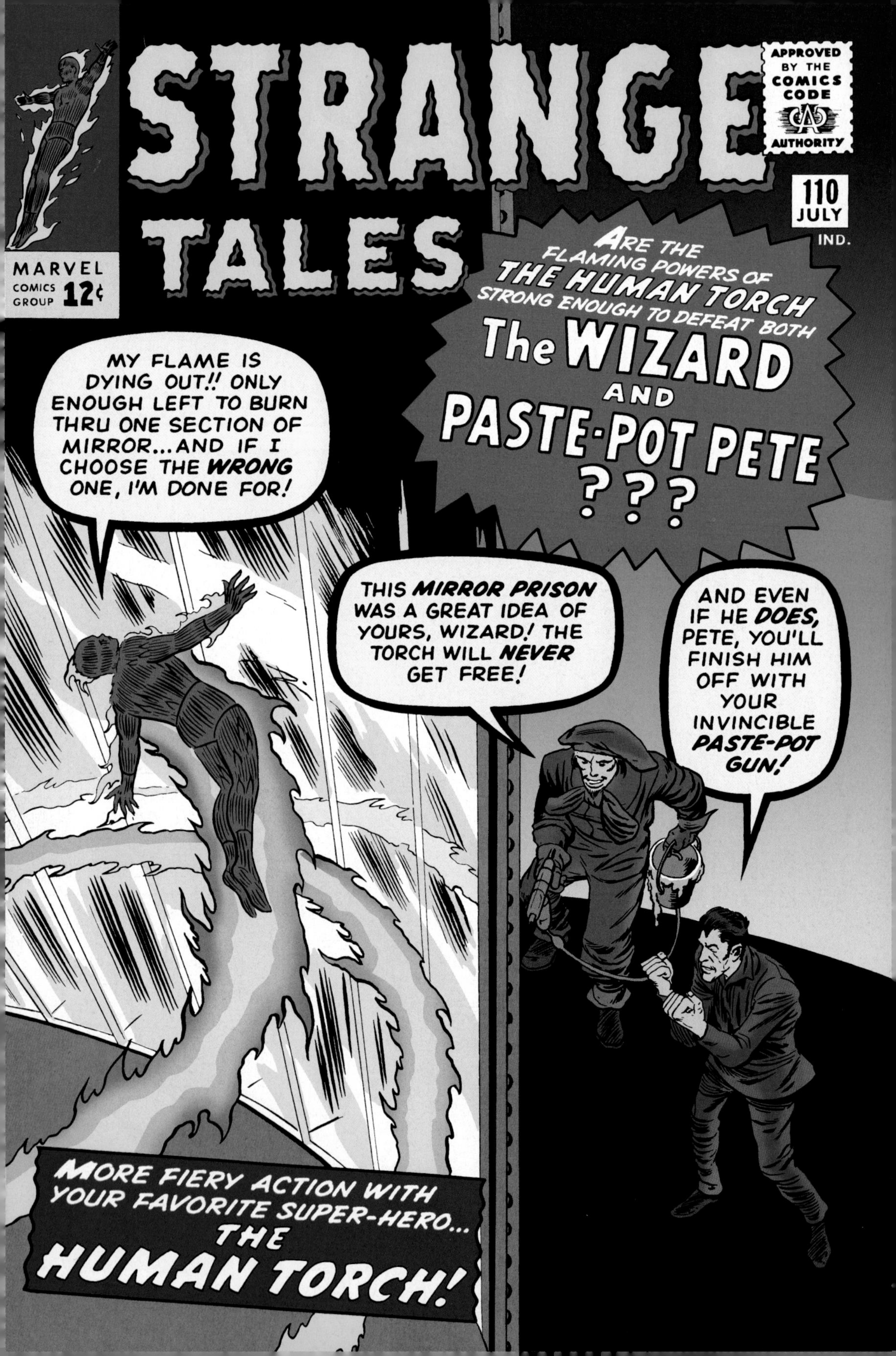
STRANGE TALES
APPROVED BY THE COMICS CODE AUTHORITY
110 JULY
IND.
MARVEL COMICS GROUP 12¢
ARE THE FLAMING POWERS OF THE HUMAN TORCH STRONG ENOUGH TO DEFEAT BOTH The WIZARD AND PASTE-POT PETE ???
MY FLAME IS DYING OUT!! ONLY ENOUGH LEFT TO BURN THRU ONE SECTION OF MIRROR...AND IF I CHOOSE THE WRONG ONE, I'M DONE FOR!
THIS MIRROR PRISON WAS A GREAT IDEA OF YOURS, WIZARD! THE TORCH WILL NEVER GET FREE!
AND EVEN IF HE DOES, PETE, YOU'LL FINISH HIM OFF WITH YOUR INVINCIBLE PASTE-POT GUN!
MORE FIERY ACTION WITH YOUR FAVORITE SUPER-HERO... THE HUMAN TORCH!

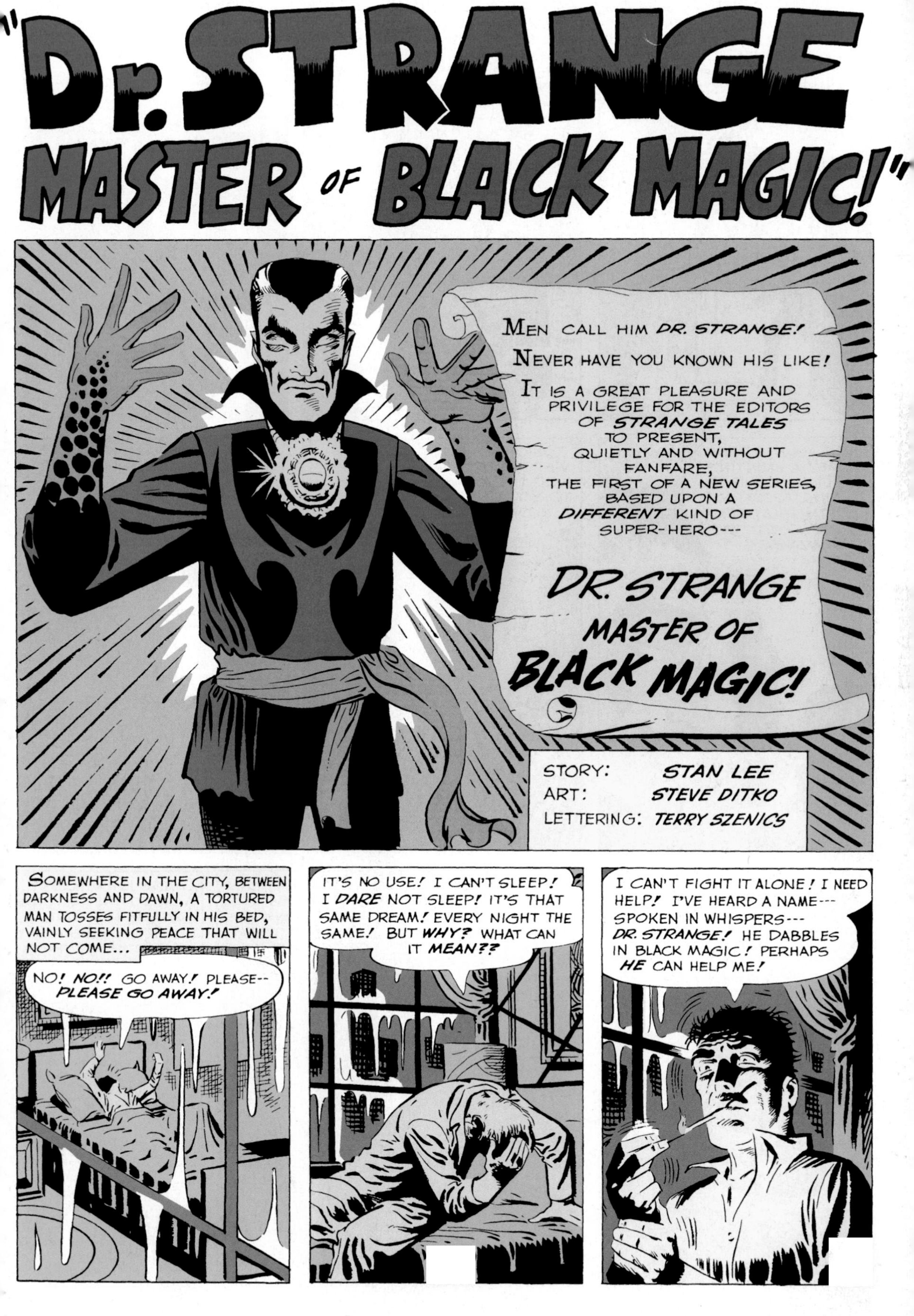
"DR. STRANGE MASTER OF BLACK MAGIC!"
MEN CALL HIM DR. STRANGE! NEVER HAVE YOU KNOWN HIS LIKE! IT IS A GREAT PLEASURE AND PRIVILEGE FOR THE EDITORS OF STRANGE TALES TO PRESENT, QUIETLY AND WITHOUT FANFARE, THE FIRST OF A NEW SERIES, BASED UPON A DIFFERENT KIND OF SUPER-HERO--- DR. STRANGE MASTER OF BLACK MAGIC!
STORY: STAN LEE
ART: STEVE DITKO
LETTERING: TERRY SZENICS
SOMEWHERE IN THE CITY, BETWEEN DARKNESS AND DAWN, A TORTURED MAN TOSSES FITFULLY IN HIS BED, VAINLY SEEKING PEACE THAT WILL NOT COME...
NO! NO!! GO AWAY! PLEASE-- PLEASE GO AWAY!
IT'S NO USE! I CAN'T SLEEP! I DARE NOT SLEEP! IT'S THAT SAME DREAM! EVERY NIGHT THE SAME! BUT WHY? WHAT CAN IT MEAN??
I CAN'T FIGHT IT ALONE! I NEED HELP! I'VE HEARD A NAME--- SPOKEN IN WHISPERS--- DR. STRANGE! HE DABBLES IN BLACK MAGIC! PERHAPS HE CAN HELP ME!

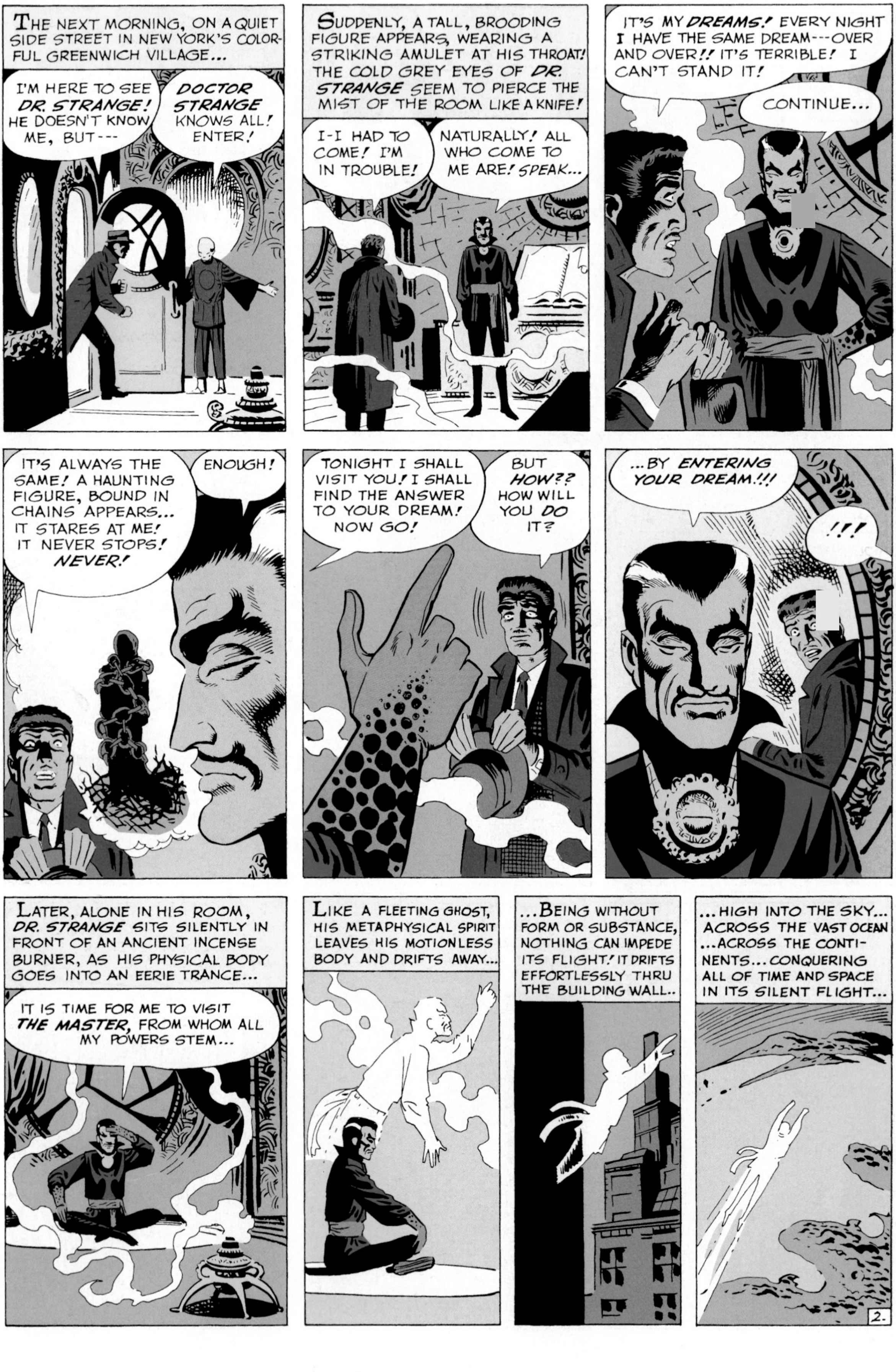
THE NEXT MORNING, ON A QUIET SIDE STREET IN NEW YORK'S COLORFUL GREENWICH VILLAGE...
I'M HERE TO SEE DR. STRANGE! HE DOESN'T KNOW ME, BUT---
DOCTOR STRANGE KNOWS ALL! ENTER!
SUDDENLY, A TALL, BROODING FIGURE APPEARS, WEARING A STRIKING AMULET AT HIS THROAT! THE COLD GREY EYES OF DR. STRANGE SEEM TO PIERCE THE MIST OF THE ROOM LIKE A KNIFE!
I-I HAD TO COME! I'M IN TROUBLE!
NATURALLY! ALL WHO COME TO ME ARE! SPEAK...
IT'S MY DREAMS! EVERY NIGHT I HAVE THE SAME DREAM---OVER AND OVER!! IT'S TERRIBLE! I CAN'T STAND IT!
CONTINUE...
IT'S ALWAYS THE SAME! A HAUNTING FIGURE, BOUND IN CHAINS APPEARS... IT STARES AT ME! IT NEVER STOPS! NEVER!
ENOUGH!
TONIGHT I SHALL VISIT YOU! I SHALL FIND THE ANSWER TO YOUR DREAM! NOW GO!
BUT HOW?? HOW WILL YOU DO IT?
...BY ENTERING YOUR DREAM!!!
!?!
LATER, ALONE IN HIS ROOM, DR. STRANGE SITS SILENTLY IN FRONT OF AN ANCIENT INCENSE BURNER, AS HIS PHYSICAL BODY GOES INTO AN EERIE TRANCE...
IT IS TIME FOR ME TO VISIT THE MASTER, FROM WHOM ALL MY POWERS STEM...
LIKE A FLEETING GHOST, HIS METAPHYSICAL SPIRIT LEAVES HIS MOTIONLESS BODY AND DRIFTS AWAY...
...BEING WITHOUT FORM OR SUBSTANCE, NOTHING CAN IMPEDE ITS FLIGHT! IT DRIFTS EFFORTLESSLY THRU THE BUILDING WALL..
...HIGH INTO THE SKY... ACROSS THE VAST OCEAN ...ACROSS THE CONTINENTS... CONQUERING ALL OF TIME AND SPACE IN ITS SILENT FLIGHT...
2.

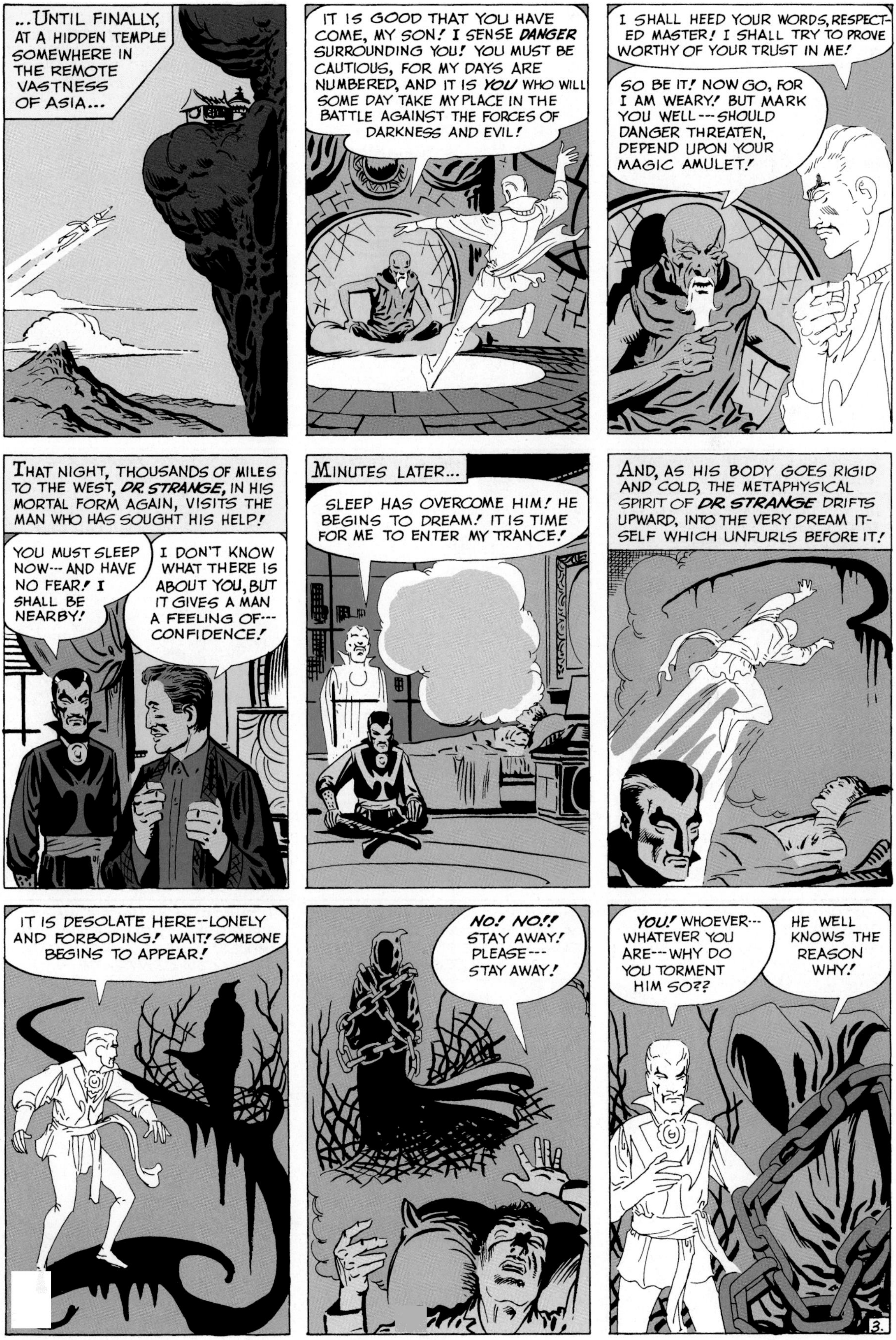

...UNTIL FINALLY, AT A HIDDEN TEMPLE SOMEWHERE IN THE REMOTE VASTNESS OF ASIA...
IT IS GOOD THAT YOU HAVE COME, MY SON! I SENSE DANGER SURROUNDING YOU! YOU MUST BE CAUTIOUS, FOR MY DAYS ARE NUMBERED, AND IT IS YOU WHO WILL SOME DAY TAKE MY PLACE IN THE BATTLE AGAINST THE FORCES OF DARKNESS AND EVIL!
I SHALL HEED YOUR WORDS, RESPECTED MASTER! I SHALL TRY TO PROVE WORTHY OF YOUR TRUST IN ME!
SO BE IT! NOW GO, FOR I AM WEARY! BUT MARK YOU WELL---SHOULD DANGER THREATEN, DEPEND UPON YOUR MAGIC AMULET!
THAT NIGHT, THOUSANDS OF MILES TO THE WEST, DR. STRANGE, IN HIS MORTAL FORM AGAIN, VISITS THE MAN WHO HAS SOUGHT HIS HELP!
YOU MUST SLEEP NOW---AND HAVE NO FEAR! I SHALL BE NEARBY!
I DON'T KNOW WHAT THERE IS ABOUT YOU, BUT IT GIVES A MAN A FEELING OF---CONFIDENCE!
MINUTES LATER...
SLEEP HAS OVERCOME HIM! HE BEGINS TO DREAM! IT IS TIME FOR ME TO ENTER MY TRANCE!
AND, AS HIS BODY GOES RIGID AND COLD, THE METAPHYSICAL SPIRIT OF DR. STRANGE DRIFTS UPWARD, INTO THE VERY DREAM ITSELF WHICH UNFURLS BEFORE IT!
IT IS DESOLATE HERE--LONELY AND FORBODING! WAIT! SOMEONE BEGINS TO APPEAR!
NO! NO!! STAY AWAY! PLEASE--- STAY AWAY!
YOU! WHOEVER---WHATEVER YOU ARE---WHY DO YOU TORMENT HIM SO??
HE WELL KNOWS THE REASON WHY!
3.

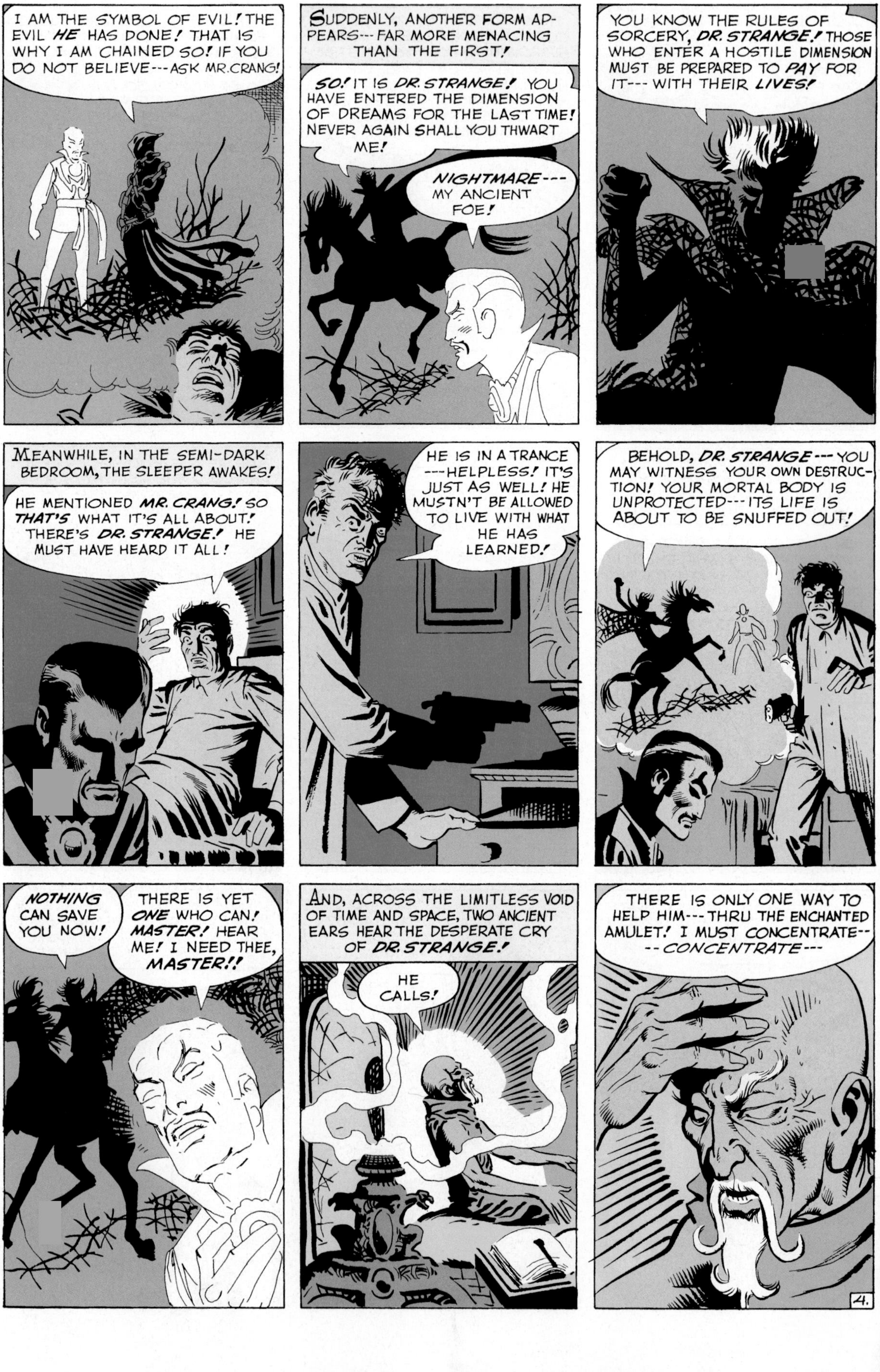

I AM THE SYMBOL OF EVIL! THE EVIL HE HAS DONE! THAT IS WHY I AM CHAINED SO! IF YOU DO NOT BELIEVE---ASK MR.CRANG!
SUDDENLY, ANOTHER FORM APPEARS--- FAR MORE MENACING THAN THE FIRST!
SO! IT IS DR. STRANGE! YOU HAVE ENTERED THE DIMENSION OF DREAMS FOR THE LAST TIME! NEVER AGAIN SHALL YOU THWART ME!
NIGHTMARE--- MY ANCIENT FOE!
YOU KNOW THE RULES OF SORCERY, DR. STRANGE! THOSE WHO ENTER A HOSTILE DIMENSION MUST BE PREPARED TO PAY FOR IT--- WITH THEIR LIVES!
MEANWHILE, IN THE SEMI-DARK BEDROOM, THE SLEEPER AWAKES!
HE MENTIONED MR. CRANG! SO THAT'S WHAT IT'S ALL ABOUT! THERE'S DR. STRANGE! HE MUST HAVE HEARD IT ALL!
HE IS IN A TRANCE ---HELPLESS! IT'S JUST AS WELL! HE MUSTN'T BE ALLOWED TO LIVE WITH WHAT HE HAS LEARNED!
BEHOLD, DR. STRANGE--- YOU MAY WITNESS YOUR OWN DESTRUCTION! YOUR MORTAL BODY IS UNPROTECTED--- ITS LIFE IS ABOUT TO BE SNUFFED OUT!
NOTHING CAN SAVE YOU NOW!
THERE IS YET ONE WHO CAN! MASTER! HEAR ME! I NEED THEE, MASTER!!
AND, ACROSS THE LIMITLESS VOID OF TIME AND SPACE, TWO ANCIENT EARS HEAR THE DESPERATE CRY OF DR. STRANGE!
HE CALLS!
THERE IS ONLY ONE WAY TO HELP HIM--- THRU THE ENCHANTED AMULET! I MUST CONCENTRATE-- --CONCENTRATE---
4.

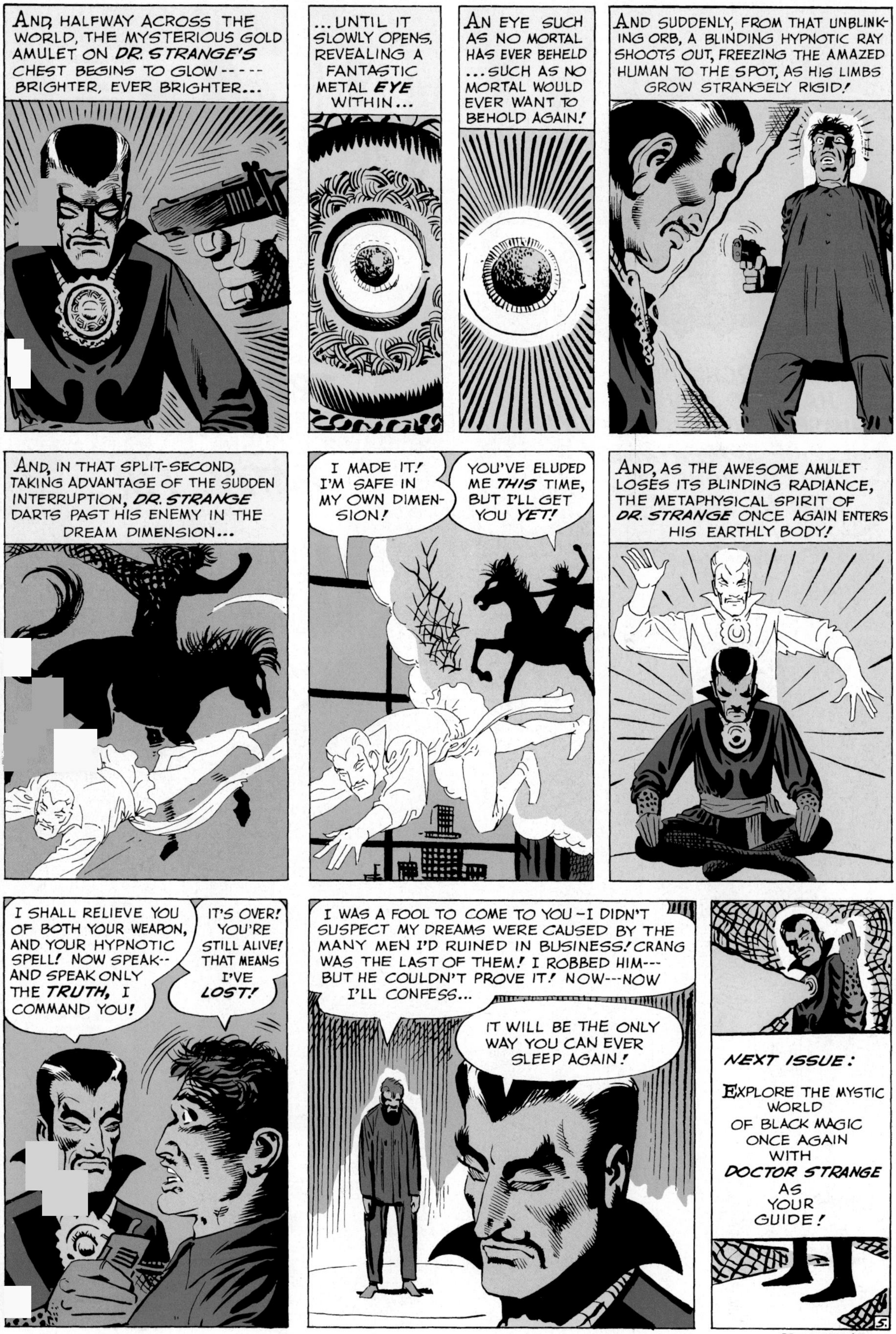
AND, HALFWAY ACROSS THE WORLD, THE MYSTERIOUS GOLD AMULET ON DR. STRANGE'S CHEST BEGINS TO GLOW----- BRIGHTER, EVER BRIGHTER...
...UNTIL IT SLOWLY OPENS, REVEALING A FANTASTIC METAL EYE WITHIN...
AN EYE SUCH AS NO MORTAL HAS EVER BEHELD ...SUCH AS NO MORTAL WOULD EVER WANT TO BEHOLD AGAIN!
AND SUDDENLY, FROM THAT UNBLINKING ORB, A BLINDING HYPNOTIC RAY SHOOTS OUT, FREEZING THE AMAZED HUMAN TO THE SPOT, AS HIS LIMBS GROW STRANGELY RIGID!
AND, IN THAT SPLIT-SECOND, TAKING ADVANTAGE OF THE SUDDEN INTERRUPTION, DR. STRANGE DARTS PAST HIS ENEMY IN THE DREAM DIMENSION...
I MADE IT! I'M SAFE IN MY OWN DIMENSION!
YOU'VE ELUDED ME THIS TIME, BUT I'LL GET YOU YET!
AND, AS THE AWESOME AMULET LOSES ITS BLINDING RADIANCE, THE METAPHYSICAL SPIRIT OF DR. STRANGE ONCE AGAIN ENTERS HIS EARTHLY BODY!
I SHALL RELIEVE YOU OF BOTH YOUR WEAPON, AND YOUR HYPNOTIC SPELL! NOW SPEAK-- AND SPEAK ONLY THE TRUTH, I COMMAND YOU!
IT'S OVER! YOU'RE STILL ALIVE! THAT MEANS I'VE LOST!
I WAS A FOOL TO COME TO YOU -I DIDN'T SUSPECT MY DREAMS WERE CAUSED BY THE MANY MEN I'D RUINED IN BUSINESS! CRANG WAS THE LAST OF THEM! I ROBBED HIM--- BUT HE COULDN'T PROVE IT! NOW---NOW I'LL CONFESS...
IT WILL BE THE ONLY WAY YOU CAN EVER SLEEP AGAIN!
NEXT ISSUE:
EXPLORE THE MYSTIC WORLD OF BLACK MAGIC ONCE AGAIN WITH DOCTOR STRANGE AS YOUR GUIDE!
S.

-THE END-

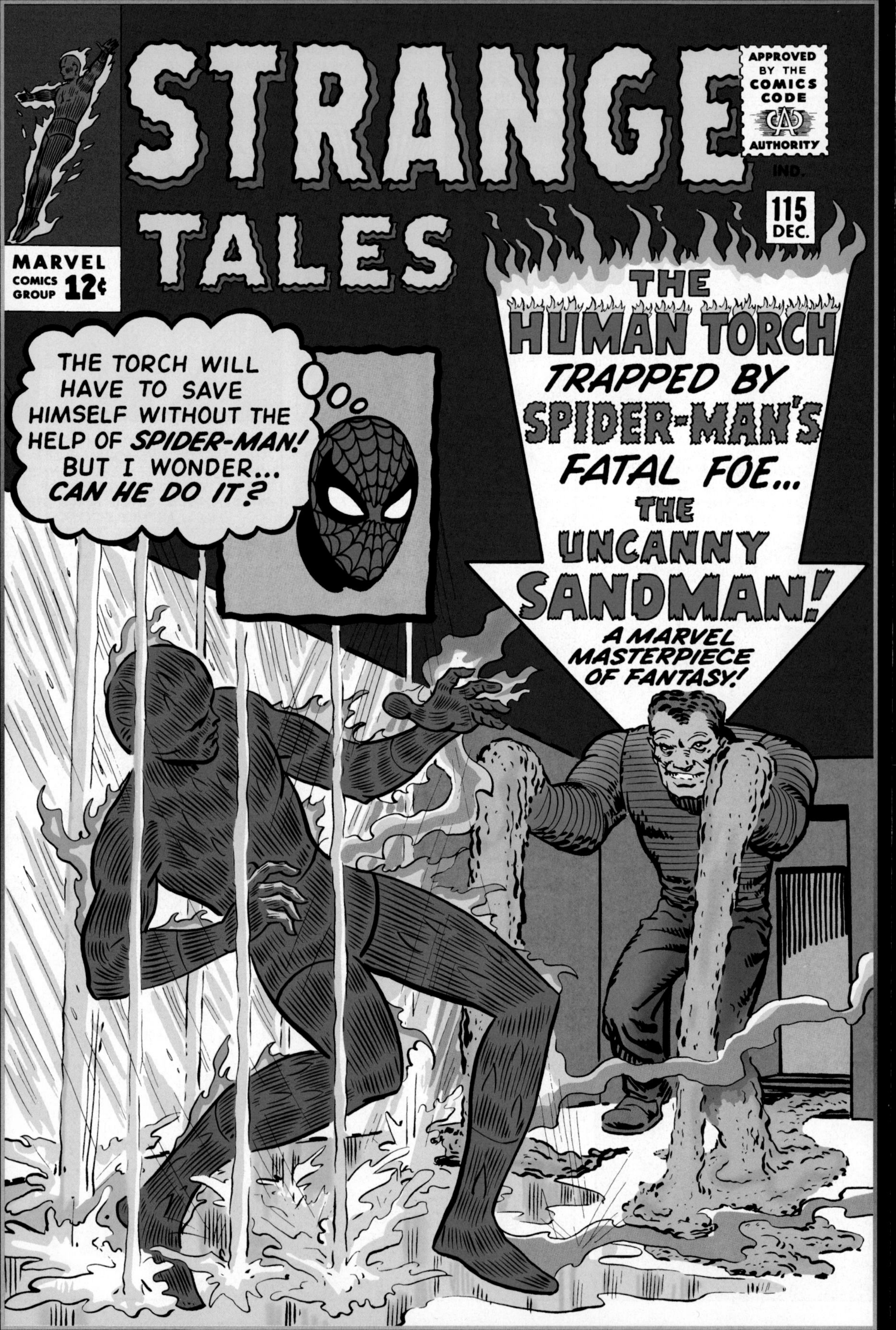

STRANGE TALES
MARVEL COMICS GROUP 12¢
APPROVED BY THE COMICS CODE AUTHORITY
IND.
115 DEC.
THE TORCH WILL HAVE TO SAVE HIMSELF WITHOUT THE HELP OF SPIDER-MAN! BUT I WONDER... CAN HE DO IT?
THE HUMAN TORCH TRAPPED BY SPIDER-MAN'S FATAL FOE... THE UNCANNY SANDMAN!
A MARVEL MASTERPIECE OF FANTASY!

IN ANSWER TO AN AVALANCHE OF REQUESTS, WE PRESENT:

"THE ORIGIN OF
Dr. STRANGE"

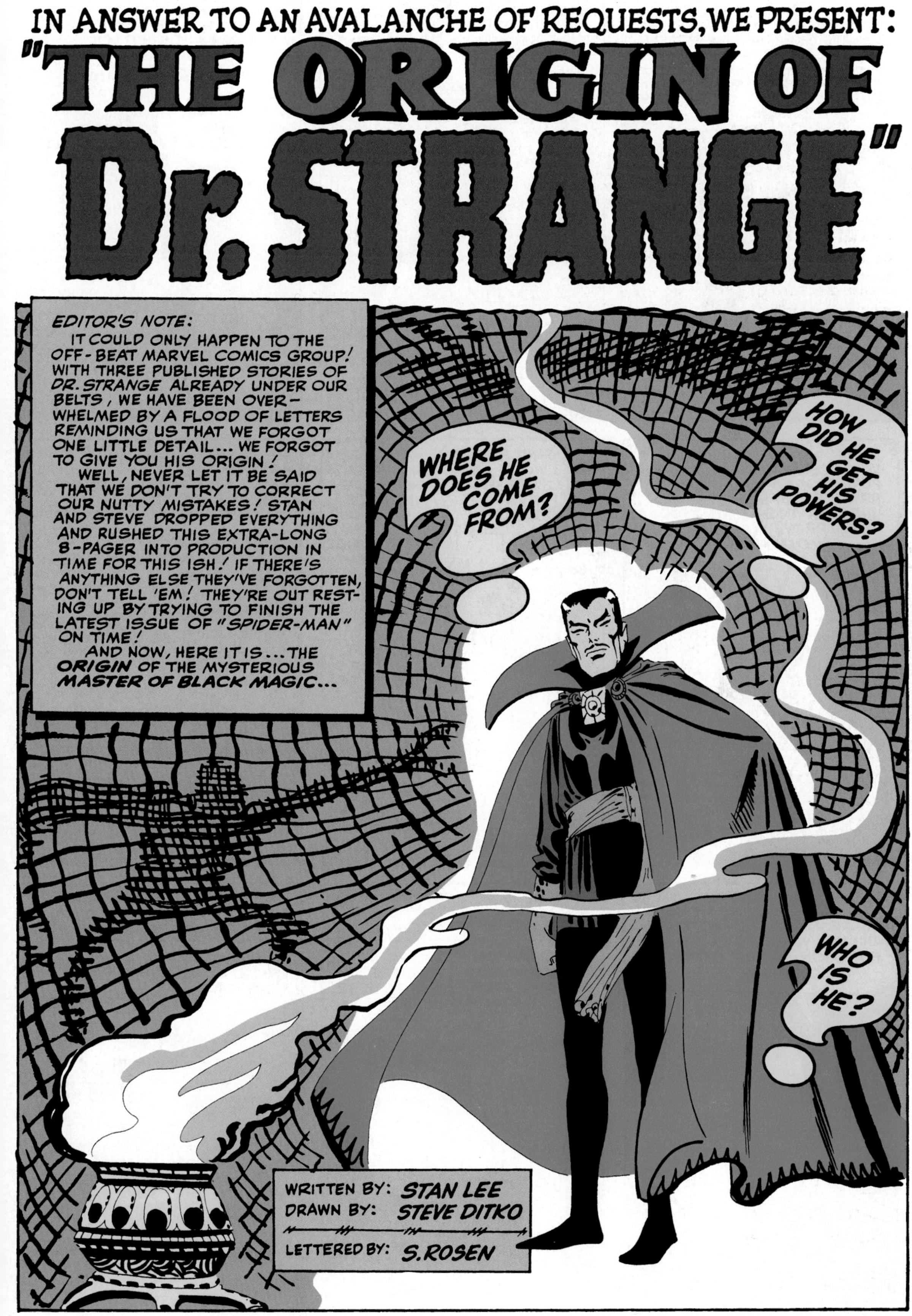
EDITOR'S NOTE:
IT COULD ONLY HAPPEN TO THE OFF-BEAT MARVEL COMICS GROUP! WITH THREE PUBLISHED STORIES OF DR. STRANGE ALREADY UNDER OUR BELTS, WE HAVE BEEN OVER-WHELMED BY A FLOOD OF LETTERS REMINDING US THAT WE FORGOT ONE LITTLE DETAIL... WE FORGOT TO GIVE YOU HIS ORIGIN!
WELL, NEVER LET IT BE SAID THAT WE DON'T TRY TO CORRECT OUR NUTTY MISTAKES! STAN AND STEVE DROPPED EVERYTHING AND RUSHED THIS EXTRA-LONG 8-PAGER INTO PRODUCTION IN TIME FOR THIS ISH! IF THERE'S ANYTHING ELSE THEY'VE FORGOTTEN, DON'T TELL 'EM! THEY'RE OUT RESTING UP BY TRYING TO FINISH THE LATEST ISSUE OF "SPIDER-MAN" ON TIME!
AND NOW, HERE IT IS... THE ORIGIN OF THE MYSTERIOUS MASTER OF BLACK MAGIC...
WHERE DOES HE COME FROM?
HOW DID HE GET HIS POWERS?
WHO IS HE?
WRITTEN BY: STAN LEE
DRAWN BY: STEVE DITKO
LETTERED BY: S. ROSEN

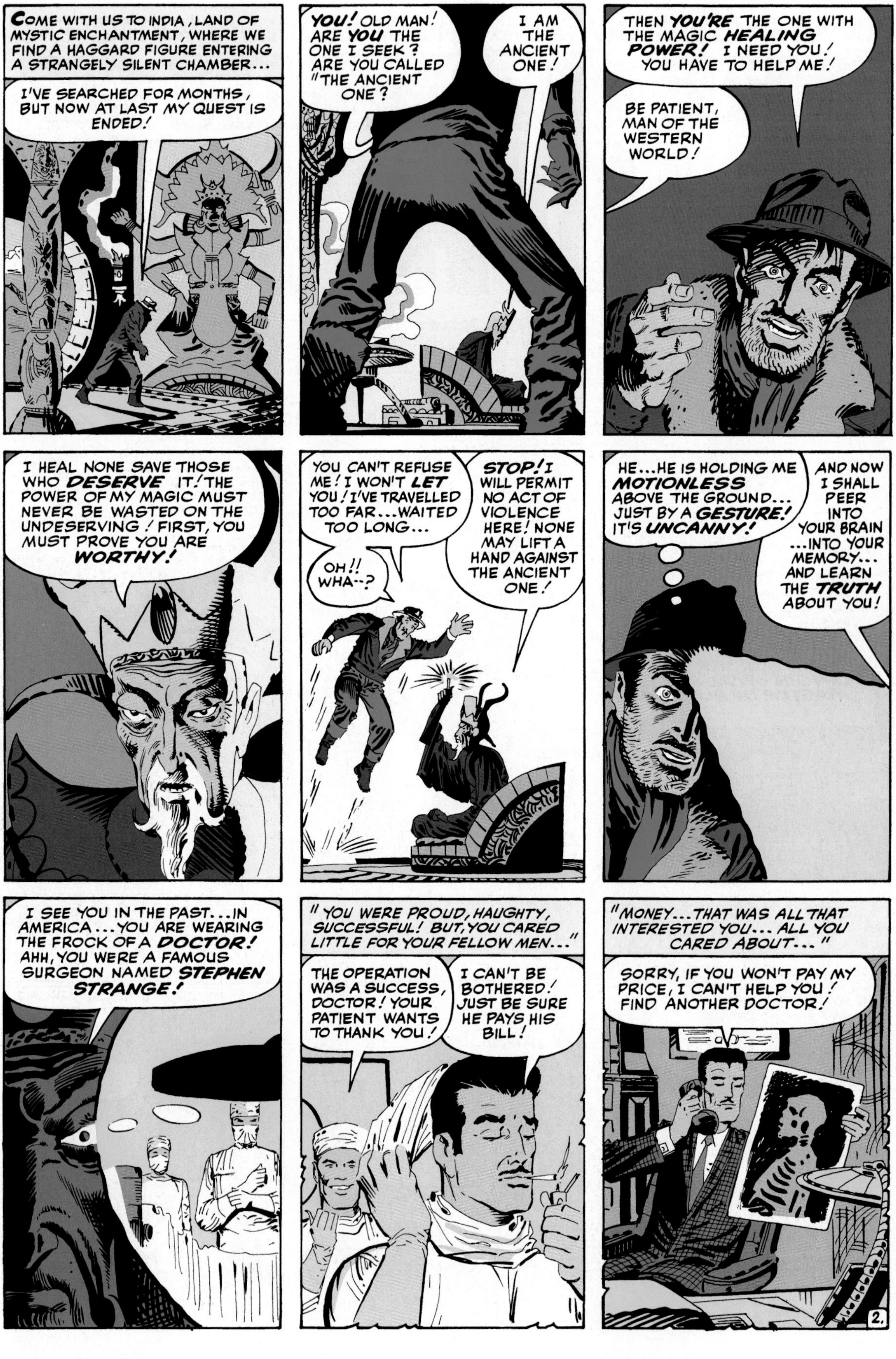
COME WITH US TO INDIA, LAND OF MYSTIC ENCHANTMENT, WHERE WE FIND A HAGGARD FIGURE ENTERING A STRANGELY SILENT CHAMBER...
I'VE SEARCHED FOR MONTHS, BUT NOW AT LAST MY QUEST IS ENDED!
YOU! OLD MAN! ARE YOU THE ONE I SEEK? ARE YOU CALLED "THE ANCIENT ONE"?
I AM THE ANCIENT ONE!
THEN YOU'RE THE ONE WITH THE MAGIC HEALING POWER! I NEED YOU! YOU HAVE TO HELP ME!
BE PATIENT, MAN OF THE WESTERN WORLD!
I HEAL NONE SAVE THOSE WHO DESERVE IT! THE POWER OF MY MAGIC MUST NEVER BE WASTED ON THE UNDESERVING! FIRST, YOU MUST PROVE YOU ARE WORTHY!
YOU CAN'T REFUSE ME! I WON'T LET YOU! I'VE TRAVELLED TOO FAR...WAITED TOO LONG...
STOP! I WILL PERMIT NO ACT OF VIOLENCE HERE! NONE MAY LIFT A HAND AGAINST THE ANCIENT ONE!
OH!! WHA--?
HE...HE IS HOLDING ME MOTIONLESS ABOVE THE GROUND... JUST BY A GESTURE! IT'S UNCANNY!
AND NOW I SHALL PEER INTO YOUR BRAIN ...INTO YOUR MEMORY... AND LEARN THE TRUTH ABOUT YOU!
I SEE YOU IN THE PAST...IN AMERICA...YOU ARE WEARING THE FROCK OF A DOCTOR! AHH, YOU WERE A FAMOUS SURGEON NAMED STEPHEN STRANGE!
"YOU WERE PROUD, HAUGHTY, SUCCESSFUL! BUT, YOU CARED LITTLE FOR YOUR FELLOW MEN..."
THE OPERATION WAS A SUCCESS, DOCTOR! YOUR PATIENT WANTS TO THANK YOU!
I CAN'T BE BOTHERED! JUST BE SURE HE PAYS HIS BILL!
"MONEY...THAT WAS ALL THAT INTERESTED YOU... ALL YOU CARED ABOUT..."
SORRY, IF YOU WON'T PAY MY PRICE, I CAN'T HELP YOU! FIND ANOTHER DOCTOR!
2.

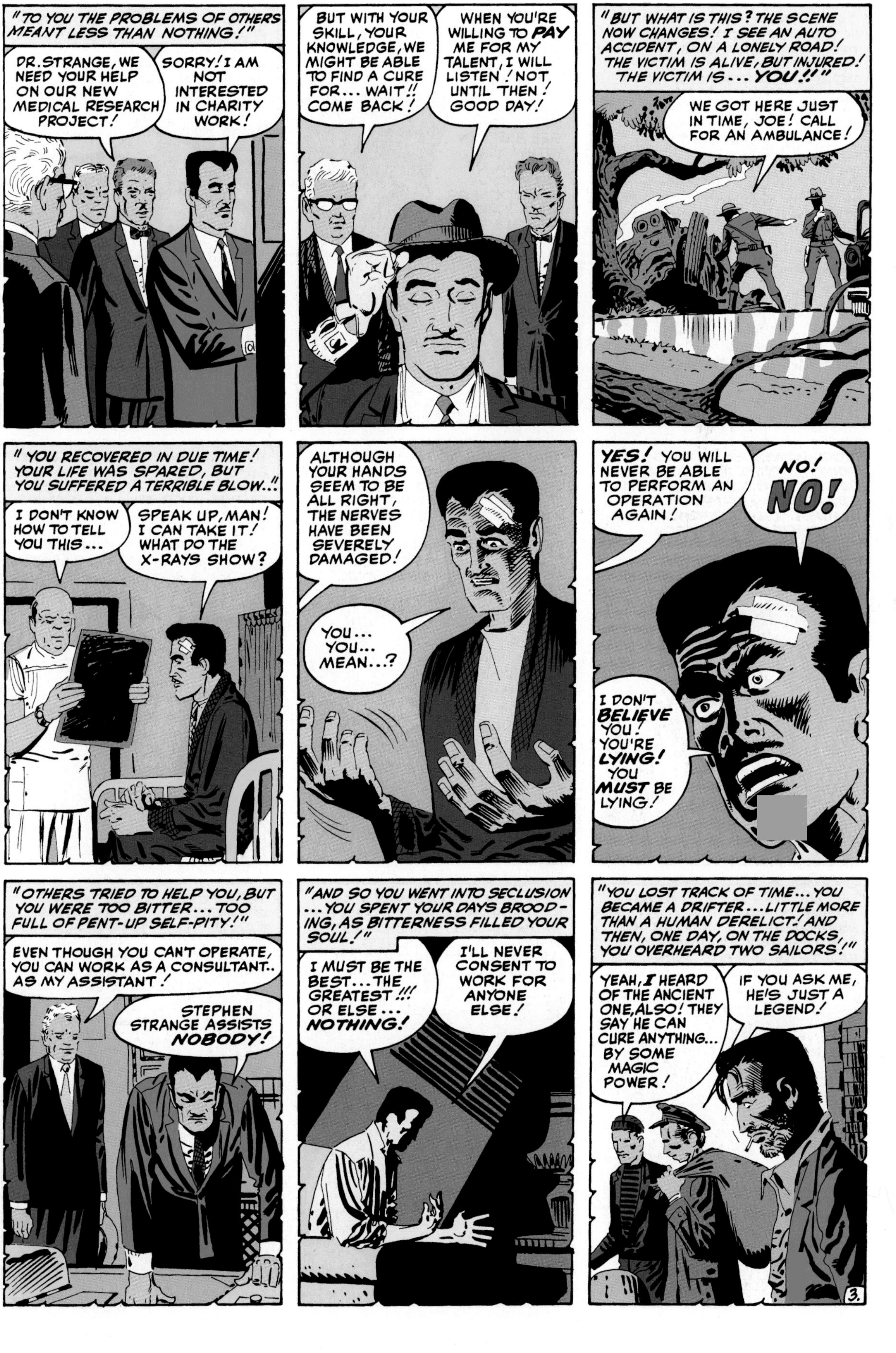
"TO YOU THE PROBLEMS OF OTHERS MEANT LESS THAN NOTHING!"
DR. STRANGE, WE NEED YOUR HELP ON OUR NEW MEDICAL RESEARCH PROJECT!
SORRY! I AM NOT INTERESTED IN CHARITY WORK!
BUT WITH YOUR SKILL, YOUR KNOWLEDGE, WE MIGHT BE ABLE TO FIND A CURE FOR... WAIT!! COME BACK!
WHEN YOU'RE WILLING TO **PAY** ME FOR MY TALENT, I WILL LISTEN! NOT UNTIL THEN! GOOD DAY!
"BUT WHAT IS THIS? THE SCENE NOW CHANGES! I SEE AN AUTO ACCIDENT, ON A LONELY ROAD! THE VICTIM IS ALIVE, BUT INJURED! THE VICTIM IS... **YOU!!**"
WE GOT HERE JUST IN TIME, JOE! CALL FOR AN AMBULANCE!
"YOU RECOVERED IN DUE TIME! YOUR LIFE WAS SPARED, BUT YOU SUFFERED A TERRIBLE BLOW..!"
I DON'T KNOW HOW TO TELL YOU THIS...
SPEAK UP, MAN! I CAN TAKE IT! WHAT DO THE X-RAYS SHOW?
ALTHOUGH YOUR HANDS SEEM TO BE ALL RIGHT, THE NERVES HAVE BEEN SEVERELY DAMAGED!
YOU... YOU... MEAN...?
YES! YOU WILL NEVER BE ABLE TO PERFORM AN OPERATION AGAIN!
NO! **NO!**
I DON'T **BELIEVE** YOU! YOU'RE **LYING!** YOU **MUST** BE LYING!
"OTHERS TRIED TO HELP YOU, BUT YOU WERE TOO BITTER... TOO FULL OF PENT-UP SELF-PITY!"
EVEN THOUGH YOU CAN'T OPERATE, YOU CAN WORK AS A CONSULTANT.. AS MY ASSISTANT!
STEPHEN STRANGE ASSISTS **NOBODY!**
"AND SO YOU WENT INTO SECLUSION ...YOU SPENT YOUR DAYS BROODING, AS BITTERNESS FILLED YOUR SOUL!"
I MUST BE THE BEST... THE GREATEST!!! OR ELSE... **NOTHING!**
I'LL NEVER CONSENT TO WORK FOR ANYONE ELSE!
"YOU LOST TRACK OF TIME... YOU BECAME A DRIFTER... LITTLE MORE THAN A HUMAN DERELICT! AND THEN, ONE DAY, ON THE DOCKS, YOU OVERHEARD TWO SAILORS!"
YEAH, **I** HEARD OF THE ANCIENT ONE, ALSO! THEY SAY HE CAN CURE ANYTHING... BY SOME MAGIC POWER!
IF YOU ASK ME, HE'S JUST A LEGEND!
3.

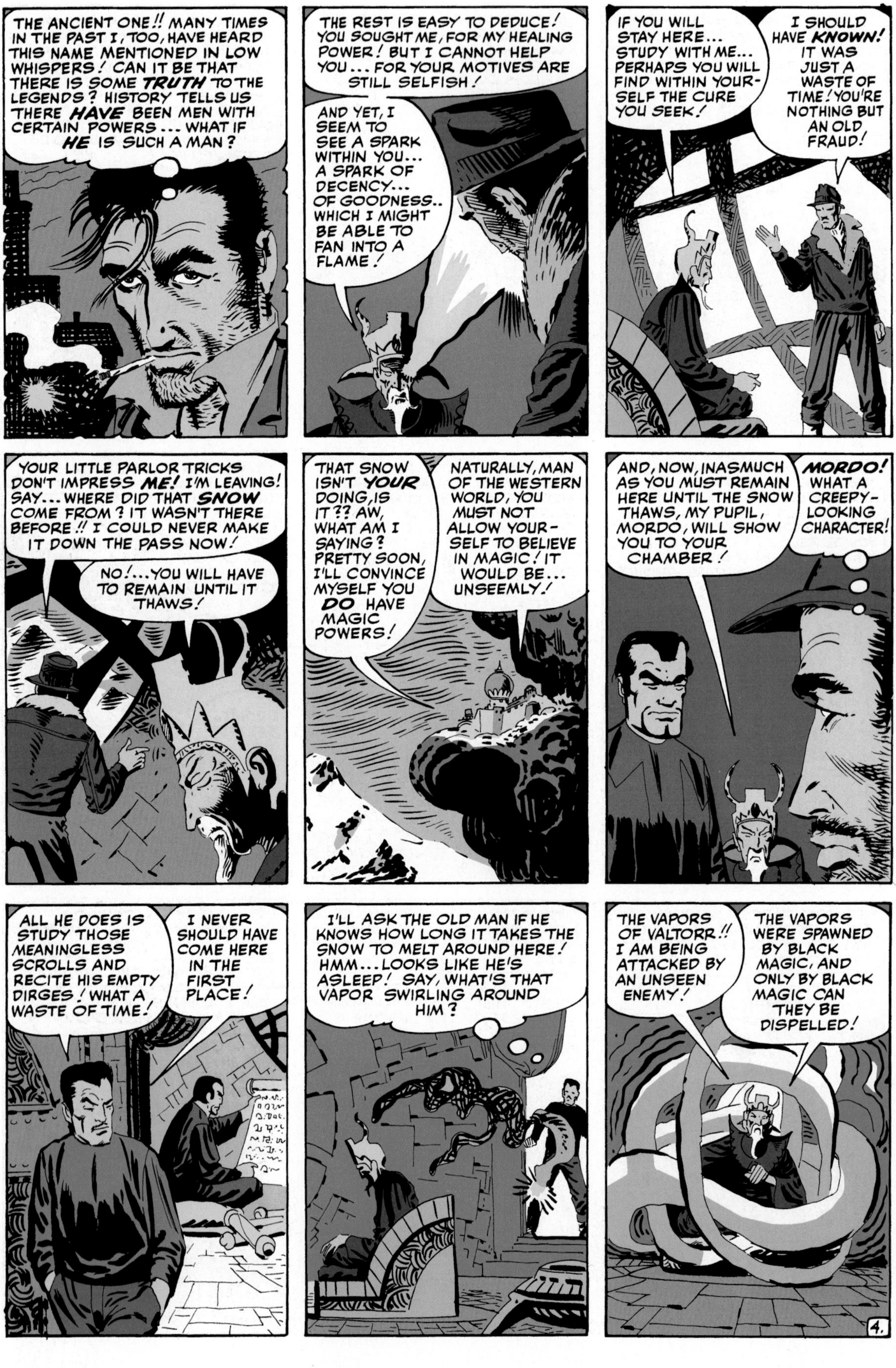

THE ANCIENT ONE!! MANY TIMES IN THE PAST I, TOO, HAVE HEARD THIS NAME MENTIONED IN LOW WHISPERS! CAN IT BE THAT THERE IS SOME TRUTH TO THE LEGENDS? HISTORY TELLS US THERE HAVE BEEN MEN WITH CERTAIN POWERS... WHAT IF HE IS SUCH A MAN?
THE REST IS EASY TO DEDUCE! YOU SOUGHT ME, FOR MY HEALING POWER! BUT I CANNOT HELP YOU... FOR YOUR MOTIVES ARE STILL SELFISH!
AND YET, I SEEM TO SEE A SPARK WITHIN YOU... A SPARK OF DECENCY... OF GOODNESS.. WHICH I MIGHT BE ABLE TO FAN INTO A FLAME!
IF YOU WILL STAY HERE... STUDY WITH ME... PERHAPS YOU WILL FIND WITHIN YOURSELF THE CURE YOU SEEK!
I SHOULD HAVE KNOWN! IT WAS JUST A WASTE OF TIME! YOU'RE NOTHING BUT AN OLD FRAUD!
YOUR LITTLE PARLOR TRICKS DON'T IMPRESS ME! I'M LEAVING! SAY... WHERE DID THAT SNOW COME FROM? IT WASN'T THERE BEFORE!! I COULD NEVER MAKE IT DOWN THE PASS NOW!
NO!... YOU WILL HAVE TO REMAIN UNTIL IT THAWS!
THAT SNOW ISN'T YOUR DOING, IS IT?? AW, WHAT AM I SAYING? PRETTY SOON, I'LL CONVINCE MYSELF YOU DO HAVE MAGIC POWERS!
NATURALLY, MAN OF THE WESTERN WORLD, YOU MUST NOT ALLOW YOURSELF TO BELIEVE IN MAGIC! IT WOULD BE... UNSEEMLY!
AND, NOW, INASMUCH AS YOU MUST REMAIN HERE UNTIL THE SNOW THAWS, MY PUPIL, MORDO, WILL SHOW YOU TO YOUR CHAMBER!
MORDO! WHAT A CREEPY-LOOKING CHARACTER!
ALL HE DOES IS STUDY THOSE MEANINGLESS SCROLLS AND RECITE HIS EMPTY DIRGES! WHAT A WASTE OF TIME!
I NEVER SHOULD HAVE COME HERE IN THE FIRST PLACE!
I'LL ASK THE OLD MAN IF HE KNOWS HOW LONG IT TAKES THE SNOW TO MELT AROUND HERE! HMM... LOOKS LIKE HE'S ASLEEP! SAY, WHAT'S THAT VAPOR SWIRLING AROUND HIM?
THE VAPORS OF VALTORR!! I AM BEING ATTACKED BY AN UNSEEN ENEMY!
THE VAPORS WERE SPAWNED BY BLACK MAGIC, AND ONLY BY BLACK MAGIC CAN THEY BE DISPELLED!
4.

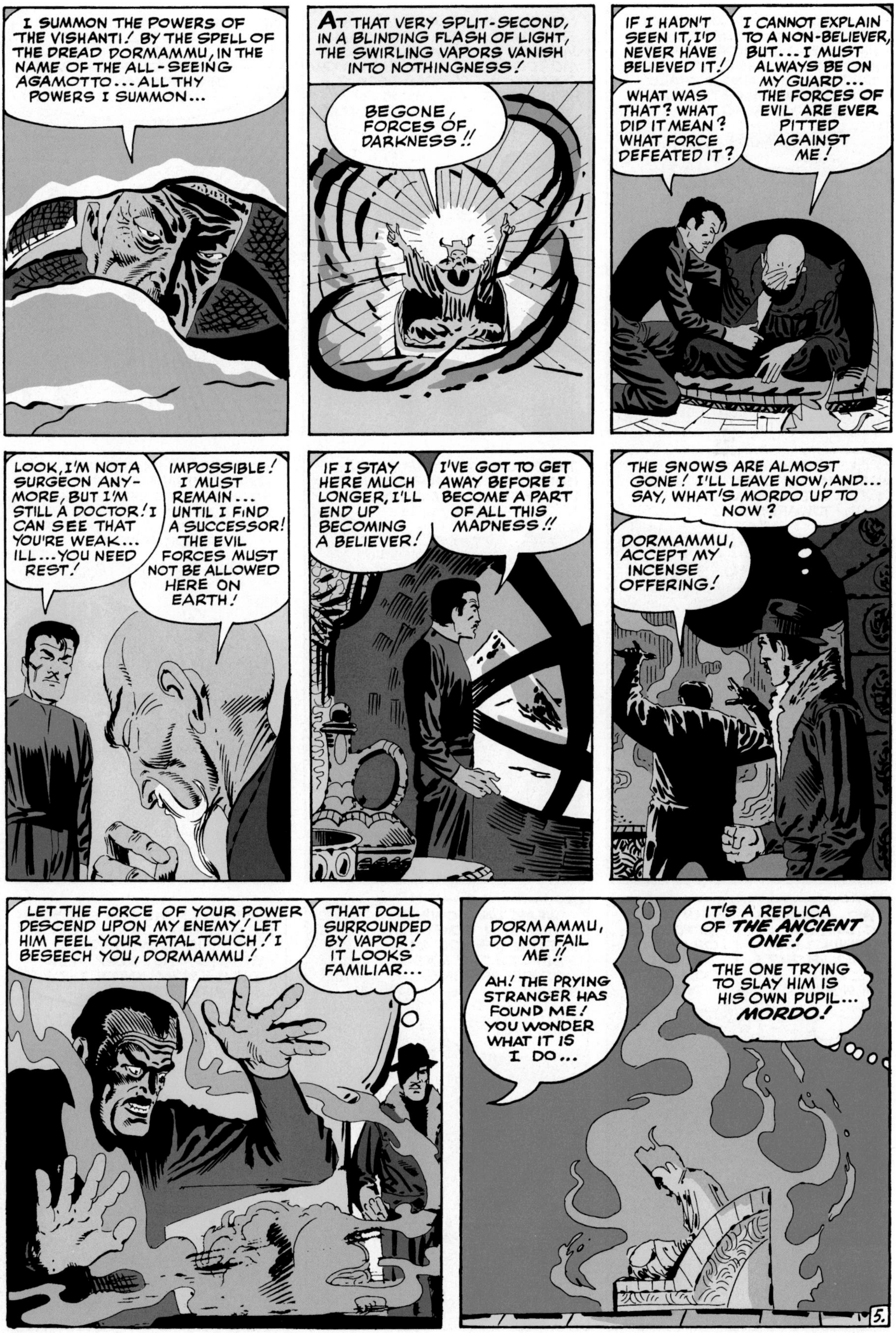
I SUMMON THE POWERS OF THE VISHANTI! BY THE SPELL OF THE DREAD DORMAMMU, IN THE NAME OF THE ALL-SEEING AGAMOTTO... ALL THY POWERS I SUMMON...
AT THAT VERY SPLIT-SECOND, IN A BLINDING FLASH OF LIGHT, THE SWIRLING VAPORS VANISH INTO NOTHINGNESS!
BEGONE, FORCES OF DARKNESS!!
IF I HADN'T SEEN IT, I'D NEVER HAVE BELIEVED IT!
WHAT WAS THAT? WHAT DID IT MEAN? WHAT FORCE DEFEATED IT?
I CANNOT EXPLAIN TO A NON-BELIEVER, BUT... I MUST ALWAYS BE ON MY GUARD... THE FORCES OF EVIL ARE EVER PITTED AGAINST ME!
LOOK, I'M NOT A SURGEON ANYMORE, BUT I'M STILL A DOCTOR! I CAN SEE THAT YOU'RE WEAK... ILL... YOU NEED REST!
IMPOSSIBLE! I MUST REMAIN... UNTIL I FIND A SUCCESSOR! THE EVIL FORCES MUST NOT BE ALLOWED HERE ON EARTH!
IF I STAY HERE MUCH LONGER, I'LL END UP BECOMING A BELIEVER!
I'VE GOT TO GET AWAY BEFORE I BECOME A PART OF ALL THIS MADNESS!!
THE SNOWS ARE ALMOST GONE! I'LL LEAVE NOW, AND... SAY, WHAT'S MORDO UP TO NOW?
DORMAMMU, ACCEPT MY INCENSE OFFERING!
LET THE FORCE OF YOUR POWER DESCEND UPON MY ENEMY! LET HIM FEEL YOUR FATAL TOUCH! I BESEECH YOU, DORMAMMU!
THAT DOLL SURROUNDED BY VAPOR! IT LOOKS FAMILIAR...
DORMAMMU, DO NOT FAIL ME!!
AH! THE PRYING STRANGER HAS FOUND ME! YOU WONDER WHAT IT IS I DO...
IT'S A REPLICA OF THE ANCIENT ONE!
THE ONE TRYING TO SLAY HIM IS HIS OWN PUPIL... MORDO!
5.

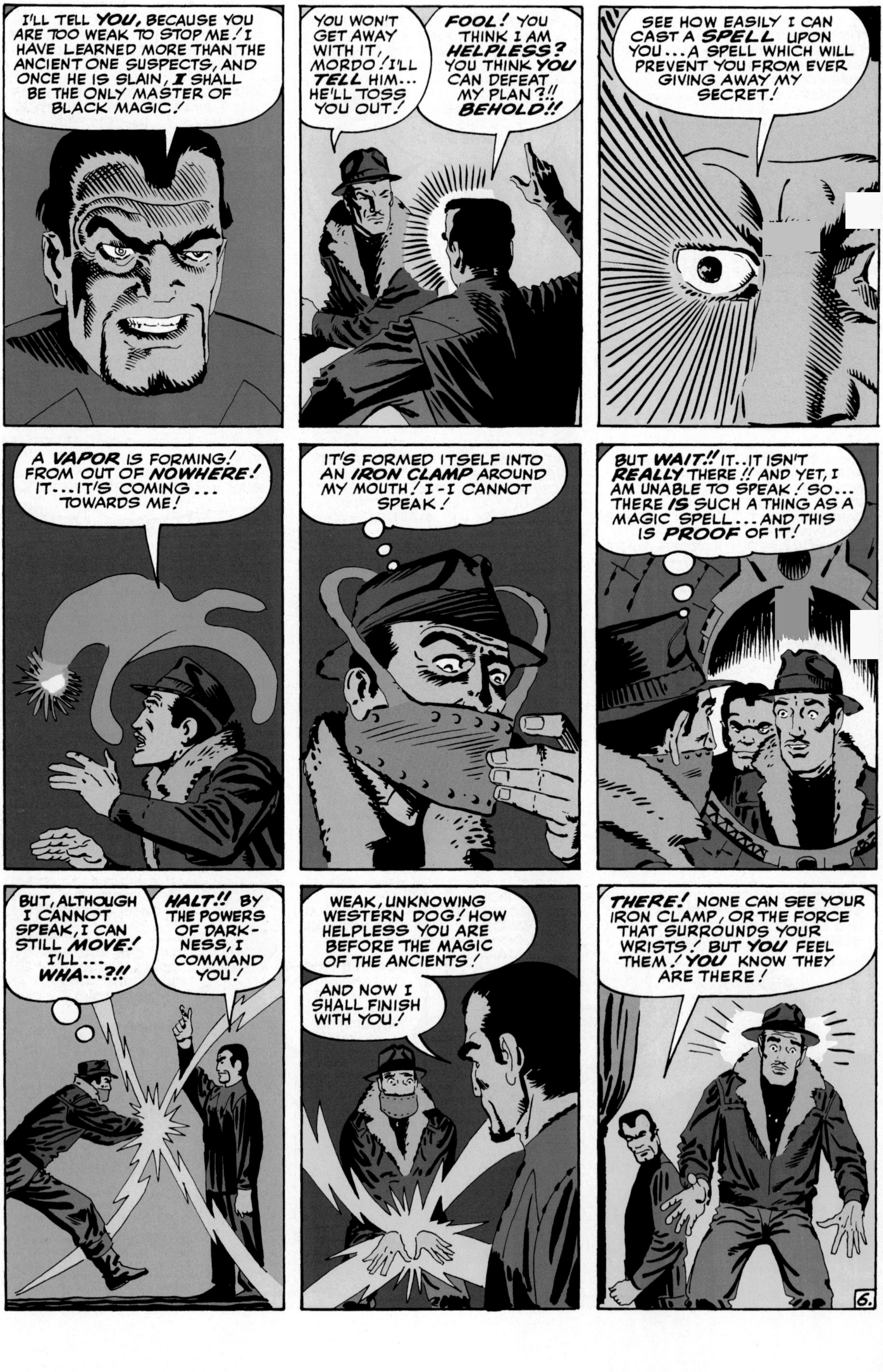

I'LL TELL YOU, BECAUSE YOU ARE TOO WEAK TO STOP ME! I HAVE LEARNED MORE THAN THE ANCIENT ONE SUSPECTS, AND ONCE HE IS SLAIN, I SHALL BE THE ONLY MASTER OF BLACK MAGIC!
YOU WON'T GET AWAY WITH IT, MORDO! I'LL TELL HIM... HE'LL TOSS YOU OUT!
FOOL! YOU THINK I AM HELPLESS? YOU THINK YOU CAN DEFEAT MY PLAN?!! BEHOLD!!
SEE HOW EASILY I CAN CAST A SPELL UPON YOU... A SPELL WHICH WILL PREVENT YOU FROM EVER GIVING AWAY MY SECRET!
A VAPOR IS FORMING! FROM OUT OF NOWHERE! IT...IT'S COMING... TOWARDS ME!
IT'S FORMED ITSELF INTO AN IRON CLAMP AROUND MY MOUTH! I-I CANNOT SPEAK!
BUT WAIT!! IT..IT ISN'T REALLY THERE!! AND YET, I AM UNABLE TO SPEAK! SO... THERE IS SUCH A THING AS A MAGIC SPELL... AND THIS IS PROOF OF IT!
BUT, ALTHOUGH I CANNOT SPEAK, I CAN STILL MOVE! I'LL... WHA...?!!
HALT!! BY THE POWERS OF DARKNESS, I COMMAND YOU!
WEAK, UNKNOWING WESTERN DOG! HOW HELPLESS YOU ARE BEFORE THE MAGIC OF THE ANCIENTS!
AND NOW I SHALL FINISH WITH YOU!
THERE! NONE CAN SEE YOUR IRON CLAMP, OR THE FORCE THAT SURROUNDS YOUR WRISTS! BUT YOU FEEL THEM! YOU KNOW THEY ARE THERE!
6.

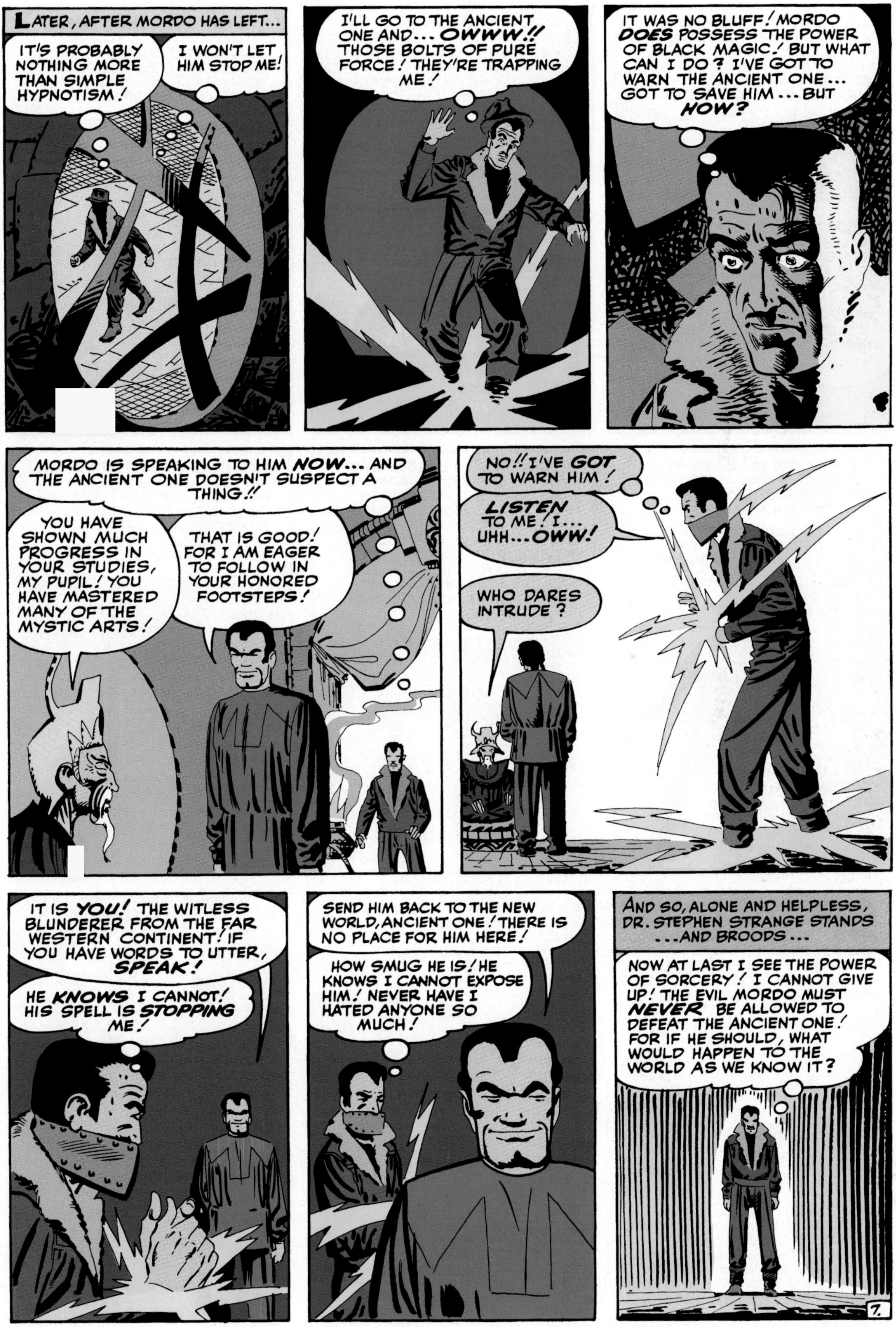
LATER, AFTER MORDO HAS LEFT...
IT'S PROBABLY NOTHING MORE THAN SIMPLE HYPNOTISM!
I WON'T LET HIM STOP ME!
I'LL GO TO THE ANCIENT ONE AND... OWWW!! THOSE BOLTS OF PURE FORCE! THEY'RE TRAPPING ME!
IT WAS NO BLUFF! MORDO DOES POSSESS THE POWER OF BLACK MAGIC! BUT WHAT CAN I DO? I'VE GOT TO WARN THE ANCIENT ONE... GOT TO SAVE HIM... BUT HOW?
MORDO IS SPEAKING TO HIM NOW... AND THE ANCIENT ONE DOESN'T SUSPECT A THING!!
YOU HAVE SHOWN MUCH PROGRESS IN YOUR STUDIES, MY PUPIL! YOU HAVE MASTERED MANY OF THE MYSTIC ARTS!
THAT IS GOOD! FOR I AM EAGER TO FOLLOW IN YOUR HONORED FOOTSTEPS!
NO!! I'VE GOT TO WARN HIM!
LISTEN TO ME! I... UHH...OWW!
WHO DARES INTRUDE?
IT IS YOU! THE WITLESS BLUNDERER FROM THE FAR WESTERN CONTINENT! IF YOU HAVE WORDS TO UTTER, SPEAK!
HE KNOWS I CANNOT! HIS SPELL IS STOPPING ME!
SEND HIM BACK TO THE NEW WORLD, ANCIENT ONE! THERE IS NO PLACE FOR HIM HERE!
HOW SMUG HE IS! HE KNOWS I CANNOT EXPOSE HIM! NEVER HAVE I HATED ANYONE SO MUCH!
AND SO, ALONE AND HELPLESS, DR. STEPHEN STRANGE STANDS ...AND BROODS...
NOW AT LAST I SEE THE POWER OF SORCERY! I CANNOT GIVE UP! THE EVIL MORDO MUST NEVER BE ALLOWED TO DEFEAT THE ANCIENT ONE! FOR IF HE SHOULD, WHAT WOULD HAPPEN TO THE WORLD AS WE KNOW IT?
7.

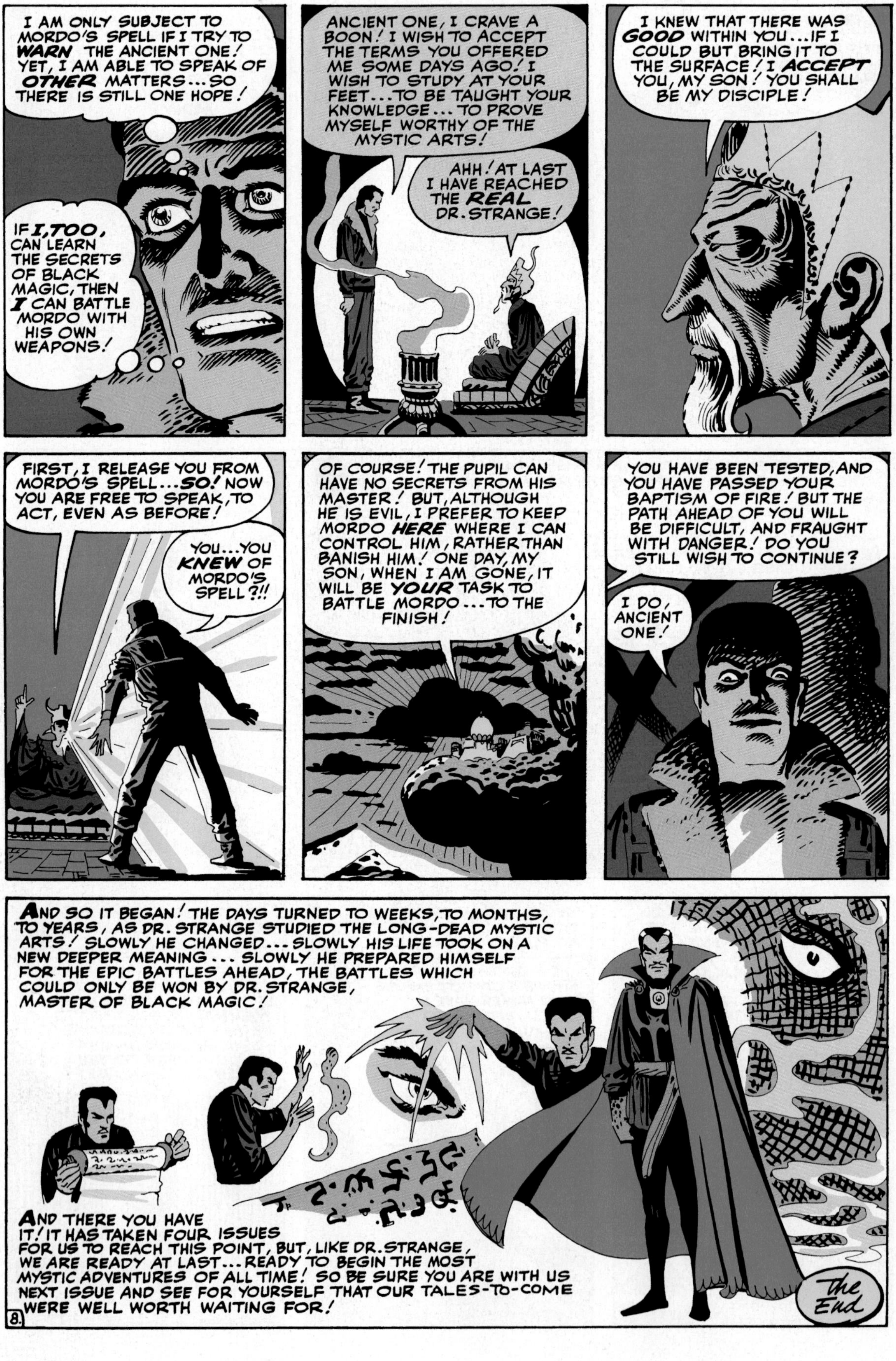
I AM ONLY SUBJECT TO MORDO'S SPELL IF I TRY TO WARN THE ANCIENT ONE! YET, I AM ABLE TO SPEAK OF OTHER MATTERS... SO THERE IS STILL ONE HOPE!
IF I, TOO, CAN LEARN THE SECRETS OF BLACK MAGIC, THEN I CAN BATTLE MORDO WITH HIS OWN WEAPONS!
ANCIENT ONE, I CRAVE A BOON! I WISH TO ACCEPT THE TERMS YOU OFFERED ME SOME DAYS AGO! I WISH TO STUDY AT YOUR FEET... TO BE TAUGHT YOUR KNOWLEDGE... TO PROVE MYSELF WORTHY OF THE MYSTIC ARTS!
AHH! AT LAST I HAVE REACHED THE REAL DR. STRANGE!
I KNEW THAT THERE WAS GOOD WITHIN YOU... IF I COULD BUT BRING IT TO THE SURFACE! I ACCEPT YOU, MY SON! YOU SHALL BE MY DISCIPLE!
FIRST, I RELEASE YOU FROM MORDO'S SPELL... SO! NOW YOU ARE FREE TO SPEAK, TO ACT, EVEN AS BEFORE!
YOU... YOU KNEW OF MORDO'S SPELL?!!
OF COURSE! THE PUPIL CAN HAVE NO SECRETS FROM HIS MASTER! BUT, ALTHOUGH HE IS EVIL, I PREFER TO KEEP MORDO HERE WHERE I CAN CONTROL HIM, RATHER THAN BANISH HIM! ONE DAY, MY SON, WHEN I AM GONE, IT WILL BE YOUR TASK TO BATTLE MORDO... TO THE FINISH!
YOU HAVE BEEN TESTED, AND YOU HAVE PASSED YOUR BAPTISM OF FIRE! BUT THE PATH AHEAD OF YOU WILL BE DIFFICULT, AND FRAUGHT WITH DANGER! DO YOU STILL WISH TO CONTINUE?
I DO, ANCIENT ONE!
AND SO IT BEGAN! THE DAYS TURNED TO WEEKS, TO MONTHS, TO YEARS, AS DR. STRANGE STUDIED THE LONG-DEAD MYSTIC ARTS! SLOWLY HE CHANGED... SLOWLY HIS LIFE TOOK ON A NEW DEEPER MEANING... SLOWLY HE PREPARED HIMSELF FOR THE EPIC BATTLES AHEAD, THE BATTLES WHICH COULD ONLY BE WON BY DR. STRANGE, MASTER OF BLACK MAGIC!
AND THERE YOU HAVE IT! IT HAS TAKEN FOUR ISSUES FOR US TO REACH THIS POINT, BUT, LIKE DR. STRANGE, WE ARE READY AT LAST... READY TO BEGIN THE MOST MYSTIC ADVENTURES OF ALL TIME! SO BE SURE YOU ARE WITH US NEXT ISSUE AND SEE FOR YOURSELF THAT OUR TALES-TO-COME WERE WELL WORTH WAITING FOR!
The End
8.

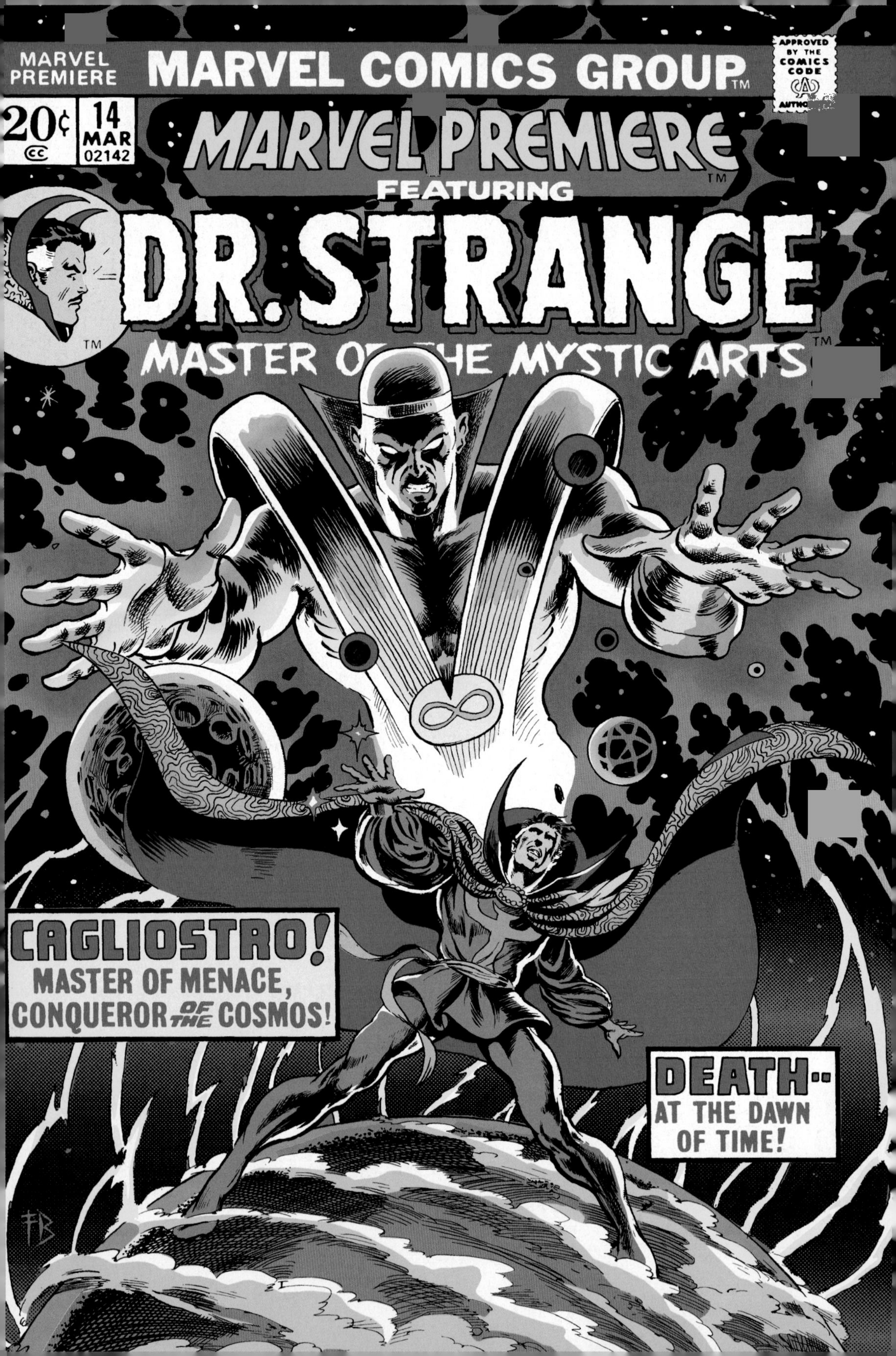

MARVEL PREMIERE
MARVEL COMICS GROUP
APPROVED BY THE COMICS CODE
20¢
14 MAR
02142
MARVEL PREMIERE
FEATURING
DR. STRANGE
MASTER OF THE MYSTIC ARTS
CAGLIOSTRO!
MASTER OF MENACE, CONQUEROR OF THE COSMOS!
DEATH--
AT THE DAWN OF TIME!

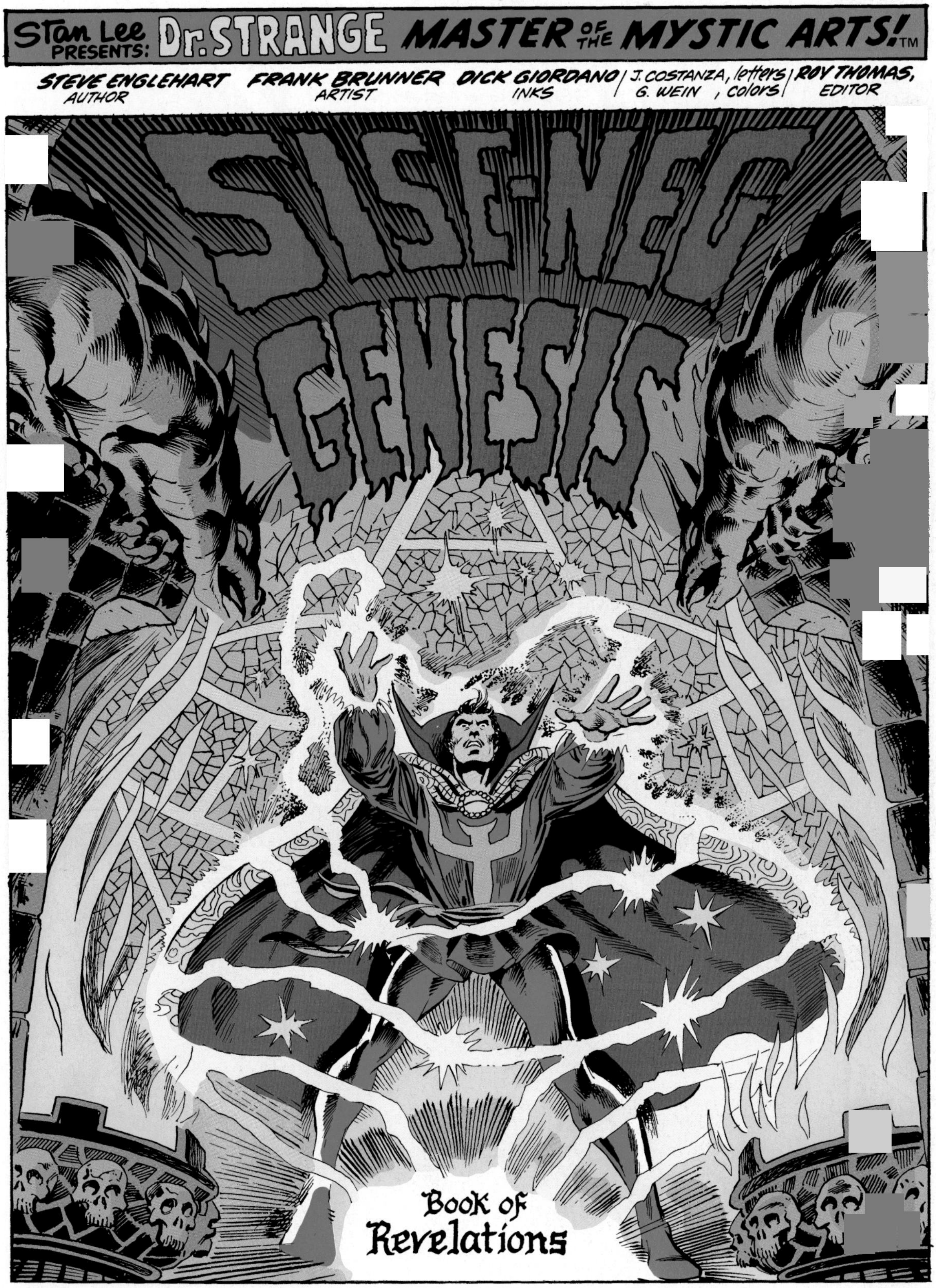

Stan Lee PRESENTS: Dr. STRANGE MASTER OF THE MYSTIC ARTS! TM
STEVE ENGLEHART AUTHOR
FRANK BRUNNER ARTIST
DICK GIORDANO INKS
J. COSTANZA, letters
G. WEIN, colors
ROY THOMAS, EDITOR
SISE-NEG GENESIS
Book of Revelations

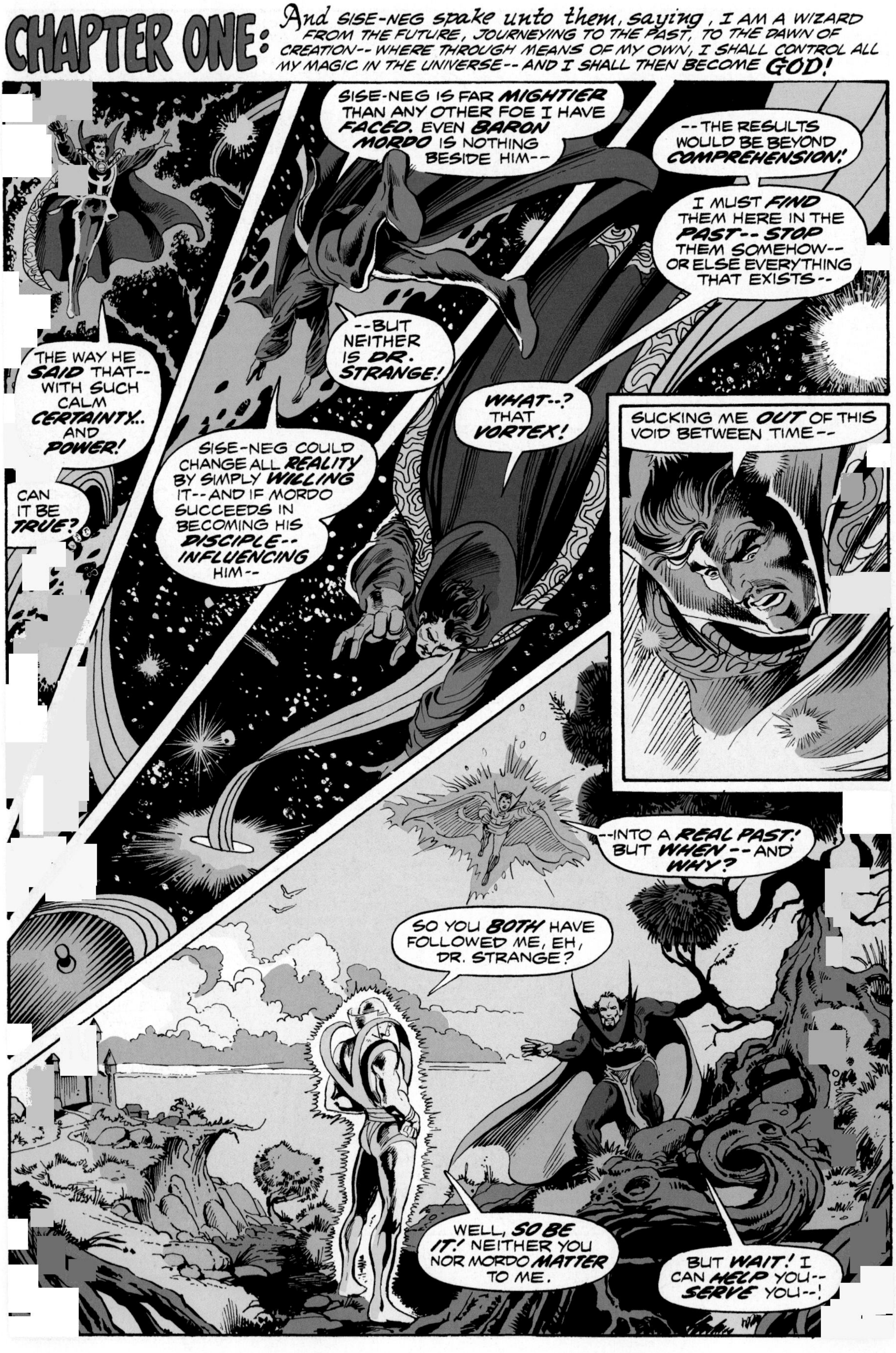
CHAPTER ONE:
And SISE-NEG spake unto them, saying, I AM A WIZARD FROM THE FUTURE, JOURNEYING TO THE PAST, TO THE DAWN OF CREATION-- WHERE THROUGH MEANS OF MY OWN, I SHALL CONTROL ALL MY MAGIC IN THE UNIVERSE-- AND I SHALL THEN BECOME GOD!
THE WAY HE SAID THAT-- WITH SUCH CALM CERTAINTY.. AND POWER!
CAN IT BE TRUE?
SISE-NEG IS FAR MIGHTIER THAN ANY OTHER FOE I HAVE FACED. EVEN BARON MORDO IS NOTHING BESIDE HIM--
--BUT NEITHER IS DR. STRANGE!
SISE-NEG COULD CHANGE ALL REALITY BY SIMPLY WILLING IT--AND IF MORDO SUCCEEDS IN BECOMING HIS DISCIPLE--INFLUENCING HIM--
--THE RESULTS WOULD BE BEYOND COMPREHENSION!
I MUST FIND THEM HERE IN THE PAST-- STOP THEM SOMEHOW-- OR ELSE EVERYTHING THAT EXISTS--
WHAT--? THAT VORTEX!
SUCKING ME OUT OF THIS VOID BETWEEN TIME--
--INTO A REAL PAST! BUT WHEN -- AND WHY?
SO YOU BOTH HAVE FOLLOWED ME, EH, DR. STRANGE?
WELL, SO BE IT! NEITHER YOU NOR MORDO MATTER TO ME.
BUT WAIT! I CAN HELP YOU-- SERVE YOU--!

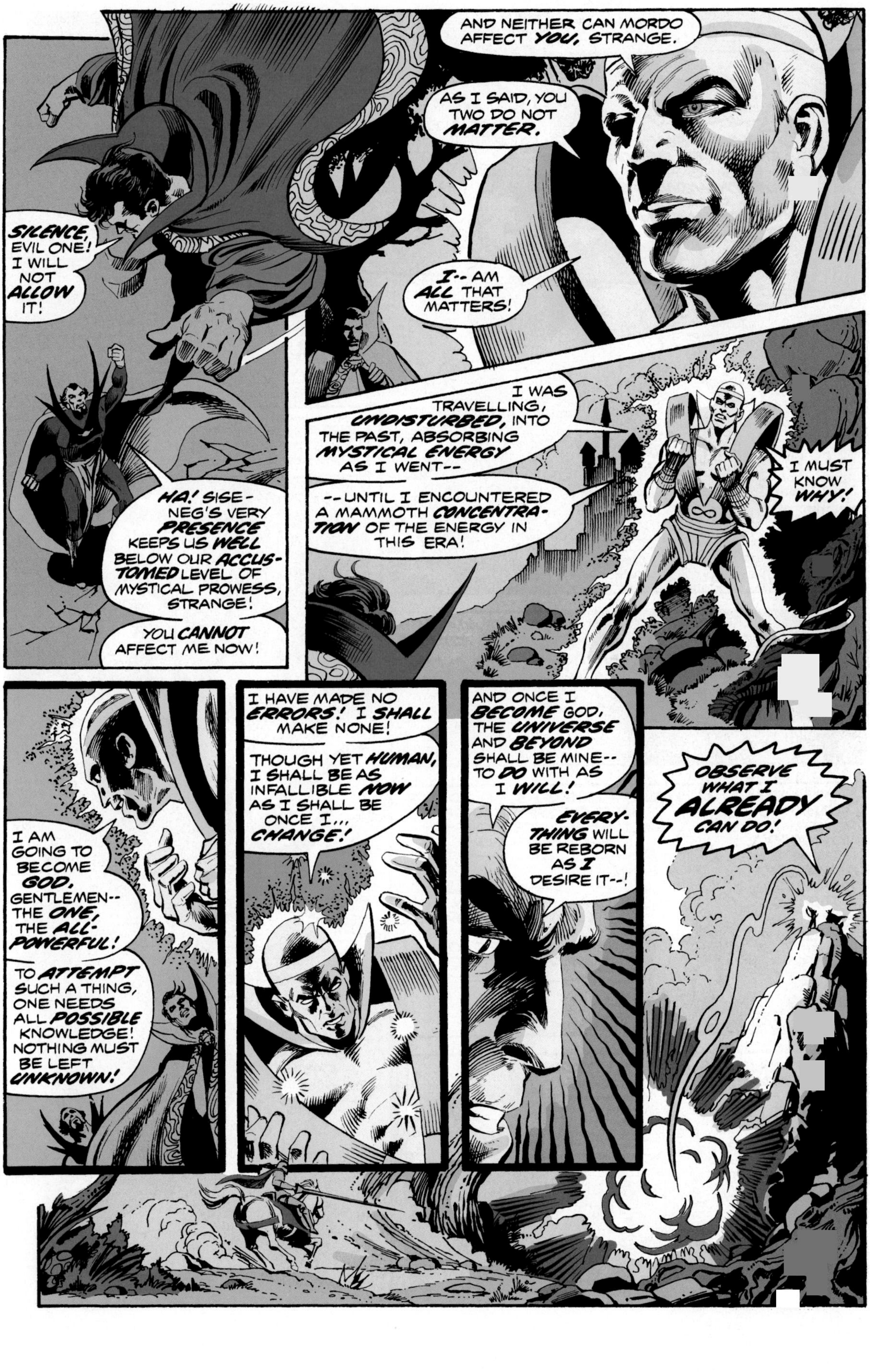
SILENCE, EVIL ONE! I WILL NOT ALLOW IT!
HA! SISENEG'S VERY PRESENCE KEEPS US WELL BELOW OUR ACCUSTOMED LEVEL OF MYSTICAL PROWESS, STRANGE!
YOU CANNOT AFFECT ME NOW!
AND NEITHER CAN MORDO AFFECT YOU, STRANGE.
AS I SAID, YOU TWO DO NOT MATTER.
I-- AM ALL THAT MATTERS!
I WAS TRAVELLING, UNDISTURBED, INTO THE PAST, ABSORBING MYSTICAL ENERGY AS I WENT--
--UNTIL I ENCOUNTERED A MAMMOTH CONCENTRATION OF THE ENERGY IN THIS ERA!
I MUST KNOW WHY!
I AM GOING TO BECOME GOD, GENTLEMEN-- THE ONE, THE ALL-POWERFUL!
TO ATTEMPT SUCH A THING, ONE NEEDS ALL POSSIBLE KNOWLEDGE! NOTHING MUST BE LEFT UNKNOWN!
I HAVE MADE NO ERRORS! I SHALL MAKE NONE!
THOUGH YET HUMAN, I SHALL BE AS INFALLIBLE NOW AS I SHALL BE ONCE I... CHANGE!
AND ONCE I BECOME GOD, THE UNIVERSE AND BEYOND SHALL BE MINE-- TO DO WITH AS I WILL!
EVERYTHING WILL BE REBORN AS I DESIRE IT--!
OBSERVE WHAT I ALREADY CAN DO!

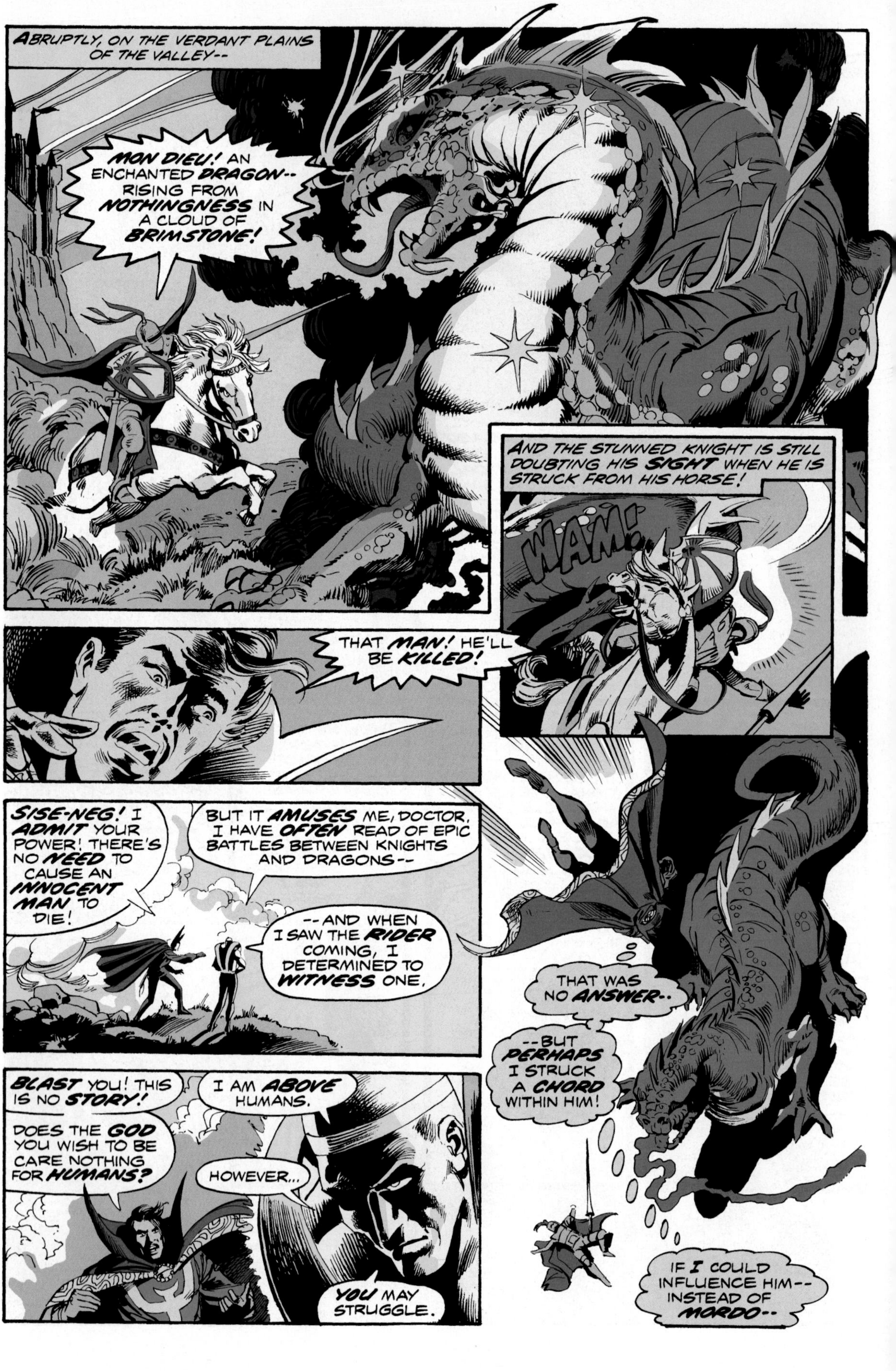
ABRUPTLY, ON THE VERDANT PLAINS OF THE VALLEY--
MON DIEU! AN ENCHANTED DRAGON-- RISING FROM NOTHINGNESS IN A CLOUD OF BRIMSTONE!
AND THE STUNNED KNIGHT IS STILL DOUBTING HIS SIGHT WHEN HE IS STRUCK FROM HIS HORSE!
WAM!
THAT MAN! HE'LL BE KILLED!
SISE-NEG! I ADMIT YOUR POWER! THERE'S NO NEED TO CAUSE AN INNOCENT MAN TO DIE!
BUT IT AMUSES ME, DOCTOR. I HAVE OFTEN READ OF EPIC BATTLES BETWEEN KNIGHTS AND DRAGONS--
--AND WHEN I SAW THE RIDER COMING, I DETERMINED TO WITNESS ONE.
THAT WAS NO ANSWER--
--BUT PERHAPS I STRUCK A CHORD WITHIN HIM!
BLAST YOU! THIS IS NO STORY!
DOES THE GOD YOU WISH TO BE CARE NOTHING FOR HUMANS?
I AM ABOVE HUMANS.
HOWEVER...
YOU MAY STRUGGLE.
IF I COULD INFLUENCE HIM-- INSTEAD OF MORDO--

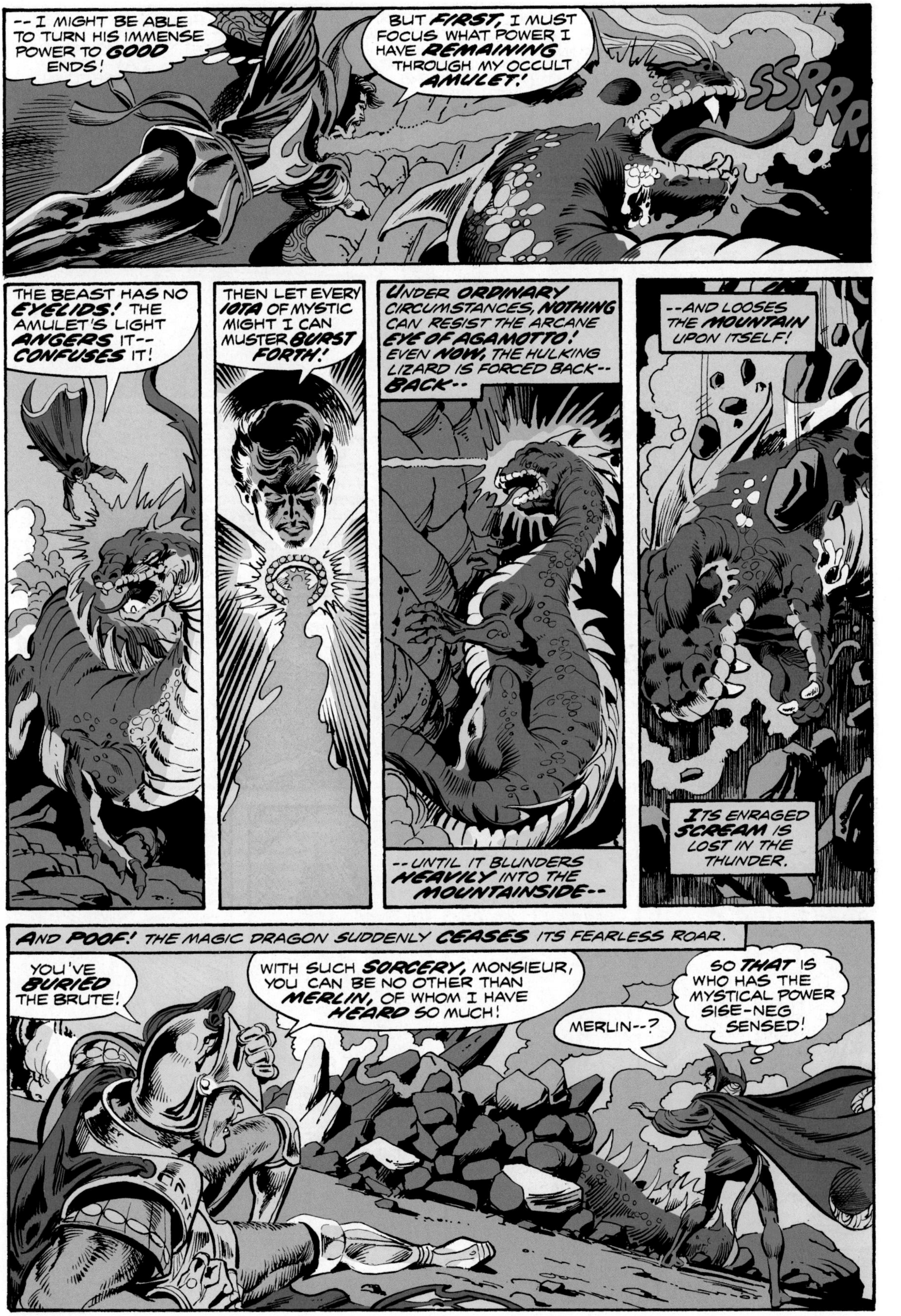

-- I MIGHT BE ABLE TO TURN HIS IMMENSE POWER TO GOOD ENDS!
BUT FIRST, I MUST FOCUS WHAT POWER I HAVE REMAINING THROUGH MY OCCULT AMULET!
SSRRR
THE BEAST HAS NO EYELIDS! THE AMULET'S LIGHT ANGERS IT-- CONFUSES IT!
THEN LET EVERY IOTA OF MYSTIC MIGHT I CAN MUSTER BURST FORTH!
UNDER ORDINARY CIRCUMSTANCES, NOTHING CAN RESIST THE ARCANE EYE OF AGAMOTTO! EVEN NOW, THE HULKING LIZARD IS FORCED BACK-- BACK--
--UNTIL IT BLUNDERS HEAVILY INTO THE MOUNTAINSIDE--
--AND LOOSES THE MOUNTAIN UPON ITSELF!
ITS ENRAGED SCREAM IS LOST IN THE THUNDER.
AND POOF! THE MAGIC DRAGON SUDDENLY CEASES ITS FEARLESS ROAR.
YOU'VE BURIED THE BRUTE!
WITH SUCH SORCERY, MONSIEUR, YOU CAN BE NO OTHER THAN MERLIN, OF WHOM I HAVE HEARD SO MUCH!
MERLIN--?
SO THAT IS WHO HAS THE MYSTICAL POWER SISE-NEG SENSED!

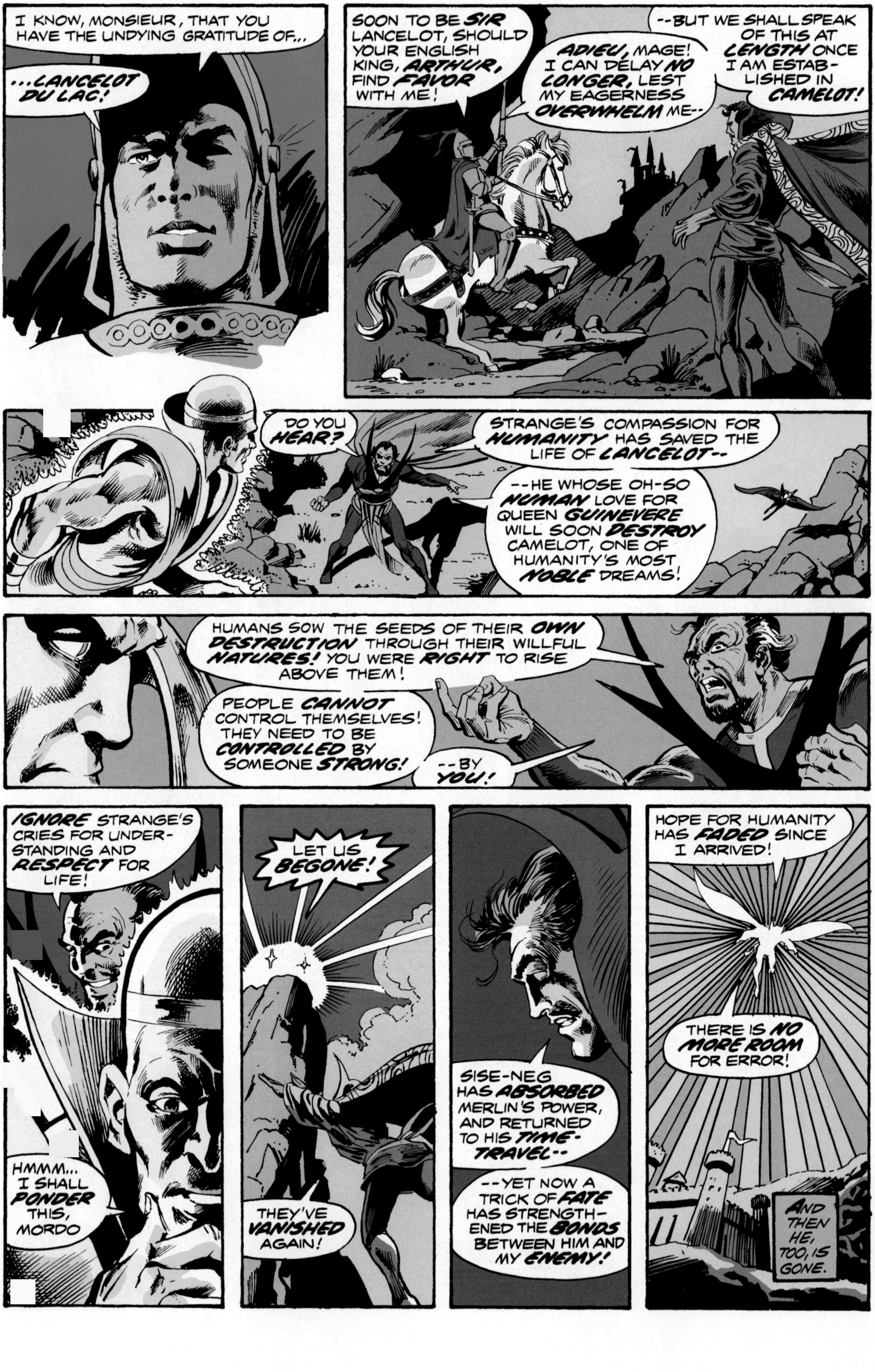
I KNOW, MONSIEUR, THAT YOU HAVE THE UNDYING GRATITUDE OF...
...LANCELOT DU LAC!
SOON TO BE SIR LANCELOT, SHOULD YOUR ENGLISH KING, ARTHUR, FIND FAVOR WITH ME!
ADIEU, MAGE! I CAN DELAY NO LONGER, LEST MY EAGERNESS OVERWHELM ME--
--BUT WE SHALL SPEAK OF THIS AT LENGTH ONCE I AM ESTABLISHED IN CAMELOT!
DO YOU HEAR?
STRANGE'S COMPASSION FOR HUMANITY HAS SAVED THE LIFE OF LANCELOT--
--HE WHOSE OH-SO HUMAN LOVE FOR QUEEN GUINEVERE WILL SOON DESTROY CAMELOT, ONE OF HUMANITY'S MOST NOBLE DREAMS!
HUMANS SOW THE SEEDS OF THEIR OWN DESTRUCTION THROUGH THEIR WILLFUL NATURES! YOU WERE RIGHT TO RISE ABOVE THEM!
PEOPLE CANNOT CONTROL THEMSELVES! THEY NEED TO BE CONTROLLED BY SOMEONE STRONG!
--BY YOU!
IGNORE STRANGE'S CRIES FOR UNDERSTANDING AND RESPECT FOR LIFE!
HMMM... I SHALL PONDER THIS, MORDO
LET US BEGONE!
THEY'VE VANISHED AGAIN!
SISE-NEG HAS ABSORBED MERLIN'S POWER, AND RETURNED TO HIS TIME-TRAVEL--
--YET NOW A TRICK OF FATE HAS STRENGTHENED THE BONDS BETWEEN HIM AND MY ENEMY!
HOPE FOR HUMANITY HAS FADED SINCE I ARRIVED!
THERE IS NO MORE ROOM FOR ERROR!
AND THEN HE, TOO, IS GONE.

CHAPTER TWO:

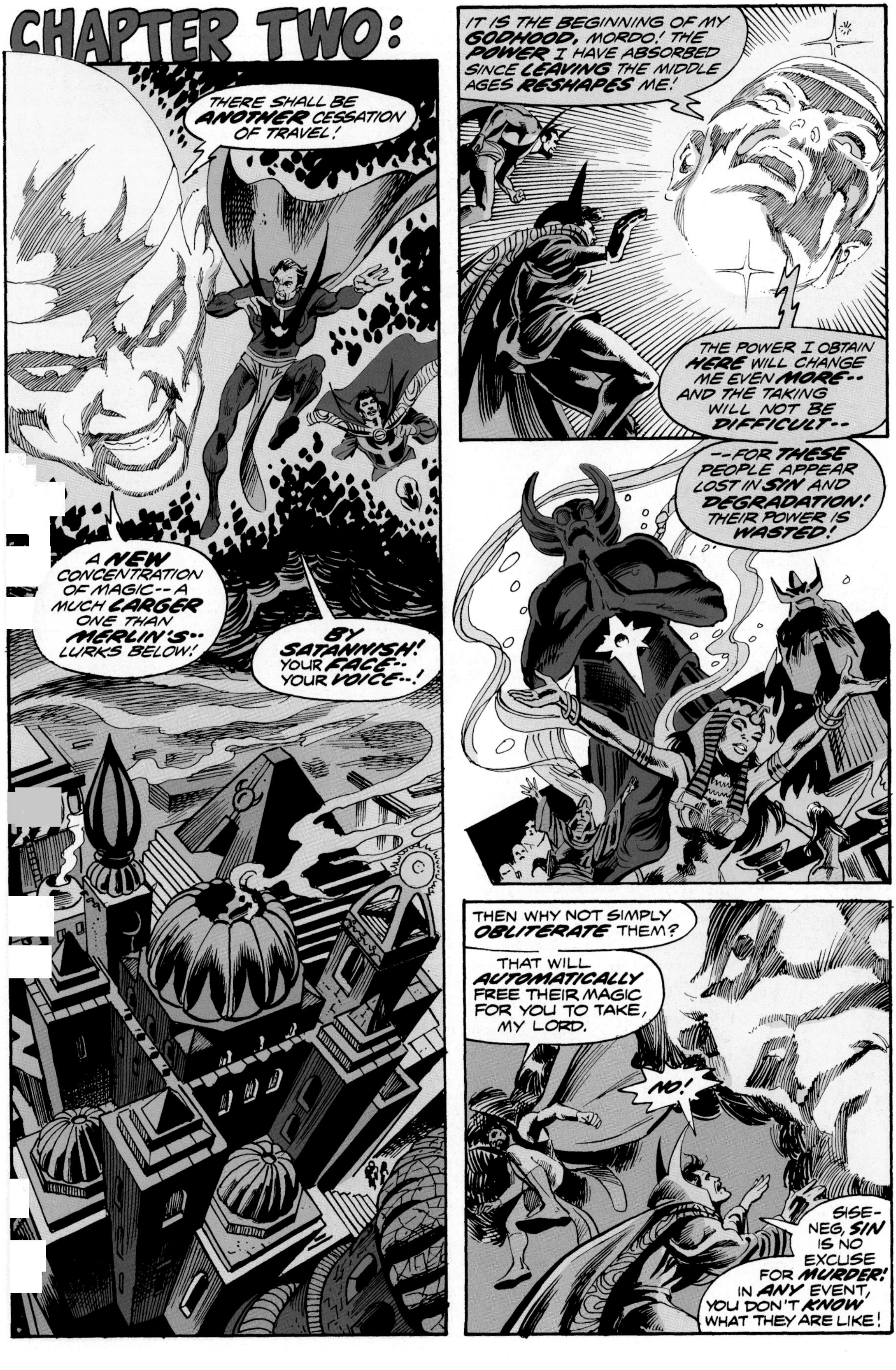
THERE SHALL BE ANOTHER CESSATION OF TRAVEL!
A NEW CONCENTRATION OF MAGIC--A MUCH LARGER ONE THAN MERLIN'S--LURKS BELOW!
BY SATANNISH! YOUR FACE--YOUR VOICE--!
IT IS THE BEGINNING OF MY GODHOOD, MORDO! THE POWER I HAVE ABSORBED SINCE LEAVING THE MIDDLE AGES RESHAPES ME!
THE POWER I OBTAIN HERE WILL CHANGE ME EVEN MORE--AND THE TAKING WILL NOT BE DIFFICULT--
--FOR THESE PEOPLE APPEAR LOST IN SIN AND DEGRADATION! THEIR POWER IS WASTED!
THEN WHY NOT SIMPLY OBLITERATE THEM?
THAT WILL AUTOMATICALLY FREE THEIR MAGIC FOR YOU TO TAKE, MY LORD.
NO!
SISENEG, SIN IS NO EXCUSE FOR MURDER! IN ANY EVENT, YOU DON'T KNOW WHAT THEY ARE LIKE!

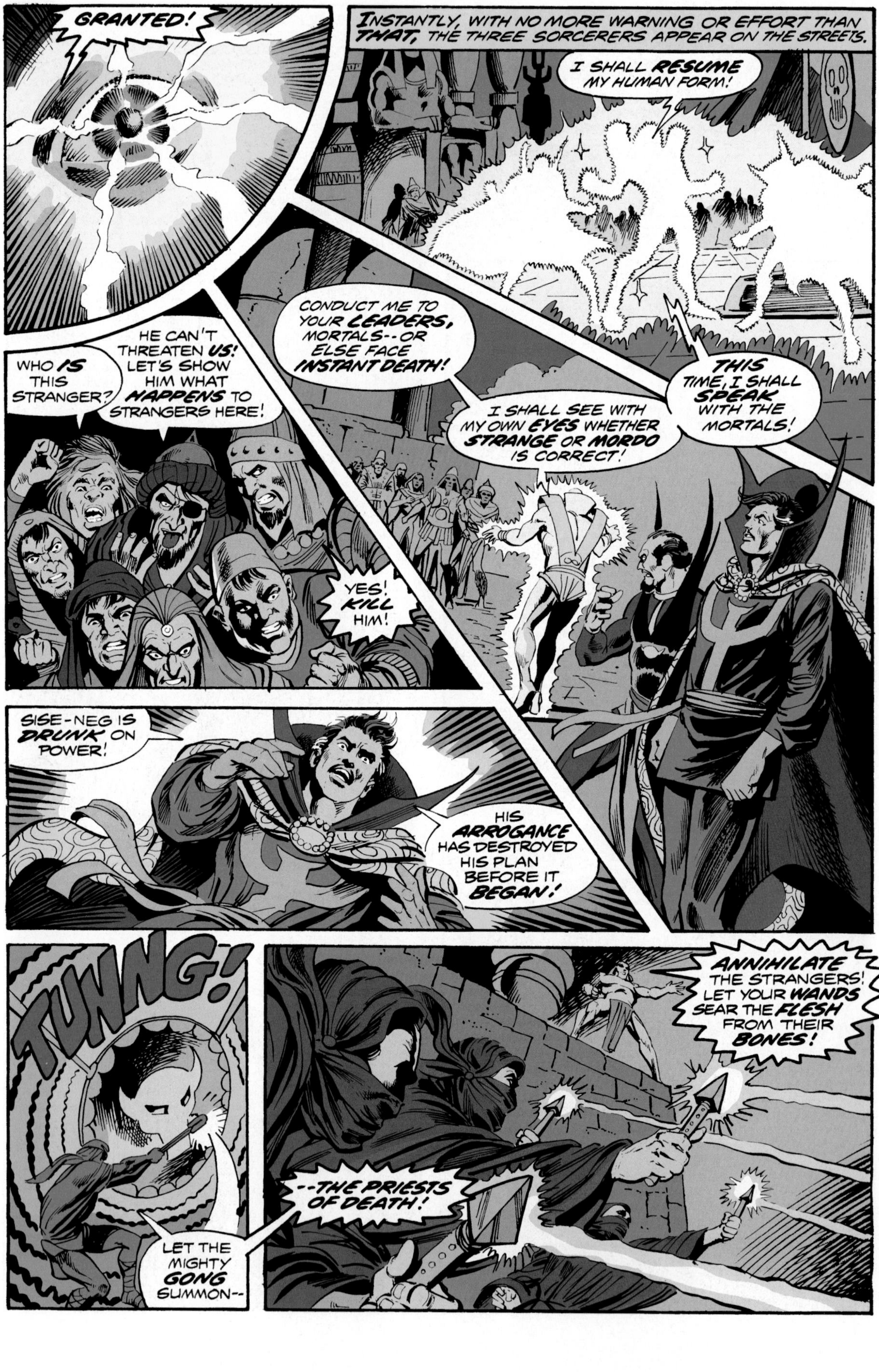

GRANTED!
INSTANTLY, WITH NO MORE WARNING OR EFFORT THAN THAT, THE THREE SORCERERS APPEAR ON THE STREETS.
I SHALL RESUME MY HUMAN FORM!
THIS TIME, I SHALL SPEAK WITH THE MORTALS!
CONDUCT ME TO YOUR LEADERS, MORTALS--OR ELSE FACE INSTANT DEATH!
I SHALL SEE WITH MY OWN EYES WHETHER STRANGE OR MORDO IS CORRECT!
WHO IS THIS STRANGER?
HE CAN'T THREATEN US! LET'S SHOW HIM WHAT HAPPENS TO STRANGERS HERE!
YES! KILL HIM!
SISE-NEG IS DRUNK ON POWER!
HIS ARROGANCE HAS DESTROYED HIS PLAN BEFORE IT BEGAN!
TUNNG!
LET THE MIGHTY GONG SUMMON--
--THE PRIESTS OF DEATH!
ANNIHILATE THE STRANGERS! LET YOUR WANDS SEAR THE FLESH FROM THEIR BONES!

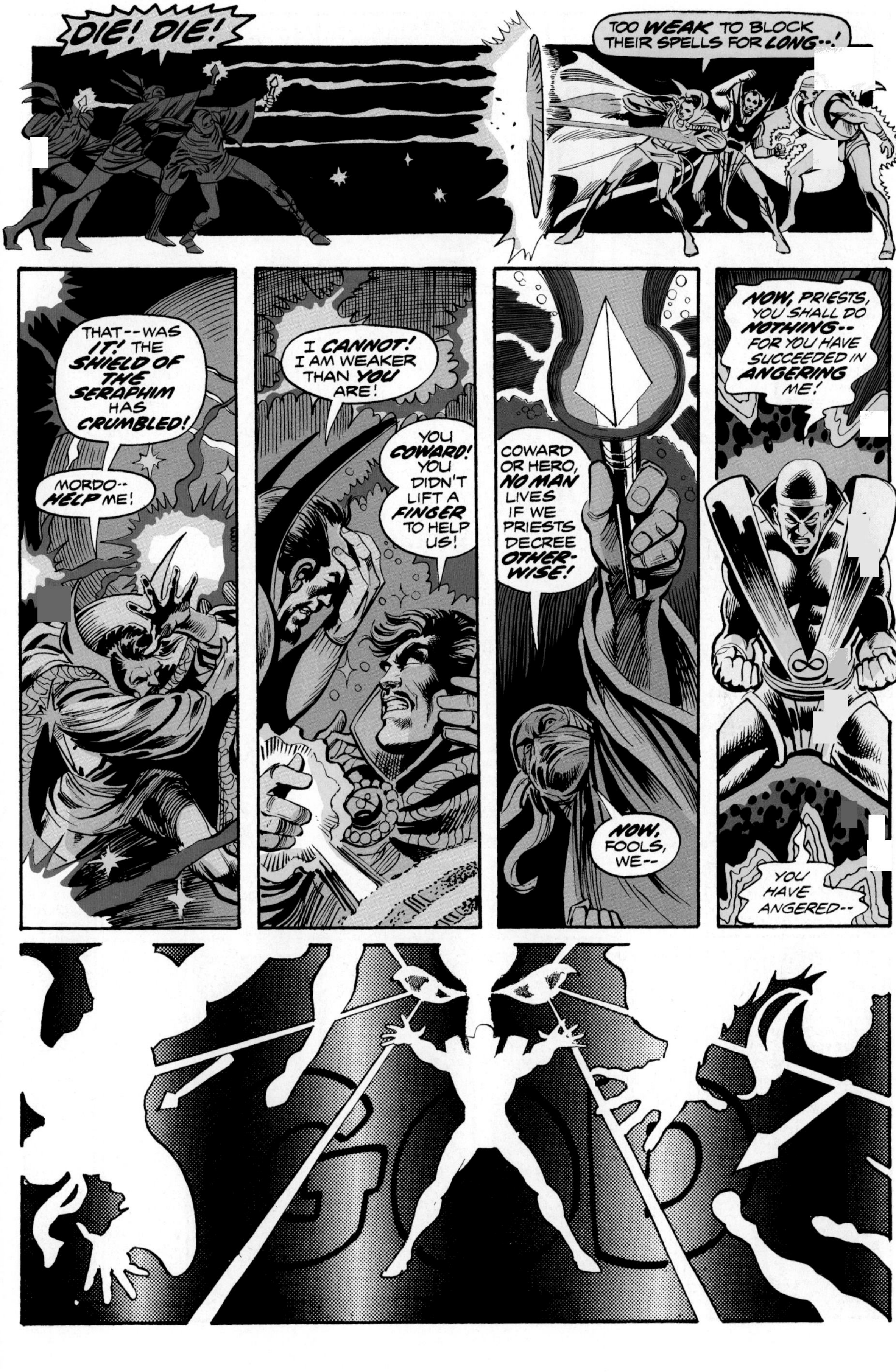
DIE! DIE!
TOO WEAK TO BLOCK THEIR SPELLS FOR LONG..!
THAT--WAS IT! THE SHIELD OF THE SERAPHIM HAS CRUMBLED!
MORDO--HELP ME!
I CANNOT! I AM WEAKER THAN YOU ARE!
YOU COWARD! YOU DIDN'T LIFT A FINGER TO HELP US!
COWARD OR HERO, NO MAN LIVES IF WE PRIESTS DECREE OTHERWISE!
NOW, FOOLS, WE--
NOW, PRIESTS, YOU SHALL DO NOTHING--FOR YOU HAVE SUCCEEDED IN ANGERING ME!
YOU HAVE ANGERED--

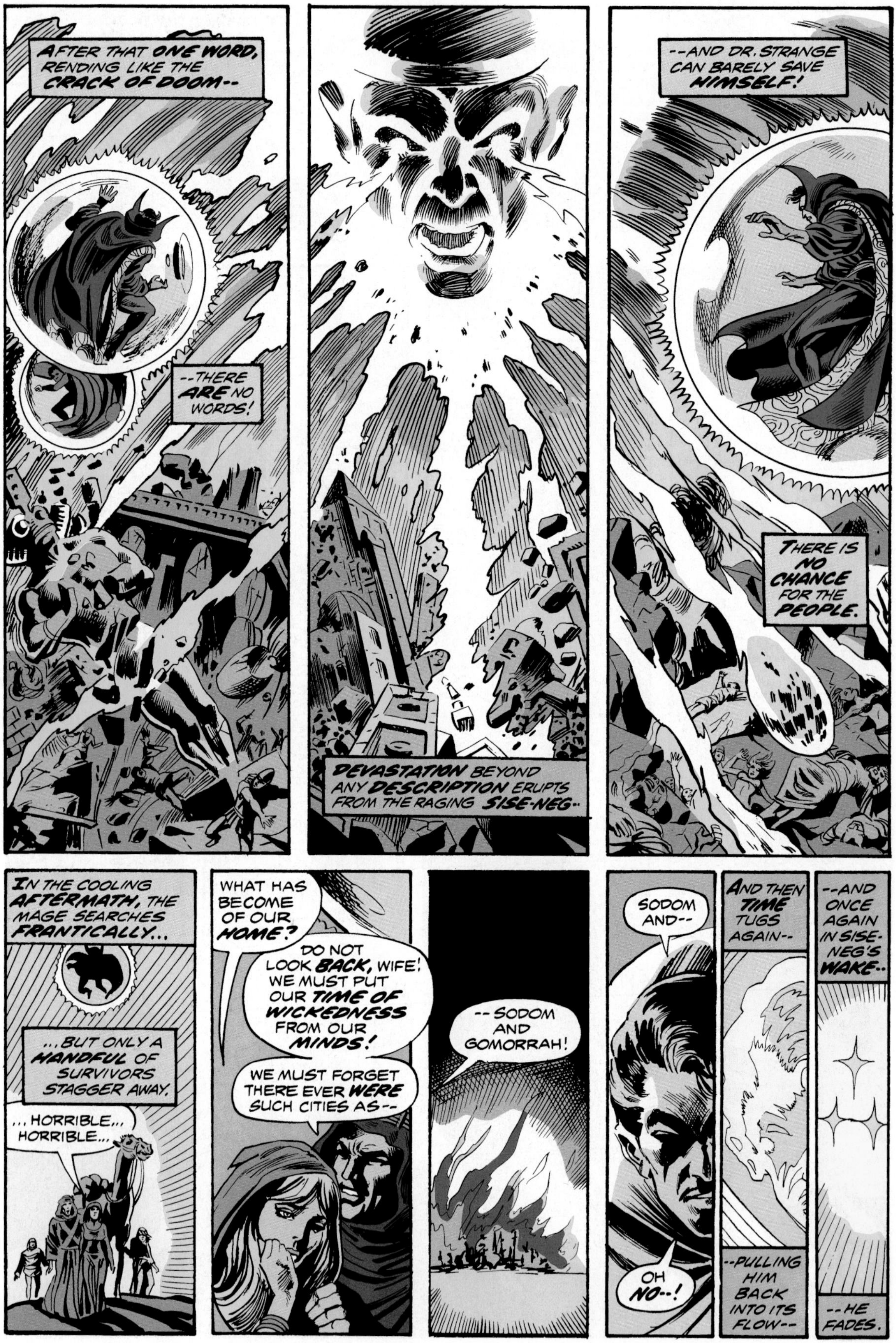
AFTER THAT ONE WORD, RENDING LIKE THE CRACK OF DOOM--
--THERE ARE NO WORDS!
DEVASTATION BEYOND ANY DESCRIPTION ERUPTS FROM THE RAGING SISE-NEG..
--AND DR. STRANGE CAN BARELY SAVE HIMSELF!
THERE IS NO CHANCE FOR THE PEOPLE.
IN THE COOLING AFTERMATH, THE MAGE SEARCHES FRANTICALLY...
...BUT ONLY A HANDFUL OF SURVIVORS STAGGER AWAY.
...HORRIBLE... HORRIBLE...
WHAT HAS BECOME OF OUR HOME?
DO NOT LOOK BACK, WIFE! WE MUST PUT OUR TIME OF WICKEDNESS FROM OUR MINDS!
WE MUST FORGET THERE EVER WERE SUCH CITIES AS--
--SODOM AND GOMORRAH!
SODOM AND--
OH NO--!
AND THEN TIME TUGS AGAIN--
--PULLING HIM BACK INTO ITS FLOW--
--AND ONCE AGAIN IN SISE-NEG'S WAKE..
--HE FADES.

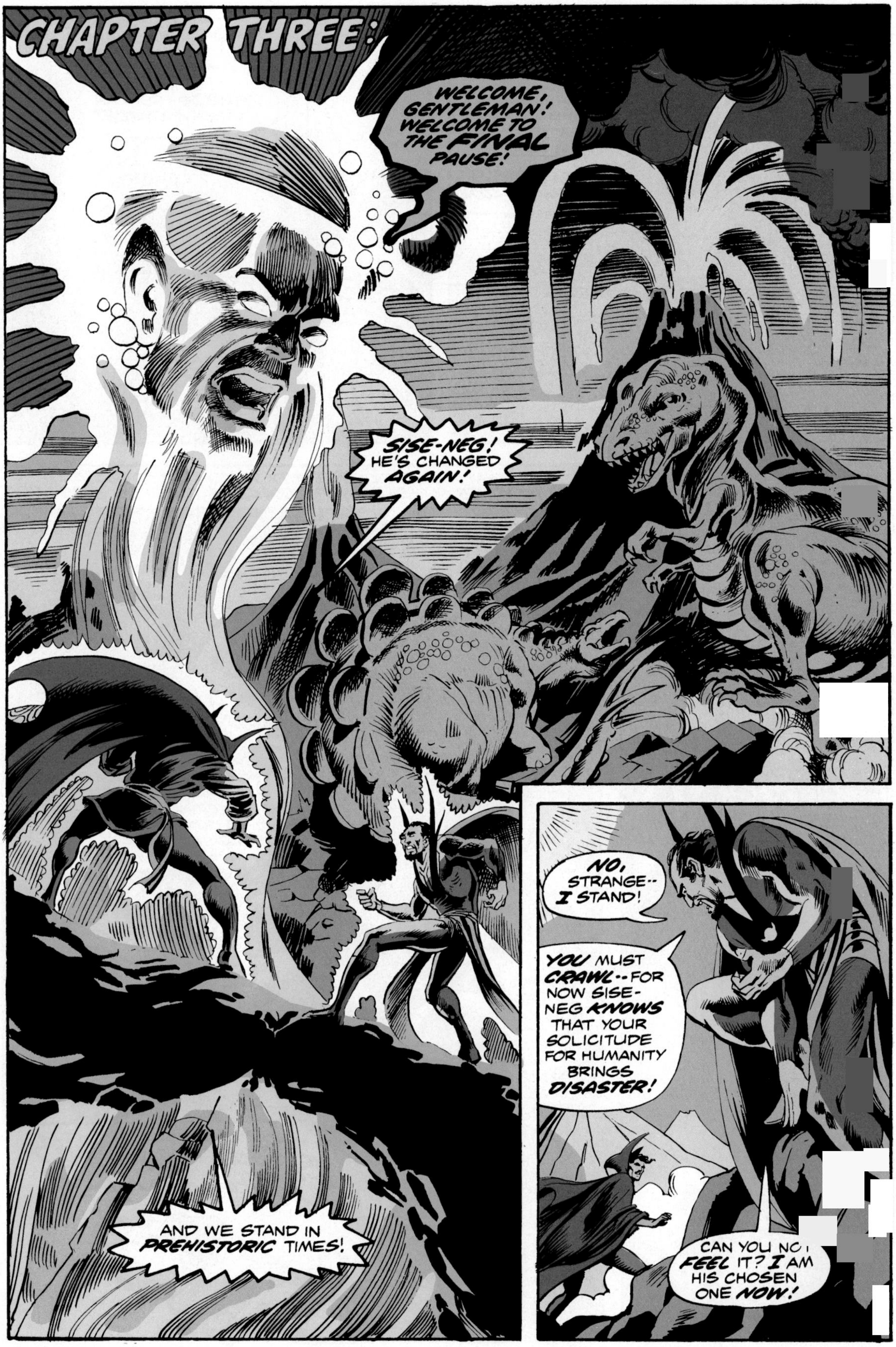
CHAPTER THREE:
WELCOME, GENTLEMAN! WELCOME TO THE FINAL PAUSE!
SISE-NEG! HE'S CHANGED AGAIN!
AND WE STAND IN PREHISTORIC TIMES!
NO, STRANGE-- I STAND!
YOU MUST CRAWL-- FOR NOW SISE-NEG KNOWS THAT YOUR SOLICITUDE FOR HUMANITY BRINGS DISASTER!
CAN YOU NOT FEEL IT? I AM HIS CHOSEN ONE NOW!

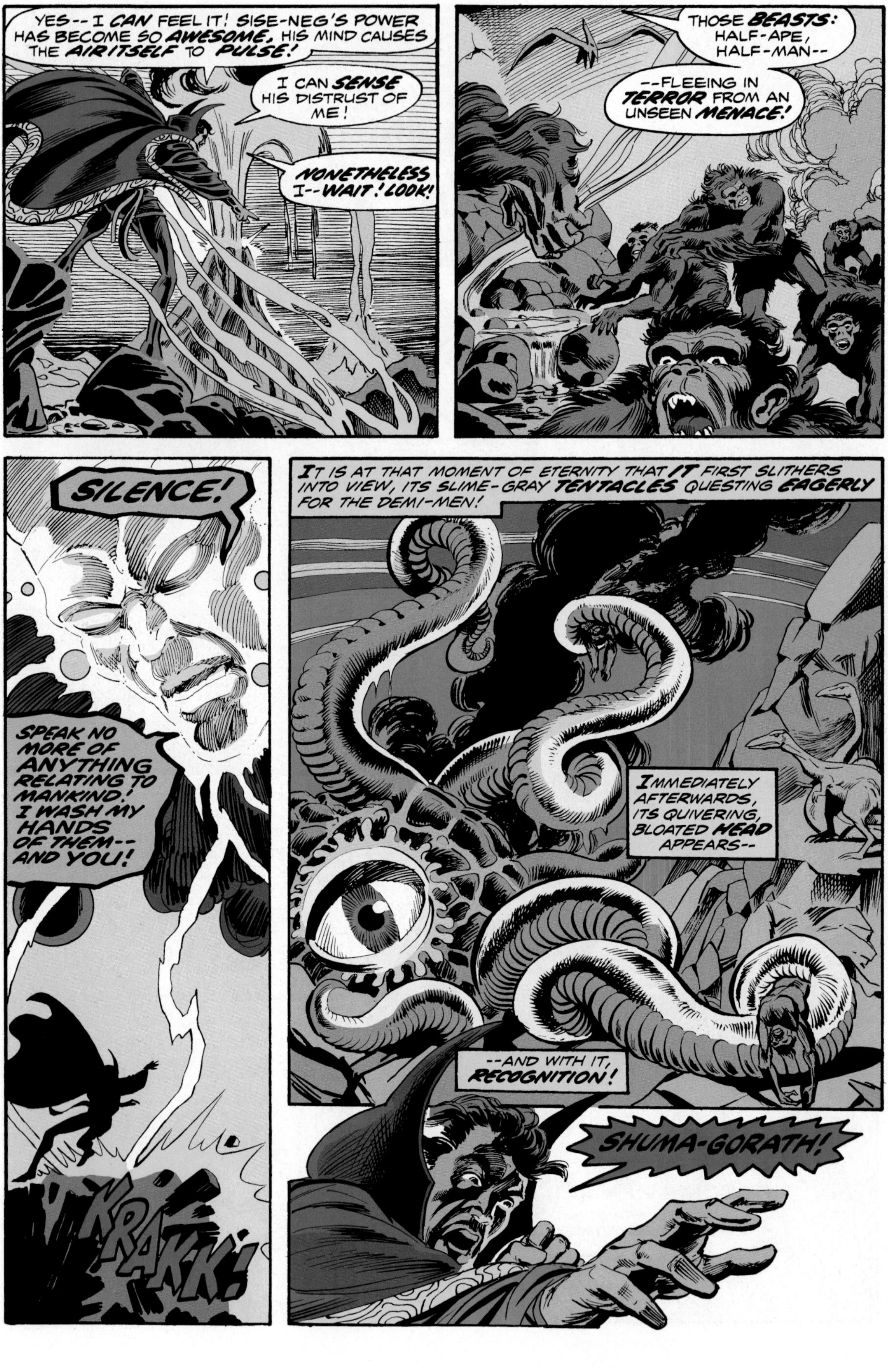
YES--I CAN FEEL IT! SISE-NEG'S POWER HAS BECOME SO AWESOME, HIS MIND CAUSES THE AIR ITSELF TO PULSE!
I CAN SENSE HIS DISTRUST OF ME!
NONETHELESS I--WAIT! LOOK!
THOSE BEASTS: HALF-APE, HALF-MAN--
--FLEEING IN TERROR FROM AN UNSEEN MENACE!
SILENCE!
SPEAK NO MORE OF ANYTHING RELATING TO MANKIND! I WASH MY HANDS OF THEM-- AND YOU!
KRAKK!
IT IS AT THAT MOMENT OF ETERNITY THAT IT FIRST SLITHERS INTO VIEW, ITS SLIME-GRAY TENTACLES QUESTING EAGERLY FOR THE DEMI-MEN!
IMMEDIATELY AFTERWARDS, ITS QUIVERING, BLOATED HEAD APPEARS--
--AND WITH IT, RECOGNITION!
SHUMA-GORATH!

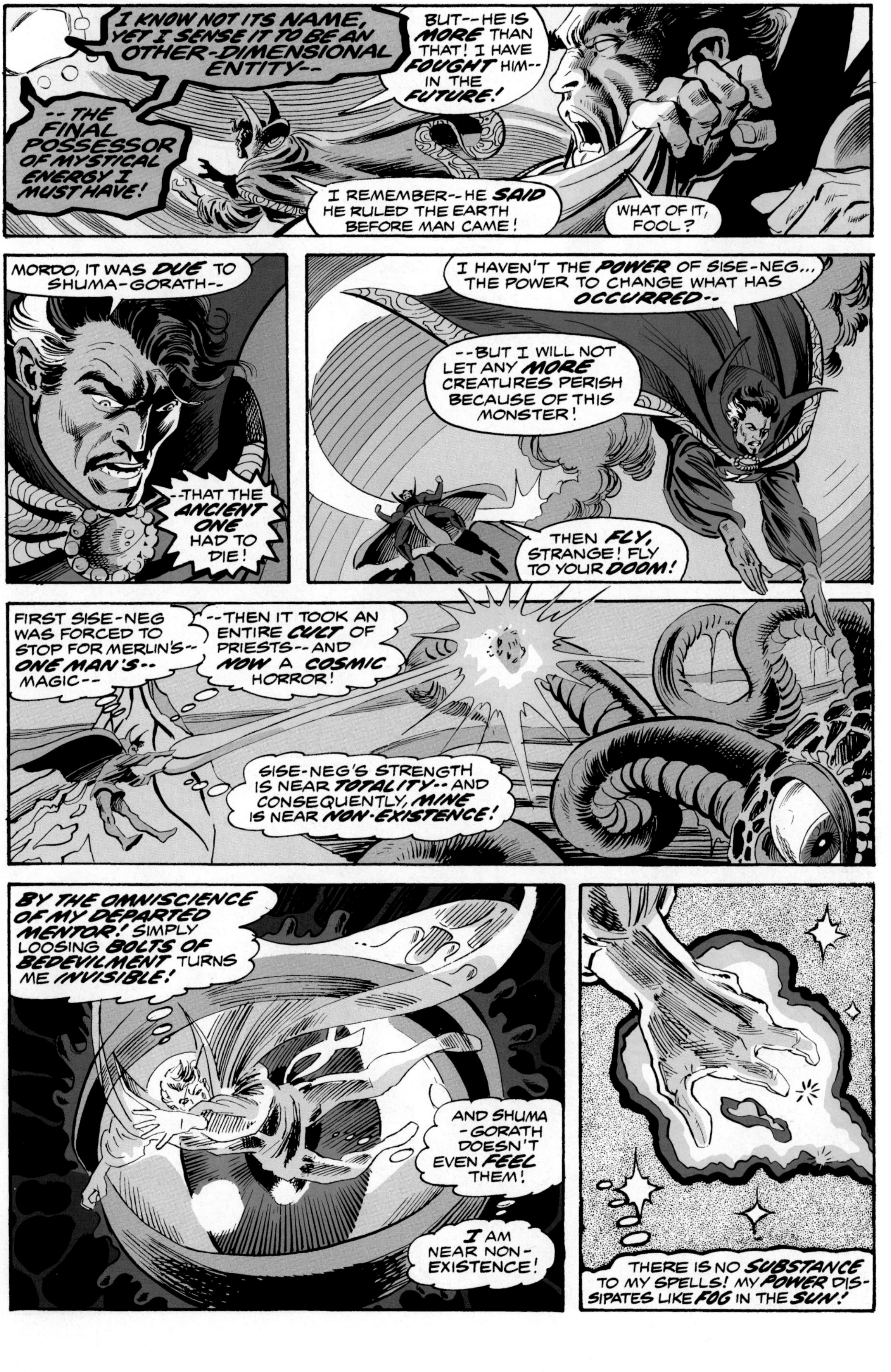
I KNOW NOT ITS NAME, YET I SENSE IT TO BE AN OTHER-DIMENSIONAL ENTITY--
--THE FINAL POSSESSOR OF MYSTICAL ENERGY I MUST HAVE!
BUT--HE IS MORE THAN THAT! I HAVE FOUGHT HIM--IN THE FUTURE!
I REMEMBER--HE SAID HE RULED THE EARTH BEFORE MAN CAME!
WHAT OF IT, FOOL?
MORDO, IT WAS DUE TO SHUMA-GORATH--
--THAT THE ANCIENT ONE HAD TO DIE!
I HAVEN'T THE POWER OF SISE-NEG... THE POWER TO CHANGE WHAT HAS OCCURRED--
--BUT I WILL NOT LET ANY MORE CREATURES PERISH BECAUSE OF THIS MONSTER!
THEN FLY, STRANGE! FLY TO YOUR DOOM!
FIRST SISE-NEG WAS FORCED TO STOP FOR MERLIN'S--ONE MAN'S--MAGIC--
--THEN IT TOOK AN ENTIRE CULT OF PRIESTS--AND NOW A COSMIC HORROR!
SISE-NEG'S STRENGTH IS NEAR TOTALITY--AND CONSEQUENTLY, MINE IS NEAR NON-EXISTENCE!
BY THE OMNISCIENCE OF MY DEPARTED MENTOR! SIMPLY LOOSING BOLTS OF BEDEVILMENT TURNS ME INVISIBLE!
AND SHUMA-GORATH DOESN'T EVEN FEEL THEM!
I AM NEAR NON-EXISTENCE!
THERE IS NO SUBSTANCE TO MY SPELLS! MY POWER DISSIPATES LIKE FOG IN THE SUN!

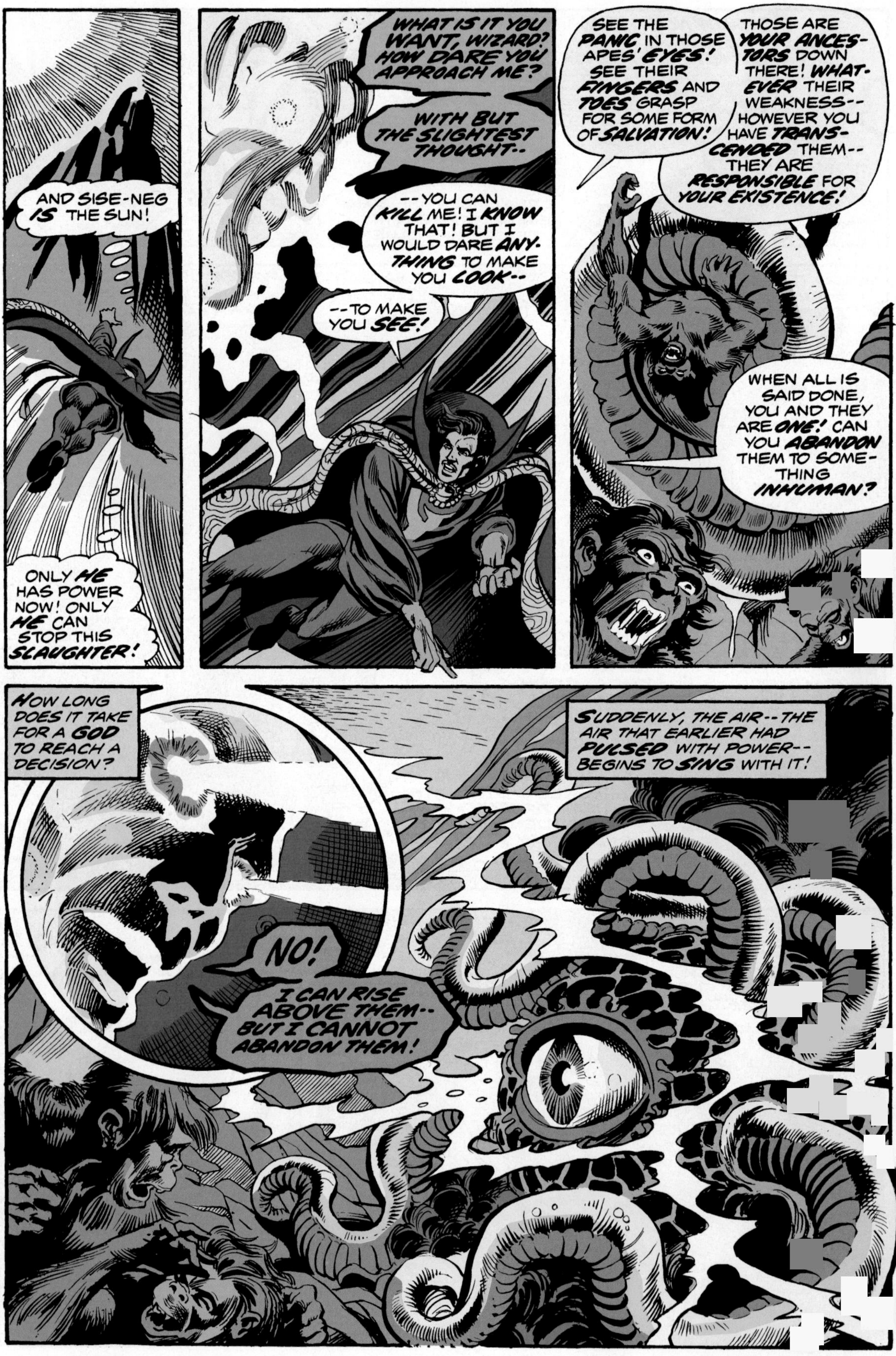
AND SISE-NEG IS THE SUN!
ONLY HE HAS POWER NOW! ONLY HE CAN STOP THIS SLAUGHTER!
WHAT IS IT YOU WANT, WIZARD? HOW DARE YOU APPROACH ME?
WITH BUT THE SLIGHTEST THOUGHT--
--YOU CAN KILL ME! I KNOW THAT! BUT I WOULD DARE ANYTHING TO MAKE YOU LOOK--
--TO MAKE YOU SEE!
SEE THE PANIC IN THOSE APES' EYES! SEE THEIR FINGERS AND TOES GRASP FOR SOME FORM OF SALVATION!
THOSE ARE YOUR ANCESTORS DOWN THERE! WHATEVER THEIR WEAKNESS-- HOWEVER YOU HAVE TRANSCENDED THEM-- THEY ARE RESPONSIBLE FOR YOUR EXISTENCE!
WHEN ALL IS SAID DONE, YOU AND THEY ARE ONE! CAN YOU ABANDON THEM TO SOMETHING INHUMAN?
HOW LONG DOES IT TAKE FOR A GOD TO REACH A DECISION?
SUDDENLY, THE AIR--THE AIR THAT EARLIER HAD PULSED WITH POWER-- BEGINS TO SING WITH IT!
NO!
I CAN RISE ABOVE THEM-- BUT I CANNOT ABANDON THEM!

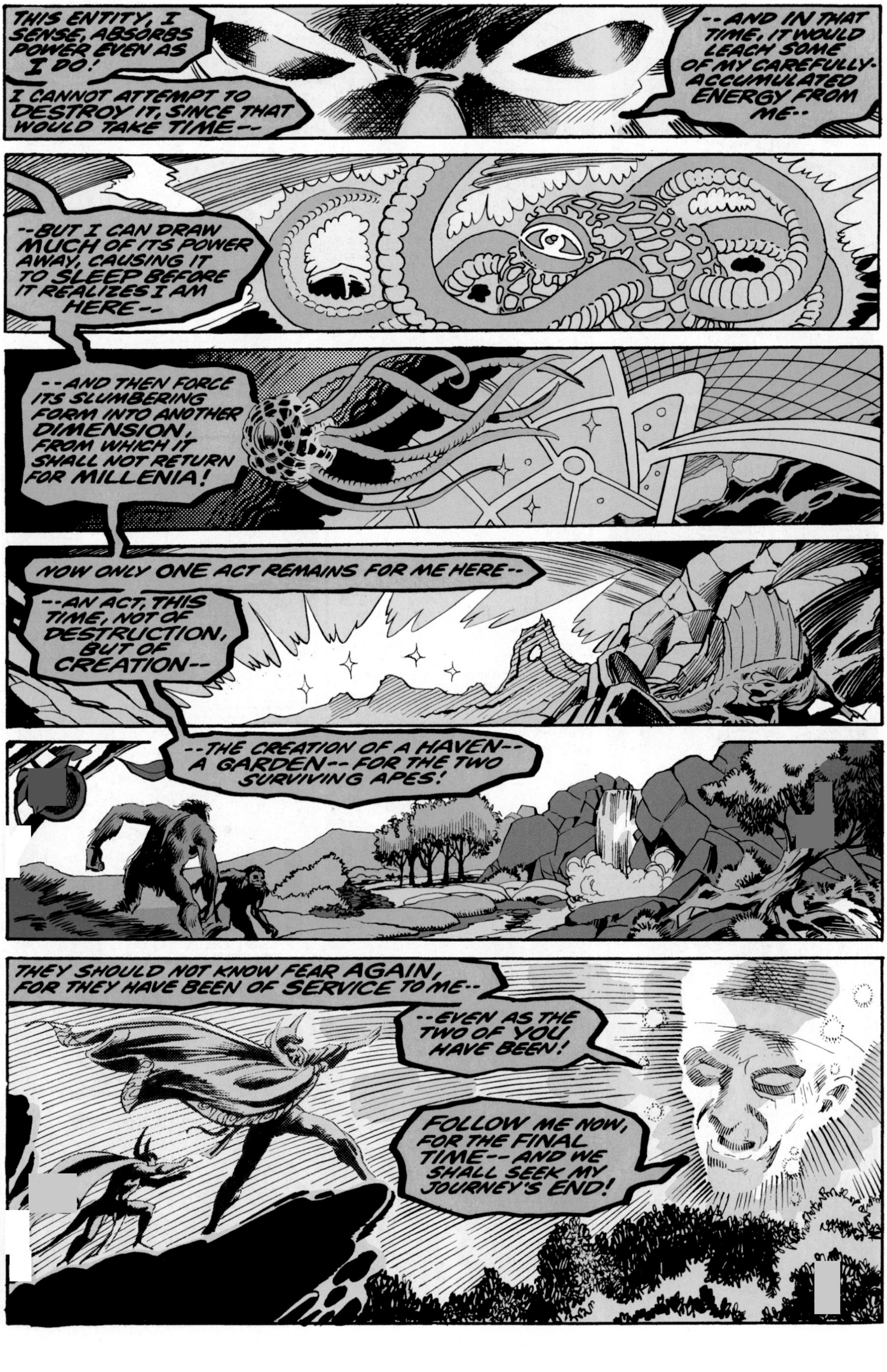
THIS ENTITY, I SENSE, ABSORBS POWER EVEN AS I DO!
I CANNOT ATTEMPT TO DESTROY IT, SINCE THAT WOULD TAKE TIME--
--AND IN THAT TIME, IT WOULD LEACH SOME OF MY CAREFULLY-ACCUMULATED ENERGY FROM ME--
--BUT I CAN DRAW MUCH OF ITS POWER AWAY, CAUSING IT TO SLEEP BEFORE IT REALIZES I AM HERE--
--AND THEN FORCE ITS SLUMBERING FORM INTO ANOTHER DIMENSION, FROM WHICH IT SHALL NOT RETURN FOR MILLENIA!
NOW ONLY ONE ACT REMAINS FOR ME HERE--
--AN ACT, THIS TIME, NOT OF DESTRUCTION, BUT OF CREATION--
--THE CREATION OF A HAVEN--A GARDEN--FOR THE TWO SURVIVING APES!
THEY SHOULD NOT KNOW FEAR AGAIN, FOR THEY HAVE BEEN OF SERVICE TO ME--
--EVEN AS THE TWO OF YOU HAVE BEEN!
FOLLOW ME NOW, FOR THE FINAL TIME--AND WE SHALL SEEK MY JOURNEY'S END!

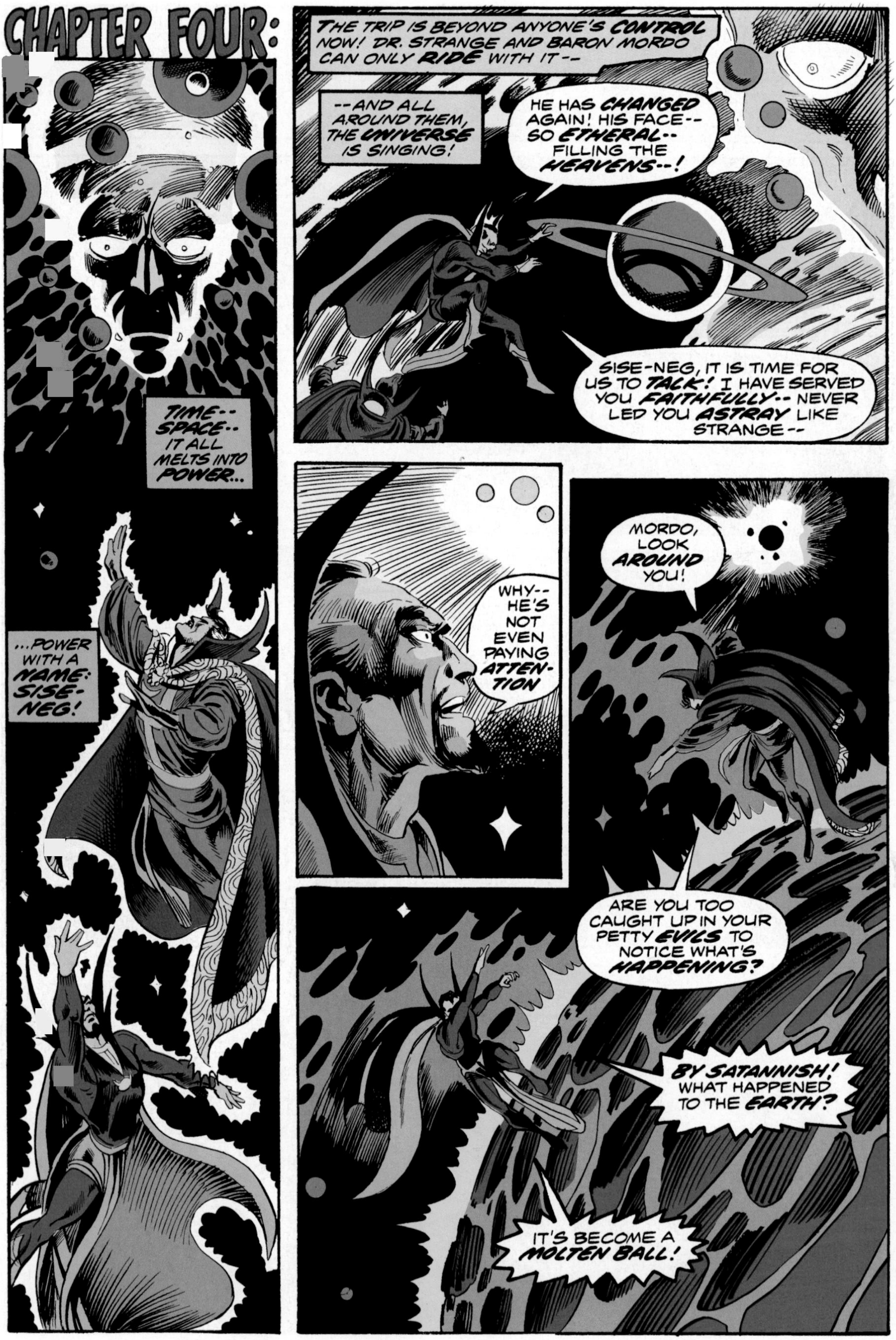
CHAPTER FOUR:
THE TRIP IS BEYOND ANYONE'S CONTROL NOW! DR. STRANGE AND BARON MORDO CAN ONLY RIDE WITH IT--
--AND ALL AROUND THEM, THE UNIVERSE IS SINGING!
HE HAS CHANGED AGAIN! HIS FACE--SO ETHERAL--FILLING THE HEAVENS--!
SISE-NEG, IT IS TIME FOR US TO TALK! I HAVE SERVED YOU FAITHFULLY--NEVER LED YOU ASTRAY LIKE STRANGE--
TIME--SPACE--IT ALL MELTS INTO POWER...
...POWER WITH A NAME: SISE-NEG!
WHY--HE'S NOT EVEN PAYING ATTEN-TION
MORDO, LOOK AROUND YOU!
ARE YOU TOO CAUGHT UP IN YOUR PETTY EVILS TO NOTICE WHAT'S HAPPENING?
BY SATANNISH! WHAT HAPPENED TO THE EARTH?
IT'S BECOME A MOLTEN BALL!

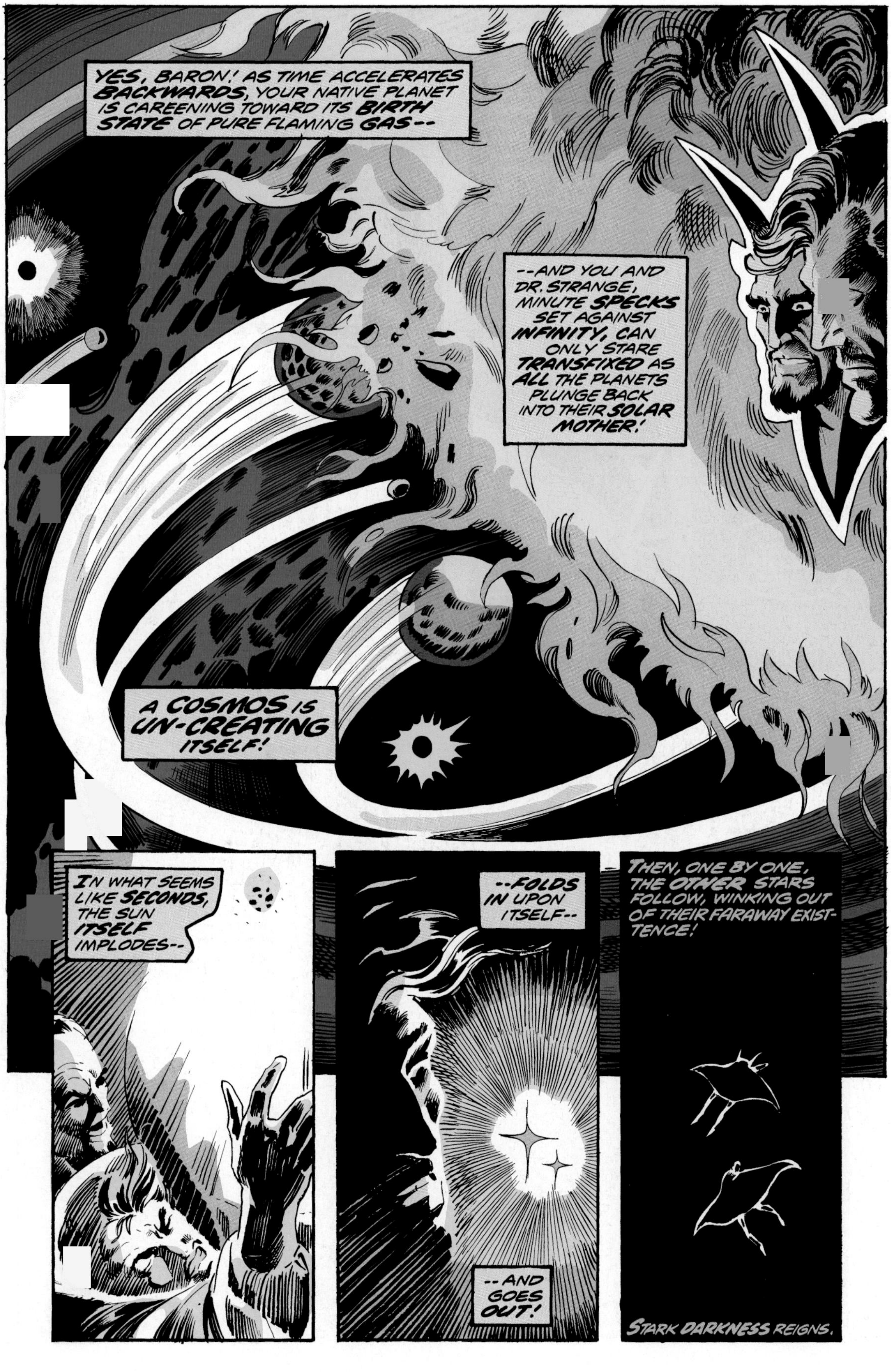
YES, BARON! AS TIME ACCELERATES BACKWARDS, YOUR NATIVE PLANET IS CAREENING TOWARD ITS BIRTH STATE OF PURE FLAMING GAS--
--AND YOU AND DR. STRANGE, MINUTE SPECKS SET AGAINST INFINITY, CAN ONLY STARE TRANSFIXED AS ALL THE PLANETS PLUNGE BACK INTO THEIR SOLAR MOTHER!
A COSMOS IS UN-CREATING ITSELF!
IN WHAT SEEMS LIKE SECONDS, THE SUN ITSELF IMPLODES--
--FOLDS IN UPON ITSELF--
--AND GOES OUT!
THEN, ONE BY ONE, THE OTHER STARS FOLLOW, WINKING OUT OF THEIR FARAWAY EXISTENCE!
STARK DARKNESS REIGNS.

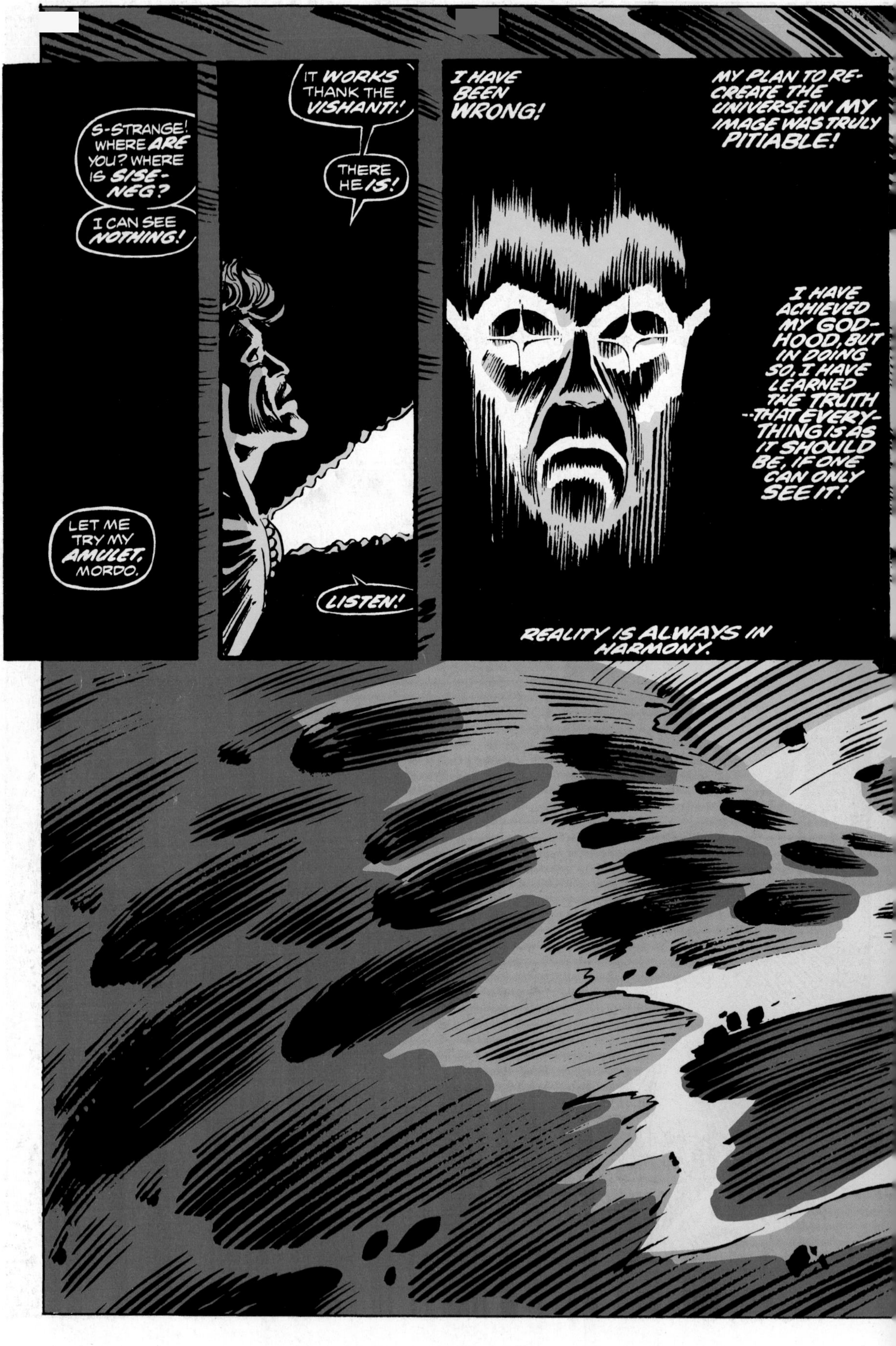
S-STRANGE! WHERE ARE YOU? WHERE IS SISE-NEG?
I CAN SEE NOTHING!
LET ME TRY MY AMULET, MORDO.
IT WORKS THANK THE VISHANTI!
THERE HE IS!
LISTEN!
I HAVE BEEN WRONG!
MY PLAN TO RE-CREATE THE UNIVERSE IN MY IMAGE WAS TRULY PITIABLE!
I HAVE ACHIEVED MY GOD-HOOD, BUT IN DOING SO, I HAVE LEARNED THE TRUTH --THAT EVERY-THING IS AS IT SHOULD BE, IF ONE CAN ONLY SEE IT!
REALITY IS ALWAYS IN HARMONY.

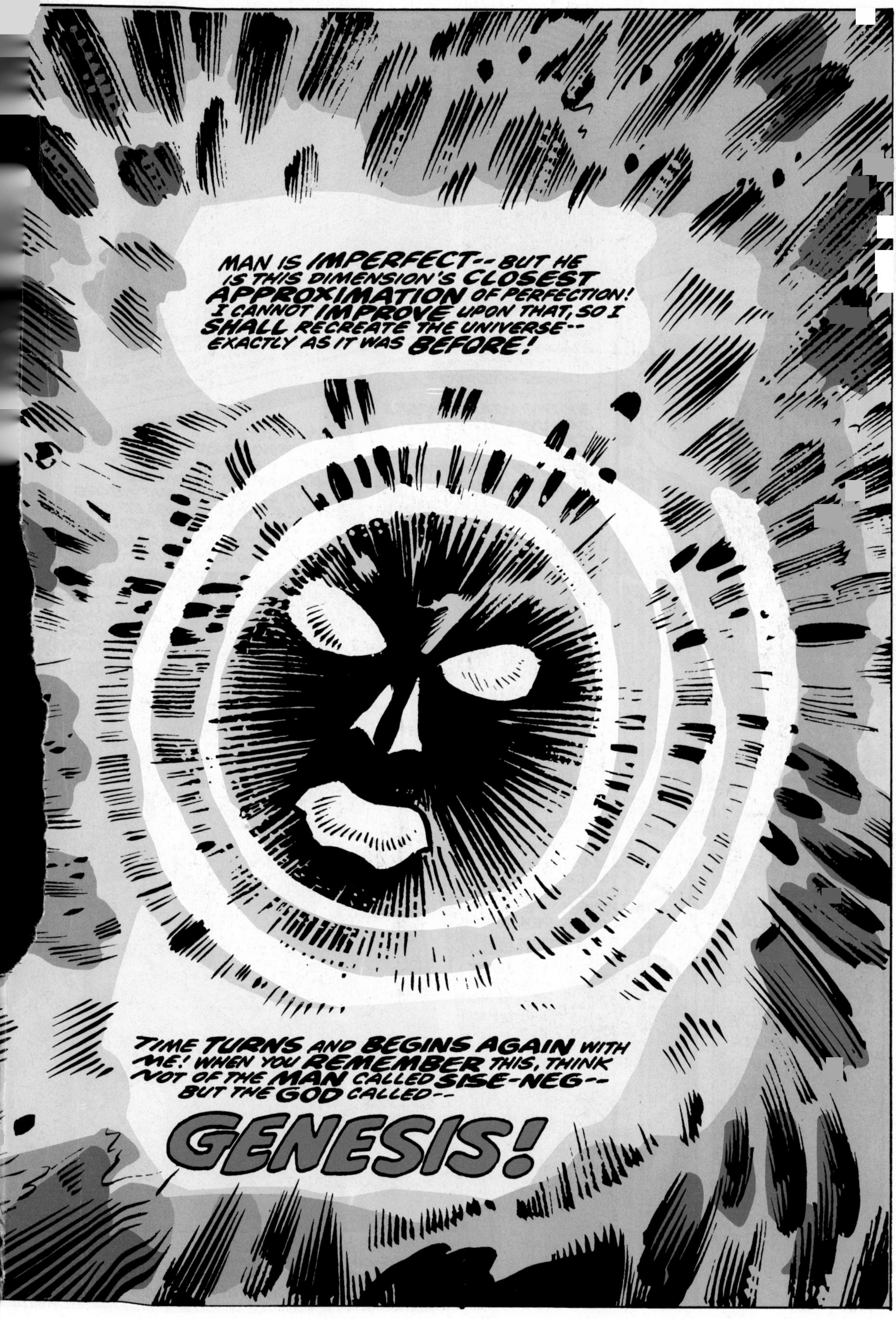
MAN IS IMPERFECT-- BUT HE IS THIS DIMENSION'S CLOSEST APPROXIMATION OF PERFECTION! I CANNOT IMPROVE UPON THAT, SO I SHALL RECREATE THE UNIVERSE-- EXACTLY AS IT WAS BEFORE!
TIME TURNS AND BEGINS AGAIN WITH ME! WHEN YOU REMEMBER THIS, THINK NOT OF THE MAN CALLED SISE-NEG-- BUT THE GOD CALLED--
GENESIS!

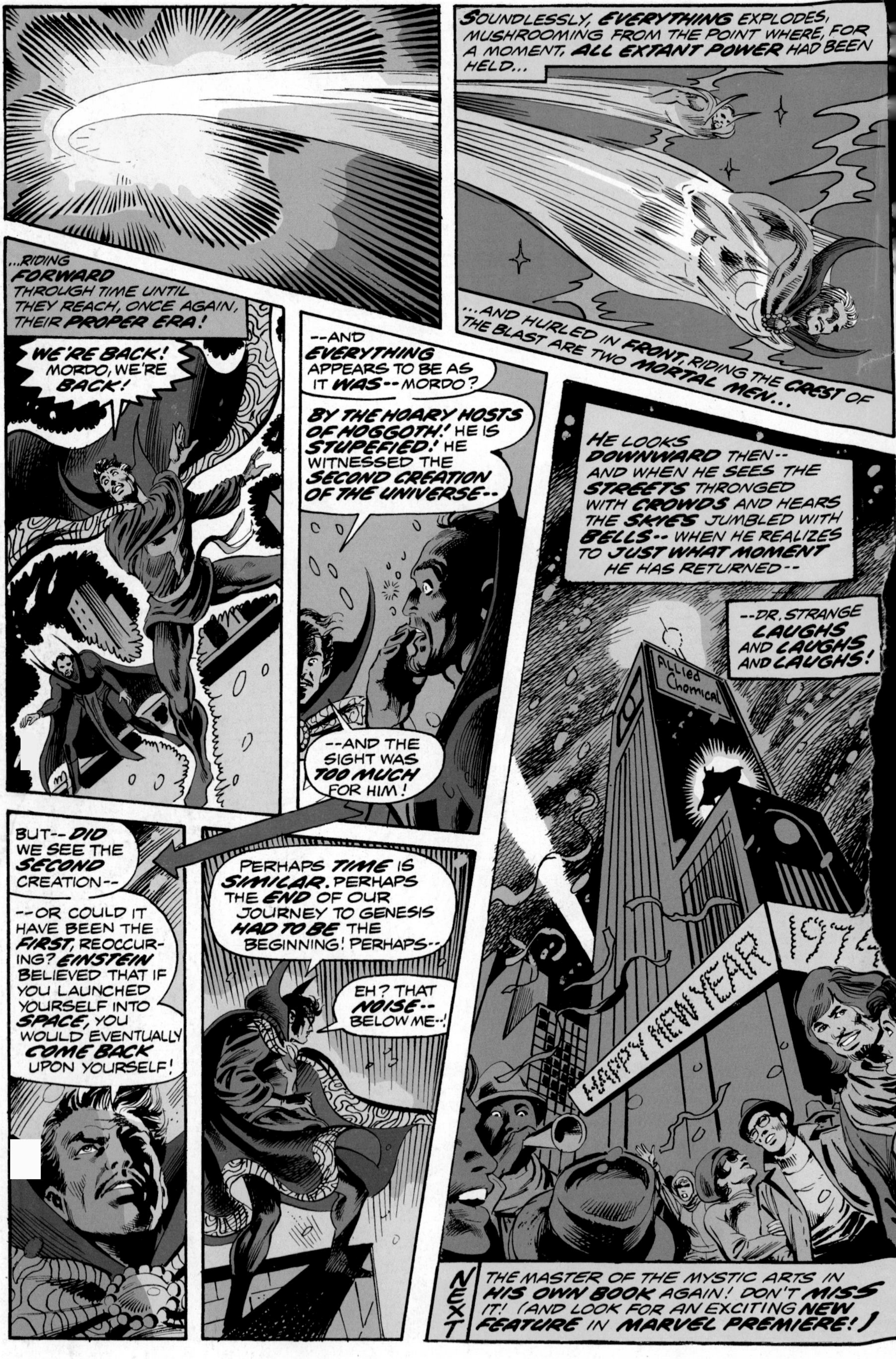
SOUNDLESSLY, EVERYTHING EXPLODES, MUSHROOMING FROM THE POINT WHERE, FOR A MOMENT, ALL EXTANT POWER HAD BEEN HELD...
...AND HURLED IN FRONT, RIDING THE CREST OF THE BLAST ARE TWO MORTAL MEN...
...RIDING FORWARD THROUGH TIME UNTIL THEY REACH, ONCE AGAIN, THEIR PROPER ERA!
WE'RE BACK! MORDO, WE'RE BACK!
--AND EVERYTHING APPEARS TO BE AS IT WAS--MORDO?
BY THE HOARY HOSTS OF HOGGOTH! HE IS STUPEFIED! HE WITNESSED THE SECOND CREATION OF THE UNIVERSE--
--AND THE SIGHT WAS TOO MUCH FOR HIM!
HE LOOKS DOWNWARD THEN--AND WHEN HE SEES THE STREETS THRONGED WITH CROWDS AND HEARS THE SKIES JUMBLED WITH BELLS--WHEN HE REALIZES TO JUST WHAT MOMENT HE HAS RETURNED--
--DR. STRANGE LAUGHS AND LAUGHS AND LAUGHS!
Allied Chemical
BUT--DID WE SEE THE SECOND CREATION--
--OR COULD IT HAVE BEEN THE FIRST, REOCCURING? EINSTEIN BELIEVED THAT IF YOU LAUNCHED YOURSELF INTO SPACE, YOU WOULD EVENTUALLY COME BACK UPON YOURSELF!
PERHAPS TIME IS SIMILAR. PERHAPS THE END OF OUR JOURNEY TO GENESIS HAD TO BE THE BEGINNING! PERHAPS--
EH? THAT NOISE--BELOW ME--!
HAPPY NEW YEAR 197
NEXT
THE MASTER OF THE MYSTIC ARTS IN HIS OWN BOOK AGAIN! DON'T MISS IT! (AND LOOK FOR AN EXCITING NEW FEATURE IN MARVEL PREMIERE!)